THE HUMAN RIGHTS ACT 1998: ENFORCING THE EUROPEAN CONVENTION IN THE DOMESTIC COURTS

THE HUMAN RIGHTS ACT 1998: ENFORCING THE EUROPEAN CONVENTION IN THE DOMESTIC COURTS

Jason Coppel

JOHN WILEY & SONS

Chichester · New York · Weinheim · Brisbane · Singapore · Toronto

National   01243 779777
International (+44) 1243 779777
e-mail (for orders and customer service enquiries):
cs-books@wiley.co.uk
Visit our Home Page on http://www.wiley.co.uk
or http://www.wiley.com

Reprinted August 2000

Other Wiley Editorial Offices

John Wiley & Sons, Inc., 605 Third Avenue,
New York, NY 10158-0012, USA

WILEY-VCH GmbH, Pallelallee 3,
D-69469 Weinheim, Germany

Jacaranda Wiley Ltd, 33 Part Road, Milton,
Queensland 4064, Australia

John Wiley & Sons (Asia) Pte Ltd, 2 Clementi Loop #02-01,
Jin Xing Distripark, Singapore 129809

John Wiley & Sons (Canada) Ltd, 22 Worcester Road,
Rexdale, Ontario M9W 1L1, Canada

British Library Cataloguing in Publication Data

A catalogue record for this book is available from the British Library

ISBN 0-471-98250-4

Typeset in 11/13pt Garamond by C.K.M. Typesetting, Salisbury, Wiltshire.
Printed and bound in Great Britain by Biddles, Guildford and King's Lynn.

This book is printed on acid-free paper responsibly manufactured from sustainable forestry, in
which at least two trees are planted for each one used for paper production.

For Sarah

THE ALEXANDER MAXWELL LAW SCHOLARSHIP TRUST

CONTENTS

Chapter 8
PERSONAL LIBERTY   207

Chapter 9

DUE PROCESS OF LAW

Chapter 11
FREEDOM OF THOUGHT, CONSCIENCE AND RELIGION

Chapter 12
FREEDOM OF EXPRESSION

PREFACE

The aim of this book is to introduce legal practitioners to the implications for everyday legal practice of the Human Rights Act 1998 and of the European Convention on Human Rights, to which it gives effect. The Convention, which has been binding on the UK since 1953, has an impact across a very wide range of legal practice areas. Police powers, criminal and civil rules of evidence and procedure, family law, planning, employment law, freedom of information, privacy, tax, education, environmental law, immigration and asylum and electoral law are only some of the affected subjects. However, notwithstanding these wide-ranging implications, the failure of successive governments to incorporate the terms of the Convention into domestic law has meant that the ECHR has been of only esoteric interest for the vast majority of practitioners.

The passage of the Human Rights Act will change all that.* Just as many practitioners were beginning to come to terms with the profound implications of European Community law, the Act has brought with it a whole new European legal system with different rights, different courts, a new body of case-law and, most confusing of all, a legal status which differs in important ways from the status accorded to EC law. This book is intended to arm practitioners with the basic tools they will need to fight cases which, pursuant to the Human Rights Act, raise issues of violation of rights conferred by the European Convention. It seeks to answer three questions for the practitioner faced with a legal problem: is there a potential European Convention aspect to the problem, what are the basic principles to consider and where can further information be found?

The book is in two parts. Part I is a general account of how the European Convention might be enforced in any particular case. Its focus is, naturally, on the meaning and effect of the Human Rights Act itself, but

---

* At the time of writing, the Human Rights Act has not been brought into force. No firm date has been set for its coming into force: there is speculation that commencement may be delayed until early in the year 2000.

it recognises that Convention rights may be enforced other than under the Act. In particular, it looks at how the Convention may take effect through the medium of EC law, and at the procedure for taking cases to the Court of Human Rights in Strasbourg. It also contains a short chapter which aims to assist with the task of legal research in Convention cases. Part II of the book looks in more detail at the particular rights which are conferred by the European Convention. It starts with an exposition of general principles of interpretation and application of substantive Convention law which may arise in every Convention case. Chapter 6 also examines the scope of the Convention right to an effective remedy, and of its prohibition of discrimination, provisions which may only be relied upon in conjunction with another substantive Convention right. Part II then moves on to analyse, in turn, each of the relevant Convention rights. The intention is not to compile a comprehensive or even a detailed account of the case-law of the Strasbourg institutions: there are other publications which succeed admirably on that count. It is, on the contrary, to set out the basic principles which fall to be applied by the Court of Human Rights in each area and to illustrate the application of these principles by examples where necessary. The examples from the case-law have been chosen deliberately to illustrate how the Convention has impacted upon English law in the past, and how it might do so in the future. On occasion, I have commented on how the current state of English law on a particular issue might measure up to the requirements of the Convention. Again, the book does not attempt a comprehensive survey of compliance of English law with the Convention, but makes appropriate comparisons by way of example only. Finally, the appendices to this book reproduce, for ease of reference, the terms of the Human Rights Act, and of the European Convention on Human Rights as modified by Protocol No. 11.

Although the Human Rights Act, and the European Convention, apply equally in Scotland and Northern Ireland, I have not presumed to comment on the implications of the Act or of the Convention for those legal systems. My aim has been to state the law as at 30 June 1998 (subject to the difficulties of accessing unreported decisions of the European Commission of Human Rights), but it has been possible to include some later developments. There are two notable exceptions to the general approach. First, the book analyses the Human Rights Act in its final, enacted form. Secondly, the enforcement machinery of the Convention has been remodelled, pursuant to Protocol No. 11 from 1 November 1998. The three-tier judicial system of Commission, Court and Committee of Ministers is to be abolished and replaced by a single Court which will exercise all judicial powers, leaving the Committee of Ministers to deal with the enforcement of Court judgments. The provisions of the

Convention are cited and described as amended by Protocol No. 11 (as, indeed, they are in the Human Rights Act).

The writing of this book was assisted by a grant from the Alexander Maxwell Law Scholarship Trust. I acknowledge with gratitude the support provided by the trustees, and the confidence which they have shown in me. Several people have given generously of their time, and their expertise, in reading and commenting on chapters of this book and in talking through with me some of the thornier issues which it raises. I would like to thank, in particular, Patrick Elias, Nina Ellin, Gillian Morris and Aidan O'Neill. Susie Hamblin, formerly of John Wiley & Sons, was unfailingly helpful and enthusiastic and, best of all, tolerant of missed deadlines. Finally, I owe more than I can say to my wife, Sarah Jarvis, who has endured countless lonely evenings and weekends in the cause of this book and can now count on my undivided attention once more.

Jason Coppel
Barrister
11 Kings Bench Walk Chambers
London

FOREWORD

Every liberal democracy must reconcile the conflict between the democratic right of the majority to exercise political power and the democratic need for individuals and minorities to have their human rights secured and respected. Since 1950, the legal system of the United Kingdom has attempted that reconciliation in a curious, hybrid fashion. On the one hand, the UK has been committed to an international treaty, the European Convention on Human Rights, which requires fundamental human rights to be secured to citizens of this country. Those rights are positive entitlements which must prevail unless in exceptional circumstances. At the same time, domestic law in this country has been beholden to a culture which recognises individuals' rights as residual only — they exist only insofar as they are not curtailed by the common law or by statute. The trumpet call, "freedom under the law", ignores that the law can sanction the invasion of basic rights. Thus the British have had to take the long road to Strasbourg to put their cases to the European Court of Human Rights with the outcome a catalogue of defeats for the United Kingdom before the Court.

The Human Rights Act represents a quantum leap forward in the protection of fundamental human rights by our domestic legal system. It enables individuals to argue for their rights and claim their remedies under the European Convention in any court or tribunal in the United Kingdom. By requiring the courts to construe and give effect to domestic legislation so far as possible in conformity with the Convention, and obliging public authorities to act consistently with Convention rights, the Act will obviate the need for recourse to Strasbourg. The Act also requires ministers to take account of the implications for human rights of new legislation, and to declare to Parliament whether or not draft bills are compatible with Convention rights. In the courts and in Parliament, the Act will promote a culture of awareness of, and respect for, fundamental human rights. It places human rights protection on a coherent footing, intellectually and morally, a footing which, I believe, will stand this country in good stead in the twenty-first century and beyond.

The far-reaching effects of the Human Rights Act represent a major challenge for British lawyers. Few, if any, practitioners can safely ignore the implications for their practices of Convention rights. However, only a small proportion of lawyers could at present claim to be familiar with the detail of the Convention system, and the rights which it confers. The Act will, therefore, require a huge investment by academic and practising lawyers in education and training in order to understand and realise its full potential.

This book will assist considerably towards that understanding. It contains a commendable analysis not only of the Act itself but also of the practice of the European Commission and Court of Human Rights in respect of each of the Convention rights given effect by the Act. Chapters 3 and 5 on the relationship between the Convention and EC law, and on legal research in Convention cases will also provide practical assistance not readily available elsewhere. The book as a whole is a concise and practical guide to the wide-ranging implications of the Human Rights Act. I recommend it as a valuable guidebook to what for many will be unfamiliar territory.

The Lord Chancellor the Rt Hon. Lord Irvine of Lairg

TABLE OF CASES

European Court of Human Rights

UK Cases

European Court of Justice Cases

Other Jurisdictions

Canada

New Zealand

TABLE OF CONVENTIONS AND TREATIES

EU Conventions and Treaties

EU Directives

Other Conventions

TABLE OF LEGISLATION

Part I

ENFORCING THE EUROPEAN CONVENTION ON HUMAN RIGHTS: MECHANICS AND GENERAL PRINCIPLES

Chapter 1
THE HUMAN RIGHTS ACT: BACKGROUND AND OVERVIEW

1. BACKGROUND

The European Convention for the Protection of Human Rights and **1.1** Fundamental Freedoms is an international treaty to which the United Kingdom was one of the original signatories in 1950. It was drawn up under the auspices of the Council of Europe, an international organisation established in 1949 to promote ideals of democracy and human rights, and to facilitate economic and social progress in the post-war era. The Convention provides for a series of fundamental rights which signatory states undertake to secure to individuals within their jurisdiction. It also sets out machinery for the enforcement of the rights which it confers, which can be used in the event of a state failing in its obligations. The UK played a major role in drafting the Convention which, by virtue of its signature by the Attlee Government, and ratification by Parliament, has been binding on the UK since it came into force in 1953. Moreover, the UK accepted at a relatively early stage the right of individual petition to the Commission of Human Rights in Strasbourg, so enabling direct action to be taken by individuals who have suffered a breach of their Convention rights.

However, despite the fact that the UK is bound to give effect to **1.2** Convention rights, and that its obligations can be enforced by individuals through the Strasbourg machinery, the influence of the Convention on domestic law and practice has been peripheral. The domestic courts have come to regard it as legitimate to refer to the provisions of the Convention in a growing range of circumstances, but the cases in which a Convention right has had a determinative impact on the outcome of the proceedings are few and far between.[1] The Convention has had a more dramatic effect in a number of cases where a defeat for the Government before the European Court of Human Rights in Strasbourg has provoked a change in domestic law in order to bring it into line with Convention requirements. Such victories, however, have been hard fought, over a period of several years, and frequently they have brought little in the way of practical benefit to the individual applicants concerned. The Court in Strasbourg frequently declines to award compensation, preferring to leave the applicant with a moral victory only. Furthermore, whilst the UK is bound to give effect to Court judgments by introducing changes in domestic law and/or practice, such changes need not have retrospective effect so as to confer any entitlement on the pioneering applicant.

1.3   The continuing marginal effect of the Convention in domestic law was due to the fact that the UK, unlike the vast majority of other signatories to the Convention, did not incorporate the provisions of the Convention into domestic law. Convention rights could be directly invoked in Strasbourg, but only in Strasbourg. Unlike many rights conferred by European Community law, Convention rights had no legal force in the domestic courts. The Human Rights Act 1998 is intended to remedy that situation, by giving to Convention rights a formal status in domestic law and, on any view, it will revolutionise the impact of the Convention upon domestic legal practice. The Convention is to become part of English law, for certain purposes at least, which can be applied and enforced in the English courts. Once the Act has entered into force, Convention rights will be capable of invocation in every court in the land, and without the need to take the long road to Strasbourg.

1.4   However, looking beyond the headline effects of the Act, the mechanism chosen for the incorporation of the Convention into domestic law is a complex one. The Human Rights Act does not amount to full incorporation but is, in many ways, a half-way house. Convention rights, although they are described by the Convention itself as "fundamental", do not trump contrary provisions in domestic legislation. The Act does not even have the power, possessed by all other primary legislation, to impliedly repeal provisions of previous statutes which are inconsistent with it. It will, nevertheless, have a profound effect upon the development and application of English law, both statutory and judge-made, and upon the outcome of many and varying types of litigation. The remainder of this

---

[1] See Klug and Starmer, "Incorporation by the Back Door?" [1996] PL 223: the authors found that the Convention had been referred to in 316 cases between 1975–1996 but had influenced the outcome in only 16 of those cases.

chapter is taken up with an overview of the main provisions of the Act. Chapter 2 then analyses the Act in more detail and looks at how it may be used in individual cases.

2. OVERVIEW OF THE HUMAN RIGHTS ACT

1.5 The Human Rights Act incorporates into domestic law most, although not all, of the rights protected by the European Convention, for limited purposes and with limited effect. It is important to note that, as its short title suggests, the Act gives "further effect" to the European Convention in domestic law but not full effect. During the passage of the Bill through Parliament, the Government rejected a proposed amendment to it which would have made clear that the relevant provisions of the Convention were now part of the domestic law of the UK.[2] The key to understanding the Act is to appreciate the various ways in which it falls short of wholesale incorporation of the Convention into domestic law.

1.6 The Convention rights to which the Act gives further effect are defined in s. 1(1): Articles 2-12 and 14 of the Convention, Articles 1-3 of the First Protocol of the Convention and Articles 1-2 of the Sixth Protocol.[3] The Act, therefore, excludes Articles 1 and 13 of the Convention which, respectively, require Contracting Parties to secure Convention rights to the individuals under their jurisdiction and to provide an effective remedy before a domestic authority for those complaining of a violation of their Convention rights. With the exception of the Sixth Protocol, the Act also excludes those rights contained in Protocols to the Convention which do not bind the UK because it has not signed and/or ratified them, although provision is made for future changes to the current position.[4] Convention rights are to be construed in accordance with the general limitations upon them which are set out in Articles 16-18 of the Convention,[5] and with such derogations and reservations as are currently in force in relation to the UK.[6] They are also to be interpreted having regard to relevant decisions of the Strasbourg institutions — the Court, the Commission and the Committee of Ministers — which the courts "must take into account" but are not formally bound by.[7]

---

[2] HL Debs., 18 November 1997, cols. 507–510.

[3] As in the Act itself, these rights are hereafter referred to as (the) Convention rights.

[4] HRA s. 1(4)–(6).

[5] As to which, see chapter 6, paras. 6.31–6.34.

[6] HRA s. 1(2); further provision is made in respect of derogations and reservations by HRA ss. 14–17, 20.

[7] HRA s. 2(1). In s. 2 and elsewhere, the Act refers to the revised text of the Convention (as modified by Protocol No. 11) which is in force from November 1998 onwards.

1.7   The limited purposes for which Convention rights may have effect are set out in ss. 3-5 and 6-9 of the Act. Section 3, which is modelled on s. 6 of the New Zealand Bill of Rights Act 1990, concerns the interpretation of legislation. The basic rule is set out in s. 3(1): primary and secondary legislation must be read in a way which is compatible with Convention rights, so far as it is possible to do so. The remainder of s. 3 then abrogates the standard rules of implied repeal insofar as the Act, and Convention rights, are concerned. The usual position is that an Act of Parliament has the effect of expressly and/or impliedly repealing previous statutes and secondary legislation insofar as it is inconsistent with them, but may itself be expressly and/or impliedly repealed by future legislation. The Human Rights Act, by contrast, cannot have the effect of expressly and/or impliedly repealing previous primary legislation.[8] It may have the effect of invalidating previous inconsistent secondary legislation, but not where it originates in primary legislation which requires that inconsistency.[9] Further, s. 3(2)(a) of the Act provides that the basic rule of interpretation applies to the interpretation of future, as well as past, primary and secondary legislation.

1.8   Where it is not possible to construe a provision of primary legislation in accordance with Convention rights (because of its plain wording), or to strike down an inconsistent provision of secondary legislation (because of primary legislation which authorises or requires the inconsistency) the courts may conclude that the relevant provision is incompatible with Convention rights. Section 4 provides for a new form of remedy to be used in such a situation, the declaration of incompatibility. The declaration of incompatibility is an option available only to the higher courts.[10] It has no concrete legal effects: s. 4(6) provides that a declaration of incompatibility has no effect on the validity, continuing operation and enforcement of the legislation in respect of which it is made and is not binding on the parties to the proceedings in which it is made. Section 5 makes provision for the Crown to intervene in cases where a court is considering whether or not to make a declaration of incompatibility.

1.9   Section 6(1) of the Act sets out the basic rule that public authorities must not act in a way which is incompatible with Convention rights. A wide range of bodies are fixed with that obligation: not only Government departments, local authorities and others who would fall within any ordinary definition of public authority but also courts and tribunals and

---

[8] HRA s. 3(2)(b).
[9] HRS s. 3(2)(c).
[10] HRA s. 4(5).

any person which has one or more functions of a public nature.[11] However, the breadth of the latter category is mitigated by s. 6(5), which provides that the Convention does not apply to the private acts of bodies which are only considered to be public authorities by virtue of the nature of one or more of their functions. Public authorities are given a defence to Convention claims: that they acted pursuant to primary legislation which was itself incompatible with Convention rights.[12]

Section 7 lays down the circumstances in which the Convention **1.10** obligations of public authorities may be enforced. First and foremost, there is an important test of *locus standi*: Convention rights may only be enforced by persons who qualify as a "victim", actual or potential, of a violation of the Convention, as that term has been defined in the Strasbourg case-law.[13] Persons with the requisite standing may attack the decisions of public authorities by way of a direct challenge, for example, by instigating proceedings for judicial review. However, reliance upon Convention rights is not restricted to that context: they may be raised in any legal proceedings, by plaintiff or defendant, applicant, appellant or respondent.[14] Consequently, the Convention may be invoked in proceedings between private persons, to which no public authority is a party; in such cases, the court is the public authority which must act consistently with the Convention.[15]

Section 8 complements ss. 6 and 7 in providing for the remedies which **1.11** may be granted in respect of the acts of public authorities which are unlawful because they breach Convention rights. The general rule is that any remedy or form of relief which is ordinarily available to a court can be applied to cases involving Convention rights.[16] That rule is subject to the important qualification that damages may only be awarded to the extent that the European Court of Human Rights would award damages if the case came before it and was decided in favour of the applicant.[17] Special provision is made in s. 9 for the availability of remedies against judicial decisions which are found to be in breach of Convention rights: subject to further provision being made, the only possible remedies are judicial review and appeal, and damages may only be claimed where there has been a breach of Article 5 of the Convention on pre-trial detention.

---

[11] HRA s. 6(3).
[12] HRA s. 6(2).
[13] HRA ss. 7(1) and (6).
[14] HRA ss. 7(1) and (5).
[15] The status of the courts as public authorities is spelled out in HRA s. 6(3)(a).
[16] HRA s. 8(1).
[17] HRA s. 8(3)–(4).

1.12   Section 11 makes clear that the right to challenge public authorities where they have acted or propose to act contrary to the Convention is strictly additional to any other rights conferred by domestic law, and that proceedings based upon Convention rights will not rule out any other proceedings which might be brought quite apart from the issue of compliance with the Convention.

1.13   Sections 12 and 13 make special provision in two areas where the Human Rights Bill came in for criticism during its passage through parliament — privacy and the press freedom, and the potential impact of Convention rights on the activities of churches and other religious organisations.

1.14   Section 10 of the Act, together with Schedule 2 thereto, provides for a fast-track procedure whereby legislation which is incompatible with Convention rights may be amended so as to remove the incompatibility. Section 10(2) is a "Henry VIII" clause: it permits the making of "remedial orders" in the form of secondary legislation which have the effect of amending or repealing primary legislation. Section 19 contains another addition to Parliamentary procedure, the statement of compatibility, whereby a Minister in charge of each new Bill to come before Parliament must assure Parliament that its provisions are compatible with Convention rights, or indicate that he is unable to make such a statement but wishes the Bill to proceed in any event.

1.15   Overall, the Human Rights Act is a revolutionary document. Quite apart from its important subject matter, the mechanics of the Act are unique in constitutional terms. However, the Act is only a few pages long and is very much a skeleton which must be fleshed out by reference to the case-law of the Commission and Court of Human Rights, and perhaps also by reference to practice in New Zealand, which has adopted a similar statute. Chapter 2 seeks to explain the central provisions of the Act, with reference to domestic, European and Commonwealth practice.

Chapter 2

USING THE HUMAN RIGHTS ACT

This chapter is concerned with the way in which the Human Rights Act, **2.1** and the European Convention, are to be applied in litigation before the English courts. It can be broken down into three parts:

- the basic parameters for the use of the Convention: which rights are available, who can rely upon them, against which persons and bodies can they be relied upon;
- the uses to which the Convention may be put in the domestic courts: statutory interpretation, review of statutes and of subordinate legislation, review of the decisons of public authorities, development of the common law and influencing the exercise of judicial discretion;
- the remedies which may be obtained where Convention rights have been breached.

1. WHICH RIGHTS HAVE BEEN INCORPORATED?

The Human Rights Act gives effect to the full range of substantive rights **2.2** contained in section I of the Convention, with the exception of Article 13.[1] Article 13 provides that everyone whose rights and freedoms are violated shall have an effective remedy before a national authority. It could have been a provision of some utility for applicants, but the Court of Human Rights has interpreted it in such a way as to remove much of its potential. In broad terms, Article 13 requires only that individuals are permitted to canvass their Convention claims in fora which have the power to take binding decisions, and the Government took the view that this requirement was met by the passage of the Act itself — henceforth, Convention

---

[1] HRA s. 1(1)(a).

claims can be canvassed in the domestic courts.[2] Whether it is correct to assume that the Act itself removes the need to incorporate Article 13 is considered further in chapter 6.[3] The Lord Chancellor noted in Parliament that the courts would be permitted by s. 2(1) of the Act to have regard to the Strasbourg case-law on Article 13.[4] It must be doubted, however, whether that case-law will necessarily be relevant in circumstances where an individual has, pursuant to the Act, no right to rely on Article 13.

2.3 The Act also excludes Article 1 from the range of provisions of the Convention to which further effect is given. Article 1 contains an undertaking that each Contracting Party shall secure Convention rights to everyone within its jurisdiction. It has been relied upon by applicants in numerous cases before the Commission and the Court of Human Rights, in particular where it is argued that the respondent state has failed to take the requisite positive measures to secure the Convention rights claimed. However, Article 1 is best characterised as an obligation entered into on the international level, between states, which does not create rights for individuals. It is therefore inappropriate for inclusion in the Act's list of Convention rights.[5]

2.4 Section 1(1) of the Act gives effect, in addition, to the rights contained in the First Protocol to the Convention (rights to property, education and free elections) and to the Sixth Protocol, which prohibits the death penalty (save in time of war). Protocols 4 and 7 to the Convention contain a variety of further rights but have not been either signed or ratified by the UK, and hence do not feature in the Act. However, ss. 1(4)-(5) make provision for their inclusion within the Act's list of Convention rights in the event that the UK decides in the future to subscribe to them. In the White Paper which preceded the Act, the Government indicated that it intended to sign and ratify Protocol No. 7 as soon as legislation can be passed which irons out certain inconsistencies between domestic law and provisions of the Protocol, notably its right of equality between spouses.[6]

2.5 It is inherent within the intention of the Act that Convention rights are to be interpreted by the English courts in the same manner as the Commission and the Court of Human Rights would interpret them. That entails the application of the limitations placed upon Convention rights by Articles 16–18 of the Convention itself, of any relevant reservations to, and

---

[2] HL Debs., 3 November 1997, col. 1308.
[3] Paras. 6.79, 6.85.
[4] HL Debs., 18 November 1997, cols. 476–477. Compare the approach of the Home Secretary, the promoter of the Human Rights Bill: HC Debs., 20 May 1998, cols. 978–987.
[5] The effects of Article 1, so far as individuals are concerned, are not lost but are incorporated into each substantive provision of section I of the Convention.
[6] *Bringing Rights Home*, Cm. 3782, paras. 4.14-4.16.

derogations from, Convention rights and of the case-law of the Strasbourg institutions.[7] Relevant case-law is not formally binding upon the English courts (in contrast to the status which is accorded to decisions of the European Court of Justice on matters of EC law) but they "must take [it] into account". Three factors explain the adoption of that formulation. First, it avoids confusion in those situations where Convention rights cannot, because of s. 3(2) of the Act, prevail over the terms of an inconsistent statutory provision. Secondly, the UK is bound under the Convention only to abide by decisions of the Court of Human Rights in cases to which it is a party.[8] A provision to the effect that the English courts are bound by the decisions of the Strasbourg Court, including, by implication, decisions in cases involving other states, would have gone further than the UK's international obligations required. Thirdly, it was thought inappropriate to bind the English courts to follow decisions from Strasbourg when neither the Strasbourg institutions themselves, nor the other state parties to the Convention, attach binding force to those decisions.[9] It is, nevertheless, envisaged that the courts will faithfully apply the Strasbourg case-law where it is relevant.[10]

Four categories of case-law are mentioned in s. 2, three of which may **2.6** well have become curiosities of history before the Act comes into force. Section 2(1)(a) refers to judgments of the Court, which have the greatest authority so far as interpretation of the Convention is concerned. Sub-sections (b) and (c) of s. 2(1) refer to decisions of the Commission of Human Rights on the merits of cases (under what used to be Article 31), and on whether or not applications are admissible (formerly Article 26) or an abuse of the right of petition (formerly Article 27(2)). Commission decisions are not authoritative, and must cede to any contrary ruling by the Court. However, in the absence of a ruling by the Court on the same or a similar issue, Commission decisions, particularly its reasoned decisions on the merits of cases, are of strong persuasive value. The same can be said of the judicial decisions of the Committee of Ministers, which are referred to in s. 2(1)(d). From 1 November 1998, the Commission of Human Rights and the judicial function of the Committee of Ministers are abolished and all judicial decision-making subsumed within a single Court. Only cases which are pending in Strasbourg and have been declared admissible by the Commission as at that date will proceed for determination by the Commission and, perhaps, the Committee of Ministers.

---

[7] HRA ss. 1(1), 1(2) and 2(1).
[8] Art. 46(1).
[9] See HL Debs., 18 November 1997, cols. 513-515.
[10] *Ibid.* at col. 515.

2. WHO CAN RELY UPON CONVENTION RIGHTS?

2.7 The question of who may rely upon Convention rights is regulated by s. 7 of the Act, which lays down the same test of *locus standi* as is applied by the Commission and Court of Human Rights.

"(1) A person who claims that a public authority has acted (or proposes to act) in a way which is made unlawful by section 6(1) may —

   (a) bring proceedings against the authority under this Act in the appropriate court or tribunal, or
   (b) rely on the Convention right or rights concerned in any legal proceedings,

but only if he is (or would be) a victim of the unlawful act.

. . .

(6) For the purposes of this section, a person is a victim of an unlawful act only if he would be a victim for the purposes of Article 34 of the Convention if proceedings were brought in the European Court of Human Rights in respect of that act."

LOCUS STANDI UNDER ARTICLE 34 OF THE CONVENTION

2.8 Article 34 of the Convention permits claims to be brought by "any person, non-governmental organisation or group of individuals claiming to be the victim of a violation" of the Convention. There is a large body of case-law, particularly decisions of the Commission on the admissibility of applications, in which the victim requirement has been elaborated.

- The Convention applies to all persons within the jurisdiction of contracting states,[11] so it is not necessary that the person claiming in respect of the unlawful act of a British authority is a UK national.
- Both natural and legal persons may invoke Convention rights.
- The "victim" of a violation of the Convention is a person who is

---

[11] Art. 1.

directly affected by the act or omission at issue.[12] In the vast majority of cases, there will be no difficulty in ascertaining whether or not a person is a victim.

- A person may be directly affected by a measure which has not actually been applied to them, but might be in the future.[13] Hence, potential, as well as actual, victims have standing under Article 34.[14]
- A person or body may claim to be a victim on the strength of a close link with the person who is immediately affected by the alleged violation. The term "indirect victim" is frequently used in this context although it is slightly misleading since the applicant must still establish that he has been "directly affected" as a result of the treatment of someone else. Claims by close relatives of victims are the most obvious example in this category.[15]
- A person ceases to be a victim if the wrong done to him has been rectified. In *Reed* v *UK*,[16] for example, the applicant complained, amongst other things, that his hearing before a prison Board of Visitors had been unfair and contrary to Article 6. The Commission ruled that, on this point, he was not a victim because the ruling of the Board had subsequently been quashed by the Divisional Court. Also, in *Frederiksen* v *Denmark*, the applicants had been dismissed for refusing to join a particular trade union. They were awarded compensation by the Danish courts up to a maximum amount of 18 months' salary but claimed that there was a breach of Article 11 on the basis that they had not been reinstated or received full compensation. The Commission found that the compensation paid was an adequate remedy in the circumstances, so that the applicants could not claim to be "victims" of a breach.[17]
- Claims may be brought (although they are not required to be brought) by a representative on behalf of a victim who lacks legal capacity, for example, a minor, or a person of unsound mind.[18] Representatives of a deceased victim may only continue with a claim

---

[12] See, for example, *Corigliano* v *Italy*, A/57, (1983) 5 EHRR 334.

[13] See, for example, *Campbell and Cosans* v *UK*, A/48, (1982) 4 EHRR 293; *Bowman* v *UK*, A/874, (1998) 26 EHRR 1.

[14] The express provision in s. 7(1) for persons who "would be" a victim is, therefore, otiose.

[15] For example, *Amekrane* v *UK*, Appl. No. 5961/72, (1973) 16 *Yearbook* 356; cf. *Winer* v *UK*, Appl. No. 10871/84, (1986) 48 D&R 154.

[16] Appl. No. 7630/76, (1979) 19 D&R 113.

[17] Appl. No. 12719/87, (1988) 56 D&R 237.

[18] See, for example, *Campbell and Cosans* v *UK*, above n. 13, a claim brought by parents on behalf of their children. See also *SD, DP and T* v *UK*, Appl. No. 23715/94, (1996) 22 EHRR CD148 (claim introduced on behalf of children by solicitor appointed by their guardian *ad litem*).

if they have an interest of their own to protect;[19] heirs may not seek to enforce rights which are personal to the deceased.[20]

- Save in those limited types of case, the Convention does not permit representative actions by interested parties — the complainant must actually be a victim and cannot simply represent others who are victims.[21] The effect is to rule out most actions by pressure groups.

2.9　　Three specific applications of the standing rules are also worthy of note.

- Where the interests of a company have been affected by the disputed measures, it is, in principle, the company which is the victim and which must bring a claim. Exceptions have been made for majority shareholders who were, in effect, carrying on their business through the company. They are considered to have a direct personal interest in the company's affairs, but minority shareholders must look to the company to claim on their behalf.[22] This remains the position, at least for claims to property rights under Article 1 of the First Protocol; more recently, the Court has drawn a distinction between property claims under Article 1 and claims under Article 6 of the Convention and permitted a minority shareholder to complain about the length of proceedings brought by him in respect of damage caused to the company.[23]
- Article 34 rarely permits trade unions to bring claims in their own right on the basis that they are the victims of measures taken against their members. The disputed measures must actually be aimed at the rights of the union; it is not sufficient that the operations of the union have been affected by restrictions upon its members.[24]
- Special allowances are made for those who claim to be victims of state surveillance, since it is frequently impossible for an individual to know, or to prove, that he is under surveillance. It will be sufficient for an individual to point to the existence of surveillance without establishing that it was actually inflicted upon him.[25] An applicant

---

[19] *X* v *Austria*, Appl. No. 8003/77, (1980) 17 D&R 80.

[20] *Kofler* v *Italy*, Appl. No. 8261/78, (1983) 30 D&R 5.

[21] See, for example, *Lindsay* v *UK*, Appl. No. 31699/96, (1997) 23 EHRR CD199.

[22] *Kaplan* v *UK*, Appl. No. 7598/76, (1982) 4 EHRR 64; *Yarrow* v *UK*, Appl. No. 9266/81 (1983) 30 D&R 155.

[23] *Neves e Silva* v *Portugal*, A/153, (1990) 13 EHRR 535.

[24] *Ahmed* v *UK*, Appl. No. 22954/93, (1995) 20 EHRR CD72.

[25] *Klass* v *Germany*, A/28, (1979-80) 2 EHRR 214.

complaining of vetting by the security services must show a "reasonable likelihood" that he has been affected.[26]

Strictly speaking, the test of standing under Article 34 is two-fold: the **2.10** claimant must be a victim, but must also fall into one of the categories of claimant listed, being a "person, non-governmental organisation or group of individuals". Accordingly, it is submitted that a claimant should not be found to be "a victim for the purposes of Article 34 of the Convention" within s. 7 of the Act unless both limbs of Article 34 are satisfied. The principal effect of the restriction of Convention claims to persons, non-governmental organisations and groups of individuals is that bodies which are themselves part of the state apparatus cannot rely upon Convention rights, since they are governmental, rather than "non-governmental", organisations. In *Ayuntamiento de M*, for example, the Commission ruled that a Spanish local authority had no standing under the Convention, being neither a non-governmental organisation nor a group of individuals.[27] Any "authority which exercises public functions" will be excluded.[28] Whilst the Commission has been reluctant to provide guidance on the status of borderline bodies, such as the BBC, which, arguably, fall into the excluded category,[29] a test focusing on the exercise of public functions appears to correspond closely with the definition of public authority in s. 6 of the Act. Therefore, any body which is bound by s. 6 to act in a way which is compatible with Convention rights may itself be excluded from relying upon Convention rights against other public authorities.

CONVENTION CLAIMS AND JUDICIAL REVIEW

The domestic rules of *locus standi* for bringing an application for judicial **2.11** review are broader than the test of standing under Article 34 of the Convention. Order 53, rule 3(5) of the Rules of the Supreme Court permits applications by any person with "a sufficient interest in the matter to

---

[26] *Hilton* v *UK*, Appl. No. 12015/86, (1988) 57 D&R 108.
[27] *Ayuntamiento de M* v *Spain*, Appl. No. 15090/89, (1991) 68 D&R 209; *Rothenthurm Commune* v *Switzerland*, Appl. No. i3252/87, (1988) 59 D&R 251. A Home Office Minister confirmed in Parliament that local authorities would be unable to claim Convention rights: HC Debs., 24 June 1998, 1084-1085.
[28] *Ibid.* at 215.
[29] *BBC* v *UK*, Appl. No. 25798/94, (1996) 21 EHRR CD93.

which the application relates", and permits challenges to be brought by pressure groups which would not be accepted in Strasbourg.[30] Organisations such as Greenpeace, the World Development Movement and the Joint Council for the Welfare of Immigrants have standing under domestic law to bring claims which are within their field of interest and activity. Section 7(3) of the Act makes it clear that in cases of overlap, where Convention rights are potentially at issue in judicial review proceedings, it is the more restrictive Convention test of standing which is to prevail:

"If the proceedings are brought on an application for judicial review, the applicant is to be taken to have a sufficient interest in relation to the unlawful activity only if he is, or would be, a victim of that act."

2.12   The effect of this approach is to produce anomalies in the standing rules according to the subject matter of the claim. An interest group may have a sufficient interest for the purposes of bringing judicial review proceedings based on fundamental common law rights, or fundamental rights contained in European Community law but may not, in the same proceedings, rely upon Convention rights.

2.13   The Government's view was that the legal activities of interest groups would not be inhibited by the adoption of the Convention rules of *locus standi*, for two reasons. First, there would always be individuals who could be put forward as "victims" of an unlawful act with their cases funded rather than fronted by an interest group. Secondly, interest groups could be permitted to intervene in Convention-based cases in the higher courts by filing *amicus* briefs.[31] The Court of Human Rights permits such interventions, and the House of Lords has also started to accept written submissions from pressure groups.[32] The Lord Chancellor told the House of Lords that the Act would permit such interventions in Convention cases notwithstanding the wording of s. 7(1) of the Act, which permits persons claiming that a public authority has acted in breach of the Convention to rely on Convention rights in any legal proceedings only if they satisfy the victim test.[33] It would have to be argued that (regardless of the content of their submissions) third party intervenors are not there to "claim" anything, but are merely seeking to assist the court.

---

[30] See generally De Smith, Woolf and Jowell, *Judicial Review of Administrative Action* (Sweet and Maxwell, 5th ed., 1995), 2-021-041.

[31] HL Debs., 24 November 1997, cols. 830–833.

[32] See *R. v Home Secretary ex parte Venables and Thompson* [1997] 3 WLR 23 (Justice); *R. v Khan (Sultan)* [1997] AC 558 (Liberty).

[33] HL Debs., 24 November 1997, cols. 833–834.

Do the Requirements of Article 34 Apply in All Convention Cases?

Section 11(2) of the Act provides: **2.14**

"A person's reliance upon a Convention right does not restrict ... his right to make any claim or bring any proceedings which he could make or bring apart from sections 7–9."

Clearly, this provision does not dispense with the victim requirement of s. 7 in cases where it would otherwise apply, but are there cases where the Convention can be relied upon "apart from" those covered by s. 7? Two possibilities can be suggested. First, the standing requirements of s. 7(1) arguably do not affect the ability of parties to rely upon the Convention in the same circumstances, and for the same purposes, as they could do prior to the passing of the Act. They would not be able to invoke Convention rights as conferred by the Act, but could argue that the requirements of the Convention are relevant, for example, to the interpretation of legislation and the development of the common law just as they were relevant before the Act. Convention-based claims which do not invoke Convention rights as such, or complain of a breach of s. 6(1) of the Act, appear to fall outside the scope of s. 7. Of course, this may be of little consolation to those persons, including interest groups, who do not satisfy the "victim" test, since the provisions of the Convention, when they were on the international plane alone, were a far less powerful means of challenge. The outcome would be anomalous but would at least avoid the perverse conclusion that the strengthening of the status of the Convention in domestic law has removed the pre-existing scope for certain parties to rely upon it.

The second possibility is based upon the duty of the courts under s. 3 of   **2.15** the Act to seek to interpret legislation in a manner which is compatible with Convention rights. It could be argued that this is a freestanding duty which applies whether or not the person who will benefit from such an interpretation is a victim. The argument is probably only sustainable in cases which do not fall squarely within s. 7 (which applies to cases involving a claim that a public authority has acted or proposes to act in breach of Convention rights). The problem is that all instances of statutory interpretation pursuant to s. 3, even in cases not involving parties who are public authorities, could be said to involve a public authority — the court — acting, or proposing to act, in breach of Convention rights, within the terms of s. 7. That is because the court may act in breach of Convention rights, contrary to s. 6(1), if it declines to interpret a statutory provision in a manner which is consistent with the Convention.[34]

3. VERTICAL AND HORIZONAL EFFECT OF CONVENTION RIGHTS

2.16   Against whom may Convention rights be invoked? The basic premise is that the Convention confers rights upon individuals which may be enforced against the state. By signing up to the Convention, the UK has accepted the obligation of securing certain rights to persons within its jurisdiction. To use the terminology which has entered the legal lexicon via EC law, the paradigm claim under the Convention is a *vertical* claim, brought by an individual to enforce obligations which are owed to him by the state and to give effect to rights which the state has promised to secure. The Convention does not envisage *horizontal* claims, by one private person or body against another, since individuals do not, *prima facie*, owe any duty to other individuals to respect their Convention rights.

2.17   This premise is reflected in s. 6 of the Act, which obliges only public authorities to respect Convention rights:

"(1) It is unlawful for a public authority to act in a way which is incompatible with a Convention right.

. . .

(3) In this section, 'public authority' includes —

   (a) a court or tribunal, and
   (b) any person certain of whose functions are functions of a public nature,

but does not include either House of Parliament or a person exercising functions in connection with proceedings in Parliament.

(4) In subsection (3) 'Parliament' does not include the House of Lords in its judicial capacity.

(5) In relation to a particular act, a person is not a public authority by virtue only of subsection (3)(b) if the nature of the act is private."

Section 7(1) goes on to provide for vertical claims, whereby individuals may challenge the acts of public authorities. However, it will be argued

---

[34] Subject to the defences set out in HRA s. 6(2).

below that the status of the courts as public authorities entails that Convention rights can be invoked also in horizontal proceedings.

STRASBOURG PRACTICE ON STATE RESPONSIBILITY

Just as there is a wealth of case-law of the Strasbourg institutions on the issue of *locus standi*, so the Commission and the Court have frequently had to decide whether the actions of a person or body can give rise to responsibility on the part of the state for breach of Convention rights.[35] In contrast with its treatment of *locus standi*, the Act does not refer directly to the Strasbourg practice on state responsibility but lays down its own definition of which persons and bodies are required to respect Convention rights. The Strasbourg case-law is, nevertheless, relevant given the overall purpose of the Act to enable individuals to rely upon Convention rights in the domestic courts in the same circumstances as they can rely upon them in Strasbourg.[36] In the light of that purpose, it would be surprising if a person or body whose actions could legitimately be attacked in Strasbourg fell outside the scope of s. 6. The converse proposition — that the range of public authorities should be no broader than the range of bodies whose actions will give rise to state responsibility in Strasbourg — may also hold good. **2.18**

SECTION 6 CLAIMS AGAINST PUBLIC AUTHORITIES

Section 6 envisages two types of public authorities: bodies which are manifestly public authorities within s. 6(1), and bodies which are not clearly within s. 6(1) but fall within the definition in s. 6(3)(b), in that they exercise one or more public functions.[37] This typology is made tolerably **2.19**

---

[35] This question is analytically different, but the underlying issue is the same. For a detailed discussion, see chapter 6, paras. 6.18–6.29.

[36] HC Debs., 24 June 1998, col. 1084 (purpose of the Act set out in a response on the issue of *locus standi*).

[37] The courts are perhaps an exception: they are mentioned specifically in s. 6(3) but, on any view, would also fall within s. 6(1). For a definition of "function" see *R v Hammersmith and Fulham LBC ex parte Hazell* [1990] 2 QB 697, 722.

clear by the wording of s. 6 itself and in particular by the fact that s. 6(3) is expressly non-exhaustive. It was also set out by the Lord Chancellor at the committee stage of the Human Rights Bill in the House of Lords. He mentioned Government departments, local authorities, the police, the courts, prisons, prison officers and immigration officers as examples of the former, obvious type of public authority.[38] Railtrack, the Press Complaints Commission, the NSPCC, private security companies managing contracted-out prisons and doctors in general practice were, in his view, public authorities by virtue only of s. 6(3)(b).[39] The White Paper also mentioned the privatised utilities as falling within that category.[40] The Home Secretary added the BBC, the Independent Television Commission (although not independent television companies), the Jockey Club, Group 4 (in its role within the police and prison service), the British Board of Film Classification and any body which regulates a profession of any kind.[41] The distinction is an important one since obvious public authorities within s. 6(1) are required to respect Convention rights in everything they do; s. 6(5) provides, however, that bodies which are public authorities by virtue only of s. 6(3)(b) have no obligation to comply with the Convention in their "private" acts.

Public functions

2.20   The first step in ascertaining whether or not a person or body is a public authority which is bound to respect Convention rights is to ask whether or not it exercises one or more "functions of a public nature". That is a pre-condition not only for the type of public authority recognised by s. 6(3)(b) but for all public authorities since it could hardly be said that a person or body was clearly a public authority within s. 6(1) if it did not exercise any public functions. At its narrowest, a public function is one of a small group of essential functions which are performed by all governments — law and order, taxation, defence of the realm and on. At its broadest, a public function is any function which is available to the public and would cover newspapers, supermarkets, window cleaners and the like.[42]

---

[38] HL Debs., 24 November 1997, cols. 796 and 811.
[39] *Ibid.* at cols. 785–786, 796, 800 and 811.
[40] Above n. 6 at para. 2.2.
[41] HC Debs., 16 February 1998, col. 778; HC Debs., 20 May 1998, col. 1015; HC Debs., 17 June 1998, cols. 410-413.
[42] One eminent former judge suggested that even Safeways supermarket could be said to be a public authority since it conducts a business of a public nature: HL Debs., 3 November 1997, col. 1294.

The notion of "functions of a public nature" appears to have been **2.21**
borrowed not from the Convention or its case-law but from the New
Zealand Bill of Rights Act 1990. Under s. 3 of that Act, the fundamental
rights conferred by it apply only in respect of acts done by the legislative,
executive, or judicial branches of the government of New Zealand or by
any person or body *in the performance of any public function*, power, or
duty conferred or imposed on that person or body by or pursuant to law
(emphasis added). There is, however, relatively little New Zealand case-
law elaborating on the definition of a public function. Three decisions are
worthy of note.

- NZ Post Ltd, the equivalent of The Post Office, has been held to fall
  within the scope of the Bill of Rights Act. Mail handling was said to be
  a public function since it was carried out for the public, in the public
  interest, by a company which, while technically separate from the
  Government, was wholly owned and ultimately controlled by it.[43]
- TV3 Network, a privately owned television company, has also been
  held to be exercising a public function on the grounds that it was
  licensed by statute and subject to obligations imposed by that statute
  in the public interest.[44]
- More recently, a state school was held to fall outside s. 3 when it
  expelled a pupil from its boarding hostel.[45] The court required a
  "close and direct relationship of agency" between the Government
  and the body in question and referred to a test of control adopted by
  the Canadian courts under the Canadian Charter of Rights and
  Freedoms. The Bill of Rights Act could not apply because there
  was no government input or control over the actions of the school
  boards of trustees with respect to the management of boarding
  establishments.[46]

It is fundamental to the New Zealand analysis of a public function that **2.22**
the function is conferred or imposed on the relevant person or body *by or
pursuant to law*. That requirement would exclude private commercial
organisations such as newspapers and supermarkets who offer their

---

[43] *Federated Farmers of NZ (Inc) v NZ Post Ltd* [1990–92] NZBORR 331.
[44] *TV3 Network v Eveready New Zealand Ltd* [1993] 3 NZLR 435. Compare HC Debs., 16 February
1998, col. 778.
[45] *M v Board of Trustees of Palmerston North Boys' High School* [1997] 2 NZLR 60.
[46] Under the Human Rights Act, the school would probably qualify as a public authority, on the basis
that education is a public function, but it could be argued that its actions in relation to boarding
accommodation are private acts and excluded by s. 6(5).

services to the public but do not exercise any measure of public authority and are not required by law to act in the public interest. The case-law of the Commission and the Court of Human Rights also provides support for the view that a person or body which has dealings with the public must have some additional, official or authoritative status if it is to be bound by the Convention.

2.23 Three lines of authority are relevant. First, the approach of the Convention to regulatory bodies. In *Casado Coca*, the Court was faced with argument as to whether the Barcelona Bar Council was a public body capable of breaching Convention rights. The Court held that its public law status, the fact that it performed functions in the public interest (the regulation of the legal profession) and that its decisions could be challenged in the courts all supported the view that it was a public authority subject to the Convention.[47] On the basis of that decision, most if not all bodies which are subject to judicial review under English law ought, in principle, to be deemed to be a public authority, exercising a public function, within s. 6 of the Act.

2.24 Secondly, the Government is liable under the Convention for the actions of a private body to which it has delegated the task of securing Convention rights. For example, the UK has been held responsible for the actions of a private school, on the basis that the state has delegated to the school the function of securing the Convention right to education.[48] Private prisons and security firms to whom the Government delegates responsibility with regard to the prohibition on inhuman and degrading treatment of prisoners under Article 3 would also fall squarely within this principle. The delegation principle probably also extends to those, arguably private, bodies which regulate Convention rights on behalf of the state, even if their function is to restrict, rather than exactly to secure, those rights. Examples would be the Press Complaints Commission, the Advertising Standards Authority and the British Board of Film Classification, whose task it is to regulate freedom of expression in the general interest.[49] Some of the bodies within the delegation principle are amenable to judicial review under domestic law, but others, for example, private schools, are not. It is the fact of delegation which is important — the Court of Human Rights is unlikely to be concerned with the way in which delegation is effected. Delegation could be achieved by law, or by

---

[47] *Casado Coca* v *Spain*, A/285, (1994) 18 EHRR 1, 20-21. See also *X* v *The Netherlands*, Appl. No. 7669/76, (1979) 15 D&R 133.
[48] *Costello-Roberts* v *UK*, A/247-C, (1995) 19 EHRR 112.
[49] On the BBFC, see *Wingrove* v *UK*, A/699, (1997) 24 EHRR 1. In that case, the BBFC restricted the applicant's freedom of expression in order to secure to others their freedom of thought, conscience and religion under Art. 9 of the Convention.

contract, or even by informal endorsement and omission by the Government to regulate the matter itself. The latter is the case with the Press Complaints Commission which has no statutory basis or contractual relationship with the Government, but which is run by the newspaper industry as an alternative to legal regulation.

Thirdly, it should not be forgotten that, according to the Commission, **2.25** bodies which "exercise public functions" do not have standing to complain about a violation of their Convention rights.[50] The Court would surely be reluctant to interpret that phrase broadly given the large number of persons and bodies which could be deprived of Convention rights as a result, including, for example, newspapers, whose freedoms the Convention holds dear. Certainly, an examination of the range of applications which have been accepted as admissible without any issue being raised as to the standing of the applicant — by newspapers, television stations, banks, building societies, supermarkets, churches, etc. — would suggest that the concept of public functions cannot mean simply functions which involve the public.

The definition of "public authority" for the purposes of s. 6, and of **2.26** "functions of a public nature" in particular, is one of the issues raised by the Act which is most in need of clarification by the English courts. Ultimately, they face an unattractive choice. A broader definition may catch bodies who would not be caught under the Strasbourg rules and disqualify important persons and bodies from protecting their own rights pursuant to s. 7 of the Act. A narrower definition, on the other hand, may give rise to arbitrary distinctions, between the BBC and commercial broadcasters, for example, or between The Stationary Office, the Government's publisher and bookseller, and its privately-owned competitors.

The two categories of public authority

Where the act complained of is a private act it will be crucial to determine **2.27** whether the body in question, which exercises public functions, is manifestly a public authority within s. 6(1), or only qualifies as a public authority by virtue of s. 6(3)(b), that is, by virtue of the fact that certain of its functions are of a public nature. Section 6(5) exempts the latter from liability for private acts.[51] The line is not easy to draw since bodies which are within s. 6(1) are manifestly public authorities partly or mainly by reason of their public functions.

---

[50] *Ayuntamiento de M v Spain*, above n. 27 at 215.
[51] HRA s. 6(5).

2.28 Various approaches could be adopted but it is submitted that practice under the Convention points to a broad category of s. 6(1) authorities with s. 6(3)(c) having very much a residual status. The reason is that the Convention does not recognise any distinction between the public and private acts of bodies for whom the state is responsible. If a body is found to be a public authority, all of its acts may be challenged in Strasbourg, including, for example, its private law relations as an employer. This principle was established in the *Swedish Engine Drivers Union* case, where the Court rejected the argument that the Convention was intended to protect the individual against the state as holder of public power, not to influence the state in its private law relations.[52] If practice under the Act is to reflect the Convention rules, all bodies which would be regarded as public authorities in Strasbourg must fall within s. 6(1), so that both their public and private acts may be challenged.

2.29 Conversely, the Commission and the Court do recognise a relatively narrow category of bodies which are private bodies but whose acts give rise to state responsibility on the ground that they are charged with exercising certain public functions. These are the bodies, such as private schools, who fall within the delegation principle outlined above. Only their public acts, that is, acts done in pursuance of their public functions, are actionable.[53] The analogy between delegate bodies and bodies which are public authorities only by virtue of s. 6(3)(b) is not exact but it is a relevant and useful tool for identifying those bodies which fall outside s. 6(1) and are public authorities only by virtue of s. 6(3)(b).[54]

2.30 The wording of s. 6 itself is supportive of this approach. Section 6(3)(b) applies to any person "certain of whose functions are functions of a public nature." It excludes, arguably, a wide range of persons or bodies *all* of whose functions are of a public nature.[55] They must fall within s. 6(1). Also, s. 6(5) excludes the private acts of those bodies who qualify as public authorities *only* by virtue of certain of their functions. They must, accordingly, have no other trappings of a public authority and, in particular, no public law status. Again, this will place a large number of persons and bodies within s. 6(1). It is submitted that s. 6(5) refers only to those persons and bodies whose legal status is wholly governed by

[52] *Swedish Engine Drivers Union* v *Sweden,* A/20, (1979–80) 1 EHRR 617, 626–627.

[53] In *Costello-Roberts,* the Court appeared to rule out liability for acts of a private school which were "merely ancillary to the educational process": above n. 48 at 132.

[54] The Home Secretary conformed that churches would be regarded as public authorities insofar as they stand in the place of the state, for example in the provision of education in church schools: HC Debs., 20 May 1998, col. 1015.

[55] There is an important distinction between functions and activities: all bodies perform activities of a private nature — employ staff, purchase stationary, etc. — but that say nothing about the nature of their functions.

private law but who perform certain tasks in conjunction with, or instead of, the state. Bodies within the Convention's delegation principle, such as private schools and private security firms working in a contracted-out prison, would be prime examples.

Private acts

The meaning of acts of a private nature under s. 6(5) is not self-evident. **2.31** However, it is submitted that there is a relationship between s. 6(5) and s. 6(3)(b) in that the nature of an act, for the purposes of s. 6(5), should be dependent upon the nature of the function in pursuance of which it is done. An act done in pursuance of a public function, for example, an assault committed by an employee of a private security firm whilst working in a contracted-out prison, would be a public act. Conversely, an assault committed by the same employee whilst guarding commercial premises would be a private act. However, there will undoubtedly be difficult cases, where an act is done partly for public and partly for private purposes, for example, the security firm's decision to dismiss the offending employee who works partly in the prison and partly at commercial premises.

Parliamentary immunity

Section 6 preserves the important English law principle of Parliamentary **2.32** immunity. Both Houses of Parliament (save for the Judicial Committee of the House of Lords) and persons exercising functions in connection with Parliamentary proceedings, are expressly excluded from the definition of public authority and so have no obligation under s. 6(1) to abide by Convention rights.[56] The freedom of Parliament to legislate, or not, as it chooses is also saved by s. 6(6) which provides that no liability can attach to a failure on the part of the Government to introduce or lay before Parliament any legislation, or to a failure on the part of Parliament to pass primary legislation or a s. 10 remedial order. The historical and political reasons for these provisions are clear enough but it should be noted that the Convention contains no equivalent doctrine of Parliamentary immunity: the legislature is part of the state and its actions or inactions may give rise to liability in the same way as those of any other state body. However,

---

[56] HRA s. 6(3)–(4).

in most if not all instances where Parliamentary immunity could be relevant, it should be possible to raise the same Convention issues by mounting a challenge to an existing law or a decision of another public authority (for example, a minister) which raises the same issues.

Indirect responsibility

2.33   Under the Convention, a public authority may be found liable for a violation of Convention rights by a private body where its actions have contributed indirectly towards it. In *López-Ostra*, for example, the applicant complained about pollution from a privately-owned waste treatment plant.[57] The Spanish Government was held responsible for the operations of the plant on the basis that the local council had made formerly public land available for its construction and had subsidised the construction works. It was also relevant that the council did nothing to tackle the problems caused by the plant and had opposed the applicant's attempts to have it closed.[58] No specific provision is made in s. 6 for this principle, which may be of considerable importance. However, indirect responsibility can be accommodated within s. 6 by an appropriate definition of the circumstances in which a public authority will be deemed to have acted in a manner which is incompatible with Convention rights.

CONVENTION CLAIMS AGAINST PRIVATE PARTIES

2.34   Section 7(1) of the Act provides that, in addition to proceedings against public authorities who are alleged to have violated Convention rights, the Convention may be relied upon "in any legal proceedings", and that would include horizontal proceedings, between two private persons or bodies. As has been noted above, the application of the Convention in horizontal cases is explained by the status of the courts as public authorities, who have a duty under s. 6(1) to act in a way which is compatible with Convention rights and so to give effect to those rights in their decisions.[59] Judicial decisions must, therefore, be consistent with the Convention, even if the proceedings are between private parties.[60]

---

[57] *López-Ostra* v *Spain*, A/303-C, (1995) 20 EHRR 277.
[58] *Ibid.* at 296–297.
[59] A similar approach is adopted in EC law: see, for example, *von Colson and Kamann* v *Land Nordrhein-Westfalen*, Case 14/83 [1984] ECR 1891.
[60] See, for example, *Hoffman* v *Austtria*, A/255-C, (1944) 17 EHRR 139.

There are many examples of claims succeeding in Strasbourg which **2.35**
have their origin in private proceedings in the domestic courts. In *Good-*
win, for example, the applicant journalist was found guilty of contempt of
court when, in the course of proceedings brought by a company against
the publishers of the magazine for which he worked, he refused to
deliver-up notes which would have revealed his source for a sensitive
story about the company.[61] He later took his case to Strasbourg and
succeeded in establishing that the court's order against him was an
unjustified restriction upon his right to freedom of expression.[62] Moreover, the British courts have in the past applied Convention principles in
horizontal disputes. An example is *Rantzen v MGN*, where the Court of
Appeal referred extensively to Article 10 of the Convention in seeking to
redefine the appropriate scope for awards of damages in libel cases.[63]
The duty of the courts to deliver fundamental rights protection in
horizontal, private law proceedings has also been recognised in certain
other common law jurisdictions, including New Zealand, upon whose Bill
of Rights the Human Rights Act is, in part, modelled.[64]

During the passage of the Act through the House of Lords, Lord **2.36**
Wakeham, the chairman of the Press Complaints Commission, proposed
an amendment which would have excluded the courts from their duty to
comply with the Convention in (horizontal) cases where the parties to the
proceedings do not include a public authority.[65] His aim was to prevent
the right to respect for private life under Article 8 from being invoked
against newspapers (although the amendment would also have prevented newspapers from asserting, in most cases, their right to freedom
of expression under Article 10). The amendment was rejected and the
Lord Chancellor emphasised that the courts must seek to give effect to
Convention rights in all cases and not only those involving public
authorities.[66] In principle, therefore, the Convention may be invoked in
horizontal proceedings where a failure by the court to apply the
Convention would give rise to a breach of one or more Convention
rights, and a claim against the UK Government in Strasbourg.

It is important to remember, however, that the invocation of the **2.37**
Convention in a private dispute does not imply that the other party has

---

[61] *X Ltd v Morgan-Grampian Ltd* [1991] 1 AC 1.
[62] *Goodwin v UK*, A/610, (1996) 22 EHRR 123.
[63] [1994] QB 670. See also *Holley v Smyth* [1998] 1 All ER 853.
[64] See *R v H* [1994] 2 NZLR 143, 147; *Capital Coast Health Ltd v New Zealand Medical Laboratory*
Workers Union Inc [1996] 1 NZLR 7. Compare the contrary position in Canada: *RWDSU v Dolphin*
Delivery Ltd (1986) 33 DLR 176.
[65] HL Debs., 24 November 1997, cols. 771–774.
[66] *Ibid.* at col. 783. However, Lord Wakeham's concerns were met elsewhere in the Act: s. 12.

any obligation to respect Convention rights. Ms Rantzen, for example, owed no duty to Mirror Group Newspapers to respect and uphold its freedom of expression. It is the court, as a public authority, which owes the duty. Many attempts to rely upon the Convention in horizontal proceedings will founder for that reason. Save where the positive obligations of the state are at issue, one individual cannot sustain a claim based upon breach of a Convention right against another. A woman who is sexually harassed by her private sector employer may have a claim under the Sex Discrimination Act but could not claim against him directly for inhuman and degrading treatment under Article 3, or breach of her right to respect for her private life under Article 8.

4. USING CONVENTION RIGHTS IN PARTICULAR CASES

2.38   Having established in a particular case that it will be possible, in principle, to rely upon Convention rights, the next step is to identify the use to which the Convention is sought to be put. Section 7 of the Act provides for two ways in which Convention rights may be used. The first is to bring proceedings, including a counterclaim or similar proceeding, against a public authority claiming that it has acted, or proposes to act,[67] in a way which is incompatible with Convention rights. Such proceedings are to be brought in the "appropriate court or tribunal" as determined by rules.[68] Only acts committed after s. 7 has come into force can be the subject of a direct challenge.[69] Secondly, a person claiming that a public authority has acted, or proposes to act in a way which is incompatible with Convention rights may rely upon those rights in "any legal proceedings".[70] By virtue of s. 7(6), that phrase encompasses a Convention-based defence or collateral challenge in proceedings brought or instigated by a public authority, and an appeal against a judicial decision. Where proceedings are brought or instigated by a public authority, acts may be challenged as incompatible with Convention rights even where they were committed before s. 7 came into force.[71]

---

[67] An unlawful act includes a failure to act: HRA s. 6(6).
[68] HRA ss. 7(1)–(2).
[69] HRA s. 22(4).
[70] HRA s. 7(1) (b).
[71] HRA s. 22(4)

Each case in which Convention rights are invoked, whether under s. **2.39**
7(1)(a) or (b), involves the courts in one or more specific uses of the
Convention. The forthcoming sections of this chapter examine the various
ways in which the Convention might be used, grouped into the following
categories:

- statutory interpretation
- judicial review of statutes
- judicial review of delegated legislation
- developing the common law
- influencing the exercise of judicial discretion
- challenging the exercise of administrative discretion

The mechanism whereby the Act incorporates Convention rights into
domestic law, in particular the inability of the Convention to override Acts
of Parliament, means that the Convention may have a greater or lesser
impact depending upon the particular way in which the court is being
asked to apply it.

5. STATUTORY INTERPRETATION

Section 3 of the Human Rights Act provides: **2.40**

"(1) So far as it is possible to do so, primary legislation and subordinate legislation must be
read and given effect in a way which is compatible with the Convention rights.

(2) This section —
  (a) applies to primary legislation and subordinate legislation whenever enacted;
  (b) does not affect the validity, continuing operation or enforcement of any incom-
      patible primary legislation; and
  (c) does not affect the validity, continuing operation or enforcement of any incom-
      patible subordinate legislation if (disregarding any possibility of revocation)
      primary legislation prevents removal of the incompatibility."

The principal mechanism whereby Convention rights are to take effect
in domestic law is a rule of statutory interpretation.[72] A large proportion of
cases which raise Convention issues will require the court to engage in a

---

[72] The term "statutory interpretation" is here used to describe the interpretation both of Acts of
Parliament and of statutory instruments.

process of construction of a statutory provision. Direct challenges to the compatibility with the Convention of primary legislation clearly require such an exercise. In addition, challenges pursuant to the Act to sub-ordinate legislation, or to the administrative acts of public authorities, will generally involve the construction of primary legislation in order to ascertain whether an alleged breach of Convention rights is authorised or required by it. When confronted with a statutory provision in domestic proceedings, the courts must, pursuant to s. 3 of the Human Rights Act, endeavour to construe it in accordance with the Convention. Even where it is argued that a statutory provision is inconsistent with, and in breach of, the Convention, the court must proceed, firstly, along the road of statutory interpretation. It is only if legislation cannot be construed consistently with the Convention that a breach will arise, and the Act instructs the courts to avoid that conclusion if possible.

2.41   Given the central role which is ascribed by the Human Rights Act to statutory interpretation, the key issue is how far the courts are obliged to go in seeking to construe legislation in a manner which is compatible with Convention rights. How strong is the interpretive obligation and when must it yield to the language of the statutory provision? The following sections will outline, briefly, the role played by the Convention in statutory interpretation before the enactment of the Human Rights Act and then analyse in more detail what has changed. It will be submitted that the role of the Convention in statutory interpretation under the Act is far more compelling than it was previously, such that many statutory provisions can, pursuant to s. 3, be read consistently with the Convention which previously would have been found to be unambiguous and beyond salvation. Further, whether or not the strength of the interpretive obligation under the Act marks any advance on the previous position, the courts are, indisputably, required to change the methodology which they have previously adopted when using the Convention for the purposes of statutory interpretation.

THE PRE-INCORPORATION POSITION

2.42   The pre-incorporation use of the Convention for statutory interpretation is exemplified by the decision of the House of Lords in *ex parte Brind*.[73] This was the case brought by a group of journalists to

---

[73] *R.* v *Home Secretary ex parte Brind* [1991] 1 AC 696.

challenge restrictions imposed by the Government on the broadcast of the voices of members of proscribed organisations, notably Sinn Fein. The statutory power under which the Government had acted, s. 29(3) of the Broadcasting Act 1981, was broadly worded. It stated:

"the Secretary of State may at any time by notice in writing require the [Independent Broadcasting] Authority to refrain from broadcasting any matter or classes of matter specified in the notice, and it shall be the duty of the Authority to comply with the notice."

Clause 13(4) of the licence and agreement governing the activities of the BBC was in similar terms. The applicants sought to quash the directives by which the Home Secretary had imposed the broadcasting restrictions, arguing, *inter alia*, that he had acted in breach of a duty to exercise his powers in accordance with the freedom of expression under Article 10 of the Convention.

2.43 It was argued, first, that there was a general presumption that Parliament did not intend to legislate in breach of its international commitments.[74] Accordingly, all legislation should be construed in conformity with the Convention if it was reasonably capable of bearing that meaning and nothing in s. 29(3) was not reasonably capable of being construed so as to further Article 10 and not to be inconsistent with it. However, Lord Bridge held that the Convention could only be used in construing provisions of domestic legislation which are ambiguous, in which case the courts will presume that Parliament intended to legislate in conformity with the Convention, not in conflict with it.[75] It was not sufficient to give rise to ambiguity that s. 29(3) conferred a discretion which was apparently unlimited ("the Secretary of State may . . . require") when everyone accepted that it could not be unlimited and that it was restricted by the principles of public law. An ambiguous provision is one which is capable of a meaning which either conforms to or conflicts with the Convention, and s. 29(3) was unambiguous on that test.[76]

2.44 The precondition that a provision must be ambiguous, in the sense expounded by Lord Bridge, before reference can be made to the Convention has been the rock upon which very many pre-incorporation Convention claims have foundered. There are numerous other examples of statutory provisions which have been held by the courts to be unambiguous and therefore not open to interpretation in line with the

---

[74] See *Garland* v *British Rail Engineering Ltd* [1983] 2 AC 751, 771 (per Lord Diplock).
[75] Above n. 73 at 747–748.
[76] *Ibid.* at 761 (per Lord Ackner).

Convention.[77] Following the enactment of the Human Rights Act, parties on the receiving end of Convention arguments may well submit that little or nothing has changed, and that it is only "possible" to read statutory provisions consistently with the Convention where, in effect, they are ambiguous.

A NEW INTERPRETIVE OBLIGATION

2.45   Section 3 requires statutory provisions to be read consistently with Convention rights "so far as it possible to do so". It is submitted that this is clearly not an invitation to continue to use the Convention only for the purposes of resolving ambiguity (if it were, it would be otiose). On the contrary, it is an instruction to construe a statutory provision in accordance with the Convention where it is capable of being so read, regardless of whether or not, considered in isolation, the provision is ambiguous in the *Brind* sense, and using, if necessary, the technique of reading-in additional words so as "read down" otherwise inconsistent provisions. On this approach, it will only be impossible to read a provision consistently with the Convention where it contains clear words which require that conclusion.

2.46   The analysis below adopts a three-fold classification of statutory provisions.

- *Category one*: provisions which are ambiguous in the *Brind* sense, in that the language employed is susceptible to at least two different meanings, one of which is consistent with the Convention. An example would be s. 10 of the Contempt of Court Act 1981, which requires a journalist to disclose his sources only where it is "in the interests of justice" that he do so. "The interests of justice" is a notoriously flexible concept which is certainly capable of being construed in any individual case so as to ensure that there is no breach of Convention rights.
- *Category two*: provisions which are not ambiguous on their face but which it is possible to read in conformity with the Convention, if necessary by the implication of additional words. The *Brind* provision, s. 29(3) of the Broadcasting Act 1981, fell into this category. Its text was broadly worded, and found by the House of

---

[77] For example, *Attorney-General* v *Associated Newspapers Ltd* [1994] 2 AC 238.

Lords to be unambiguous. However, there was nothing express in the text of the provision, or in the scheme of the Act, which would have prevented it from being read and applied consistently with the Convention by the implication of a Parliamentary intention and/or of additional words to that effect. The problem was, rather, that the implication that Parliament had intended s. 29(3) to be so read and applied was illegitimate where the Convention had not been incorporated into domestic law.

- *Category three*: provisions which are not ambiguous and which, to the contrary, evince a clear intention for an interpretation which does not conform to the Convention. On any view, it is not possible to interpret such provisions in accordance with Convention rights. An example is s. 434 of the Companies Act 1985 which was found to breach Article 6 of the Convention in *Saunders*.[78] It required persons questioned by DTi company inspectors to answer questions and produce documents on pain of being held in contempt of court. It was clear and uncompromising and not capable of being saved by interpretation but only by repeal.

According to *Brind*, only category one provisions must be read consistently with the Convention. It will be submitted that the rule of interpretation contained in s. 3 of the Human Rights Act requires, further, that category two provisions are also construed so as to be compatible with the requirements of the Convention. The effect of s. 3(2)(b) of the Act is to exclude category three provisions from the reach of the Convention; it will remain for Parliament to take the necessary action. Various lines of argument can be put forward in support of this view of s. 3: **2.47**

- It is required by the wording of the section itself, as explained in Parliament.
- It is based upon well-established principles of the common law which apply when construing statutory provisions in the light of fundamental rights norms which have the status of domestic law.
- It has been adopted by the New Zealand courts in interpreting s. 4 of the New Zealand Bill of Rights Act 1990, which is phrased in similar terms.
- It is consistent with the approach adopted by the domestic courts when giving effect to the analogous obligation to interpret statutory provisions so that they are compatible with rules of EC law.

---

[78] *Saunders v UK*, A/702, (1997) 23 EHRR 313.

THE WORDING OF S. 3

2.48   Section 3 of the Act does not expressly require that a statutory provision must be ambiguous before it can legitimately be read in conformity with the Convention, although it would have been a simple matter to give statutory effect to the *Brind* test. Arguably, it would be surprising if there were any such requirement, either express or implied, within s. 3 since the ruling in *Brind* was premised on the view that the Convention formed no part of domestic law. As a result of the Act, the Convention now does form part of domestic law, for limited purposes at least, and it would be most odd if its incorporation had made absolutely no difference. Certainly, the White Paper which preceded the Act did not subscribe to that conservative view: it stated that s. 3 "goes far beyond the present rule which enables the courts to take the Convention into account in resolving any ambiguity in a legislative provision." [79]

2.49   The use of the word "possible", as opposed to "natural" or "reasonable", within s. 3 has changed the nature of the interpretive exercise. [80] The courts are not required to search for the true meaning of a statutory provision, having regard to the precise words used and to the background intention of Parliament to legislate in accordance with its international obligations. Rather, s. 3 instructs them to seek out a possible meaning which would prevent a finding of breach of the Convention. [81] It is submitted that it is "possible" to read a statutory provision in accordance with the Convention if it can bear that meaning once it has been subjected to all legitimate interpretive techniques, including, where necessary, the implication of additional words. The result of such an approach would be that in virtually all cases primary legislation will be capable of interpretation in line with the Convention. [82]

FUNDAMENTAL RIGHTS IN DOMESTIC LAW

2.50   There are notable pre-incorporation examples of the courts perceiving a stronger interpretive obligation than that permitted by *Brind*. The *dictum*

---

[79] Above n. 6 at para. 2.7. See also HC Debs., 3 June 1998, col. 426.

[80] It is notable that the Government rejected an attempt to amend s. 3 so as to impose an obligation to interpret statutory provisions in accordance with the Convention only where it is "reasonable" to do so: HL Debs., 18 November 1997, cols. 533–536.

[81] See Lord Cooke of Thorndon, HL Debs., 3 November 1997, col. 1272; Lord Steyn, "Incorporation and Devolution — A Few Reflections on the Changing Scene" [1998] EHRLR 193, 199.

[82] HL Debs., 5 February 1998, col. 840; HC Debs., 16 February 1998, col. 780.

of Lord Diplock in *Garland*, which was relied upon by the applicants in *Brind* for their broad presumption of compliance with the Convention, suggests that a statute should be construed so as to conform with an international treaty where it is reasonably capable of bearing that meaning, and contains no suggestion that it applies only to ambiguous provisions. The leading text on judicial review describes the *Brind* approach as unorthodox and lists an impressive body of extra-judicial support for the *Garland* test.[83] However, judicial invocation of the *Garland* test has been at best sporadic.[84]

It is submitted that the pre-Human Rights Act authorities on the use of **2.51** the Convention for the purposes of statutory interpretation are no longer authoritative or even relevant since they are premised on the Convention having the status of an unincorporated international treaty and forming no part of domestic law. Rather, the relevant cases are those which deal with the situation where a statutory provision is sought to be interpreted consistently with a fundamental rights norm which does form part of domestic law. There are two distinct but related lines of authority on fundamental rights which are incorporated into domestic law: cases where the courts have reviewed statutory provisions against fundamental rights contained in the common law, and the jurisprudence of the Privy Council when interpreting fundamental rights norms contained in the constitutions of former British territories overseas.

Fundamental common law rights

Perhaps the best examples of statutory provisions being read so as to **2.52** conform to a fundamental right contained in the common law have occurred in the context of prisoners' correspondence with their legal advisors. The fundamental right at issue in the leading cases was the right of unimpeded access to a court, described by the Court of Appeal in *ex parte Leech* as "a constitutional right", which incorporates a right of unimpeded access to a solicitor for the purpose of receiving advice and

---

[83] De Smith, Woolf and Jowell, above n. 30 at 6–052.
[84] See, for example, Brooke LJ in *R.* v. *Radio Authority ex parte Bull* [1997] 2 All ER 561, 578–579, citing *Garland* as the correct approach to be adopted when construing statutory provisions in line with the Convention.

assistance in connection with proposed or ongoing proceedings.[85] The primary statutory power at issue was s. 47(1) of the Prison Act 1952:

"The Secretary of State may make rules for the regulation and management of prisons, remand centres, detention centres and youth custody centres respectively, and for the classification, treatment, employment, discipline and control of persons required to be detained therein."

This section provides the legal basis for the adoption of the Prison Rules, which are a statutory instrument, and of standing orders and circulars which supplement and explain the Prison Rules.

2.53   In *Raymond* v *Honey*, a prisoner sought to commit the governor of his prison for contempt of court after the governor had stopped two letters from the prisoner to his solicitor. The first concerned ongoing legal proceedings; the second contained an application to commit the governor and deputy-governor for contempt by reason of the earlier interference.[86] Lord Wilberforce held that s. 47, which concerned the regulation and management of prisons, was "quite insufficient" to authorise hindrance or interference with so basic a right as that of access to the courts. That statutory power, although broadly worded, was limited by implication such that it did not authorise an infringement of a fundamental right contained in domestic law. Lord Bridge also found s. 47 to be "manifestly insufficient" for imposing fetters on the right of access of prisoners to the courts.[87] In *Leech*, the Court of Appeal understood the ratio of *Raymond* v *Honey* to be that the right of unimpeded access to the court could be restricted only by express enactment or by necessary implication. As to the latter, it noted that "the more fundamental the right interfered with, and the more drastic the interference, the more difficult becomes the implication."[88] The applicant prisoner had complained that his correspondence with his solicitor was being censored, pursuant to rule 33(3) of the Prison Rules, which expressly empowered prison governors to intercept, read or examine and, if necessary, stop prisoners' correspondence including correspondence with a legal advisor. Rule 33(3) was subject to a limited exception in rule 37A, whereby correspondence with a legal advisor in connection with ongoing proceedings could not be stopped unless the governor had reason to suppose that it contained matter which did not relate to the proceedings. The Court of Appeal

---

[85] *R.* v *Home Secretary ex parte Leech* [1994] QB 198, 210.
[86] [1983] 1 AC 1.
[87] *Ibid.* at 13, 15.
[88] Above n. 85 at 209–210.

followed *Raymond* v *Honey* in ruling that s. 47(1) could not be read as authorising a rule which created an impediment to the free flow of communications between a solicitor and his client about contemplated legal proceedings.[89] It found that rule 33(3) imposed an unnecessary fetter on prisoners' rights, which had not been authorised either expressly or by necessary implication and was therefore *ultra vires*.[90]

Section 47(1) of the Prisons Act 1952 falls within category two in the **2.54** classification adopted above. It is as broad as the provision which was at issue in *Brind*, and no more ambiguous. It was, nevertheless, capable of being read consistently with the fundamental principle of free access to the courts, provided that the correct starting point was adoped. Another leading example of statutory interpretation so as to preclude interference with the fundamental common law right of access to the courts is *ex parte Witham*, a challenge to subordinate legislation which removed the exemption from court fees enjoyed by litigants in person on income support.[91] The relevant enabling power was s. 130 of the Supreme Court Act 1980, which provides, in general terms, that the Lord Chancellor has the power to prescribe court fees. There is nothing in s. 130 which precludes measures interfering with the right of access to the courts but the starting point of the court was, as in *Leech*, precisely the opposite: such an interference was unjustified in the absence of clear authorisation. Indeed, Laws J went further than *Leech* and doubted whether it would be possible for such authorisation to be provided by necessary implication: that class of case was, in his view, a class with no members.[92] It is submitted that *Witham* might provide an ideal model for statutory interpretation pursuant to s. 3 HRA.

There is, in short, a presumption that a statutory provision should be **2.55** read as complying with the fundamental principles of the common law, rebuttable by clear words or necessary implication only in "a rare case".[93] That principle applies not only where the statutory provision conflicts directly with an established right but also where it indirectly defeats the right by making the exercise of the right difficult or impossible.[94]

Whilst the prisoners' cases and *Witham* concerned a particular right **2.56** contained in domestic law, it is clear that they express a principle of

---

[89] See also *R.* v *Home Secretary ex parte Anderson* [1984] QB 778.
[90] *Leech* was distinguished by the Court of Appeal in *R.* v *Home Secreatary ex parte Simms, The Times,* 9 December 1997 (standing orders restricting visiting to prisoners by journalists); cf *Bamber* v *UK,* Appl. No. 33742, [1998] EHRLR 110.
[91] *R.* v *Lord Chancellor ex parte Witham* [1997] 2 All ER 778.
[92] *Ibid.* at 787–788.
[93] *Leech,* above n. 85 at 212.
[94] *R.* v *Secretary of State for Social Security ex parte Joint Council for the Welfare of Immigrants* [1996] 4 All ER 385.

application to all common law rights. In *ex parte Bull*, Brooke LJ gave judicial approval to a passage contained in a leading text which stated the general rule that Parliament does not intend to deprive the subject of his or her common-law rights except where this is made clear by express words or by necessary implication.[95] Moreover, according to the leading work on statutory interpretation, there is a general "principle against doubtful penalisation",[96] which extends to statutory as well as common law rights.[97] Convention rights are, of course, somewhat different from common law or other statutory rights, because they are only incorporated into domestic law to a limited extent and for limited purposes. However, it is submitted that the same principles should apply to them since, under s. 3 of the Act, one of the purposes for which they are incorporated into domestic law is to inform statutory interpretation.

Fundamental rights in the Privy Council

2.57 The Privy Council has, on a number of occasions, addressed issues of statutory construction in the light of fundamental rights rules which are incorporated into overseas constitutions. A leading example is *Attorney-General of the Gambia* v *Jobe*, which concerned the validity of special powers and procedures enacted to deal with offences of misappropriation of public funds and property.[98] A defendant to an offence of theft from a public bank claimed that the special powers and procedures were void as contrary to guarantees of personal liberty and property rights contained in the constitution of the Gambia. In interpreting the relevant statutory provisions, many of which appeared, when considered in isolation, to violate the claimed constitutional rights, the Privy Council applied a presumption that the statute was intended to comply with fundamental rights. Given that presumption, the omission of the draftsman to provide in express terms for the necessary safeguards upon police action could be rectified by incorporating, by necessary implication, words which would rescue most, although not all, of the powers from invalidity. For example, the Act conferred upon the police the power to

---

[95] Above n. 84 at 578, citing De Smith, Woolf and Jowell *Judicial Review of Administrative Action* (5th ed., 1995). See also per Lord Blackburn in *Metropolitan Asylum District Managers* v *Hill* (1881) 6 App. Cas. 193, 208; per Lord Donaldson in *Re O* [1991] 2 WLR 475, 480 on the common law rule against self-incrimination.
[96] Bennion, *Statutory Interpretation: A Code* (Butterworths, 3rd ed., 1997), Part XVII.
[97] See, recently, *ex parte JCWI*, above n. 94.
[98] [1984] AC 689.

apply to a magistrate to freeze the bank accounts of suspects and banks were required not to pay any money out of a frozen account unless authorised in writing by the Inspector General of Police. Their Lordships inferred that a magistrate granting a freezing order would be obliged to lay down conditions in respect of payments out of the frozen account, and the Inspector General of Police would act as a mere rubber stamp, approving payments which complied with those conditions.[99] This was certainly not obvious from the legislation, but was a necessary addition if the relevant provision was not to be held unconstitutional.

The approach to statutory interpretation adopted by the Privy Council **2.58** in *Jobe* was prompted in part by the consideration that the legislation would be void if the appropriate implications were not made, and the Gambian Parliament could not have intended to pass a statute which was void. Similar considerations will apply under the regime of the Human Rights Act. Provisions of primary legislation which conflict with Convention rights are not thereby void, but the declaration of incompatibility, the remedy provided by s. 4 of the Act for use in that situation, is intended very much as a last resort.[100] Moreover, legislation which is passed after the Human Rights Act comes into force will generally be preceded by a statement of compatibility, in which Parliament is assured that the legislation does not conflict with the Convention.[101] It will thus be difficult to assume that Parliament intended otherwise.

THE INTERPRETIVE OBLIGATION IN EC LAW

It is a well-established principle of European Community law that **2.59** domestic courts are under an obligation to interpret provisions of domestic law consistently with EC law, so far as it is possible to do so.[102] These are, of course, the very words used in s. 3 of the Act and it is submitted that there is a strong identity between the interpretive obligation imposed on the courts by s. 3 and that which they have been applying for some time, pursuant to EC law. Given that, it is highly significant that the EC law obligation extends far beyond the sympathetic construction of ambiguous legislation. On the contrary, it is clear from

---

[99] *Ibid.* at 699–701.
[100] HL Debs., 18 November 1997, cols. 535–536.
[101] HRA s. 19.
[102] *Marleasing* v *La Comercial Internacional de Alimentación,* Case C-106/89 [1990] ECR I-4135.
   See chapter 3, paras. 3.18–3.23.

Litster, amongst other cases, that provisions which are not ambiguous, in the sense of having two or more permissible meanings, may be read consistently with EC law by the implication of appropriate words into the statutory text.[103]

2.60 In *Litster*, the House of Lords was required to apply reg. 5 of the Transfer of Undertakings (Protection of Employment) Regulations 1981, which has the effect, on the transfer of a business, of transferring to the new owner the contracts of employment of employees who are "employed [in an undertaking] immediately before the transfer." The European Court of Justice had interpreted the equivalent provision of the Acquired Rights Directive to mean that employees who are dismissed because of an impending transfer (an eventuality which is prohibited by the Directive) must be considered still to be employed in the business at the time of the transfer. In order to comply with the ECJ's interpretation, and despite the unambiguous wording of reg. 5, the House of Lords implied an additional clause into the text, so that reg. 5 applied to transfer the employment of those employees who were employed "immediately before the transfer *or would have been so employed if they had not been unfairly dismissed [by reason of the transfer]*".[104] The implication of appropriate language into the text of an apparently unambiguous provision was a departure from a line of earlier English cases which had emphasised the need for ambiguity in a statutory provision before Community law could be invoked.[105]

THE NEW ZEALAND MODEL

2.61 Sections 4 and 6 of the New Zealand Bill of Rights Act 1990 provide as follows:

"4. No court shall, in relation to any enactment (whether passed or made before or after the commencement of this Bill of Rights),

(a) Hold any provision of the enactment to be impliedly repealed or revoked, or to be in any way invalid or ineffective; or

---

[103] *Litster* v *Forth Dry Dock and Forth Estuary Engineering* [1990] 1 AC 546, 559.
[104] *Ibid.* at 558 (Lord Templeman) and 577 (Lord Oliver).
[105] For example, *Haughton* v *Olau Lines (UK) Ltd* [1986] 1 WLR 504. Another good example of the required approach under EC law is *R.* v *Secretary of State for the Environment ex parte Greenpeace* [1994] 4 All ER 352.

(b) Decline to apply any provision of this enactment —

> by reason only that the provision is inconsistent with any provision of this Bill of Rights.

> . . .

6. Wherever an enactment can be given a meaning that is consistent with the rights and freedoms contained in this Bill of Rights, that meaning shall be preferred to any other meaning."

The parallels between these provisions and s. 3 of the Human Rights Act are obvious. Whilst the Government has not stated in terms that the New Zealand legislation was adopted as the model for the Act, there can be little doubt that that was the case.[106] Accordingly, the case-law of the New Zealand courts on s. 6 of the New Zealand Act is a legitimate, and important, source of authority as to the limits of the interpretive obligation laid down by s. 3 of the Human Rights Act. It is worthy of note that Lord Cooke of Thorndon, formerly President of the New Zealand Court of Appeal, stated during the Second Reading debate on the Human Rights Bill that s. 3(1) "is, if anything, slightly stronger than the corresponding New Zealand section".[107] The New Zealand case-law is, on that view, a useful starting-point, but not the last word, on s. 3. Human rights challenges to legislation have been relatively scarce in New Zealand since the passing of the 1990 Act; the majority of cases in which the Bill of Rights has been invoked have concerned the compatibility with it of administrative action. There is not, as yet, a landmark ruling which analyses in detail the workings of s. 6, but it has been applied in a sufficient number of cases for a coherent pattern to be discerned. That pattern is consistent with the approach suggested above: in the New Zealand courts, both category one and category two provisions will be read consistently with the Bill of Rights.

In *Rangi*, the New Zealand Court of Appeal was faced with a category **2.62** one provision.[108] Section 202A(4)(a) of the Crimes Act 1961 rendered liable to imprisonment anyone "who without lawful authority or reasonable excuse, has with him in any public place any knife or offensive weapon or disabling substance." The accused had been convicted on the basis of a direction from the trial judge that the onus was on him to prove lawful authority or reasonable excuse. He argued on appeal that the burden upon him could be an evidential burden only, such that he had

---

[106] The White Paper gives a clear hint to this effect: above n. 6 at paras. 2.10–2.15.
[107] HL Debs., 3 November 1997, col. 1273.
[108] *R.* v *Rangi* [1992] 1 NZLR 385.

only to point to a sufficient foundation of fact upon which a defence might be based, rather than having to prove his defence on the balance of probabilities. He relied upon s. 25(c) of the Bill of Rights Act, which lays down the right to be presumed innocent until proven guilty. The Court held that the language of the Crimes Act was "neutral" as to the burden of proof. Accordingly, it was susceptible to an interpretation which accorded with the rights and freedoms contained in the Bill of Rights Act, and the conviction was quashed.

2.63   Conversely, s. 6 will not assist where a provision is clearly not in conformity with the Bill of Rights (category three). In *Phillips*, the defendant challenged his conviction under s. 6(6) of the Misuse of Drugs Act 1975 which created a presumption "until the contrary is proved" that an accused in possession of 28 grams or more of cannabis possesses it for an illegal purpose. It was argued that in order to accord with the presumption of innocence under s. 25(c) of the Bill of Rights Act, "until the contrary is proved" ought to be interpreted as meaning "unless sufficient evidence is given to the contrary". As in *Rangi*, which was decided subsequently, the defendant's aim was to reduce the burden on him to an evidential burden only. In *Phillips*, however, the Court of Appeal refused to give the wording of the offence what it viewed as a "strained and unnatural interpretation" in order to make it conform to the Bill of Rights Act.[109] The contrast between the two cases is clear: in *Rangi*, the relevant provision made no mention of the burden of proof but in *Phillips*, the burden of proof was expressly dealt with, and was placed upon the accused.

2.64   The interesting and important issue is how the New Zealand courts apply s. 6 to category two provisions, those which are silent on the fundamental rights issue with which the court is concerned but which, with the implication of appropriate words, could be read consistently with rights guarantees. It appears that their approach is indeed to "read down" category two provisions, implying limitations which safeguard the fundamental rights guaranteed in the Bill of Rights Act. In *Ministry of Transport v Noort*,[110] for example, the Court of Appeal was faced with a conflict between provisions enabling the police to take breath and blood tests from persons suspected of drink-driving and the rights enshrined in s. 23(1)(b) of the Bill of Rights Act to "consult and instruct a lawyer without delay and to be informed of that right". The complex provisions of the Transport Act governing the administration of alcohol tests did not expressly permit the suspect to consult a lawyer and were, to some

---

[109] See also *TV3 Network Services Ltd* v *R* [1993] 3 NZLR 421 and *Temese* v *Police* (1992) 9 CRNZ 425.
[110] [1992] 3 NZLR 260.

extent, at odds with the exercise of that right, since it was clearly the policy of the legislation that delays in the testing process should be minimised. Four out of five judges held, nevertheless, that a limited opportunity to consult a lawyer by telephone should be read into the legislation so that it did not conflict with s. 23(1)(b). Richardson J's approach was to ask whether the Transport Act ousted, by necessary implication, the right to consult a lawyer. He noted that whilst a suspect taken to a testing station may be required "forthwith" to provide a breath or blood test, there was no requirement that he proceed "forthwith" to the testing station.[111] There was, on that basis, time to seek legal advice, and so no ouster.[112]

2.65 The overall approach of the New Zealand Court of Appeal was reminiscent of that adopted in *Raymond* v *Honey* and in *Leech* in relation to another facet of the right to consult a lawyer. Whether or not a statutory provision can be interpreted in a way which is consistent with the Bill of Rights Act does not depend upon textual ambiguity. Certainly, no textual ambiguity, as such, was argued for in *Noort*, or relied upon by any of the judges in the majority. The issue, rather, is whether the legislation, expressly or by necessary implication, excludes or restricts a fundamental right. If it does not, then the legislation will be deemed capable of a meaning which is consistent with the Bill of Rights Act, and appropriate words will be implied to that effect. That approach is further exemplified by the subsequent decision of the Court of Appeal in *R* v *Laugalis*.[113] The Misuse of Drugs Act 1975 was again at issue, this time for its authorisation, in s. 18(2), of searches for drugs without a warrant. The defendant, whose car had been searched pursuant to that provision, complained that the search was in breach of s. 21 of the Bill of Rights Act, which provides for protection against "unreasonable search and seizure". The Court of Appeal agreed: there had been ample time for the police to obtain a warrant, so search without a warrant had been unnecessary and "unreasonable". Hardie Boys J accepted that his approach effectively wrote into s. 18(2) a restriction which Parliament had not thought appropriate to enact. However, he held that it was justified as necessary in order to preserve the force of the guarantee contained in the Bill of Rights Act, consistently with s. 6 of that Act.[114]

2.66 Hence, under the New Zealand model, appropriate exceptions or qualifications can and should be read into a statutory provision unless

---

[111] *Ibid.* at 284.
[112] The reasoning of the other judges in the majority, whilst informative, was influenced by the role of s. 5 of the New Zealand Act, which has no equivalent in the Human Rights Act.
[113] (1993) 10 CRNZ 350.
[114] *Ibid.* at 356.

it is clear in its limitation of fundamental rights. Category two provisions will be rescued from inconsistency with fundamental rights guarantees, even, as in *Laugalis*, where the exception or qualification is not justified by any evidence of Parliamentary intention.

SUMMARY

2.67 Section 3, read in isolation, does not, it is submitted, either require or permit the interpretation of statutory provisions in accordance with the Convention only where they are ambiguous, which was the established pre-incorporation approach. That conclusion becomes inescapable when reference is made to the previous practice of the courts in the various fields set out above. The rule of construction which has been applied in the context of domestic fundamental rights guarantees and of EC law will uphold fundamental rights unless the legislation is unambiguously to the opposite effect, thereby saving statutory provisions in categories one and two. New Zealand law, upon which s. 3 of the Act was modelled, confirms that analysis. Moreover, in the case of legislation passed after the Human Rights Act, the courts must have regard to a specific intention of Parliament to comply with Convention rights, save in the exceptional case where a statement of compatibility has not been made. It will, therefore, be all the more legitimate to imply necessary safeguards into broadly worded statutory provisions.

RECOURSE TO HANSARD

2.68 The landmark decision of the House of Lords in *Pepper* v *Hart* has opened the way for the use of Hansard for the purposes of discerning the intention of Parliament in a wide range of cases.[115] The use of Hansard in human rights cases may, however, give rise to special problems, because the conferral upon a statutory provision of an interpretation which is consistent with the Convention, perhaps through the implication of appropriate words, may run totally contrary to the intention of Parliament as revealed in the columns of Hansard. This problem should

---

[115] [1993] AC 593.

not arise in relation to legislation passed after the Human Rights Act, which will have been subjected to pre-legislative scrutiny for compliance with Convention rights and, in most if not all cases, accompanied by a statement of compatibility. It is legislation bearing upon Convention rights which was already in existence prior to the passing of the Act, and which may have been enacted with little regard to the Convention, which will raise the awkward questions. Put shortly, the issue is this: where, as a matter of language, a statutory provision can be given a meaning which is consistent with the Convention, should that meaning be defeated by evidence from Hansard that Parliament in fact intended something different?

Pepper v *Hart* requires three conditions to be satisfied before Hansard **2.69** may be used as an aid to interpretation: the legislation at issue is ambiguous or obscure or leads to absurdity; the material relied upon consists of the statements of a Minister or other promoter of the Bill; and the statements are clear.[116] It is at least arguable that, on the basis of these criteria, recourse to Hansard is unlikely to be appropriate in Convention cases. If the rule of construction applied under s. 3 is as suggested above, a statutory provision must clearly infringe the Convention if it is not to be read consistently with it. A finding of ambiguity sufficient for *Pepper* v *Hart* purposes should, on that analysis, result in an interpretation which conforms to the Convention, without the need to refer to Hansard.

On the assumption that Hansard does feature in at least some human **2.70** rights cases, it is submitted that little if any weight should be attributed to it and that the general intention of Parliament expressed in the Human Rights Act, that statutes be construed in conformity with Convention rights, should prevail over the specific intention expressed by the Minister introducing the relevant Bill in Parliament. If it is possible to construe the language of the statute in accordance with the Convention then, it is submitted, Hansard should not be permitted to alter the outcome.

That proposition is consistent with the scheme of s. 3, which is **2.71** concerned with "possible" meanings; recourse to Hansard, in contrast, aims to discern the *true* meaning of legislation through discovering the historical intention of the legislature. It is also soundly based in the decision of the Court of Appeal in *Rantzen*.[117] The issue in that case was the scope of the Court's power to substitute a lower award of damages for libel than that which had been set by a jury. The power to substitute a lower award was introduced by s. 8 of the Courts and Legal Services Act

---

[116] *Ibid.* at 634.
[117] Above n. 63.

1990 in the very limited circumstances where the Court of Appeal previously had the power to order a new trial. The then Lord Chancellor, Lord Mackay of Clashfern, told Parliament in plain terms that s. 8 would not affect the range of circumstances in which the Court of Appeal could interfere with a jury award but only broaden the range of options available to it once it had decided to interfere.[118]

2.72   The Court of Appeal in *Rantzen* agreed with the defendant newspaper that Article 10 of the Convention required a lower threshold, and a more interventionist approach, when deciding whether to make a substitute award than that which had existed in relation to ordering a new trial. It was faced, therefore, with a direct conflict between what it saw as the requirements of the Convention and the intention of Parliament as revealed by Hansard. It chose to give effect to the former, and to ignore the latter. It conceded that the Lord Chancellor's speech did not lend support to the newspaper's arguments (a hefty under-statement) but held that s. 8 should be interpreted so as to permit a closer scrutiny of jury awards than had hitherto been the case.[119]

A CHANGE OF METHOD

2.73   Whether or not the court's obligation to give effect to the Convention is now stronger and more effective than the rule expressed in *Brind*, it is clear that s. 3 of the Act requires a change in the methodology to be adopted where the Convention is relied upon as an aid to statutory interpretation. Under the pre-incorporation approach, a statutory provision is to be examined in isolation for signs of ambiguity. It is only if ambiguity, in the sense of two or more possible alternative meanings, can be identified that it is permissible even to look at what the substantive requirements of the Convention might be.[120] Under s. 3 of the Act, it is submitted that this methodology must be turned on its head. The first port of call must be the Convention itself, in order to determine what it requires in the circumstances of the particular case. Once the requirements of the Convention have been identified, the court should then seek to apply them in the light of the relevant domestic provisions, and endeavour to construe the latter in accordance with the former. The reason is that it is

---

[118] HL Debs., 20 February 1990, at cols. 170–171.
[119] Above n. 63 at 687, 692; cf *R. v Broadcasting Complaints Commission ex parte Barclay* [1997] EMLR 62.
[120] For example, per Lord Donaldson in *ex parte Brind* [1991] 1 AC 696, 718.

only possible properly to judge whether the domestic provision can be given a meaning which is compatible with Convention rights once it is known what the Convention actually requires. This approach is now commonplace where the courts are applying the interpretive obligation which is imposed by EC law.[121]

6. CHALLENGING PRIMARY LEGISLATION WHICH CONTRAVENES CONVENTION RIGHTS

Where it is impossible to interpret the provisions of an Act of Parliament **2.74** so as to accord with Convention rights, there is, by definition, a breach of the Convention. What are the courts to do in those circumstances? Pursuant to s. 3(2)(b), a court faced with a direct conflict between primary legislation and a Convention right must give effect to the legislation: a breach of Convention rights cannot affect the "validity, continuing operation or enforcement of any incompatible primary legislation".[122]

The pre-eminent status of primary legislation may frustrate not only **2.75** direct challenges to Acts of Parliament but also challenges to subordinate legislation and to the administrative acts of public authorities. Section 3(2)(c) saves subordinate legislation which is incompatible with Convention rights where it is *intra vires* its enabling power: the governing primary legislation will prevent the court from removing the incompatibility.[123] Section 6(2) negates the duty of public authorities to act in a way which is compatible with Convention rights where their actions are required by primary legislation, or are taken pursuant to primary legislation which is itself in breach of the Convention. It is important to note that primary legislation will take precedence over Convention rights whether it was passed before or after the Human Rights Act: s. 3(2) does not distinguish between primary legislation according to when it was passed and so deprives the Act of the power usually possessed by statutes to impliedly repeal previous statutes with which it is inconsistent. It is important to note that s. 21 of the Act defines primary legislation so as to confer pre-eminent status not only upon Acts of Parliament but also upon a variety of other measures including Orders in Council made in

---

[121] See, for example, *Adams v Lancashire CC* [1996] ICR 935; aff'd [1997] ICR 834.
[122] Compare the treatment of directly effective provisions of EC law which override inconsistent domestic legislation: s. 2 of the European Communities Act 1972; *R. v Secretary of State for Transport ex parte Factortame* [1990] 2 AC 85 and [1991] 1 AC 603.
[123] See, paras. 2.86–2.88.

exercise of the Royal Prerogative and subordinate legislation which brings into force or amends any primary legislation.

THE DECLARATION OF INCOMPATIBILITY

2.76 Section 4 of the Human Rights Act provides for a new remedy which will be available to certain courts in the event that Convention rights are frustrated by primary or subordinate legislation. This is the declaration of incompatibility, whereby the court may make a formal finding that Convention rights have been breached, albeit that it is unable to do anything concrete to remedy the breach. It can be made where the court is satisfied that a provision of primary legislation is incompatible with Convention rights,[124] or that a provision of subordinate legislation is incompatible with Convention rights and primary legislation prevents the removal of the incompatibility.[125] It is also implicit within s. 4(1) that a declaration of incompatibility may also be made where the otherwise unlawful acts of public authorities are rescued by the terms of primary legislation under s. 6(2) (since, in such cases, the court has "determine[d] whether a provision of primary legislation is compatible with Convention rights.") It would appear that a s. 4 declaration can be made by the court of its own motion and does not have to be requested by any of the parties to the proceedings. Like all declarations, it is a discretionary remedy and whilst the Government anticipated that the courts would, in general, make a declaration of incompatibility where there were grounds for it, it also recognised that there may be circumstances in a particular case which militate against the exercise of the s. 4 power.[126] For example, a declaration might not be appropriate where a declaration in similar terms has been made in another case and is under appeal, or the Government has indicated its intention to take remedial action so as to give effect to it.

2.77 The declaration has no formal legal effect, either on the outcome of the case, or on the continuing force of the legislation at issue. Section 4(6) provides:

"A declaration [of incompatibility] —

(a) does not affect the validity, continuing operation or enforcement of the provision in respect of which it is given; and

(b) is not binding on the parties to the proceedings in which it is made."

---

[124] HRA s. 4(2).
[125] HRA s. 4(4).
[126] HL Debs., 18 November 1997, col. 546.

The only substantive effect of a declaration of incompatibility is formally to draw the attention of the executive to a breach of the Convention and to provoke a decision as to whether or not the law should be changed. Section 10 of the Act, which permits (but does not require) the Government to take remedial action in the form of subordinate legislation to bring domestic law into line with the Convention, is triggered where a statutory provision is declared incompatible pursuant to s. 4.[127] Under s. 5, the Crown is entitled to notice that a declaration of incompatibility is under consideration and, by giving notice to the relevant court, to be joined as a party to proceedings. As a result, the Government will be able to make representations as to the compatibility with the Convention of legislative provisions which are under challenge, and to seek to appeal any decision to make a s. 4 declaration, even in criminal cases, where the Crown does not generally have the right of appeal.[128]

The power to make a declaration of incompatibility is conferred only upon the higher courts: the High Court, Court of Appeal, House of Lords, Privy Council and Courts-Martial Appeal Court.[129] This is perhaps surprising, since the duty to interpret legislation so as to conform to Convention rights is placed upon all courts, and lower courts, in particular, criminal trial courts, which are not included within s. 4, will be faced with the same issues as higher courts and the same obligation to give precedence to primary legislation. They will, no doubt, have to make rulings in terms which recognise a breach of Convention rights, but will be unable to make a formal declaration to that effect. Their exclusion from s. 4 is perhaps explained by the consequences which follow where a court is considering whether or not to make a declaration of incompatibility and where a declaration of incompatibility is actually made. It may have been thought desirable to avoid the need for, and the expense of, Crown intervention in lower court hearings and to exclude the possibility of formal pressure for legislative change arising out of the decisions of magistrates' courts, employment tribunals and the like. This way, the Government will only be troubled where an issue of compatibility raised in the lower courts has also been considered on appeal.

2.78

---

[127] The Government may also take remedial action where a breach of the Convention has been brought to its attention by a judgment of the Court of Human Rights: HRA s. 10(1)(b).

[128] HRA s. 5(4)

[129] HRA s. 4(5).

7. CHALLENGES TO SUBORDINATE LEGISLATION

2.79 Subordinate legislation may take a wide variety of forms, including certain Orders in Council, orders, rules, regulations, schemes, warrants, byelaws and other instruments made under primary legislation.[130] Even where it has been approved by both Houses of Parliament, subordinate legislation has, under conventional principles of administrative law, none of the immunity which is accorded to primary legislation.[131] It may be subjected to judicial review, declared invalid and, in some circumstances, quashed; alternatively, it may be held invalid pursuant to a collateral challenge in private law proceedings.

2.80 Where it appears that subordinate legislation is incompatible with Convention rights, the first line of argument is, as with primary legislation, that there is, in fact, no incompatibility because the relevant provisions can be read in a way which is consistent with the Convention. If, however, it is not possible to avoid a finding of breach, a legal challenge to the subordinate legislation may be brought pursuant to s. 7 of the Act. First, under s. 7(1)(a), a direct challenge could be mounted alleging that the Minister, or other public authority, responsible for the subordinate legislation, has acted unlawfully, contrary to s. 6(1), by exercising a power to make it in a manner which is incompatible with Convention rights. Alternatively, where the issue of compatibility of subordinate legislation with Convention rights arises in proceedings which do not involve the authority responsible for the legislation, a collateral challenge may be brought pursuant to s. 7(1)(b).

2.81 Whether the challenge to subordinate legislation is direct or collateral, the court will have to consider the effect of s. 3(1)(c) of the Act, which preserves the validity of incompatible subordinate legislation where the primary legislation under which it was made "prevents removal of the incompatibility". The primacy thus accorded to Acts of Parliament means that any Convention-based challenge to subordinate legislation raises a question of *vires*. A breach of Convention rights by subordinate legislation which is authorised by and consistent with its enabling power, that is, which is *intra vires*, is protected from challenge and can result only in a declaration of incompatibility. It is submitted, however, that s. 3(1)(c) will operate to save incompatible subordinate legislation only in exceptional cases. The vast majority of provisions in primary legislation which

---

[130] Legislation passed by the Welsh National Assembly is subordinate legislation.
[131] Wade and Forsyth, *Administrative Law* (Oxford, 7th ed., 1994) at 874.

authorise the making of delegated legislation are phrased in very general terms and, with the appropriate implication, can be read so that they do not authorise breach of Convention rights. In *Leech*, the Court of Appeal held that enabling provisions would be less likely than other provisions to be found to authorise a breach of a fundamental right. The right in that case, it will be recalled, was the right of access to the courts and the enabling provision at issue was s. 47(1) of the Prison Act 1952, authorising the Home Secretary to make rules for the regulation and management of prisons etc. Could s. 47(1) be interpreted as authorising the making of rules which infringed the right of free access to the courts? The Court of Appeal stated:

"It will be a rare case in which it could be held that such a fundamental right was by necessary implication abolished or limited by statute. It will, we suggest be an even rarer case in which it could be held that a statute authorised by necessary implication the abolition or limitation of so fundamental a right by subordinate legislation." [132]

According to the Court of Appeal, the presumption against statutory interference with vested common law rights was accompanied by a presumption against a statute authorising interference with a vested common law right by subordinate legislation. *Leech*, as noted above, expresses a principle which applies to all fundamental rights protected by the common law and indeed to rights conferred by statute, including, it is submitted, Convention rights.

Where a provision of subordinate legislation is found to be incompatible with Convention rights, the court must ascertain whether it can be severed from the rest of the instrument. The test of severance is not the textual "blue-pencil" test familiar in private law, whereby the offending words are deleted provided that what remains of the text is grammatical and coherent. Rather, the issue is whether the removal or modification of the *ultra vires* provision will produce so substantially different a law that it cannot safely be assumed that the legislation would have been made at all.[133] Following this exercise, the court will proceed to declare invalid and/or quash the relevant provisions under conventional principles of administrative law, or, where the subordinate legislation is *intra vires* its enabling power, to consider whether or not a declaration of incompatibility should be granted.

2.82

---

[132] Above n. 85 at 212.
[133] A test of "substantial severability": see *DPP* v *Hutchinson* [1990] 2 AC 783, 811.

8. CHALLENGING ACTS OF PUBLIC AUTHORITIES

2.83 Review of decision-making by public bodies is likely to be the area in which the Human Rights Act has the greatest impact. Experience in both New Zealand and Canada demonstrates that the majority of cases raising human rights issues are challenges to administrative decisions and practices rather than to legislation. The position following the enactment of the Human Rights Act is, in short, that infringement of the Convention has become a legitimate ground of legal challenge to the exercise of administrative discretion. Challenges may be direct, under s. 7(1)(a), notably by way of judicial review, or indirect, under s. 7(1)(b), for example, where the actions of the police are criticised by way of defence to criminal charges.

THE PRE-INCORPORATION POSITION

2.84 Prior to the Human Rights Act, judicial review was one of the least fruitful areas for Convention-based claims. The leading case on the pre-incorporation position is *Brind*, in which the applicants argued that the Home Secretary was obliged to have regard to Article 10 of the Convention when exercising his discretion to issue directives under the Broadcasting Act.[134] The blunt response to this argument, as identified by Neill LJ in *ex parte NALGO*, went as follows:

"Article 10 is not part of English domestic law. It is therefore not necessary for the minister when exercising an administrative discretion conferred upon him by Parliament to exercise that discretion in accordance with the provisions of Article 10. Nor will a court when reviewing the decision of the minister interfere with it on the ground that he did not have regard to the provisions of Article 10." [135]

This broad principle was, however, subject to the exception that an administrative decision could be scrutinised for compliance with the Convention where it was taken pursuant to legislation which had been

---

[134] Above n. 73.
[135] *R. v Secretary of State for the Environment ex parte National and Local Government Officer Association* (1993) 5 Admin LR 785, 797.

enacted for the purpose of bringing domestic law into line with the Convention.[136] A further, more limited exception arose where the decision maker professed to have taken account of the Convention in his deliberations.[137]

Where the Convention could not directly be put in issue, the courts nevertheless made encouraging noises about the special importance attached to human rights protection. Lord Bridge, in *Bugdaycay*, called for "the most anxious scrutiny" where a decision affected the right to life, the most fundamental of human rights.[138] In *Brind*, even though the European Convention did not apply, Lord Bridge started from the premise "that any restriction of the right to freedom of expression requires to be justified and that nothing less than an important competing public interest will be sufficient to justify it".[139] The most authoritative recent ruling on this issue was that of Sir Thomas Bingham MR in *ex parte Smith*, the first round of challenges to the policy of discharging homosexuals from the armed forces.[140] Both the Divisional Court and the Court of Appeal concluded that the *Wednesbury* test of irrationality must apply to review of the policy, and that it could only be struck down if the justification for it "outrageously defies logic or accepted moral standards".[141] The policy survived, but the Master of the Rolls did give some special credence to the human rights element of the case:

2.85

"The court may not interfere with the exercise of an administrative discretion on substantive grounds save where the court is satisfied that the decision is unreasonable in the sense that it is beyond the range of responses open to a reasonable decision-maker. But in judging whether the decision-maker has exceeded this margin of appreciation the human rights context is important. The more substantial the interference with human rights, the more the court will require by way of justification before it is satisfied that the decision is reasonable in the sense outlined above." [142]

THE NEW METHOD

Under the Human Rights Act, the general rule is that administrative decisions must not infringe Convention rights. Pursuant to s. 6(1) of the

2.86

---

[136] See, for example, *R. v Home Secretary ex parte Norney* (1995) 7 Admin LR 861.
[137] *R v Home Secretary ex parte Launder* [1997] 3 All ER 961.
[138] *R. v Home Secretary ex parte Bugdaycay* [1987] AC 514, 531.
[139] Above n. 73 at 749.
[140] [1996] QB 517.
[141] *Ibid.* at 540 (per Simon Brown LJ).
[142] *Ibid.* at 554.

Act, Convention rights have been incorporated into domestic law for the purposes of regulating the decision-making of public authorities, which are placed under an express duty not to act in a way which is incompatible with them. However, consistent with the scheme of preserving the overriding force of primary legislation, the Act does not allow Convention rights simply to trump contrary decisions by public authorities in all cases. Section 6(2) provides:

"(2) Subsection (1) does not apply to an act if—

  (a) as the result of one or more provisions of primary legislation, the authority could not have acted differently; or
  (b) in the case of one or more provisions of, or made under, primary legislation which cannot be read or given effect in a way which is compatible with Convention rights, the authority was acting so as to give effect to or enforce those provisions."

Section 6(2) recognises that, as with subordinate legislation, administrative acts which are incompatible with the Convention may be authorised or required by primary legislation. If that is so, it is in truth the legislation which is incompatible with Convention rights, and the Convention rights cannot prevail. Hence, public authorities are offered a two-fold defence: that an act in breach of Convention rights was required by, or was taken pursuant to, statutory powers which themselves breach Convention rights.[143] The provision of such a defence was essential in order to preserve the continuing affect of incompatible primary legislation. Otherwise, public authorities would be prevented from implementing or acting pursuant to, such legislation.

2.87 Section 6(2)(a) is of narrow application: it is not often that an authority will, in truth, be *required* to act inconsistently with the Convention. Where, as is often the case, an authority has statutory powers which it may use or not use at its discretion, s. 6(2)(a) would probably not apply, because the authority could legitimately have decided not to act at all. Notably, s. 6(2)(a) would apply to judicial decisions which are required to cause breach of the Convention by incompatible primary legislation. By contrast, the defence set out in s. 6(2)(b) will frequently be available, at least in theory, since a great number of public authorities are creatures of statute who will only ever be acting pursuant to statutory powers.

---

[143] "Primary legislation" is defined to include Orders in Council made pursuant to the royal prerogative: HRA s. 21(1).

The key issue under both limbs of s. 6(2) will be whether or not the   **2.88**
underlying statutory powers are themselves incompatible with Convention rights, and, in answering that question, the courts will apply the
approach to statutory interpretation laid down in s. 3 of the Act. In
practice, the s. 6(2) defence should succeed only rarely: most statutory
powers are phrased in general terms and could be exercised either
consistently or inconsistently with the Convention. Following the analysis
of s. 3 set out above, such powers should not be interpreted as permitting
an infringement of Convention rights. On the rare occasion when a
s. 6(2) defence does succeed, the court will, by definition, have ruled
upon the compatibility of legislation with Convention rights, and will
therefore have the option of making a declaration of incompatibility
under s. 4.

THE INTENSITY OF REVIEW FOR BREACH OF CONVENTION RIGHTS

Breach of Convention rights is a ground of review of administrative action   **2.89**
which is not only novel but is also fundamentally different in nature from
the traditional *Wednesbury* approach. *Wednesbury* review stresses the
wide discretion of the decision-maker and will only impugn a decision on
its merits where it is so unreasonable that no reasonable decision-maker
could have made it.[144] The difference between review for compliance
with the European Convention and *Wednesbury* review has been
described by various judges as the exercise of a primary as opposed to
a secondary judgment.[145] In *Smith*, Simon Brown LJ upheld the validity of
the armed forces' policy with some reluctance, and contrasted the role of
the court were the European Convention to be directly at issue. He stated:

"If the Convention for the Protection of Human Rights and Fundamental Freedoms were
part of our law and we were accordingly entitled to ask whether the policy answers a
pressing social need and whether the restriction on human rights involved can be shown
to be proportionate to its benefits, then clearly the primary judgment (subject only to a
limited 'margin of appreciation') would be for us and not for others; the constitutional

---

[144] *Associated Provincial Picture Houses* v *Wednesbury Corporation* [1948] 1 KB 223, 230 (per Lord
  Greene MR).
[145] See *ex parte Smith*, above n. 140 at 541 (per Simon Brown LJ); Lord Bridge in *Brind*, above n. 73
  at 749.

balance would shift. But that is not the position. In exercising merely a secondary judgment, this court is bound, even though adjudicating in a human rights context, to act with some reticence."[146]

2.90   Another illustration of the different nature of the enquiry necessitated by a Convention challenge is the *Chahal* case, which resulted, ultimately, in defeat for the UK before the Court of Human Rights.[147] Chahal was a Sikh nationalist who claimed that deporting him to India, as the Home Secretary intended, would be likely to result in his detention, torture and possible death. The Court of Human Rights held that Article 3 of the Convention prohibited deportation to a country where there was a real risk of ill-treatment, and that Chahal had established that there was such a risk. The English courts, in contrast, were able to require only that the Home Secretary had weighed up the risk to the individual against the public good, and, given that balancing exercise, could intervene only if the outcome was irrational or based upon a misdirection of law.[148] In the event, the latter enquiry was precluded by the invocation by the Home Secretary of national security considerations. Had Chahal been able to rely upon Article 3 in the English courts, the nature of their enquiry would have been different, and much more rigorous.

2.91   The intensity of the review function called for under the Convention and the extent to which the Convention margin of appreciation differs from a *Wednesbury* test are important issues which will play a significant role in determining the potency of Convention rights in the domestic courts. They are, however, general issues which affect not only judicial review of administrative action but all cases where the court is called upon to identify the requirements of the Convention. As such, they are dealt with separately, and in more detail, below.

9. DEVELOPMENT OF THE COMMON LAW

2.92   Virtually all, if not all, of the rights protected by the European Convention raise issues which are governed to some extent at least by the common law.[149] The interpretation and development of the common law will, therefore, play an important role in securing Convention rights in this

---

[146] *Ibid.*
[147] *Chahal* v *UK*, A/697, (1997) 23 EHRR 413.
[148] *R.* v *Home Secretary ex parte Chahal* [1995] 1 WLR 526.
[149] The "common law" is here used to denote judge-made rules in general, and no distinction is drawn between common law and equitable rules.

country. Crucially, the Human Rights Act does not protect the common law from the effects of the Convention in the same way as it does Acts of Parliament. The result is that, in theory at least, Convention rights should prevail over common law rules.

In fact, the development of the common law was one area where the **2.93** relevance of the Convention was already widely accepted even before incorporation. This was primarily because the courts have been persuaded that a good many Convention rights are already reflected in, and protected by, the common law. The right to life, protection from inhuman and degrading treatment, access to the courts, freedom of thought, conscience and religion and freedom of expression are only some of the Convention rights identified as having a counterpart in the common law.[150] Admittedly, some judges have used this insight as an excuse for ignoring the Convention altogether; admittedly also, judicial faith in the common law as the safeguard of Convention rights has not always proved justified when cases have reached Strasbourg. Nevertheless, the principle that the Convention is relevant to the development of the common law is well-established. The leading case is perhaps *Derbyshire CC v Times Newspapers Ltd*, in which the Court of Appeal used Article 10 of the Convention as a basis for its conclusion that the common law of defamation would not permit a public body to sue for libel in order to vindicate its governing reputation.[151] Balcombe LJ held that:

"Where the law is uncertain, it must be right for the court to approach the issue before it with a predilection to ensure that our law should not involve a breach of article 10."[152]

Pursuant to s. 6 of the Act, the courts are under a duty to act in a way **2.94** which is compatible with Convention rights when they interpret and apply common law rules in cases before them. As has been explained above, the status of the courts as public authorities within s. 6 entails that Convention rights must be considered in all cases, including purely private proceedings and not only those to which one or more public authorities is a party. In all cases raising common law issues, a party may seek to preclude restrictions on Convention rights by arguing that the court ought to apply the common law in the appropriate way.

---

[150] See, for example, *R. v Cambridge DHA ex parte B* [1995] 1 FLR 1055 (Art. 2); *R. v Home Secretary ex parte Togher*, unreported judgement of the Court of Appeal, 1 February 1995 (Art. 3); *Raymond v Honey*, above n. 86 (Art. 6); *R. v Home Secretary ex parte Moon* (1996) 8 Admin LR 477 (Art. 9); *Attorney-General v Guardian Newspapers Ltd (No. 2)* [1990] 1 AC 109 (Art. 10).
[151] [1992] QB 770.
[152] *Ibid.* at 812. See also *R. v Chief Metropolitan Stipendiary Magistrate ex parte Choudhury* [1991] 1 QB 429.

2.95   The easy case is where, as the Court of Appeal found in *Derbyshire*, the common law position on a particular point is ambiguous or uncertain: the Convention-friendly approach can then be adopted without difficulty. Of course, ambiguity is an even more fluid and subjective concept when it is applied to the corpus of the common law than it is in the context of statutory language. The sheer volume of authorities, not only from this country but also from other common law jurisdictions, and the inter-pretive tools which permit the courts to distinguish on their facts cases which might otherwise appear to be binding, may give rise to ambiguity or uncertainty in the common law even in apparently clear-cut cases. There are few cases in which the authorities are all one way, and the quest for uncertainty will undoubtedly be assisted by the conviction that some Convention rights are already reflected in the common law. The *Derbyshire* case is a good example of how ambiguity in the law may be very much a matter of opinion. Morland, J, the first instance judge, had reviewed the conflicting authorities and found the common law to be clear in allowing the plaintiff local authority to maintain its libel action.[153] The Court of Appeal found unanimously that the common law was unclear on that point.

2.96   There will, however, be some cases where the common law is firmly settled, and that settled position is incompatible with the Convention. A number of pre-incorporation authorities indicate that in those circum-stances the courts may be reluctant to "develop" the common law in the radical way required to uphold Convention rights. In *Choudhury*, the Divisional Court, having found the common law to be clear in its restriction of the offence of blasphemy to protection of the Christian religion, stated:

> "In our judgment, where the law is clear, it is not the proper function of the court to extend it; particularly is this so in criminal cases where offences cannot be retrospectively created. It is in that circumstance the function of Parliament alone to change the law." [154]

2.97   In the civil sphere, Sir Robert Megarry VC in *Malone* found the common law in its present state to be deficient because it could not be invoked so as to protect the plaintiff's privacy from invasion in the form of telephone tapping. He also agreed with the plaintiff that the current state of the law was almost certainly in breach of Article 8 of the Convention (a view which was later confirmed by the Court of Human Rights). He felt that the common law would be "sufficiently fertile" to prohibit telephone

---

[153] [1992] QB 770, 788.
[154] Above n. 152 at 447. See also *R.* v *Knuller* [1973] AC 435, 490 per Lord Simon.

tapping save in suitably limited classes of case, but was not suitable for framing the safeguards which must exist when tapping is justified. Overall, regulation of telephone tapping was, in his view, "essentially a matter for Parliament, not the courts".[155] Protection of privacy is likely to figure prominently amongst early attempts to invoke Convention rights in order to supplement existing common law safeguards. However, it may be that incremental development of the common law in that direction will be precluded by recent rulings which have proclaimed the absence of any right of privacy in English law, and the inability of the courts to remedy the situation.[156]

2.98   The flexibility of the common law and its capacity to generate hitherto unknown causes of action should not be underestimated. However, where the changes demanded by the Convention are too dramatic to be accommodated within the existing framework of the common law, an alternative approach would be to identify a statutory rule derived from the Human Rights Act which takes precedence over the common law. Hence, a plaintiff whose privacy had been invaded would argue, on the one hand, that the common law could support a claim for invasion of privacy (either directly or through other, pre-existing remedies) but, in the alternative, that the Act has given rise to what is, in effect, a new statutory tort of breach of the right to respect for private and family life under Article 8 of the Convention. If the common law is inadequate to protect Convention rights and cannot be developed in the appropriate way, there is no need to wait for Parliament to act, as suggested in *Choudhury* and *Malone.* Parliament has already acted, by passing the Human Rights Act.

2.99   During the passage of the legislation through Parliament, the Lord Chancellor sought to head off criticism that the Bill could empower the courts to create a new tort of privacy, arguing that the courts would not be permitted to fill gaps in the existing common law protection accorded to Convention rights:

"I would not agree with the proposition that the courts as public authorities will be obliged to fashion a law on privacy because of the terms of the Bill. That is simply not so. If it were so, whenever a law cannot be found either in the statute book or as a rule of common law to protect a Convention right, the courts would in effect be obliged to legislate by way of judicial decision and to make one. That is not the true position. If it were — in my view, it is not — the courts would also have in effect to legislate where Parliament had acted, but incompatibly with the Convention . . .

---

[155] *Malone* v *MPC* [1979] Ch. 344, 380.
[156] *Kaye* v *Robertson* [1991] FSR 62, 71; *R.* v *Broadcasting Complaints Commission ex parte Barclay* [1997] EMLR 62, 69.

In my opinion, the court is not obliged to remedy the failure by legislating via the common law either where a Convention right is infringed by incompatible legislation, or where, because of the absence of legislation — say, privacy legislation — a Convention right is left unprotected. In my view, the courts may not act as legislators and grant new remedies for infringement of Convention rights unless the common law itself enables them to develop new rights or remedies."[157]

It is, of course, likely that much judicial protection of Convention rights under the common law can and will be achieved through traditional common law techniques, and through the incremental development of long-established causes of action. However, beyond that, it is difficult to agree with the Lord Chancellor's analysis. There is a distinction between the courts acting (or "legislating") in a manner which is inconsistent with primary legislation, and the courts acting in a manner which is not, because no relevant primary legislation exists. That distinction is reflected in s. 6 of the Act, which removes the courts' obligation to act in a manner which is compatible with Convention rights where primary legislation stands in the way. In the absence of primary legislation, however, there is nothing to mitigate the courts' obligation to give effect to Convention rights, even if that requires "judicial legislation". Whilst the Act seeks to preserve the legal effect of clearly incompatible primary legislation, it places no express limit on the extent to which the settled approach of the common law may be modified.

2.100   It can be said, however, that the situation in which the court is asked to intervene so as to fill a gap in the law is less likely to give rise to obligations under s. 6(1) of the Act. That is because of the distinction drawn by the Convention between negative and positive obligations. In certain cases, s. 6(1) is engaged because a court order may constitute a unjustified state restriction on Convention rights. For example, the contempt order issued by the English courts in *X* v *Morgan Grampian* was held by the Court of Human Rights in *Goodwin* to be a breach of the applicant's right to freedom of expression.[158] That was a breach of the UK's negative obligations to refrain from interfering with Convention rights. In other cases, the argument will be that the court must act in order to fulfil its positive obligations under the Convention to protect Convention rights from interference not by a public authority but by private persons (the classic case being the protection of privacy against media intrusion). The Convention permits states a wide discretion in deciding how to satisfy positive obligations and it is not necessarily a breach of

---

[157] HL Debs., 24 November 1997, col. 785.
[158] Above n. 61 and 62.

positive obligations to fail to do so through the courts in any given case. The Convention requires that domestic law as a whole is examined when considering the extent to which a particular right is protected. Also, it emphasises the structural merits and demerits of the system: it is not necessarily a breach of the Convention where an individual fails to obtain the benefit of a particular remedy on the facts of his case provided that a remedy is, in principle available, to someone in his position.[159]

10. INFLUENCING THE EXERCISE OF JUDICIAL DISCRETION

The outcome of a wide range of cases which raise Convention issues may be determined by the exercise of judicial discretion. In the criminal law, for example, the judge has a discretion to exclude evidence which would have a significant adverse effect on the fairness of proceedings,[160] and to direct the members of the jury that they may draw inferences from the silence of the accused under interrogation or at trial.[161] Both of these matters fall at least within Article 6 of the Convention. In the civil sphere, the grant of injunctions, perhaps to restrain freedom of expression, rests upon the exercise of judicial discretion. Under the Human Rights Act, the key issue is whether the courts are now obliged in all cases to exercise their discretion so as to comply with Convention requirements.   **2.101**

Even before the Convention was incorporated into domestic law, the courts were receptive to arguments that the requirements of the Convention should be a material factor in the exercise of their discretion. *Rantzen* v *MGN* is a good example of the exercise of judicial discretion (to overturn excessive awards of libel damages) in accordance with the perceived requirements of the Convention.[162] Another civil law example is the corpus of case-law on the courts' inherent jurisdiction to grant injunctions restraining publicity about the care and upbringing of children over whose welfare they are exercising a supervisory role, which gives due weight to the requirements of freedom of expression under Article 10.[163]   **2.102**

---

[159] See, for example, *Stewart-Brady* v *UK,* Appl. No. 27436/95, (1997) 24 EHRR CD38.
[160] Section 78 of the Police and Criminal Evidence Act 1978.
[161] Sections 34–37 of the Criminal Justice and Public Order Act 1994.
[162] Above n. 63; see also *Holley* v *Smyth*, above n. 63.
[163] See, for example, *In re W* [1992] 1 WLR 100, 103. Compare *R.* v *Central Independent Television* [1994] 3 WLR 20; *In re Z* [1996] 2 WLR 88.

2.103   There has been less enthusiasm for the Convention in the criminal law field. In *Khan*, for example, the House of Lords has recently addressed the issue of the effect of breach of the Convention upon the discretion of a trial judge to exclude evidence under s. 78 of PACE.[164] The evidence in question was gathered by the police using a covert listening device. Given the absence at the relevant time of legislative safeguards on such activities,[165] there had undoubtedly been a breach of the accused's right to privacy under Article 8 of the Convention (although their Lordships did not decide the latter issue). The evidence, which was the only evidence against the accused, was admissible, but should the judge have exercised his discretion under s. 78 to exclude it? The Convention was accorded only a lukewarm welcome: it was relevant only because Article 6 embodied many of the principles of English law and of our concept of justice. Hence, the trial judge should consider an apparent breach of the Convention in the gathering of evidence, just as he should consider an apparent breach of the law of a foreign country, but it would be inappropriate for him to decide whether there had actually been a breach, or to exclude evidence solely on that basis.[166]

2.104   Under s. 6(1) of the Act, the courts, as public authorities, have a duty in domestic law to exercise their discretion in such a way as to protect Convention rights. In principle, injunctions should not be granted where to do so would contravene the right to freedom of expression, evidence should be excluded where its admission would prejudice the right to a fair trial under Article 6, and so on. However, the sympathetic exercise of judicial discretion is not permissible in all cases to prevent a breach of the Convention. According to s. 6(2), the duty to exercise discretion in accordance with the Convention does not operate where the court is applying, or giving effect to, primary legislation which is itself incompatible with the Convention. If the relevant infringement of Convention rights arises directly from the terms of a statute, the use of judicial discretion to remedy the situation may amount to ignoring, or repealing, the statute. That is specifically prohibited by s. 3(2)(b) and (c) of the Act.

2.105   *R.* v *Morrissey and Staines*, a pre-incorporation case, illustrates the point. The Court of Appeal was faced with two defendants who had been convicted under insider-dealing legislation on the basis of evidence which they been obliged to give to DTi inspectors.[167] In *Saunders* v *UK*,

---

[164] Above n. 32.
[165] See now the Police Act 1997.
[166] Above n. 32 at 580–581 (per Lord Nolan).
[167] *The Times*, 1 May 1997.

the Court of Human Rights had found that provisions in the Companies Act 1985 which required cooperation with the inspectors and allowed evidence given by an accused to the inspectors to be used against him at trial, were in breach of Article 6 of the Convention. In the light of the *Saunders* decision, it was argued that the evidence given to the inspectors by Morrissey and Staines should be excluded under s. 78 of PACE. The Court of Appeal refused to exclude the evidence. The Financial Services Act 1986 expressly authorised the use of such evidence and this amounted to a statutory presumption that, absent special features, it was to be treated as fair. There were no special features to distinguish the present case from any other case, and if the evidence was excluded in the present case, it would have to be excluded in all cases. That, according to the Court, would amount to the repeal of an English statutory provision in deference to a ruling of the Court of Human Rights which does not have direct effect and which, as a matter of strict law, is irrelevant. Of course, under ss. 2, 3 and 6 of the Act, rulings of the Court of Human Rights will have effect in domestic law but they will not have effect sufficient to overrule a statutory provision which is clearly to the opposite effect. The upshot is that the exercise of judicial discretion in the way suggested by the Convention is not an automatic solution: much depends on the construction of the relevant statutory powers.

11. IDENTIFYING THE REQUIREMENTS OF THE CONVENTION

In every case where the Convention is invoked, whether for the purposes **2.106** of statutory interpretation, judicial review of administrative action, developing the common law, etc., the court will be obliged to decide what exactly the Convention requires. The identification of the demands of the Convention is a task which is arguably prior to that of ascertaining whether a statutory provision can be construed in accordance with those demands, whether the common law can be developed accordingly, whether administrative action has infringed Convention rights and so on. Section 2 of the Human Rights Act requires the English courts to take account of the Strasbourg case-law when interpreting Convention rights, so that, in theory, Convention rights will be interpreted in the same way by the domestic courts as they would be before the Court of Human Rights. Chapter 6, entitled "General Principles of the Law of the Convention" contains a detailed analysis of the general issues which arise in most if not all Convention cases, regardless of the particular right or rights which are at stake. Three are worthy of brief mention at this stage.

INTERPRETATION OF THE CONVENTION

2.107 First, the way in which the provisions of the Convention are to be interpreted differs greatly from the way in which an English court would approach a domestic statute. In particular, interpretation of the Convention is teleological and dynamic, rather than literal and historic. It is likely also that the English courts will view the Human Rights Act as a domestic constitutional document, and adopt interpretive methods which are consistent with that status. The classic statement of the required approach is that of Lord Wilberforce in *Minister of Home Affairs* v *Fisher*.[168] In interpreting one of the human rights provisions of the Bermudan Constitution, he referred to its origins in the European Convention and the UN Universal Declaration of Human Rights and then stated:

"These antecedents, and the form of Chapter I itself, call for a generous interpretation avoiding what has been called the 'austerity of tabulated legalism', suitable to give to individuals the full measure of the fundamental rights and freedoms referred to." [169]

PROPORTIONALITY

2.108 Secondly, the Human Rights Act has given further effect in domestic law to the principle of proportionality, which is a vital component of the test of necessity of restrictions upon Convention rights and which has up to now been accorded only limited recognition in the English courts.[170] The essence of proportionality, as applied by the Court of Human Rights, is that a measure must impose no greater restriction upon a Convention right than is absolutely necessary in order to achieve its objectives (although in fact a number of distinct tests can be identified, all of

---

[168] [1980] AC 319, 328.
[169] This *dictum* has been relied upon by the Canadian and the New Zealand courts in interpreting their respective bills of rights. See further *Ministry of Transport* v *Naort,* above n. 110 at 271 and *R.* v *Big M Drug Mart Ltd* (1985) 18 DLR (4th) 321, 360.
[170] See *Brind*, above n. 73 and *NALGO*, above n. 135.

which are described by the Court as measures of proportionality).[171] The various facets of the Court's principle of proportionality are examined in chapter 6. It may well be that the difficulties in identifying a consistent and coherent approach on the part of Court will cause domestic judges to adopt the clearer, three-fold test of proportionality which has been adopted by the European Court of Justice and other constitutional courts. This would require that a measure is carefully designed to achieve a legitimate aim or objective, that it is the least restrictive means possible of achieving that objective and that it does not have an excessive or disproportionate effect on the interests of affected persons.[172] Many of the questions raised by a proportionality test are foreign to the traditional *Wednesbury* approach to judicial review, which emphasises the autonomy of the decision-maker, but they will have to be asked if the Convention is to be applied correctly.

THE MARGIN OF APPRECIATION

A significant proportion of Convention cases, notably those under Articles 8–11, raise, and indeed turn on, the issue of the margin of appreciation of states. In most cases, the applicant will be able to establish that a Convention right has been restricted, and it will fall to the state to justify the restriction as one which is "necessary in a democratic society". One of the most important components of the necessity analysis is the proportionality test and in each case the authority has an area of discretion, a margin of appreciation, within which it may legitimately consider a restriction to be necessary. Only if it steps outside the permitted area of discretion will it be found to have breached the Convention. Two particular issues arise: is the margin of appreciation doctrine relevant in domestic Convention claims, and if so, how does it differ from the usual approach of the domestic courts to judicial review of state action?   **2.109**

On one view, the margin of appreciation doctrine should not apply at all in the domestic courts. It is nowhere express in the Convention, but has been invented and developed in the case-law of the Court of Human Rights as a means of delimiting the supervisory role of an international court. Strictly speaking, the doctrine is suitable for application only by the Court of Human Rights, since it is based upon the view that national and   **2.110**

---

[171] See chapter 6, paras. 6.45–6.53.
[172] Opinion of Advocate General Van Gerven in *SPUC* v *Grogan,* Case C-159/90 [1991] ECR I-4865, 4719-20. See also *E.* v *Oakes* (1986) 26 DLR (4th) 200, 227–28 (Supreme Court of Canada).

local authorities have a greater knowledge of, and ability to judge, conditions in their national/regional/local area than do the judges sitting in Strasbourg. That basis for the margin of appreciation, which is particularly explicit in the Court's judgments on freedom of artistic expression,[173] is, arguably, specific to the Court and does not imply that a similar doctrine should be applied in the domestic courts.

2.111   It is submitted, however, that the margin of appreciation doctrine, as it is applied by the Court of Human Rights, is highly relevant to Convention claims brought in the domestic courts. It could be argued that the margin of appreciation is directly relevant in that because an individual claiming that his Convention rights have been infringed must submit that the Court of Human Rights would find that his rights have been infringed. His rights are, after all, Convention rights, to be interpreted in accordance with the case-law of the Court, not purely domestic law rights which are framed in identical terms. In submitting that his case would succeed were it brought before the Court, he must necessarily account for the Court's application of the margin of appreciation doctrine, and argue that if his rights are not upheld in the domestic courts, they will be restricted in a way which falls outside the margin of appreciation, and breaches the Convention. This argument is, however, conceptually flawed as it fails to distinguish between the obligations of domestic public authorities to respect Convention rights, and the supervisory role of the Court of Human Rights in making sure that they have done so.[173a] It is also problematic in that it involves a direct and unmodified application of the Court's margin of appreciation doctrine which, as noted above, is specific to the status of the Court of Human Rights as an international tribunal, remote from local conditions.

2.112   A stronger argument is that, even if *the margin of appreciation* as applied by the Court is rejected as inappropriate, it is inescapable that *a margin of appreciation* must be allowed where the decisions of public authorities are challenged in the courts. Just as national and local authorities have a greater expertise than international judges, so they also have a more intimate knowledge of their day-to-day activities, and of whether particular restrictions are necessary, than do the domestic judiciary (not to mention, in many cases, a democratic mandate). That indeed is the doctrine which lies at the heart of the English public law tradition. If it is accepted that an area of discretion should be allowed to the decision-maker in Convention claims, the Court's margin of appreciation is surely the most obvious source of authority on how that

---

[173] See, for example, *Wingrove v UK*, A/699, (1997) 24 EHRR 1, 20–21.
[173a] See *Attorney General of Hong Kong v Lee Kwong-Kut* [1993] AC 951, per Lord Woolf at 966-967.

area of discretion ought to be delimited. Where the Court of Human Rights allows only a narrow margin of appreciation (for example, in cases concerning the freedom of the press), so the domestic courts should also be more interventionist in that field than, say, where property rights, or obscenity laws are concerned (where the Court is traditionally more forgiving). Indeed, were the domestic courts to depart from the practice of the Court, there would be a risk of them refusing to uphold Convention rights in circumstances which would amount to a breach, by the courts themselves, of the requirements of the Convention, contrary to s. 6(1) of the Human Rights Act. Hence, it would only be legitimate for the domestic courts to formulate their own margin of appreciation doctrine insofar as it is more favourable to individuals than the practice of the Court of Human Rights. The Court's case-law remains relevant also in cases where the domestic courts may wish to allow a margin of appreciation or legitimate area of discretion which is narrower than that which would be allowed by the Court of Human Rights in similar circumstances. That is because the matters taken into account by the Court in assessing the Convention criteria of necessity and proportionality should guide the domestic courts in making their own assessment.

The next issue is how much latitude the legislator or decision-maker **2.113** has in assessing the necessity of restrictions on Convention rights. Translated into domestic legal parlance, how does the margin of appreciation compare to the deferential *Wednesbury* approach, whereby a decision will only be found to be unlawful if it is so badly wrong that no reasonable decision-maker could have taken it? The *Wednesbury* test is, of course, a public law test, but respondents to Convention claims will no doubt seek to invoke the sentiments which underlie it wherever the court is called upon to assess the legality of an authority's actions under the Convention.

There is certainly some encouragement in the pre-Human Rights Act **2.114** case-law for the view that the margin of appreciation under the Convention is simply the *Wednesbury* test writ large, and requires no more active an approach than would be usual in public law.[174] However, the test of necessity, incorporating the margin of appreciation doctrine, is, in truth, an altogether different test from the *Wednesbury* approach to limitations upon fundamental rights. It requires the exercise of a primary rather than a secondary judgment by the court, it is more flexible, and it will come down on the side of the applicant in far more cases than will a test of irrationality. A number of specific differences can be pinpointed between

---

[174] See, for example, *R.* v *Home Secretary ex parte Patel* [1995] Imm AR 223, 230; *R.* v *Home Secretary ex parte Mbatube* [1996] Imm AR 184, 188.

the necessity/margin of appreciation test under the Convention and the yardstick of irrationality in domestic administrative law.

The threshold for review

2.115   In domestic law, a decision is irrational, or *Wednesbury* unreasonable, if it "outrageously defies logic or accepted moral standards". The margin of appreciation doctrine is not so forgiving. The Court has stated on innumerable occasions that the existence of a margin of appreciation "does not mean that the supervision is limited to ascertaining whether the respondent State exercised its discretion reasonably, carefully and in good faith".[175] Conversely, a reasonable, careful and *bona fide* exercise of discretion will always be sufficient to pass a conventional test of irrationality. However, the margin of appreciation doctrine comes close to a test of irrationality in the field of property rights under Article 1 of the First Protocol. Where property rights have been interfered with pursuant to a choice of social or economic policy, the Court will not interfere unless the state's actions have been "manifestly unreasonable".[176] There are clear parallels between the Court's approach in cases such as *James* and *Lithgow* and the so-called super-*Wednesbury* test labelled by Simon Brown LJ in *ex parte Smith*.[177]

A variable standard

2.116   The margin of appreciation is very definitely a variable standard. It is wide, for example, where moral judgments are concerned, but narrow where the state seeks to restrict political speech. Predicting how widely the margin of appreciation will be drawn is indeed the most difficult aspect of advising on cases which are before, or may go before, the Strasbourg institutions. The irrationality yardstick, on the other hand, is far more rigid. On the super-*Wednesbury* test, it is an even higher standard in cases involving a choice of national economic policy under Parliamentary supervision. The threshold of unreasonableness is not, however, lower in human rights cases;[178] still less is it lower in some human rights cases than in others.

---

[175] See, for example, *Vogt* v *Germany*, A/323, (1996) 21 EHRR 205, 235.
[176] *James* v *UK*, A/98, (1986) 8 EHRR 123, 144; *Lithgow* v *UK*, A/102, (1986) 8 EHRR 329, 373.
[177] Above n. 140 at 541.
[178] per Neill LJ in *NALGO*, above n. 135 at 801.

The hierarchy of values

The Convention's necessity test requires of the decision-maker a qualita-   **2.117**
tively different reasoning process from that deemed sufficient under the
Wednesbury approach. Following cases such as *Brind* and *Smith*, the
decision-maker in a human rights case is obliged by English administrative law to cite an important competing public interest and to strike a
balance between the right at issue and the public interest. The balance
struck can only be challenged if it outrageously defies logic or accepted
moral standards. Under the Convention, however, there can be no
question of balancing two equal but competing interests — the individual
right is fundamental. In the first *Sunday Times* case, the Court clearly
stated that the criterion of necessity under the Convention did not involve
a choice between two conflicting principles; rather it involved a single,
fundamental principle (freedom of expression) which could only be
compromised on a small number of narrowly defined grounds.[179]

Review of the facts

Genuine and searching review of the facts behind a decision is generally   **2.118**
excluded by the *Wednesbury* test: the decision-maker's assessment of
the facts must be accepted unless it is irrational. However, the Convention
requires the courts to assess whether a decision-maker has based its
decisions upon "an acceptable assessment of the relevant facts." [180] There
are indeed a number of cases in which a state has failed to satisfy the
Court that its view of the facts was sustainable.[181]

Evidence

The "primary judgment" to be exercised by the court under the Conven-   **2.119**
tion test of necessity entails, therefore, a more rigorous jurisdiction to
review on the facts, and also a more searching analysis of the conclusions
drawn by the decision-maker from the relevant facts. This has an impact
on the character and the extent of the evidence which will need to be put
before the court in Convention cases. In *Smith*, all three members of the
Court of Appeal noted that the evidence which had been put before it for

---

[179] *Sunday Times* v *UK*, A/30, (1979–80) 2 EHRR 245, 281.
[180] See, for example, *Vogt* v *Germany*, above n. 175 at 235.
[181] See, for example, *Autronic* v *Switzerland*, A/178, (1990) 12 EHRR 485.

the purposes of the irrationality challenge was not sufficient to enable it to form a view on the issue of compatibility of the policy with the Convention.[182] The "primary jurisdiction" to be exercised under the Convention would require different evidence and submissions as compared with the "secondary or review jurisdiction" under the *Wednesbury* approach. Henry LJ went on to mention the possibility of hearing submissions from interested third parties in the form of a "Brandeis brief".[183]

The burden of proof

2.120 A person challenging a decision or a piece of delegated legislation under principles of domestic public law bears the burden of proof to the ordinary civil standard. Under the Convention, however, the burden of proof is on the respondent to justify any restriction upon Convention rights, and the necessity of any restriction must be "convincingly established",[184] arguably a more onerous burden than the ordinary civil standard.

2.121 In summary, it would be complacent in the extreme to believe that where the Convention allows a margin of appreciation the courts are restricted to performing the same, limited task as they perform when applying the *Wednesbury* test of irrationality. The Convention requires the court to make a primary judgment, subject to a limited margin of appreciation;[185] the existence of a margin of appreciation does not convert the primary judgment into a *Wednesbury*-type secondary judgment.

12. SPECIAL PROVISION FOR FREEDOM OF EXPRESSION AND FREEDOM OF RELIGION

2.122 Sections 12 and 13 of the Act make special provision for two Convention rights, freedom of expression and freedom of religion. Both provisions

---

[182] Above n. 140 at 558, 564 and 565.
[183] *Ibid.* at 564. This possibility was also mentioned by the Lord Chancellor during the passage through Parliament of the Human Rights Bill: above n. 33.
[184] See, for example, *Barthold* v *Germany,* A/90, (1985) 7 EHRR 383, 403.
[185] Per Simon Brown LJ in *Smith*, above n. 140 at 543.

were professed by the Government merely to clarify the existing case-law of the Convention and not to depart from it. On that basis, the provisions are otiose and add nothing to ss. 1 and 2, which incorporate Articles 9 and 10 of the Convention and require British courts to take account of Convention case-law in interpreting them. That, of course, begs the question as to why they were inserted in the Bill in the first place, the answer to which is to be found in the realm of practical politics. The provisions on freedom of expression were a direct result of concerns expressed by the Press Complaints Commission, and by the Opposition, that the Bill, by giving further effect to the Convention right to respect for private and family life under Article 8, amounted to a privacy law which would frustrate the activities of the press. (Indeed, the Government was quite open about the fact that s. 12 had been drafted in consultation with the Press Complaints Commission.) Section 13 on freedom of thought, conscience and religion is a response to concerns that Convention rights would enable individuals to force churches and other religious organisations to act in a way which is contrary to their beliefs — same sex marriages was one example which figured prominently. It replaces much lengthier amendments made to the Bill by the House of Lords.

2.123

Section 12 does not mention Article 8 or privacy, and is cast in broad terms such that it applies not only where a right to privacy is asserted but wherever freedom of expression might be affected by judicial action.[186] Therefore, whilst it is a direct response to worries about prior restraints on publication by the press of material which intrudes into private life, it will also assist the press where other interests are asserted in opposition to publication (such as commercial confidentiality) and indeed where the press itself takes action in order to allow publication of otherwise prohibited material. In fact, s.12 is broad enough to apply to cases raising issues of freedom of expression which do not involve the press at all. Section 12 makes two adjustments to the domestic law which governs the granting of *ex parte* injunctions. First, where an application is made ex parte, relief is not to be granted unless the court is satisfied that all practical steps have been taken to notify the defendant/respondent or there are compelling reasons why the defendant/respondent should not be notified (s. 12(2)). That is a more rigid rule than that which currently governs applications for *ex parte* relief. Second, an applicant for injunctive relief (whether *ex parte* or *inter partes*) will not succeed on the basis of the normal standard of a "serious issue to be tried" but must go further and show that he is "likely" to succeed.[187]

---

[186] HRA, s. 12(1).
[187] HRA, s. 12(3), cf *American Cyanamid v Ethicon* [1975] AC 396.

2.124   Section 12 then proceeds to instruct the courts as to the important factors to be taken into account when deciding a case which affects the right to freedom of expression. They must have particular regard to the importance of that right, and where journalistic, literary or artistic material is concerned, must consider the extent to which the material is already in the public domain, or is about to be placed in the public domain and the extent to which it would be "in the public interest for the material to be published".[188] "Any relevant privacy code" must be considered in determining the latter issues; depending upon the medium of expression, this may involve rules drafted and policed by bodies such as the Press Complaints Commission, the Broadcasting Complaints Commission and the Independent Television Commission. It is submitted that these provisions do indeed correspond to the case-law of the Court of Human Rights on freedom of expression, which emphasises the importance of that right, condemns, save in exceptional circumstances, prior restraints on publication and permits restrictions on freedom of expression only on narrowly defined public interest grounds.

2.125   Section 13 seeks to reassure churches and other religious organisations, and their considerable band of supporters in Parliament, that they have little to fear from the Human Rights Act. The concerns which were originally expressed on their behalf and which led to amendment of the Bill by the House of Lords were undoubtedly an over-reaction to the prospect of Convention rights becoming justiciable in the domestic courts. Churches and religious organisations would constitute public authorities under s. 6 (and so be vulnerable to challenge) in very limited circumstances, primarily where they exercise functions which otherwise would be exercised by state organisations (for example, performing marriages and running schools). Even in those limited spheres, however, it is difficult to envisage the Convention giving rise to fundamental challenges to the way in which matters are currently handled. For example, the right to marry under Article 12 of the Convention extends only to traditional, and not to same sex, marriages. Challenges would be most likely in reliance upon arts. 8 and 10, the rights to respect for private life and freedom of expression, which specifically permit restrictions in the interests of the "rights of others", including the right to freedom of thought, conscience and religion under Article 9. Section 13 instructs the courts to have particular regard to the importance of Article 9 rights, but that is no more nor less than they would have been obliged to do in any event.

---

[188] HRA, s. 12(4).

13. PROCEDURE AND REMEDIES FOR BREACH OF CONVENTION RIGHTS

The Act itself says little about the procedures to be adopted in claims **2.126** which rely upon Convention rights, although further rules are to be added by rules of court. One important procedural provision is s. 7(5), which lays down a time limit of one year for Convention claims beginning with the date on which the act complained of took place. However, the effect of the one year limitation period is restricted in three ways. First, it only applies to claims brought under s. 7(1)(a), that is, direct challenges to public authorities. Second, it is a default provision which applies only where no stricter time limit already exists for that form of direct challenge. Hence, it does not displace the three month time limit for applications for judicial review. Third, the limit itself is not absolute but may be displaced where the court or tribunal thinks it equitable to do so. The Act does not enumerate any circumstances or factors which would point to an extension of time being granted, preferring to leave it to the courts to address the issue on a case by case basis. No doubt the courts will be urged to have regard to similar provisions for extension of time under the Sex Discrimination Act 1975, the Race Relations Act 1976 and the Disability Discrimination Act 1995.[189]

The general approach adopted by the Human Rights Act is that the **2.127** courts should have exactly the same remedial powers where Convention rights are at issue as they do in other cases. Section 8(1) provides:

"In relation to any act (or proposed act) of a public authority which the court finds is (or would be) unlawful,[190] it may grant such relief or remedy, or make such order, within its powers at it considers just and appropriate."

This is not surprising since in the vast majority of cases, Convention rights will be given effect through the interpretation of domestic legislation, and so within the existing parameters of English law. There are two exceptions to the general approach, where the Act makes special provision for remedies. The first is the declaration of incompatibility under s. 4 of the Act, which is a new remedy, albeit one which has no legal effect between the parties and can only operate to put pressure on the Government to change the law. The second area where special provision

---

[189] SDA, s. 76(5); RRA, s. 68(6); DDA, Sch. 3, para. 3(2). A Government minister referred expressly to the Sex Discrimination Act at the Committee stage in the House of Commons: HC Debs., 24 June 1998, col. 1097.
[190] An unlawful act is one which is incompatible with a Convention right, contrary to s. 6(1): s. 8(5).

is made is that of the award of damages for the act of a public authority which breaches Convention rights. Here, the Act incorporates the principles adopted by the Court of Human Rights when it awards compensation, or "just satisfaction" as it is known in the Convention system. Section 8 provides further:

"(3) No award of damages is to be made unless, taking account of all the circumstances of the case, including —

(a) any other relief or remedy granted, or order made, in relation to the act in question (by that or any other court), and
(b) the consequences of any decision (of that or any other court) in respect of that act

the court is satisfied that the award is necessary to afford just satisfaction to the person in whose favour it is made.

(4) In determining —

(a) whether to award damages, or
(b) the amount of an award,

the court must take into account the principles applied by the European Court of Human Rights in relation to the award of compensation under Article 41 of the Convention."

2.128   A preliminary point to note is that not all courts will have jurisdiction to award damages for breach of a Convention right, and two sets of proceedings will sometimes be necessary — one to establish that a Convention right has been breached and a second to obtain damages. Pursuant to s. 8(2), only those courts which have the power to award damages in civil proceedings may award damages for breach of a Convention right: criminal courts are, therefore, excluded. Duplication of proceedings may also arise in other contexts. For example, in judicial review proceedings, it is well-established that the Divisional Court is only able to award damages where there has been misfeasance in public office. Financial liability under the Convention is not so limited and it is unclear whether a person who establishes in judicial review proceedings that a Convention right has been breached, in circumstances which do not amount to misfeasance, may also claim damages in those proceedings for breach of the right. It is submitted that the courts would be keen to avoid the alternative scenario, whereby a separate claim for damages in the ordinary civil courts must be launched once the judicial review proceedings are completed. Section 8(5)(b) applies to damages awards for breach of Convention rights the provisions of the Civil Liability (Contribution) Act 1978, such that public authorities will be able to argue that claimants have themselves contributed to the loss which they have suffered as a result of breach of their Convention rights. It is also conceivable that public authorities which have incurred liability for breach of Convention rights despite having followed, in good faith, the apparent requirements of domestic legislation might seek to blame central government for their predicament.

Section 9 of the Act makes special provision where remedies are sought in respect of a decision of a court or tribunal which has acted in breach of Convention rights.[191] A direct challenge to such a decision under s. 7(1)(a) can only be brought by way of an appeal or, where otherwise permitted under domestic law, an application for judicial review, and liability for breach of s. 6(1) can never be personal.[192] No damages may be awarded in respect of the unlawful decision of a court, save where a person has been detained contrary to Article 5 of the Convention.[193] The exception reflects the requirements of Article 5(5), but it is hard to see any basis in the Convention for the general rule. Just satisfaction may be awarded by the Court of Human Rights where the applicant has suffered as a result of a judicial decision, just as where other branches of the state are at fault.

2.129

JUST SATISFACTION UNDER THE CONVENTION

The key issue so far as damages claims are concerned is undoubtedly the ambit of the remedy of just satisfaction under Article 41 of the Convention — when it will be awarded, and how much can be recovered. Just satisfaction covers three types of loss: pecuniary damage, non-pecuniary damage and costs. Only the award of damages is subject to Convention principles and the Act leaves intact the jurisdiction of the domestic courts to award costs. Hence it must be assumed that the courts will continue to award costs in the usual way and that only the approach of the Court of Human Rights to pecuniary and non-pecuniary damage is relevant. However, it is one thing to advert to the approach of the Court of Human Rights and quite another to predict how that approach would be applied by the Court in any given case. Beyond stating that it adopts an equitable approach, the Court has nowhere set out in any detail the principles which it applies in awarding just satisfaction and it is submitted that domestic judges are likely to have great difficulty in arriving at any firm conclusions on what the Court would have done if the instant case

2.130

---

[191] "Court" is also defined to include a justice of the peace and a justice's clerk: HRA s. 9(5).
[192] HRA s. 9(1)–(2), (4).
[193] HRA s. 9(3).

had come before it. Some very basic ground-rules can be gleaned from the case-law; after that, it is a matter of analysing specific awards made in analogous cases.[193a]

2.131   There are no apparent limits upon the types of loss and damage which can be compensated under Article 41. The Court draws a distinction between pecuniary and non-pecuniary damage. Pecuniary damage is the loss or damage to real or personal property (including damage to one's business and loss of money generally). Non-pecuniary damage is damage to the person and to interests which do not have an obvious money value. The most common type of claim under this head is for damages for anxiety and distress. Nor is there any upper limit on what can be awarded, and very large payments are occasionally ordered by the Court, particularly in cases involving the confiscation of property contrary to Article 1 of the First Protocol.[194] On average, however, awards are modest. The Court employs two particular principles which go to reduce the value of claims.

Causation

2.132   The first is a strict requirement of causation: there must be a direct causal link between a violation of the Convention and financial loss to the applicant. This requirement gives rise to particular difficulties for applicants who have suffered breaches of their procedural rights, for example under Article 6 of the Convention, since the Court is often reluctant to find that the outcome of their case would have been any different if fair procedures had been followed. In *Saunders*, for example, the applicant succeeded in establishing a breach of Article 6 following the use in criminal proceedings against him of self-incriminating evidence given under duress to DTi inspectors. The criminal proceedings had resulted in conviction for Mr Saunders and a five year jail sentence and he made a substantial claim for, *inter alia*, lost earnings arising out of his trial and imprisonment. The Court refused to award any compensation, principally because it felt unable to speculate as to whether the exclusion of the offending evidence from the criminal trial would have made any difference to the outcome of the trial.[195] Similarly, in *Findlay*, the applicant won his Article 6 claim on the basis of manifest shortcomings in the procedural rules attaching to court martials.[196] He claimed over £400,000 for loss of income caused by

---

[193a] A good synopsis of the case law of the Court on just satisfaction appears in Part III of Reid, *A Practical Guide to the European Convention on Human Rights* (Sweet & Maxwell, 1998).

[194] For example, *Stran Greek Refineries v Greece*, A/301-B, (1995) 19 EHRR 293.

[195] *Saunders v UK*, above n. 78.

[196] *Findlay v UK*, A/734, (1997) 23 EHRR 221.

his discharge from the army, but again the Court held that it could not speculate as to what the outcome of the court-martial proceedings would have been if they had fulfilled the requirements of Article 6(1). His claim for damages for distress was also rejected for that reason: he may have been discharged and suffered the same level of distress even if the proceedings against him had been fairly conducted.[197]

The uniform application of a strict rule of causation, whatever its intrinsic rectitude, would at least have the merit of certainty. Unfortunately, there is another line of cases where the Court has adopted a rather different approach, and compensated the applicant for the loss of the opportunity of a different outcome. In *McMichael*, for example, the applicants' complaint was that they had been refused access to relevant documents during care proceedings.[198] The Government argued that no compensation should be awarded because it was impossible to maintain that the outcome of the proceedings would have been any different if the documents had been handed over. In contrast to its approach in *Saunders* and *Findlay*, the Court reasoned that it could not be said with certainty that no practical benefit could have accrued to the applicants if the procedural deficiencies had not existed. Also, it was material that some of the distress which the applicants had suffered flowed directly from their inability to see the documents and reports in question and did not depend on the outcome of proceedings.[199] In *Weeks*, where there was a breach of Article 5 as a result of the failure to provide a remedy whereby the applicant's continuing detention might be reviewed, the Court awarded compensation on the basis that the possibility of an earlier release following an appropriate procedure could not be excluded.[200] It is in truth very difficult to find any rational basis for predicting when the loss of a chance approach will prevail, and justify compensation. It is, in the circumstances, tempting to conclude that the Court is swayed merely by its own instinctive view of the personal merits of particular applicants.   **2.133**

Necessity

The fact that compensation should only be awarded "if necessary" gives the Court a wide discretion to do justice in the circumstances of each case. Put bluntly, it will not award compensation to undeserving applicants,   **2.134**

---

[197] *Ibid.* at 246–247. Another example is *Maxwell* v *UK*, A/300-C, (1995) 19 EHRR 97.
[198] *McMichael* v *UK*, A/307-B, (1995) 20 EHRR 205.
[199] *Ibid.* at 243–244. The Court awarded £8,000.
[200] A/145-A (1988) at 9.

even in cases of serious violation of Convention rights. In *McCann*, for example, the Court found a breach of the right to life under Article 2 arising out of the killing by the SAS in Gibraltar of three suspected IRA terrorists. There could hardly be a more serious violation of the Convention, but no compensation was awarded in the light of the Court's finding that the three had been intending to plant a bomb.[201] *McCann* is a rare example of the Court being explicit about its motivations for refusing to award compensation. There are numerous cases where convicted criminals have established a breach of their Convention rights yet been refused compensation on the grounds that the decision itself constituted sufficient redress.[202] Equally, the Court is quick to recognise that certain claims are brought in order to establish a legal principle, rather than for financial gain, and to withhold compensation accordingly. That would explain the outcome in *Goodwin* where the applicant journalist had been found guilty of contempt of court after refusing to disclose evidence of his sources for a controversial story. He succeeded in a claim under Article 10 and claimed £15,000 for mental anguish, shock, dismay and anxiety. The Court held that its finding of breach of Article 10 was adequate satisfaction; a financial award was not necessary.[203]

Quantum of damages

2.135   Where it is necessary to award compensation for loss which has been caused by a breach of the Convention, the next step is to seek to value the loss and damage which has been suffered. Again, there are no firm principles to be found in the Strasbourg case-law. Occasionally, the Court resorts to expert evidence.[204] More often, it awards a global sum without descending to details of how that sum was calculated, or the evidence which it has relied upon. In *Halford*, for example, the applicant had suffered an intrusion into her private life through the monitoring of private telephone calls on her office phone. She claimed damages for distress and anxiety and was awarded £10,000. The Court did not cite any medical evidence or, indeed, give any indication at all as to how it had arrived at that figure.[205] The

---

[201] *McCann* v *UK*, A/324, (1996) 21 EHRR 97.
[202] For example, *Welch* v *UK*, A/307-A, (1995) 20 EHRR 247; *Murray (John)* v *UK*, A/593, (1996) 22 EHRR 29; *Hussein* v *UK*, A/599, (1996) 22 EHRR 1.
[203] *Goodwin* v *UK*, above n. 61.
[204] For example, *Papamichalopoulos* v *Greece*, A/260-B, (1995) 21 EHRR 439.
[205] *Halford* v *UK*, A/773, (1997) 25 EHRR 523. See also *Schuler-Zgraggen* v *Switzerland*, A/305-A, (1995) 21 EHRR 404.

Court's rather haphazard approach should not, however, prevent the English courts from using more analytical methods of damages assessment.

Further approximate justice may be achieved through the use of a **2.136** discretionary power to award interest on compensation. The award of interest appears to be particularly appropriate where property has been confiscated by the state. Overall it has been awarded in only a minority of cases. In most English courts and tribunals, interest on compensation is virtually automatic, but it is submitted that their usual approach may have to give way in Convention claims. That is because interest is a component of damages, rather than a separate head of claim, and, pursuant to s. 8(3)-(4), damages as a whole can only be awarded in line with the approach of the Court of Human Rights.

14. REMEDIAL ORDERS

Whilst the Human Rights Act does not have the effect of invalidating **2.137** provisions of primary legislation which are incompatible with Convention rights, it recognizes that the UK remains under an international law obligation to repeal or amend such legislation. Section 10(2) of the Act is a Henry VIII clause: it permits Ministers to use subordinare legislation for the purposes of amending primary legislation which is considered to be in breach of the Convention. It may be triggered in two ways. First, where a particular piece of legislation has been the subject of a declaration of incompatibility under s. 4, provided that the appeal process in respect of that declaration has been exhausted.[206] Secondly, a decision of the Court of Human Rights may draw attention to inconsistency between domestic legislation and the requirements of the Convention.[207] In either case, the Minister in question must consider that there are "compelling reasons" for proceeding under s. 10. Presumably, breach of the Convention will be generally compelling enough reason for amending legislation but that requirement refers also to the perceived imperative of proceeding under the Henry VIII clause rather than by further primary legislation. Section 10 may also be used to cure defects within subordinate legislation where such defects cannot be removed by virtue of incompatible primary legislation.[208]

---

[206] HRA, s. 10(1).
[207] HRA, s. 10(2).
[208] HRA, s. 10(3).

2.138   Schedule 2 to the Act makes further provision in relation to remedial orders. It deals primarily with the Parliamentary procedure which must be employed in making a remedial order.[209] Notably, it also provides that remedial orders may have retroactive effect (although not such as to create retrospective criminal liability).[210]

15. SCRUTINY OF LEGISLATION

2.139   It is well-known that government departments commonly vet draft legislation for compliance with the Convention, but the Act gives new impetus to pre-legislative scrutiny. Section 19 creates a new addition to Parliamentary procedure, the statement of compatibility. This is a written statement to be made by a Minister in charge of each new Bill confirming that the provisions of the Bill are compatible with Convention rights. In the unlikely event that the provisions of a Bill are thought by the Minister not to be compatible with Convention rights, or where the position is unclear, a statement must be made to the effect that the Government wishes the Bill to proceed in any event. A similar provision exists in the New Zealand Bill of Rights, s. 7 of which places an obligation upon the Attorney-General to bring to Parliament's attention any conflict between draft legislation and human rights guarantees. The New Zealand courts have rejected the argument that the provisions relating to Parliamentary scrutiny of legislation confer rights on individuals, such that a failure to notify a breach of the Bill of Rights Act might render legislation invalid.[211]

2.140   The White Paper which preceded the Act also proposed the establishment of a Joint Committee on Human Rights of both Houses of Parliament, with continuing responsibility to monitor the operation of the Human Rights Act. The Committee could also consider what should be done about judicial declarations that the Convention has been breached by primary legislation. One of the first tasks of the Committee, if it is established, will be to consider whether or not a Human Rights Commission should be created, with the task of promoting public awareness of Convention rights and of sponsoring important human rights litigation. The Equal Opportunities Commission and the Commission for Racial Equality perform similar functions under the Sex Discrimination Act 1975

---

[209] Paragraphs 2–6 of Schedule 2.
[210] Paragraphs 1(1)(b) and 1(3) of Schedule 2.
[211] *Mangawaro Enterprises Ltd* v *A-G* [1994] 2 NZLR 451.

and the Race Relations Act 1976, and one option would have been for the Act to subsume those bodies within a single human rights agency. Ultimately, the Government decided not to establish a Human Rights Commission at the outset of the life of the Act, but it expressed the wish in its White Paper that the matter be considered by the proposed Parliamentary Joint Committee.[212]

16. FURTHER READING

Blake, "Judicial Review of Discretion in Human Rights Cases" [1997] EHRLR 391 **2.141**

Hunt, *Using Human Rights Law in English Courts*, Hart Publishing, (1997)

Hunt, "The 'Horizontal Effect' of the Human Rights Act" [1998] PL 423

Huscroft and Rishworth, *Rights and Freedoms — the New Zealand Bill of Rights Act 1990 and the Human Rights Act 1993*, Brooker's Wellington (1995)

Irvine, "The Development of Human Rights in Britain" [1998] PL 221

Laws, "*The Limitations of Human Rights*" [1998] PL 254

Mowbray, "The European Court of Human Rights' Approach to Just Satisfaction" [1997] PL 647

Reid, *A Practical Guide to the European Convention on Human Rights*, Sweet & Maxwell (1998), Part III on Just Satisfaction

Taggart, "Tugging on Superman's Cape: Lessons from Experience with the New Zealand Bill of Rights Act 1990" [1998] PL 266

---

[212] Above n. 6 at paras. 3.8–3.12.

Chapter 3

THE CONVENTION AND EUROPEAN COMMUNITY LAW

Although this book is primarily concerned with the enforcement of the **3.1** European Convention through the Human Rights Act 1998, it would be incomplete without an examination of the ways in which the Convention can be enforced through the medium of European Community law. In many cases, the Human Rights Act and the European Communities Act 1972 offer alternative or complementary means of challenge to legislation and administrative decisions; in others, EC law will avail the individual where the Convention, and the Human Rights Act, cannot. Both avenues should, therefore, be considered.

1. TWO EUROPEAN LEGAL SYSTEMS

The Council of Europe, which was responsible for drafting and adopting **3.2** the European Convention on Human Rights, and is in charge of its continuing enforcement, is entirely separate from the European Union. The European Union was founded as the European Economic Community (EEC, also known as the Common Market) by the Treaty of Rome in 1957, as a free trade area comprising six European states. Since then, it has undergone considerable changes. In terms of membership, there are now 15 Member States (including the UK, as of 1973) with plans to co-opt many more. The EEC has become the European Community, which is now only one pillar of the European Union, and the EU as a whole is much more than simply a free trade area. Few areas of domestic law are untouched by the law of the European Union, and EC legislation is the dominant influence in a whole range of areas of legal practice including employment law, immigration, inter-state trade, environmental law and competition law.

3.3 Confusion between the Council of Europe and the European Union is understandable. The range of labels which can be applied to trans-European political institutions is limited and the Council of Europe and its Committee of Ministers are easily mistaken for the Council of Ministers and the European Council, two important bodies within the institutional framework of the EU. Also, lawyers tend to talk of "European law" as if there were only one trans-national European legal order. However, it is vital to differentiate between the law of the European Union, and the law of the European Convention. The two legal systems are vastly different in content, and take effect in the domestic courts in entirely different ways. European Convention rights, as incorporated into domestic law by the Human Rights Act, have significantly less legal force than EC law rights, which are given effect through the European Communities Act 1972.[1]

3.4 There is, nevertheless, some degree of overlap between the two systems, in particular since the EU professes to adhere to the principles laid down in the European Convention. The result is that in some situations, EC law can be used as a powerful medium through which European Convention rights may be given effect in the UK, regardless of the strictures of the Human Rights Act. This chapter examines the relationship between the EU and the European Convention legal system, the various methods by which EC law can be given effect in the UK and finally, the range of situations in which EC law can be adopted as an aid to the enforcement of the Convention.

2. THE RELATIONSHIP BETWEEN EC LAW AND THE LAW OF THE ECHR

3.5 Since the adoption of the Maastricht Treaty on European Union (TEU) in 1993, the EU has had a firm constitutional commitment to respect for the principles of fundamental rights which are enshrined in the European Convention. Article F2 TEU states:

"The Union shall respect fundamental rights, as guaranteed by the European Convention for the Protection of Human Rights and Fundamental Freedoms signed in Rome on 4 November 1950 and as they result from the constitutional traditions common to the Member States, as general principles of Community law."[2]

---

[1] The term "EC law" is used throughout, since the EC is the pillar of the European Union under which the vast majority of legislation is adopted, and the vast majority of European Court of Justice decisions are delivered.

[2] By virtue of Art. L, Art. F.2(1) is non-justiciable.

Also, Article F.2(1) contains a commitment by states to exercise powers **3.6**
relating to, *inter alia*, asylum and immigration, in conformity with the
European Convention on Human Rights. The Treaty amendments agreed
at the Amsterdam summit in May 1997 strengthen this commitment. A
new Article F1 is to be added, to the effect that the EU is founded upon the
principles of liberty, democracy, respect for human rights and fundamental freedoms, and the rule of law. A new Article Fa will give the
Member States power to take action against any EU member which is
seen to be consistently violating one or more of those principles.

Given that the European Convention had already been finalised seven **3.7**
years before the Common Market was established in 1957, the adoption in
1993 of a constitutional commitment to respect for human rights might be
viewed as coming rather late in the day. However, despite the lack of an
explicit reference in the Treaty text to human rights standards, the
European Court of Justice has, since the late 1960s, sought to assert its
human rights credentials, and those of the EC as a whole, by establishing
respect for human rights as one of the general principles of EC law.[3] More
recently, it has taken to referring explicitly to the European Convention as
the most important source from which EC human rights principles are
drawn. In one recent judgment it formulated its position in this way:

"As the Court has consistently held, fundamental rights form an integral part of the general
principles of Community law whose observance the Court ensures. For that purpose, the
Court draws inspiration from the constitutional traditions common to the Member States
and from the guidelines supplied by international treaties for the protection of human
rights on which the Member States have collaborated or of which they are signatories. The
[European] Convention has special significance in that respect. As the Court has also held,
it follows that measures are not acceptable in the Community which are incompatible with
observance of the human rights thus recognized and guaranteed."[4]

Human rights principles, and the law of the European Convention, **3.8**
have been used before the European Court of Justice in three specific
ways. First, to influence the way in which EC legislation is interpreted. In
P v S and Cornwall County Council, for example, the issue was whether
the EC Equal Treatment Directive, which prohibits sex discrimination in
employment matters, should be interpreted as extending to discrimination against transsexuals. Both the Court's Advocate General and the
Court itself referred to case-law of the Court of Human Rights on the
protection of transsexuals before finding that such discrimination was

---

[3] The first case is *Stauder v City of Ulm*, Case 29/69 [1969] ECR 419. See also *Nold v Commission*,
  Case 4/73 [1974] ECR 491; *Hauer v Rheinland-Pfalz*, Case 44/70 [1979] ECR 3737.
[4] *Kremzow v Austria*, Case C-299/95 [1997] ECR I-2629.

indeed prohibited under EC law.[5] Similarly, in *Grant* v *South West Trains*, the ECJ drew support from the Strasbourg case-law for its decision that discrimination on grounds of sexuality was not covered by the Equal Treatment Directive.[6] Secondly, human rights principles have been used to challenge the legislative and administrative acts of the EC institutions. A recent example is *X* v *Commission*, in which the Commission had ordered a blood test designed to indicate the presence of AIDS to be carried out on a sample provided by a job applicant who had refused to undergo an AIDS screening test. The Court held that the Commission had infringed the applicant's right to respect for his private life as embodied in Article 8 of the Convention.[7]

3.9   Thirdly, and most significantly, the Court of Justice has indicated that legislation and administrative action at national level may be reviewed for compliance with human rights principles where it constitutes an implementation of EC law or otherwise falls within the scope of EC law. The ambit of these important terms is examined in greater detail below. In *R.* v *Kirk*, for example, a Danish fisherman was convicted under a British fishing restriction which was held by the Court to have been invalid at the time it was adopted. The restriction was subsequently given retrospective approval by the Council of Ministers but that approval could not be relied upon against Mr Kirk since this would amount to giving retroactive effect to penal legislation, contrary to Article 7 of the Convention.[8]

3.10   Whilst the Court of Justice has sought to ensure respect within the EC for the rights laid down in the Convention, it is important to note that it does not appear to apply the Convention as such, or at least to apply it in the same way that the European Court of Human Rights applies it. The ECJ recognises the same rights as its counterpart in Strasbourg — the right to respect for private and family life, the right to property, etc. — and will hold, on occasion, that those rights have been breached. It does not, however, apply the wording and methodology of the Convention and the European Court of Human Rights by, for example, deciding whether a restriction on respect for private life has been adopted pursuant to one of the exceptions enumerated in Article 8(2), fulfils a pressing social need and otherwise falls within the "margin of appreciation" In fact, it has adopted its own test for assessing whether a restriction can be justified. The Court of Justice has ruled (in the context of the right to respect for

---

[5] Case C-13/94 [1996] ECR I-2143.
[6] Case C-249/96, [1998] ECR I-449.
[7] Case C-404/92-P [1994] ECR I-4737.
[8] Case 63/83 [1984] ECR 2689.

private life and the right to protection of medical confidentiality):

"Those rights, however, do not constitute unfettered prerogatives and may be restricted, provided that the restrictions in fact correspond to objectives of general interest pursued by the Community and that they do not constitute, with regard to the objectives pursued, a disproportionate and intolerable interference which infringes upon the very substance of the rights guaranteed." [9]

This formulation is similar to, but noticeably less stringent than, the approach adopted by the Court of Human Rights. The category of "objectives of general interest" is open-ended, unlike the specific grounds for restriction set out in, for example, Article 8(2). There is no requirement that a "pressing social need" for restriction must be established;[10] the import of the Court's approach is that any restriction which is convenient for the purposes of achieving a worthy objective is acceptable. Also, the rule that a restriction must not infringe upon the very substance of the right concerned falls some way short of the Convention's insistence rule that a restriction upon a fundamental right must go no further than is necessary to achieve its objectives.

The ECJ's apparently less stringent approach to the fundamental rights **3.11** guarantees set out in the Convention has resulted in only a handful of successes for individuals seeking to rely upon their Convention rights in opposition to rules and regulations in the EC law sphere. Not surprisingly, it has also given rise to inconsistencies between the level of protection for those rights which is offered by the ECJ and that guaranteed by the Court of Human Rights. In *Hoechst*,[11] for example, the Court of Justice refused to accept that a right to respect for the home could extend to business premises. A few months earlier, the Court of Human Rights had applied Article 8 of the Convention to premises which were used both for residential and business purposes;[12] a few years later, it indicated conclusively that business premises were protected as "the home".[13] In one instance, the two Courts arrived at different conclusions in respect of virtually the same subject matter. In *SPUC* v *Grogan*, the Court of Justice was faced with a challenge to Irish restrictions upon dissemination by a student organisation of information on how to obtain abortions in

---

[9] See, for example, *Commission* v *Germany*, Case C-62/90 [1992] ECR I-2575, 2609. For a confirmation in the English courts that the Court of Justice does not recognise fundamental rights to be absolute, see *R.* v *Chief Constable of Sussex ex parte International Traders' Ferry* decision of 11 November 1998 (HL).

[10] Compare, for example, *Handyside* v *UK*, A/24, (1979–80) 1 EHRR 737, 754.

[11] *Hoechst* v *Commission*, Case 46/87 [1989] ECR 2859.

[12] *Chappell* v *UK*, A/152, (1990) 12 EHRR 1.

[13] *Niemietz* v *Germany*, A/251-B, (1993) 16 EHRR 97, 112.

England (abortion being prohibited in Ireland itself).[14] The Court ruled that EC law, and in particular Article 59 of the Treaty of Rome which guarantees the free movement of services, did not protect individual rights to distribute, or to receive, the disputed information. Conversely, in *Open Door Counselling and Dublin Well Woman v Ireland*, the Court of Human Rights found that identical restrictions, this time upon counselling centres, amounted to an unjustifiable infringement of the applicants' freedom of expression in imparting the information, and of the freedom of their clients to receive the information.[15]

3.12   The only sure way to iron out inconsistencies between EC law and the law of the ECHR would be for the European Union to sign up to the Convention. Given that all of the Member States of the EU are parties to the Convention and that the EU is, in any event, bound by the tenets of the European Convention through the general principles of EC law, two of the most obvious obstacles to accession can be discounted. However, in a recent advisory opinion, the Court of Justice held that the constitution of the EU as laid down in the Treaty on European Union would not, expressly or impliedly, permit accession.[16] An amendment to the Treaty would be required, but is in practice unlikely given the opposition to accession of certain states, including the UK. No such amendment was agreed at the recent Amsterdam summit.

3.13   In the absence of accession by the EU, the Strasbourg Commission will not entertain complaints about decisions taken by EU institutions.[17] This reluctance extends to the situation where complaint is made about a national measure which has been taken in order to implement or give effect to an EC decision. In *M & Co v Germany*,[18] the Commission rejected a complaint from a company about action taken by the German authorities to implement a fine imposed upon the company by the EC Commission in competition law proceedings. According to the company, the proceedings were in breach of Article 6 of the Convention since the Commission had acted as both prosecutor and judge, and the German authorities could not lawfully seek to give effect to the outcome of those proceedings. The Commission held that the German Government was responsible for all acts or omissions violating the Convention regardless of whether they were a consequence of its domestic law or of its international obligations. However, acts resulting from powers transferred

---

[14] Case C-159/90 [1991] ECR I-4685.
[15] A/246, (1993) 15 EHRR 244.
[16] Opinion 2/94, *Re Accession by the Communities to the Convention for the Protection of Human Rights and Fundamental Freedoms* [1996] ECR I-1759.
[17] *CFDT v EC*, Appl. No. 8030/77, (1978) 13 D&R 231.
[18] Appl. No. 13258/87, (1990) 64 D&R 138.

to the EC could not be challenged under the Convention because the EC legal system provided equivalent human rights protection. The latter conclusion is certainly questionable given the scope for inconsistency between the level of fundamental rights protection afforded by EC law and that required by the Convention. Nevertheless, it is clear, following *M & Co*, that legislative and administrative acts of the domestic authorities which are taken in order to implement EC law should be challenged under EC law rather than under the Convention as such.

3. ENFORCING EC LAW IN DOMESTIC COURTS

There are various methods by which EC law can be enforced in the English courts, not all of which will be available in any one case.   **3.14**

THE MECHANISM OF IMPLEMENTATION

The mechanism through which EC law is given effect in the domestic courts is set out in the European Communities Act 1972. Section 2(1) of the 1972 Act states: **3.15**

"All such rights, powers, liabilities, obligations, restrictions from time to time created or arising by or under the Treaties, and all such remedies and procedures from time to time provided for by or under the Treaties, as in accordance with the Treaties are without further enactment to be given legal effect or used in the United Kingdom shall be recognised and available in law, and be enforced, allowed and followed accordingly; and the expression 'enforceable Community law right' and similar expressions shall be read as referring to one to which this subsection applies."

Section 2(4) provides that "any enactment passed or to be passed ... shall be construed and have effect subject to the foregoing provisions of this section" (subject, therefore, to enforceable Community law rights).

Those rights under EC law which are "without further enactment to be given legal effect", also referred to in s. 2(1) as "enforceable Community law rights" are known in EC law as directly effective (or directly enforceable) rights. Not all provisions of Community law are directly effective but those which are must take precedence over conflicting provisions of domestic law. The rule that EC law is supreme over domestic law was   **3.16** well-established long before the UK joined the EC, and has been reiterated on regular occasions since.[19] In the light of that rule, the effect of s. 2 is to insert an implied term into each and every domestic statutory provision, whether passed before or after the European Communities Act, to the effect that it is to be read without prejudice to directly effective Community law rights.[20]

3.17   The rulings of the European Court of Justice are given effect in domestic law by s. 3 of the ECA which states:

"(1) For the purposes of all legal proceedings any question as to the meaning or effect of any of the Treaties, or as to the validity, meaning or effect of any Community instrument, shall be treated as a question of law (and, if not referred to the European Court, be for determination as such in accordance with the principles laid down by and any relevant decisions of the European Court or any court attached thereto).

(2) Judicial notice shall be taken of the Treaties, of the Official Journal of the Communities and of any decision of, or expression of opinion by, the European Court or any court attached thereto on any such question as aforesaid."

Section 3 modifies the usual rule that issues of foreign law are to be treated by our courts as issues of fact. Its effect is that domestic courts will take notice of, and follow, relevant decisions of the European Court of Justice, which will take precedence over conflicting domestic authorities.[21]

IMPLEMENTATION BY INTERPRETATION

3.18   The first, and most common, way in which EC law rights are given effect in our domestic courts is through interpretation of provisions of national law in such a way that they conform to the relevant EC rules, also known as indirect effect. In every case, recourse must first be had to the remedy of interpretation since other remedies are only available in the event of a breach of Community law,[22] and if a potential inconsistency between national law and Community law can be resolved through interpretation, there is no breach. It is a longstanding principle of the common law that

---

[19] *Costa v ENEL*, Case 6/64 [1964] ECR 585; *R. v Secretary of State for Transport ex parte Factortame (No. 2)*, Case C-213/89 [1990] ECR I-2433.
[20] per Lord Bridge in *R. v Secretary of State for Transport ex parte Factortame* [1990] 2 AC 85, 140.
[21] Similar provision is made in s. 2 HRA for the decisions of the European Court and Commission of Human Rights.
[22] See *Blaik v Post Office* [1994] IRLR 280, relying upon *Pickstone v Freemans plc* [1989] AC 68.

the courts will presume Parliament to have intended to legislate in accordance with, rather than contrary to, its international commitments and will construe ambiguous legislation accordingly.[23] However, a succession of Court of Justice rulings has elevated this principle of construction to new heights. According to the ECJ, British courts have a duty, under Article 5 of the Treaty,[24] to interpret national law so far as possible in conformity with provisions of EC law.[25]

Two standard restrictions upon the application of the common law rule do not apply to the discharge of the EC duty of interpretation. The first is the rule that recourse should only be had to extraneous sources if, viewed in isolation, the statutory provision is ambiguous. A provision of domestic legislation must be read in conformity with EC law if it is reasonably capable of bearing that meaning. This goes much further than a pre-condition of ambiguity and amounts to a rule that an interpretation consistent with EC law must be preferred save where there is clear language to the contrary. The rule is clearly illustrated by the case of *Litster* v *Forth Dry Dock and Forth Estuary Engineering*, in which the House of Lords demonstrated a willingness to insert words into an apparently unambiguous statutory instrument in order to make it comply with an EC Directive.[26] Regulation 5 of the Transfer of Undertakings (Protection of Employment) Regulations 1981 has the effect, on the transfer of a business, of transferring to the new owner the contracts of employment of employees who are employed in the business immediately before the time of the transfer. The TUPE Regulations give effect in domestic law to the EC Acquired Rights Directive.[27] The applicants in *Litster* had been employed in the First Respondent's business which went into receivership and whose assets were sold to the Second Respondent (the transferee of the business). They were (unfairly) dismissed one hour before the transfer and sought to claim both against their former employer, which was insolvent, and against the transferee, which was not. They had clearly not been employed in the business "*immediately before the transfer*" within the terms of reg. 5(3) and it appeared,

3.19

---

[23] For example, *Salomon* v *Commissioners for Customs and Excise* [1967] 2 QB 116.

[24] Art. 5 provides that "Member States shall take all appropriate measures, whether general or particular, to ensure fulfilment of the obligations arising out of this Treaty or resulting from action taken by the institutions of the Community. They shall facilitate the achievement of the Community's tasks. They shall abstain from any measure which could jeopardise the attainment of the objectives of this Treaty."

[25] *Marleasing* v *La Comercial Internacional de Alimentación*, Case C-106/89 [1990] ECR I-4135; *Criminal Proceedings against Arcaro*, Case C-168/95 [1996] ECR I-4705.

[26] [1990] 1 AC 546.

[27] Directive 77/187/EEC.

therefore, that their employment and/or responsibility for their dismissal could not transfer to the Second Respondent.

3.20   However, the European Court of Justice had interpreted the equivalent provision of the Acquired Rights Directive to mean that employees who are dismissed because of an impending transfer (an eventuality which is prohibited by the Directive) must be considered still to be employed in the business at the time of the transfer. Despite the unambiguous wording of reg. 5, the House of Lords implied an additional clause, so that reg. 5 applied to transfer the employment of those employees who were employed "immediately before the transfer *or would have been so employed if they had not been unfairly dismissed [by reason of the transfer]*". Lord Oliver stated:

> "If legislation can reasonably be construed so as to conform with [EC] obligations — obligations which are to be ascertained not only from the wording of the relevant Directive but also from the interpretation placed upon it by the European Court of Justice at Luxembourg — such a purposive construction will be applied even though, perhaps, it may involve some departure from the strict and literal application of the words which the legislature has elected to use. . . . *Pickstone v Freemans plc* [1989] AC 66 has established that the greater flexibility available to the court in applying a purposive construction to legislation designed to give effect to the United Kingdom's Treaty obligations to the Community enables the court, where necessary, to supply by implication words appropriate to comply with those obligations . . . Having regard to the manifest purpose of the Regulations, I do not, for my part, feel inhibited from making such an implication in the instant case." [28]

On the basis of *Litster*, the test is whether a particular reading of the provision is at all possible, using, if necessary additional words, not whether it is invited by the terms of the provision.[29]

3.21   It will be noted from Lord Oliver's comments that the departure from the traditional common law search for ambiguity in the statute also necessitates a change of method on the part of the courts. It is no longer appropriate to first construe statutory provisions in isolation, without reference to the relevant EC law. Rather, the court should first construe EC law, in order to establish the meaning which is required to be given to the domestic statute, and then proceed to examine whether the statute can in fact be given that meaning. Another good example of the required approach is *Adams v Lancashire CC*, in which the plaintiffs'

---

[28] [1990] 1 AC 546, 559 and 577.
[29] *Litster* supersedes earlier cases such as *Haughton v Olau Lines (UK)* [1986] 1 WLR 504 which emphasised the need for ambiguity in the statutory provision before Community law could be invoked. See also *R. v Secretary of State for the Environment ex parte Greenpeace* [1994] 4 All ER 352.

argument that the TUPE regulations operated to transfer to their new employer an entitlement to accrue an occupational pension were examined solely in the light of the text of the Acquired Rights Directive and before attempting to construe the domestic legislation.[30]

3.22 The second point is that the duty to interpret national law consistently with EC law applies whether the statutory provision was passed before or after the EC rule with which it must comply. Domestic courts have been much happier to give effect to a Parliamentary intention to comply with an EC rule where they are dealing with legislation which specifically intends to implement the rule into domestic law (as in *Litster*), and which was drafted with that rule in mind.[31] However, the EC law duty is equally strong where the legislation has been passed before the adoption of the EC rule and where legislation post-dates the EC rule but does not specifically intend to implement it. The courts must in all cases presume, as did the House of Lords in *Litster*, that Parliament intended to comply with the EC law rule, regardless of the background to the legislation.[32] This principle was accepted by the House of Lords in *Webb* v *EMO Air Cargo* in the context of the Sex Discrimination Act, which had been passed before, and without reference to, the EC Equal Treatment Directive.[33] Following a ruling by the European Court of Justice, Lord Keith, giving judgment for the second time in the case, demonstrated a determination to construe the Act consistently with the Directive which was as unwavering as that shown by Lord Oliver in *Litster* when dealing with implementing legislation.[34]

3.23 The obligation to interpret domestic legislation in conformity with EC law is limited, first, by the wording of the legislation itself: legislation which is plainly at odds with EC law need not be distorted in order to comply with it. The ECJ has also ruled that national legislation should not be interpreted in accordance with EC law in such a way as to impose, or aggravate, criminal liability where the extent of such liability was not already clearly apparent. To do so would be to contravene the prohibition in Article 7 of the Convention on retroactive criminal legislation.[35] Recently, in *Arcaro*, the ECJ appeared to lay down a further limitation, ruling that the obligation of a national court to refer to an EC Directive when interpreting the relevant rules of its national law ceases to apply

---

[30] [1997] ICR 834.
[31] Contrast *Duke* v *Reliance Systems* [1988] AC 618.
[32] *Wagnet Miret* v *Fondo de Garantía Salarial*, Case C-334/92 [1993] ECR I-6911, 6932.
[33] [1933] ICR 175, 186.
[34] [1995] ICR 1021.
[35] See, for example, *Criminal Proceedings* v *Kolpinghuis Nijmegan*, Case 80/86 [1987] ECR 3969; *Arcaro*, above n. 25.

where it would lead to the imposition on an individual of an obligation laid down by a directive which has not been transposed.[36] Taken at face value, the Court's ruling would have the effect of emasculating the doctrine of indirect effect since, in most cases, including *Litster*, the purpose of invoking it is precisely to impose upon individuals obligations additional to those which appear to be contained in national law read in isolation. It is difficult to say whether that was indeed the Court's intention, and the precise effect of the *Arcaro* decision remains to be clarified.

DIRECT EFFECT OF EC LAW

3.24 Where domestic legislation cannot be interpreted consistently with an EC rule, there is, by definition, a breach of, or conflict with, EC law. In such circumstances, it may be that the individual can give effect to EC law by invoking directly effective rights which, as noted above, will take precedence over conflicting provisions of domestic legislation. It is important to note, however, that a provision of primary legislation so displaced is not thereby struck down or erased from the statute book. The ECJ insists only that the provision cannot be applied in the instant case,[37] and as a matter of domestic law the courts have no power to annul primary legislation. It remains for the legislature to amend or repeal the offending text. The position is different so far as secondary legislation is concerned; a statutory instrument which infringes Community law is thereby *ultra vires* and can be quashed.

3.25   Not all provisions of EC law confer directly effective rights. The test for direct effect is two-fold. First, the provision must be "unconditional" and "sufficiently clear and precise". The former means that the provision must impose a complete legal obligation which is not subject to further explanation or elaboration by the Government or the EC. The latter means, in essence, that it must be possible to tell from the provision exactly whom is meant to be liable, to whom and for what. It is always advisable to check whether a provision has been given direct effect in the past before embarking on the task of assessing *de novo* whether it meets those criteria.

---

[36] *Ibid.* at 4730.
[37] See *Amministrazione delle Finanze dello Stato* v *Simmenthal*, Case 106/77 [1978] ECR 629; *ex parte Factortame, (No. 2)* above n. 19.

Secondly, the provision must be of a type which is inherently capable **3.26**
of having direct effect as against the party against whom it is to be
invoked.

- Many of the articles of the Treaty can only be directly enforced
  against state bodies, because they only impose duties upon the state
  (for example, those concerning customs duties and free movement
  of goods).
- The Treaty provisions on free movement of persons and services
  (Articles 48, 52 and 59) can be directly enforced against the state and
  against private, rule-making bodies.
- Certain Treaty articles, such as Article 119 on equal pay, can be
  directly enforced both vertically, against the state, and horizontally,
  against private companies and individuals.
- The main competition law provisions, Articles 85 and 86, can only be
  directly enforced against "undertakings", that is, private (non-state)
  businesses.
- Provisions of EC Directives can only have direct eect as against state
  bodies.[38]
- Rights deriving from general principles of EC law, including the
  general principle of respect for fundamental rights as laid down in
  the European Convention, are, *ipso facto*, directly eective.

"The state", for the purposes of direct effect, is broadly defined, and
extends to bodies who carry out public functions and which have been
granted special powers for that purpose.[39]

In many cases, the invocation of a directly effective EC law right will **3.27**
have the effect of removing an obstacle to the award of a financial remedy
under domestic law. In *Marshall* v *Southampton Area Health Authority*,[40] for example, a nurse challenged the decision of her employer to
make her retire at the age of 60, even though her male colleagues were
permitted to remain at work until age 65. She claimed for sex discrimination, and relied upon Article 5 of the EC Equal Treatment Directive to
override s. 6(4) of the Sex Discrimination Act 1975, which excluded
claims in respect of provision for retirement. The way was then open for
her to claim damages for sex discrimination under the Act.

In other cases, the use of a directly effective EC law right will not lead **3.28**
to a specific financial remedy in domestic law but may give rise to a

---

[38] *Dori* v *Recreb*, Case C-91/92 [1994] ECR I-3325.
[39] *Foster* v *British Gas* [1991] 2 AC 306; *NUT* v *St Marys School* [1997] ICR 334.
[40] Case 152/84 [1986] ECR 723; [1986] ICR 335.

Community law right to damages against the Government, akin to a claim for breach of statutory duty. Such damages claims will be decided according to the principles recently laid down by the Court of Justice in the *Factortame* and *British Telecom* cases.[41] A breach of Community law by the state which causes loss to an individual will not, *ipso facto*, give rise to a right in damages. The rule of Community law at issue must be intended to confer rights upon that individual (rather than upon a category of individuals into which he does not fall) and the breach must be "sufficiently serious". The latter means, in essence, that the error on the part of the state must be a major error, having regard to the state of Community law at the time. An error caused by the adoption of an interpretation of Community law which is understandable but which ultimately turns out to be incorrect will not suffice. A failure to take steps to implement an EC Directive into domestic law within the time limit allowed for its implementation is, *per se*, a sufficiently serious breach.[42]

DAMAGES CLAIMS FOR BREACH OF EC LAW

3.29   Certain individuals will be unable to give effect to their EC law rights either by way of interpretation of domestic law, or by invoking a directly effective right. In the *Francovich* case,[43] for example, the claimants could not rely upon interpretation because, their government having wholly failed to implement the relevant EC Directive, there was no suitable national provision to interpret. Nor did they have any directly effective rights since the provision upon which they sought to rely was not sufficiently clear and precise. Their remedy was to sue the Italian Government for damages for the loss caused to them by its failure to implement Community law. The same criteria as above apply — the provision relied upon must be intended to confer rights upon the claimant, the failure to give effect to EC law must be sufficiently serious, and there must be a causal link between the breach of EC law and the loss suffered. *Francovich* being a case of total failure to implement a directive within the time limit, the breach was automatically considered to be sufficiently serious.

---

[41] *R.* v *Secretary of State for Transport ex parte Factortame (No. 4)*, Case C-48/93 [1996] ECR I-1029; *R.* v *HM Treasury ex parte British Telecommunications plc*, Case C-392/93 [1996] ECR I-1631.
[42] *Dillenkofer* v *Germany*, Case C-178/94 [1996] ECR I-4845.
[43] Cases C-6&9/90 [1991] ECR I-5357.

4. ENFORCING CONVENTION RIGHTS THROUGH EC LAW

Having outlined the methods which can be adopted to give effect to rights **3.30** conferred by EC law, the next stage is to analyse the circumstances in which Convention rights can be enforced via an EC law claim. It should be noted that there is authority in both England and Scotland to the effect that the European Convention does not form part of the law of the European Community and so does not fall to be applied by British courts as part of their duties under EC law.[44] As will become obvious, subsequent practice in the Court of Justice, and indeed subsequent Treaty amendments, have rendered this position untenable.

Whether or not EC law can be invoked as an aid to the enforcement of **3.31** the Convention is, in any individual case, an important preliminary enquiry. This is because the various mechanisms available for the enforcement of EC law are, in some respects, at least as powerful, and in others, much more powerful, than those available under the Human Rights Act for giving effect to the Convention. It is not yet clear how exactly the courts will apply the rule in s. 3 HRA that domestic legislation should, as far as possible, be interpreted in line with the Convention. There is good reason to suppose that the practice under EC law demonstrated in cases such as *Litster* will be adopted as a model but if the courts do not go so far, the *Litster* approach will at least be available where the Convention is invoked in the EC law context. The courts will be asked to interpret domestic legislation so as to conform with the general principle of respect for human rights within the EC, using if necessary, the technique of implying suitable additional words.

It is, however, the remedy of direct effect of EC law which should prove **3.32** the real attraction to Convention claimants. The rule that directly effective EC law rights must take precedence over inconsistent domestic legislation is in marked contrast to the approach adopted by the Human Rights Act. Many had indeed hoped that the Convention would be given "direct effect" on the EC model so as to be capable of overriding statutes which fail to respect Convention rights. Section 3 HRA provides, however, that violation of Convention rights does not affect the validity of incompatible primary legislation (or of subordinate legislation where primary legislation prevents the removal of the incompatibility). Fundamental rights, as

---

[44] *Allgemeine Gold* v *Commissioners for Customs and Excise* [1978] 2 CMLR, aff'd [1980] QB 390; *Kaur* v *Lord Advocate* [1980] 3 CMLR 79.

general principles of EC law, are directly effective rights and any provision of domestic legislation which is in conflict with a fundamental right as it is protected in EC law must be disapplied by the court, and later amended or repealed by the legislature.

3.33   As noted above, the Court of Justice has frequently expressed the view that measures which do not properly respect human rights standards "are not acceptable in the Community". It could be argued that this principle, combined with the duty of domestic courts under Article 5 of the Treaty on European Union to take all steps necessary to give effect to Community law, is sufficient to impose a general requirement that the courts give effect to the Convention, as a matter of EC law. Such a requirement would amount to incorporation of the European Convention via the European Communities Act. The closest that the English courts have come to accepting this argument is the decision of the Court of Appeal in *ex parte Phull.*[45] It did not dissent from the proposition that the European Convention could be invoked by persons exercising their EC law rights of free movement but the point was irrelevant since the applicant had, in its view, no rights under EC law.[46] In the absence of a firmly established general rule, the present position is that Convention rights can only be enforced through the medium of EC law in certain defined situations, and on a case-by-case basis.

IMPLEMENTING MEASURES

3.34   Legislation, whether primary or secondary, and administrative actions which are intended specifically to give effect to a provision of EC law must comply with European Convention standards. Many thousands of such measures are taken each year. The leading case on implementing measures is *Wachauf* v *Germany.*[47] Wachauf was a tenant farmer who had acquired a Community milk quota. An EC regulation provided that a milk quota would transfer upon the sale, lease or inheritance of the land to which it was attached unless and until it was surrendered, and compensation would be payable if the quota was surrendered to the

---

[45] *R.* v *Home Secretary ex parte Phull* [1996] Imm AR 72, 79.
[46] See also *R.* v *Home Secretary ex parte Payne* [1995] Imm AR 48.
[47] Case 5/88 [1989] ECR 2609. Arguably, there were other previous examples, but none in which the principle was spelled out: see, for example, *R.* v *Kirk,* above n. 8 and *UNECTEF* v *Heylens,* Case 249/86 [1987] ECR 4097. *Wachauf* was followed in *R.* v *Minister of Agriculture ex parte Bostock,* Case 2/92 [1994] ECR I-955.

state. However, the German rules implementing the EC regulation made the payment of compensation for a surrendered quota conditional upon the consent to surrender of the owner of the land, which consent was not forthcoming from Wachauf's landlord. He was, therefore, faced with having to vacate the farm (his lease having expired) without receiving compensation for the surrender of his quota. He complained that this situation was contrary to his fundamental right to property.

The Court of Justice held: **3.35**

"[I]t must be observed that the Community rules which, upon the expiry of the lease, had the effect of depriving the lessee, without compensation, of the fruits of his labour and of his investments in the tenanted holding would be incompatible with the requirements of the protection of fundamental rights in the Community legal order. Since those require-ments are also binding upon Member States when they implement Community rules, the Member States must, as far as possible, apply those rules in accordance with those requirements."

Advocate General Jacobs had earlier pointed out that the Community legislator was bound by the principle of respect for property rights. So far as he was concerned, it was self-evident that Member States, when acting in pursuance of powers granted under Community law, should be bound by the same constraints.[48] The Court ultimately ruled that the EC regula-tion did not contravene the right to property, since it provided ample scope for a regime which would leave farmers adequately compensated. The German rules were at fault, and the German courts later annulled the rule in question and awarded compensation.[49]

It will be recalled that a significant amount of British legislation stands   **3.36** as implementation of EC law even though it was passed prior to the relevant EC instrument. A prominent example is the Sex Discrimination Act, which constitutes part of the implementation in Great Britain of the Equal Treatment Directive. The duty arising from *Wachauf*, arguably, extends to this category of legislation and is not restricted to measures taken under the specific authority of the European Communities Act. It should also be noted that the effect of the decision of the Strasbourg Commission in *M and Co* v *Germany*,[50] which is outlined above, may well be that domestic measures implementing EC law cannot, in any event, be challenged under the Convention as such. They must, therefore, be challenged pursuant to EC law, as applied in *Wachauf*.

---

[48] [1989] ECR 2609, 2629 (para. 22 of his Opinion).
[49] *Re the Küchenhof Farm* [1990] 2 CMLR 289.
[50] Above n. 18.

MEASURES "WITHIN THE SCOPE OF COMMUNITY LAW"

3.37   The Court of Justice has also laid down a more general rule that national measures which fall within the scope of EC law must comply with fundamental rights standards. In *ERT*, the Court was faced with a challenge to a state television monopoly in force in Greece by a local television station which had been broadcasting in contravention of it.[51] The monopoly was found to infringe the right of the television station to provide broadcasting services, contrary to Article 59 of the Treaty, and the issue arose as to whether the monopoly rules constituted a permissible derogation from that freedom on the grounds of public policy, public security and/or public health.[52] One of the arguments against that proposition was that the monopoly infringed rights to freedom of expression under Article 10 of the Convention. Having outlined the status of fundamental rights protection as a general principle of the Community legal order, the Court stated:

> "As the Court has held, it has no power to examine the compatibility with the European Convention on Human Rights of national rules which do not fall within the scope of Community law. On the other hand, where such rules do fall within the scope of Community law, and reference is made to the Court of Justice for a preliminary ruling, it must provide all the criteria of interpretation needed by the national court to determine whether those rules are compatible with the fundamental rights the observance of which the Court ensures and which derive in particular from the European Convention on Human Rights.
>
> In particular, where a Member State relies on the combined provisions of Articles 56 and 66 in order to justify rules which are likely to obstruct the exercise of the freedom to provide services, such justification, provided for by Community law, must be interpreted in the light of the general principles of law and in particular of fundamental rights. Thus the national rules in question can fall under the exceptions provided by the combined provisions of Articles 56 and 66 only if they are compatible with the fundamental rights the observance of which is ensured by the Court." [53]

In short, national rules which fall "within the scope of Community law" are contrary to Community law if they do not comply in all respects with the principles of fundamental rights laid down in the European Convention.

---

[51] *Elliniki Radiophonia Tileorassi* v *Dimotiki Etairia Pliroforissis and Sotorios Kouvelas,* Case C-260/89 [1991] ECR I-2925.
[52] Art. 66 of the Treaty, which refers in turn to Art. 56.
[53] *Ibid.* at 2964.

The key issue is then which measures fall within the scope of Community law and which fall outside it. *ERT* tells us that a particular example of a measure falling within the scope of Community law is one which derogates from a right of free movement conferred by the Treaty. The Treaty freedoms — freedom of movement of goods, capital and workers; freedom of establishment and freedom to provide and receive services — are all subject to the right of Member States to derogate from their terms on grounds of public policy, public security and/or public health.[54] Derogating measures can be taken by central Government, or indeed by any other branch of the state apparatus,[55] and it has been accepted in the English courts that such derogations must be validated for compliance with the European Convention. In *U* v *W*, for example, the High Court followed *ERT* in examining whether s. 28(3) of the Human Fertilisation and Embryology Act 1990 was compatible with the right to respect for family life under Article 8 of the Convention (it was).[56] Also, in *ex parte Adams*, the Divisional Court accepted the need to assess whether the exclusion order imposed upon the leader of Sinn Fein was a proportionate restriction upon his freedom of expression under Article 10 of the Convention.[57] No reference was made to *ERT*, but *Adams* stands as authority for the validity of a Convention-based approach to restrictions upon EC law rights of free movement.

3.38

In *ERT*, the measure derogating from free movement of services was, for the Court, only one particular example of a measure falling within the scope of EC law which would be subject to validation for compliance with fundamental rights. It is less easy to formulate a principle which could be used for identifying other such measures. On a broad view, a national measure which is adopted in a field of law which is subject to regulation by the EC falls within the scope of EC law.[58] It could be said, for example, that EC law regulates trade, or immigration, or employment practices so that domestic measures within those spheres fall within the scope of EC law. This would have the result of rendering vast swathes of domestic rules and regulations subject to validation under the Convention. It seems

3.39

---

[54] See Arts. 36, 48(4), 56 and 66.
[55] For an example of a public policy derogation by a Chief Constable, see *ex parte International Traders Ferry*, above n. 9.
[56] [1997] 2 CMLR 431. The correct approach was agreed between the parties and did not fall to be decided by the Court.
[57] [1995] AllER (EC) 177. A reference was made to the ECJ but subsequently withdrawn when the exclusion order was lifted.
[58] See the decision of the Court of Justice in *Phil Collins v Intrat Handelsgessellschaft*, Case C-92/92 [1993] ECR I-5145, which provides some support for this view albeit in the slightly different context of Art. 6 of the treaty, which prohibits discrimination on grounds of nationality "within the field of application of" the Treaty.

clear, however, that the Court of Justice would not go so far, as illustrated by three recent cases.

- In *Perfili*, the measure in question was a rule of Italian civil procedure which required a party wishing to make a civil claim in the context of criminal proceedings to take steps to confer a special power of attorney on his legal representative. The Italian court was concerned that Lloyd's of London, who wished to bring a civil claim against Perfili but had not complied with the rule, had been disadvantaged because no equivalent rule existed in English law. The Court noted that rules restricting the legal remedies open to an English insurance company trading in Italy would fall to be examined under Articles 52 or 59 of the Treaty on freedom of establishment and freedom to provide services. However, those provisions were only concerned with national measures which produced a disparity of treatment between home and foreign nationals (not the case here), and not with disparities which existed between Member States. Therefore, the Italian rule fell outside the scope of Community law and could not be validated for compliance with Article 6 of the Convention.[59]
- In *Maurin*, the defendant was prosecuted for selling goods after their use-by date had expired. At his trial, he argued that the police report used against him had not been signed, and that there would be a breach of Article 6 of the Convention, and so of Community law, were it to be admitted in evidence. There is an EC directive concerned with the regulation of the labelling of foodstuffs, which requires that a use-by date be displayed. However, the issues raised in the case were found to fall outside the scope of Community law because the directive did not seek in any way to regulate the procedure whereby traders offering goods for sale after their use-by date should be penalised. That was a matter left entirely to the Member States.[60]
- In *Kremzow*, the plaintiff had been sentenced to life imprisonment for murder following a trial which was found by the European Court of Human Rights to be in breach of Article 6 of the Convention.[61] When he subsequently claimed damages in respect of his unlawful imprisonment, the Austrian court referred to the ECJ a variety of questions regarding the interpretation of Article 6. It was argued that the Court should answer them, because Kremzow, as an EU citizen, had free movement rights which had been frustrated by his

---

[59] Case C-177/94 [1996] ECR 161.
[60] Case C-144/95 [1996] ECR I-2910.
[61] *Kremzow* v *Austria*, A/268-B, (1994) 17 EHRR 322.

imprisonment. The Court, however, found that the matters raised fell outside the scope of Community law. As an Austrian citizen detained in Austria, Kremzow had not exercised any free movement rights and a purely hypothetical prospect of him doing so was not sufficient. Also, the national laws under which he had been convicted (regarding murder and illegal possession of a firearm) were not designed to secure compliance with rules of Community law.[62]

Insofar as it is possible to formulate a single test, it appears that a measure will fall within the scope of EC law if, in principle, a specific provision of EC law applies to regulate the matters covered by it. This is so even if, on the facts of the case, there has been no breach of Community law, fundamental rights issues aside. The line can be a thin one. In *Kremzow*, the Court relied upon the well-worn principle that a national of a Member State who has not exercised his rights of free movement cannot rely upon EC free movement rules against his own Government. The position would, however, be different, and Community law would apply, if Kremzow had been a national of another EU Member State, or even if he had worked abroad in another EU country before returning to Austria.[63] In those circumstances, imprisonment would be a restriction upon free movement rights (albeit one which might be justified on grounds of public policy); it would fall within the scope of Community law and would therefore have to be validated under the Convention. That analysis is in line with the views of Advocate General Jacobs in *Konstantinidis*, who argued that an EU national going to work in another Member State is entitled to assume that he will be treated in accordance with a common code of fundamental values, in particular those laid down in the ECHR.[64] **3.40**

The issue of when a measure falls within the scope of Community law and therefore becomes subject to the general principles of Community law was recently examined by Laws J in the context of the EC law general principle of equality.[65] He held that a measure fell to be validated according to general principles only if it is "taken pursuant to Community law", that is, pursuant to a duty to implement Community law, or to a permission to derogate from Community law. Underlying his reasoning was the proposition that general principles of Community law have been **3.41**

---

[62] *Kremzow v Austria*, above n. 4. See also *Annibaldi v Sindaco des Comune di Guidonia*, Case C-309/96 [1997] ECR I-7493.
[63] See *R. v Home Secrtary et parte Surinder Singh*. Case C-370/90 [1992] ECR I-4269.
[64] Case C-168-91 [1993] ECR I-1191, 1211-1212; see also *ex parte Phull*, above n. 45.
[65] *R. v Ministry of Agriculture ex parte First City Trading* [1997] 1 CMLR 250. See also *R. v Commissioners for Customs and Excise ex parte Lunn Poly*, decision of 2 April 1998.

devised by the Court of Justice and necessarily have a more limited field of application than principles which are expressly set out in the Treaty.

3.42   It is submitted that his view is too narrow. It reflects the factual situations which existed in *Wachauf* and *ERT,* but does not reflect the broader statement of principle made by the Court in the latter case. In *ERT,* the instant situation of a derogation from the freedom to provide services was stated to be a particular example of the principle that measures within the scope of Community law would be validated for compliance with fundamental rights and so, by implication, with other general principles. Also, the proposition that general principles of EC law have a more limited scope of application is unsupported by authority (and none was cited for it). It could not, in any event, apply to respect for fundamental rights because that principle is expressly set out in the Treaty. A large proportion of those measures falling within the scope of EC law are taken either in implementation of EC law (depending how broadly that term is defined), or by way of permitted derogation from it. There is nevertheless a significant third category of measures which regulate an area also covered by EC law but which do not implement or derogate from EC law in any real sense. If the views of Laws J were to be applied to the principle of respect for fundamental rights, certain of those measures would, it is submitted, be wrongly excluded from the EC law obligation to comply with the ECHR.

WHAT IS THE STANDARD?

3.43   Once it has been established that a national measure must, as a matter of Community law, conform to fundamental rights principles, it remains to pinpoint the level of protection which Community law confers. There are two possible approaches. On the one hand, it could be argued that since the EU is committed to upholding fundamental rights "as guaranteed by the European Convention", EC law must give at least as much protection to a given right as the Convention does. This approach would require the application of the text of the Convention, in the same manner as it is applied by the Strasbourg institutions, in an attempt to arrive at a result which is at least as favourable to the individual as that which would be produced in Strasbourg.

3.44   Thus far, the Court of Justice has not applied the Convention as such, but has developed its own approach, particularly with regard to acceptable limitations on recognised rights (see above). This alternative, Community approach to the protection of Convention rights was recognised by the Court of Appeal in the *International Traders Ferry* case.[66] There is, however, good reason to suppose that the Court of Justice might adjust its approach in the future so as to follow more closely the principles of the Convention. Such an adjustment would be in keeping with the Treaty commitment to respect the Convention which was agreed at Maastricht and strengthened at Amsterdam. Most of the relevant cases in this field arose before the Treaty was modified in that respect. Also, the Court of Justice has, in a handful of recent cases, been asked specifically to interpret provisions of the Convention (for example, *Kremzow, Maurin*). It has thus far declined to do so, not on the grounds that it would be inappropriate, as a matter of principle, for it to do so, but because the particular domestic measures at issue fell outside the scope of Community law. It is only a matter of time before the Court is asked to interpret the Convention in a case which cannot be disposed of on that ground.

Finally, it is noteworthy that the Court of Justice in *Wachauf* described **3.45** the duty of Member States as that of applying Community rules "as far as possible" in line with fundamental rights standards. This potential escape route has not been explored further in subsequent case-law and it would be surprising if the Court were to confirm that respect for Convention rights should be limited in this way. It remains, nevertheless, as a basis for the argument that a fundamental right ought not to be upheld in a particular case.

5. FURTHER READING

Burrows, "The European Union and the European Convention" in Dickson (ed.) *Human Rights and the European Convention* (Sweet & Maxwell, 1997).

Grief, *EC Law and Human Rights* (Longman, 1998).

Grief, "The Domestic Impact of the European Convention on Human Rights as Mediated through Community Law" [1991] PL 555

Neuwahl and Rosas (eds), *The European Union and Human Rights* (Kluwer, 1995)

---

[66] Above n. 9.

Chapter 4

TAKING A CASE TO STRASBOURG

1. WHEN WILL IT BE NECESSARY TO APPLY TO STRASBOURG?

The main reason for the enactment of the Human Rights Act was the **4.1** desire to enable Convention-based claims to be resolved in the domestic courts without the need for recourse to Strasbourg. In 1996–97, 451 applications against the UK were registered in Strasbourg. The Act ought, in theory, to have the effect of substantially reducing this number, but the need to go to Strasbourg will certainly not be eliminated altogether. Other European states which have incorporated the Convention into their domestic law continue to receive their share of applications. It may be that the Human Rights Act will raise awareness of the rights and freedoms which the Convention guarantees and so give rise to a far greater number of claims, only some of which will be vindicated in the domestic courts. Applying to Strasbourg remains an option, as a final level of appeal, and any lawyer embarking upon a Convention claim in the English courts should be aware of the procedure which may ultimately have to be adopted before the Court of Human Rights.

There are two principal situations in which recourse to Strasbourg will **4.2** be necessary. The first is where a party has claimed certain rights under the Convention in the domestic courts and the courts have ruled that the Convention does not have the effect contended for. The interpretation given to provisions of the Convention by domestic judges can then be challenged in Strasbourg. The vast majority of applications from other countries which have incorporated the Convention into their domestic law arise in this way. The institutional position of the Court in Strasbourg may make the domestic courts less willing to uphold Convention claims. Where points of European Community law are raised, the domestic court has the option of referring the matter for the guidance of the European Court of Justice under Article 177 of the EC Treaty. No such procedure is available under the Convention and the only way of seeking to put a matter before the Court of Human Rights is to rule against the individual claimant in the expectation that a petition will be lodged in Strasbourg once judicial remedies in this country have been exhausted.

4.3   The second situation in which applications to Strasbourg may result is where the courts have accepted that domestic law is in conflict with the Convention but are unable to grant a remedy because of the overriding terms of primary legislation.[1] In those circumstances, the higher courts may make a declaration of incompatibility, pursuant to s. 4 of the Human Rights Act. Where such a declaration is made, the Government may take remedial action to amend the offending legislation so as to remove the incompatibility, but need not do so, and need not do so with retrospective effect.[2] In the absence of remedial action with retrospective effect, the individual claimant will usually have no substantive remedy for the breach of his Convention rights, and may lodge an application in Strasbourg in the hope of forcing a change in the law and/or gaining an award of compensation.

2. WHAT CAN BE GAINED FROM WINNING IN STRASBOURG?

4.4   Applications are pursued in Strasbourg for a variety of reasons: to obtain a declaration that rights have been violated; to secure a particular remedy or form of treatment in the domestic legal system; to ensure that the law is changed, to recover financial compensation; or a combination of the above. However, victory before the Court guarantees only a declaration that the UK Government has acted in breach of the Convention. Nothing else can be taken for granted. Most applicants will have sought a particular form of substantive relief in the domestic courts, but an application to Strasbourg cannot be treated as an extension of that quest. The role of the Court of Human Rights is to provide a remedy in respect of a breach of Convention rights which has already occurred. It

---

[1] HRA ss. 3(2) and 6(2).
[2] HRA ss. 10–11.

has no power to give directions as to how a particular individual ought to be treated in the future. The Court's ruling may result in a change in the law but this need have prospective effect only — remedies in respect of past actions are limited to a declaration and compensation if appropriate. In only a few decided cases will the successful applicant obtain through the Court exactly the same relief as should have been granted in a British court. An example would be where the object of a claim is to avoid deportation and the deportation order has been stayed pending the outcome of proceedings in Strasbourg. In such a case, a declaration by the Court that deportation would breach the Convention will be sufficient to ensure the lifting of the order.

4.5 In some cases, however, the Court's ruling may be used as a basis for a further attempt in the domestic courts to secure the applicant's fundamental objectives, particularly since s. 2 of the Act gives legal force to the decisions of the Court. In *Findlay*, for example, the applicant had been convicted by a court-martial and sentenced to two years' imprisonment following an episode of violence which occurred whilst he was suffering from post-traumatic stress disorder. He failed in his attempts to get his conviction overturned and took his case to Strasbourg, where the Court ruled that the court-martial system of dispensing justice in the armed forces infringed the right to a fair trial in Article 6. It was unable to accede to his request that his conviction be quashed, and awarded him only a sum in respect of costs and expenses.[3] The Ministry of Defence had changed the court-martial system whilst the case was pending in Strasbourg but nothing in the Court's ruling obliged the Army Council to reconsider Mr Findlay's case, and it refused to do so. However, the Court's decision did provide the basis for an application for judicial review of the Army Council's refusal to reconsider.[4] In criminal cases, a finding by the Court of Human Rights of a breach of Article 6 may lead to the reference of a case to the Court of Appeal, and the subsequent review of a conviction.

4.6 Many of the cases which go to Strasbourg are "test cases" whose primary intention is to secure a change in the law for the future. The Government has an obligation to secure Convention rights to individuals within its jurisdiction and if the Court finds that a particular law or practice is contrary to the Convention, the Government is obliged to ensure that that law or practice is changed. It should be noted, however, that success in Strasbourg will not necessarily produce the change in the law which is desired by the applicant, partly because the Court has no power to give

---

[3] *Findlay* v *UK*, A/734, (1997) 23 EHRR 221.
[4] *R.* v *MOD ex parte Findlay*, unreported decision of 18 August 1997.

directions to defeated states as to how to comply with its decisions. In one British case, the Court found that the Immigration Rules were discriminatory, contrary to Articles 8 and 14 of the Convention, in that they allowed entry to wives of immigrants, but not to husbands of wives already settled in the UK. The Government's response was to remove the discriminatory effect not by extending the permission to husbands, but by removing the existing permission from wives.[5]

4.7 The Court has a discretion under Article 41 of the Convention to award compensation, and most applications do incorporate a claim for compensation (termed "just satisfaction").[6] In some cases, the applicant's claim in the domestic courts has been for money only, so it is possible that victory before the Court will result in a complete remedy. However, a successful applicant will not necessarily receive a financial award, even where loss has demonstrably been suffered, and the levels of award are, in general, lower than equivalent awards under domestic law. A successful applicant may also be awarded some or all of the costs of the application (although not those of any domestic proceedings).[7] Compensation and costs are discussed further below.

4.8 The major disadvantage of applying to Strasbourg is the length of time which it takes for an application to be determined, averaging over five years from the presentation of a petition to a decision of the Court. All interested parties, including the Council of Europe itself agree that such delays are unacceptable: it has frequently been suggested that delays of this order would indeed fall foul of the provisions of Article 6 of the Convention which guarantee a hearing within a reasonable time. In exceptional, very urgent, cases, an expedited procedure may be adopted. In *D v UK*, for example, the applicant was suffering from AIDS and had a very limited life expectancy, although even then his application took almost 15 months from registration to determination by the Court.[8] From 1 November 1998, the institutional structure of the Convention system is to be radically altered, with the abolition of the Commission and the absorption of its functions into a single Court. One of the primary motivations behind the new structure was a desire to streamline the procedure for considering cases and to shorten the period of time presently required to obtain a decision. It will take several years to assess whether this aim has been achieved.

---

[5] *Abdullaziz, Cabales and Balkandali* v *UK*, A/94, (1985) 7 EHRR 471.
[6] Reference are to provisions of the Convention text as amended by Protocol No. 11, with effect from 1 November 1998.
[7] Costs are never awarded against an applicant.
[8] A/758, (1997) 24 EHRR 423.

Finally, it should be noted that a significant proportion of applications to **4.9**
Strasbourg are compromised by the Government before a final decision is
handed down. There is a stage in the Convention procedure, immediately
after an application has been declared admissible, which is devoted
specifically to exploring the possibility of settlement, but in practice a
settlement could be agreed at any time. Many applicants obtain the remedy
which they have sought all along via the settlement procedure.

3. OVERVIEW OF THE STRASBOURG PROCEDURE

This book has been written at a time when the Strasbourg procedure is in **4.10**
the process of undergoing a dramatic reform, with the replacement of the
current two-tier system of Commission and Court with a re-constituted
single Court. The new institutional structure is set out in Protocol No. 11 to
the Convention, which has effect from 1 November 1998. The Protocol
No. 11 structure will hereafter be referred to as "the new system". The
"old system" will remain relevant for some time after that since there are
transitional provisions in Article 5 of Protocol No. 11 pursuant to which
cases which had been declared admissible before the Protocol came into
force will continue to be handled by the Commission, under the old
system. However, applications from the UK arising after the entry into
force of the Human Rights Act will not be affected by it. Accordingly, this
account of the Strasbourg procedure will be based on the new system
although reference will be made, where appropriate, to the old system.

Under the old system, applications were made to the Commission, **4.11**
which determined, first, whether or not they were admissible. If an
application was admissible, the Commission would attempt to promote
a settlement between the parties, and, failing that, proceed to find the
facts and to reach a decision on the merits of the case, known as an Article
31 report. From the Commission, cases could then be referred to the Court
for decision, or, occasionally, to the Committee of Ministers (which
would, generally, rubber-stamp the Commission's findings). Under Protocol No. 11, the new single Court will be composed of Grand Chambers
(eleven judges), Chambers (seven judges) and Committees (three
judges). A Committee appointed from within a Chamber will weed out
those cases which are obviously inadmissible. The Chamber itself will
take a formal decision on the admissibility of those applications which
survive the initial filtering process. If an application is admissible, the
Chamber will proceed to examine the facts and the merits, and seek a

friendly settlement. If no settlement is possible, the Chamber will adopt a decision on the merits of the case, although it will have the option to transfer the case to a Grand Chamber for decision, if neither party objects. There is also provision, in exceptional cases, for either party to appeal a decision of a Chamber to a Grand Chamber.

4. REPRESENTATION AND FEES

4.12 The rules of procedure of the new Court cannot be adopted until the Court is constituted following the coming into force of Protocol No. 11. The detailed rules which will apply to matters such as representation and legal aid are, for that reason, uncertain, but it is expected that the new Court will follow broadly the same approach as its predecessor. At present, applicants may be represented before the Court by a lawyer authorised to practice in any of the Convention states and resident in the territory of one of them. Leave of the President of the Court must be sought if the applicant is to appear in person, or wishes to be represented by a non-lawyer, or a lawyer from outside Convention territory.[9]

4.13   Litigation in Strasbourg is, in most cases, relatively inexpensive when compared with proceedings in the domestic courts. Although there may be significant expenditure involved in travelling to Strasbourg, oral hearings, which demand a disproportionate share of fees in domestic cases, are very short and most of the work is done on paper. Domestic legal aid is not available for proceedings in Strasbourg, although conditional fee arrangements may be used as an alternative.[10] It is possible, however, to obtain legal aid from the Council of Europe, dependent upon the means of the applicant, which must be declared on a form obtainable from the Council of Europe and verified by the Legal Aid Assessment Office. Council of Europe legal aid is granted only rarely: in 1996, the Commission granted legal aid for only 77 cases out of a total of 4,758. Even where it is granted, there are two important limitations on its scope. First, financial assistance will not be granted for the initial stage of drafting the application. Secondly, the sums awarded do not by any means reflect the true cost of representation. Awards are made on a piece-work basis, with specific amounts payable for each stage of the proceedings, regardless of the time spent, or of the fees actually incurred. Awards may,

---

[9] Rule 30(1) of the old Court's Rule of Procedure.
[10] Conditional Fee Agreements Order 1998, SI 1998/1860. Under para. 4 of the Order, fees may be increased by up to 100%.

however, extend to cover reasonable travelling expenses and a subsistence allowance for applicants and their representatives, which may be of significant assistance.

5. INITIATING A CLAIM

Cases in Strasbourg are formally commenced by the filing of an application. The application should be drafted in accordance with a standard form, which can be obtained from the Council of Europe. There is a time limit for making applications of six months, within which the Court must be notified of the substance of a claim (see below). The contents of the application and the initial stages of the proceedings are confidential and can only be publicised once an application has been declared inadmissible, or has been accepted as admissible and settlement negotiations have failed. Applications have been struck out, as an abuse of the right of petition, in cases where applicants have disseminated details of their claim prematurely.   **4.14**

6. INTERIM MEASURES

The lodging of an application in Strasbourg will not necessarily protect the applicant's legal position in the UK. In *Uppal* v *Home Office*, Sir Robert Megarry VC held that Article 34 of the Convention (formerly Article 25(1)), which obliges states not to hinder the effective exercise of the right of petition, did not require that a deportation order be stayed pending the hearing of an application by the Commission.[11] Pending proceedings in Strasbourg may, however, be relevant to the exercise of the court's discretion to grant a stay, particularly where the applicant's basic rights under Articles 2 and 3 of the Convention are at issue. More recently, in *Sarbjit Kaur*, Jowitt J ruled that English courts have no jurisdiction to grant an injunction to restrain deportation pending the outcome of a petition to Strasbourg.[12] The fact that a petition has been submitted may have a greater aura following the Human Rights Act, but the strict legal position   **4.15**

---

[11] *The Times*, 21 October 1978.
[12] *R.* v *Home Secretary ex parte Sarbjit Kaur* [1996] Imm AR 359. The protection of EC law rights of free movement would, however, justify the granting of an injunction.

remains unchanged. The Act will confer legal effect upon the decisions of the Commission and the Court but says nothing about the situation where the Court has been seised of an application but has not yet decided it.

4.16   Therefore, once proceedings have been commenced, it may be necessary to seek interim measures to protect an applicant's position while his application is being determined. The process may take some years from start to finish and for certain applicants, particularly those at risk of ill-treatment or deportation, obtaining interim relief may be central to their cause. Under the new system, the Chamber of the Court to which a case is allocated will have the power to indicate to the parties any interim measures the adoption of which seems desirable in the interests of the parties or the proper conduct of proceedings before it. Interim measures will only be appropriate where the applicant can present evidence that irreparable harm will be suffered if the respondent Government proceeds as planned.

4.17   The Court may only *indicate* appropriate measures; it has no power to *order* them. Its rules of procedure, which are part of the internal rules of administration of the Council of Europe, are not legally binding upon states, who are not obliged to take the measures indicated. In *Cruz Varas* v *Sweden*,[13] the Court ruled that a failure to comply with the Commission's indication that an applicant should not be deported could not amount to a breach of Article 34 of the Convention, or of any other provision. Nor will a failure by the Government to respect a request for interim measures give rise to any legal rights in the domestic courts. In practice however, such requests are generally obeyed: the Court in *Cruz Varas* referred to a record of "almost total compliance" with indications as to interim measures.[14] Certainly, the practice of the British Government has been to comply with the indications of the Court.

7. THE DUTY NOT TO HINDER THE RIGHT OF PETITION

4.18   The procedures laid down by the Convention for the bringing of claims are strengthened by a duty placed upon states not to hinder in any way the effective exercise of the right to make an application.[15] Individual

---

[13] A/201, (1992) 14 EHRR 1.
[14] *Ibid.* at 42.
[15] Article 34.

applicants have a correlative right to complain about interferences with their right of petition. In *Cruz Varas*, the Court rejected the claim that the expulsion of one of the applicants from Sweden to Chile had hindered his right of petition. It found that the applicant's absence from Europe had not materially hindered the presentation of his case. Article 34 has also been raised in cases where prison authorities have intercepted the applicant's correspondence with the Commission.[16]

8. WHEN WILL A CLAIM BE ADMISSIBLE?

The vast majority of applications to Strasbourg are rejected as inadmissible. Out of 451 cases registered against the UK in 1997, 411 did not pass the admissibility stage.[17] An application which is obviously without merit may be rejected on paper following examination by a committee of three judges formed from within the Chamber of the Court to which it has been assigned.[18] Alternatively, where there is some prospect of an application being declared admissible, it will go before the Chamber as a whole for a ruling.[19] The Chamber will request the written observations of the Government, and then of the applicant, and may also require an oral hearing before reaching its decision on admissibility. In important cases, the Chamber may relinquish its jurisdiction to the Grand Chamber of the Court at the admissibility stage, or at any stage prior to giving final judgment.[20] Even where an application is formally declared admissible, the Court retains a residual power to reject it at any stage on the grounds that one of the admissibility criteria has not, on closer examination, been fulfilled. A decision that an application is inadmissible, at whatever stage of the proceedings, is final and cannot be appealed.

4.19

The principal grounds on which applications are rejected as inadmissible are standing, time limits, exhaustion of domestic remedies, "compatibility" with the Convention, or because they are "manifestly ill-founded".

4.20

---

[16] For example, *Cambell* v *UK*, A/223, (1993) 15 EHRR 137.
[17] A handful of these cases were struck out rather than being declared inadmissible as such.
[18] Art. 28.
[19] Art. 29(1).
[20] Art. 30.

LOCUS STANDI

4.21   Applications may be made by "any person, non-governmental organisation or group of individuals claiming to be the victim of a violation" of the
Convention.[21] The scope of the "victim" test of standing, which has been
incorporated within the Human Rights Act,[22] is considered in detail in
chapter 2.

EXHAUSTION OF DOMESTIC REMEDIES

4.22   According to Article 35(1), the Court will not examine a matter until "all
domestic remedies have been exhausted, according to the generally
recognised rules of international law". This restriction, which, as the
Convention suggests, is a general rule applicable to remedies under
international law, is designed to give the respondent state every opportunity to remedy the alleged violation within its own legal system.[23]
Applicants must provide in their application information to satisfy the
Court that this requirement has been fulfilled (or will be fulfilled by the
time the Court comes to rule upon admissibility). The onus is then upon
the Government to show, if it wishes, that domestic remedies have not
been exhausted. The exhaustion requirement may be waived by the
Government and if the issue is not pursued at the admissibility stage it
cannot be raised later in the proceedings. Now that Convention claims
can be brought in the English courts, the temptation to apply to
Strasbourg before matters have fully run their course domestically will
be much reduced. However, there will continue to be cases which go
straight to Strasbourg, for example, where it is felt that a domestic statute
clearly excludes the Convention right claimed.

4.23   The basic rule is that all remedies which could provide redress for the
alleged violation of the Convention must be pursued. Appropriate
proceedings must be commenced in the domestic courts and appealed
to the highest level. In the English legal system, this is usually the House
of Lords. Where the Court of Appeal has refused leave to appeal, the

---

[21] Art. 34.
[22] HRA s. 7(1).
[23] There is no requirement to exhaust *international* remedies (for example, the UN Human Rights
Committee, or the International Labour Organisation).

House of Lords should be petitioned for leave. In some cases, a lower court is the highest court of appeal; for example, the Divisional Court has an unreviewable power to certify in criminal proceedings that there exists a point for consideration by the House of Lords. In pursuing their remedies in domestic law, applicants are expected to respect domestic procedural rules, in particular time limits for appealing, so there is no exhaustion where the applicant has lost the opportunity to appeal because of a missed time limit. Where there is a choice of procedures open to claimants in domestic law, no criticism can be made that one procedure was adopted where the other was more appropriate, provided that the national courts have, in substance, been given the opportunity to redress the breach complained of.[24]

4.24 Domestic remedies must be used in order to air the substance of a complaint under the Convention, although this need not be done by raising provisions of the Convention in terms. For example, a plaintiff may pursue a nuisance claim through the English system without relying upon Article 8 of the Convention, and will not be penalised when he raises Article 8 for the first time in his application to Strasbourg. The issue of exhaustion is assessed as at the time when the matter is considered in Strasbourg and not the point at which the application is made. It is possible, therefore, for an application to be submitted before an appeal has run its course in the UK, so long as the appeal has been decided against the applicant by the time of the admissibility decision. On the other hand, where domestic law changes, and a new remedy becomes available after the application has been submitted, the applicant will not be penalised.

4.25 The rigours of the basic requirement of exhaustion are mitigated by the application of various exceptions, in particular the principle that only remedies which are adequate (in theory) and effective (in practice) need to be exhausted. Certain remedies are deemed to be inherently incapable of providing adequate and effective redress.

- Remedies which do not permit the individual to assert a legal right but only to appeal to the discretion of the relevant authorities are, in general, ineffective. Therefore, a convicted criminal who wishes to complain about the conduct of his trial must go to the Court of Appeal, and if possible, the House of Lords, but need not apply for a royal pardon.

---

[24] *López Ostra v Spain*, A/303-C, (1995) 20 EHRR 277, 293.

- The scope of a remedy may be so uncertain as to render it inherently ineffective and so not worthy of exhaustion. In *Winer*, uncertainty was the basis of the Commission's decision to reject the Government's argument that an applicant who complained of infringement of privacy should have brought a claim in the English courts for breach of confidence.[25] The Commission adopted the views of the English Law Commission, which had criticised the law of confidence and recommended that the remedy be put on a statutory footing. However, the Commission's approach is itself uncertain. More recently, in *Spencer*, it distinguished *Winer* and found that a claim for breach of confidence should have been brought, notwithstanding that nothing had yet been done to implement the Law Commission's recommendations.[26]
- Ombudsman procedures are not adequate and effective.
- The possibility of asking an authority to reconsider its decision does not amount to an effective remedy.[27]
- The remedy of appeal from a tribunal decision to an appeal tribunal which will act only upon errors of law may be effective depending upon the exact nature of the applicant's complaint: if the complaint relates to findings of fact, or to the state of the law correctly found by the tribunal, the avenue of an appeal will not have to be exhausted.
- Similarly, judicial review may be considered to be effective or ineffective for the purposes of Article 35(1) depending upon the particular decision at issue. For example, a decision to refuse political asylum should be challenged by way of judicial review,[28] but in certain other cases, judicial review will offer no possibility of success and need not be exhausted.[29]
- Domestic remedies will be deemed to be ineffective where the complaint is of an administrative practice (such as mistreatment in custody) which is condoned at the highest level of government.[30]

4.26   Even remedies which are not inherently inadequate or ineffective need not be pursued if, according to settled legal opinion, the claim is bound to be rejected. Uncertainty as to the chances of success of a claim, or of an appeal, may range across a broad spectrum, from a mere doubt to a certainty of failure, and it may be difficult to assess when the prospects are

[25] *Winer* v *UK*, Appl. No. 10871/84, (1986) 48 D&R 158, 169–170.
[26] *Spencer* v *UK*, Appl. No. 28851/95, (1998) 25 EHRR CD 105.
[27] *G* v *UK*, Appl. No. 11932/86, (1988) 56 D&R 199.
[28] *M* v *UK*, Appl. No. 12268/86, (1988) 57 D&R 136.
[29] For example, *G* v *UK*, above n. 27.
[30] *Donnelly* v *UK*, Appl. No. 4477/72, (1975) 4 D&R 4.

sufficiently dim to justify an application to Strasbourg rather than further proceedings in the domestic courts. Recent case-law indicates that potential applicants should err on the side of caution. The Commission's view has been that in common law systems, where legal principles are developed through case-law, it is generally incumbent on an aggrieved individual to allow the courts to develop existing rights through interpretation.[31] In *Whiteside*, for example, the applicant had been refused an injunction in the county court protecting her from harassment by her former partner. She did not appeal to the Court of Appeal, citing serious doubts as to her prospects of success. There were, however, two conflicting Court of Appeal decisions on the issue of harassment and the Commission rejected her claim on the grounds of non-exhaustion. In *Spencer*, the Commission also took a tough line, rejecting the applications for failure to exhaust domestic remedies even though there was no legal precedent for the domestic claim, and much law to the contrary.[32]

4.27 Where the Government claims that domestic remedies have not been exhausted, the burden rests upon it to demonstrate that there was a remedy which was effective in theory and in practice. It must show that the remedy was accessible and capable of providing redress in respect of the applicant's complaints and that it offered reasonable prospects of success. Once that burden has been discharged, it then falls to the applicant to demonstrate that the remedy had in fact been exhausted, or was for some reason inadequate or ineffective in the circumstances of his case.[33]

TIME LIMITS

4.28 Claims must be made "within a period of six months from the date on which the final decision was taken".[34] Time starts to run from the final decision in the process of exhaustion of effective domestic remedies, or, more accurately, from the date upon which the applicant (or his lawyer) becomes aware of the final decision.[35] For example, time would start to run on the date when a litigant is informed that the House of Lords has dismissed his appeal, or has rejected his petition for leave to appeal the decision of the Court of Appeal. Time does not start from the date of the

---

[31] *Whiteside v UK*, Appl. No. 20357/92, (1994) 76-A D&R 80, 88.
[32] Above n. 26.
[33] *Akdivar v Turkey*, A/657, (1997) 23 EHRR 143, 185.
[34] Article 35.
[35] See *X v France*, Appl. No. 9908/82, (1983) 32 D&R 266.

outcome of an *ineffective* remedy (which need not have been exhausted), and where there is doubt as to the status of the remedy, a protective application to the Court should be made. Where there are no effective domestic remedies to exhaust, time starts to run from the date of the act complained of (or, in other words, the date when the applicant became a "victim"). Again, the start of the six month period will be delayed where the applicant does not become aware of the act immediately.[36] Where the applicant complains of a state of affairs or a continuing act, the time limit will only operate once it has come to an end. Therefore, there are no time constraints where the complaint is about the existence of a statute which might be applied to the applicant in the future.

4.29   Within six months of the date upon which time starts to run, the applicant must communicate the substance of the complaint to the Court. It is not necessary that an application be drafted and formally registered within the time limit but only that the Court is informed, in writing, of the identity of the applicant and the measure(s) about which he wishes to complain. A telephone call is not sufficient. The text of the Convention does not provide for time to be extended, or for claims to be accepted out of time. The Commission did in fact reserve to itself the power to rule that the six month period had been interrupted or suspended due to special circumstances but it seems that it must be virtually impossible for the applicant to comply with the time limit (for example, because of physical incapacity) if a plea of special circumstances is to succeed.[37]

MISCELLANEOUS GROUNDS OF INADMISSIBILITY

4.30   The Convention only permits complaints about the actions of the state and state bodies, not about those of private individuals. The range of bodies for whose actions the state is responsible, and the scope of the state's positive obligations to protect individuals from the actions of other individuals, are examined in more detail in chapter 6. A application may be rejected as inadmissible if it claims a right which is not contained within the Convention (such an application may also be rejected on the

---

[36] See *Hilton* v *UK*, Appl. No. 12015/86, (1988) 57 D&R 108 where more than nine years elapsed before the applicant became aware that her right to respect for her private life under Article 8 had been breached by the security services.

[37] A number of unreported cases on this issue are set out in col. 5 of the *Digest of Strasbourg Case-Law Relating to the European Convention on Human Rights*, pp. 328–332.

basis that it is manifestly ill-founded), or if it is substantially the same as a previous petition to the Commission or to another international organisation. Abuse of the right of petition is another, rather vague, ground of inadmissibility which may cover anything from to failure to respond to communications from the secretariat in Strasbourg, to failure to respect the confidentiality of the proceedings, to the use of abusive language in a petition.

"MANIFESTLY ILL-FOUNDED"

The vast majority of applications rejected as inadmissible fail on the **4.31** ground that they are manifestly ill-founded.[38] Rejection on this ground implies that the application does not disclose even an arguable case,[39] and as such is similar in spirit to the power of the English courts to strike out claims which disclose no reasonable cause of action. However, this power has been applied much more stringently than might have been expected, and an applicant, in reality, has to demonstrate reasonably good prospects of winning the case before it will be allowed to proceed. Many decisions to the effect that an application is manifestly ill-founded are marginal; others are reached by a majority vote (a factor which in itself would suggest that the case is at least arguable). It must be assumed that the Chambers of the Court will continue to reject applications as manifestly ill-founded in much the same manner as the Commission has done.

9. STRIKING OUT OF APPLICATIONS

In addition to the power to reject an application as inadmissible, at any **4.32** stage of the proceedings, the Court retains the power to strike out an application.[40] The power may be exercised where it appears that the applicant does not wish to pursue it, where the matter has been resolved, or if further examination is not justified "for any other reason".

---

[38] Article 35(3).
[39] See *Boyle and Rice* v *UK*, A/131, (1988) 10 EHRR 425.
[40] Art. 38.

10. ORAL HEARINGS

4.33   Assuming that an application survives rejection on the papers, there will often but not always be an oral hearing for the purposes of determining admissibility, and clarifying any issues of fact which need to be resolved before a decision on the merits of an application can be taken. It cannot be predicted how exactly the Chambers of the Court will conduct admissibility hearings. The practice of the Commission, which no doubt will be taken as a starting point, was to hold short hearings, usually lasting no more than two hours, which took the format of an opening address by each party followed by questions from the Commissioners. Often, the parties were provided in advance with a list of the questions with which the Commission was concerned, so enabling them to focus their arguments. After the hearing, and usually later on the same day, the parties were informed whether or not the application was to be allowed to proceed. If an application is declared admissible, the Court will move on to investigate the facts, and to seek to broker a friendly settlement.

11. FINDING THE FACTS

4.34   The Chamber of the Court to which an application is assigned inherits the duty of the Commission to investigate the facts of a case with a view to laying the ground for a decision on its merits. Many cases will not raise material disputes of fact between the parties, and a report can be prepared from the papers. However, where significant issues of fact do arise, there is a broad power to conduct an investigation, which the Government is required to facilitate.[41] The investigation may, exceptionally, involve the hearing of witness evidence. Under the old system, the establishment and verification of facts was primarily a matter for the Commission, rather than for the Court. However, the Court was not bound by the Commission's findings of fact and retained the exceptional power to disagree with the Commission and make its own findings. The same division of power will doubtless continue as between the Chamber and Grand Chamber of the Court, should a case be appealed.

----

[41] Art. 38(1)(a).

12. FRIENDLY SETTLEMENT PROCEDURE

Approximately one in eight of those applications which are declared **4.35** admissible are settled and never proceed to a final decision.[42] The Court, like the Commission before it, is required to use its good offices in order to facilitate settlement, and it would be wise to continue the Commission's practice of seeking to induce settlement by indicating informally to the parties its provisional views of the merits of the case. Terms of settlement may range from the payment of compensation and/or costs to a granting of a permission or facility sought to an undertaking from the Government that it will change an administrative practice, or introduce legislation to change the law.

13. THE MERITS OF THE CASE

Under the new system, the Chamber of the Court which has declared an **4.36** application case to be admissible will proceed to take a decision on its merits.[43] The previous practice of the Court of permitting interventions from other states and from interested third parties (in particular pressure groups such as Amnesty International) has been enshrined in Article 36 of the amended text of the Convention. The Chamber's decision is, potentially, a final decision, with full legal effect, subject to the possibility of appeal to a Grand Chamber of the Court (comprising 17 judges rather than seven). Either party to the case may (within three months) request a referral to the Grand Chamber, and a panel of five judges sits to determine whether a referral may proceed. The appeal procedure is intended to be reserved for "exceptional cases" which raise a "serious question affecting the interpretation or application of the Convention" or "a serious issue of general importance".[44] It is likely that a large number of requests for referral to the Grand Chamber will be made by disappointed parties and it remains to be seen how strictly these criteria will be interpreted. If the reform of the Convention machinery is to achieve its aim of dealing

---

[42] Up to the end of 1996, 324 friendly settlements were reached, compared with 2,324 cases in which the Commission went on to take a formal decision on their merits.
[43] Under Art. 29(3), the admissibility and merits decisions are to be taken separately, save in exceptional circumstances
[44] Art. 43.

quickly and efficiently with an increasing case-load, it is vital that only the most important of cases are heard a second time.

14. REMEDIES

4.37   The basic remedy available under the Convention is a declaration by the Court to the effect that there has been a violation of its terms. The Court has no power to go further and order that specific steps are taken by the state concerned so as to rectify the violation (save for the payment of compensation, considered below) or to ensure that such a violation is not repeated in the future. By signing up to the Convention, the Government has committed itself to give effect to the rulings of the Court within its domestic legal system,[45] but it is up to the Government, and not the Court, to decide how this should be done. In some cases, legislation has been the inevitable outcome of an adverse decision by the Court; in others, a change in administrative practice, perhaps by the issue of revised guidance, has been sufficient.

4.38   Article 41 of the Convention provides:

"If the Court finds that there has been a violation of the Convention and the protocols thereto, and if the internal law of the High Contracting Party concerned allows only partial reparation to be made, the Court shall, if necessary, afford just satisfaction to the injured party."

"Just satisfaction" means compensation and/or costs. The condition precedent to the award of just satisfaction, that domestic law allows only partial reparation to be made, has thus far caused no difficulty so far as English domestic law is concerned. That was because, prior to incorporation, the decisions of the Court had no status in domestic law and could not provide the basis for a claim for a remedy before the English courts. Under the regime of the Human Rights Act, domestic courts must take account of the decisions of the Court,[46] and there may be cases where they will be able to grant a remedy consequent upon a decision of the Court. The issue will then arise as to whether or not the remedies available amount to full or only partial reparation. Certain types of breach of the Convention are not capable of full reparation, for example, deprivation of liberty contrary to Article 5 and interference with freedom

---

[45] Art. 46(1).
[46] HRA s. 2(1).

of expression.[47] The principles governing the award of compensation under Article 41 have been incorporated into s. 8 of the Human Rights Act and are discussed in chapter 2.

A detailed breakdown of the costs claimed must be submitted to the **4.39** Court in advance of its decision on the merits of a case, and may include the costs incurred in domestic proceedings prior to the application to Strasbourg. The Court does not adopt the standard English law approach of costs following the event. The applicant will never have to pay the cost of the respondent state, even if the application wholly fails. Where the application succeeds on one or more grounds but fails on others the Court will take an equitable approach, awarding a proportion only of the costs claimed.

Once the basic parameters of the costs award are determined, the Court **4.40** will examine whether the costs claim submitted by the applicant is excessive and, if it is, to assess a lower award on an equitable (that is, broad brush) basis. The rule is that costs must be actually incurred, necessarily incurred and be reasonable as to quantum, and the Court's scrutiny is frequently exacting. A recent example is the *Halford* case in which the applicant won a claim for breach of Article 8 after her police employers had tapped her office telephone line.[48] She claimed solicitors' costs of £119,500 and expenses of £7,500, plus counsel's fees of £14,875 and expenses of £1,000, all exclusive of VAT. The Government argued that the solicitors' costs were excessive: they represented over 500 hours, work on the case at the rate of £239 per hour whereas the appropriate rate in domestic proceedings would be £120-150 per hour. Also, the Government submitted that 500 hours was much more work than necessary and criticised the length of the documentation submitted on behalf of Ms Halford, noting that much of it concerned issues of no, or only peripheral, relevance. The Court agreed, and awarded £25,000 plus VAT "on an equitable basis".

The enforcement of Court judgments is the responsibility of the **4.41** Committee of Ministers,[49] which in each case of default will enquire of the respondent state what steps have been taken to give effect to the Court's decision. The incorporation of the Convention into English law at least gives the judgments of the Court some formal legal status in the UK, and in some cases, individuals, including the applicant, may be able to jump-start the enforcement process by using a Court ruling to gain the relief which they seek in the domestic courts. In others, however, there

---

[47] *De Wilde, Ooms and Versyp* v *Belgium*, A/14 (1972) at 10; *Sunday Times* v *UK*, A/38 (1980) at 8–9.
[48] *Halford* v *UK*, A/773, (1997) 24 EHRR 524.
[49] Art. 46(2).

will be nothing to be done except await a change in the law in compliance with the Court's ruling, a change which will usually not be retrospective and so may not assist the applicant who secured the change in the first place.

15. FURTHER READING

Clements, *European Human Rights: Taking a Case under the Convention* (Sweet and Maxwell, 1994).

Krüger and Nørgaard, "The Right of Application" in Macdonald, Matscher and Petzold (eds), *The European System for the Protection of Human Rights* (Kluwer, 1993).

Roue and Schlette, "The Protection of Individual Rights in Europe after the Eleventh Protocol to the ECHR" (1998) 23 ELRev. HRC 3

Zwart, *The Admissibility of Human Rights Petitions* (Kluwer, 1994).

Chapter 5

EUROPEAN CONVENTION LEGAL RESEARCH

Legal research into the European Convention on Human Rights is by no 5.1
means a straightforward matter. It has become somewhat easier in the
very recent past due to the publication of new and revised secondary
sources (text-books, journals, etc.) but, compared with subject areas in
domestic law and with European Community law, it remains obscure and
difficult to penetrate. There are at least three reasons for this. The first is
that there is no comprehensive reporting system for cases decided under
the Convention. The decisions of the Court are certainly reported in full,
but those of the Commission, which are far more numerous and as a result
more likely to be directly on point, are reported only systematically. Nor
have the cases decided under the Convention been recorded on CD-ROM
or other accessible electronic format (even LEXIS), which would ease
considerably the process of research. The problems of collating primary
sources are multiplied several times over when it comes to obtaining
copies of other international treaties, resolutions or case-law which might
be relevant to the presentation of a Convention case.

Secondly, there is simply not the same range of primary and secondary 5.2
material available on the Convention as has become available in other
fields. There is only one official and one unofficial set of dedicated ECHR
case reports. The range of text-books has expanded markedly but it is fair
to say that the available texts are aimed primarily at the student market
and place little emphasis on the needs of the practitioner. The coverage of
the Convention in legal journals has also improved, due mainly to the
arrival of a specialist European human rights law journal, but again it still
lags some way behind comparable areas of study.

The third reason for the difficulties which lawyers encounter in 5.3
conducting research into the Convention is the lack of coverage in law
libraries of the appropriate materials. Few libraries carry any more than
the unofficial European Human Rights Reports and perhaps a basic text or
two; copies of the official reports are certainly few and far between. By

contrast, the presence of European Community legal materials in our law libraries has been placed on a much more secure footing by the creation of over 40 European Documentation Centres which receive them as a matter of course. Many of these centres complement their coverage of EC law with European Convention materials, but the latter are not received automatically and are, accordingly, less secure.

5.4   The bibliography sections at the end of various chapters of this book aim to point the reader towards a more specialised and detailed treatment of some or all of the aspects of the subject matter of that chapter. This chapter describes how primary sources may be located, summarises the secondary material which is currently available and then addresses the issue of research into other international legal sources which may be relevant to the interpretation of provisions of the Convention.

1. PRIMARY SOURCES

TREATIES, LEGISLATION, ETC.

5.5   The basic primary source is, of course, the Convention itself. With effect from November 1998, the text of the Convention has been substantially amended, pursuant to Protocol No. 11. The revised text of the Convention, along with the Protocols to it, is reprinted at appendix II of this book. Other important primary sources, including the rules of procedure of the Court are printed in an official publication — *European Convention on Human Rights: Collected Texts* (Council of Europe Press, 1995), and also in the *Yearbook of the European Convention on Human Rights*. The full text of the Convention, the Protocols and the rules of Court can also be found on the internet web-site of the Court of Human Rights, the address of which is www.dhcour.coe.fr.

5.6   Whilst the text of the Convention itself changes only rarely, the attitude of the UK Government towards certain provisions, as reflected in reservations and derogations, may be more fluid. The Government may decide to ratify further protocols, or to withdraw and/or to submit new or revised reservations or derogations to the substantive provisions of the Convention, in particular, having regard to the security situation in Northern Ireland, Articles 5 and 6. All ratifications and reservations are recorded in the *Yearbook* and those concerning the UK at least will also appear in the Bulletin section of the *European Human Rights Law Review*. The *European Law Review*'s annual Human Rights Survey contains tables indicating which protocols are in force in the UK.

Occasionally, it may be necessary to refer to the Convention's *travaux*   **5.7**
préparatoires for the purposes of interpreting a particular provision.
These are printed in *Collected Edition of the Travaux Préparatoires*
(Martinus Nijhoff, 1975). There is no secondary legislation as such
issued under the Convention. The nearest equivalent is perhaps the
resolutions of the Parliamentary Assembly of the Council of Europe,
which may influence the interpretation of the Convention by the
Strasbourg institutions. These are re-printed in the Council of Europe's
Yearbook.

Case-law

The case-law of the Convention falls into three categories, decisions of the   **5.8**
Court, of the Commission and of the Committee of Ministers. Commission
decisions can be further broken down into decisions on admissibility and
decisions on the merits. The official reports of the decisions of the Court
of Human Rights give to each decision a chronological number and
decisions are then referenced according to that number and their date.
The official reports are in two series, A and B. Series A contains the actual
decisions; Series B contains pleadings, records of oral arguments and
other relevant documents. Series B is many years behind Series A and it
must be doubted whether it will ever be feasible (or indeed desirable)
to update it. To take an example, the official reference for the Court's
decision in *Young, James and Webster* v *UK*, the landmark case on
freedom of association which concerned the closed shop at British Rail, is
A/44 (1981).
   The full text of all Court decisions has recently become available on
the Court's web-site (www.dhcour.coe.fr).
   Decisions of the Court are selectively reported in the *European Human*   **5.9**
Rights Reports (EHRR), the major set of unofficial reports. The *European*
Human Rights Law Review carries relatively full summaries of most Court
decisions, which appear more quickly than in the EHRR. Briefer summaries of decisions appear occasionally in *The Times* and *Current Law*
(under the subject heading "Human Rights", not "European Law"). The
Human Rights Case Digest (Sweet and Maxwell) references every decision of the Court from 1996 onwards, but has only a brief summary of
each one. The *Digest of Strasbourg Case-Law Relating to the European*
Convention on Human Rights (Carl Heymanns Verlag) is the most
comprehensive unofficial source in terms of cases covered, but it
reproduces only limited extracts from decisions and is not up to date.

A more recent but less comprehensive attempt to achieve the same objective for Court decisions is Kempees, *A Systematic Guide to the Case-Law of the European Court of Human Rights 1960-94* (Kluwer, 1996). Another, reasonably up-to-date source for Court decisions is the series of press releases issued by the Council of Europe which contain lengthy, unofficial summaries. Few libraries subscribe to them but they are published on the Court's web-site.

5.10   There is no comprehensive source, official or unofficial, for decisions of the Commission. The official series of reports is entitled *Decisions and Reports of the European Commission on Human Rights* (D&R). It is now published four times a year and contains a selection of admissibility decisions as well as reports of friendly settlements and Commission decisions on the merits of cases which are not referred to the Court (if a case is referred to the Court, the Commission decision on the merits will appear in the official report of the Court's decision; it will also be included with a Court report in the unofficial *European Human Rights Reports*). Volume 76 D&R onwards is split into parts A and B. Part A is published first and contains the text of decisions in their original language (English or French); part B contains reports of the same cases translated into the other language and follows later. Applications to the Commission are given serial numbers composed of two figures, a sequential number allocated according to the time when it was received, and the year in which it was received. For example, the reference for *Brind* v *UK*, the case in which journalists sought to continue their challenge to a ban on broadcasting the voices of members of *Sinn Fein* is Appl. No. 18714/91, (1994) 77-A D&R 42. The Decisions and Reports series commenced in 1975. The official reports for Commission cases before that date is entitled *Collection of Decisions of the European Commission of Human Rights* (CD).

5.11   There are a variety of other sources for Commission decisions. Commission cases reported in the Decisions and Reports series from 1986 onwards can be accrued on the Court's web-site using the HUDOC search engine. The Commission's internet site (www.dhcommhr.coe.fr) gives the full text of its reports on the merits of cases from 1997 onwards, but not of its more numerous decisions on admissibility. The best unofficial sources are the *European Human Rights Reports* and the *European Human Rights Law Review.* From 1993, the *European Human Rights Reports* contain a dedicated Commission Supplement (EHRR CD) which reports a broad range of Commission decisions both on admissibility and on the merits. Volumes from 1979-1992 contain some Commission decisions and reports, particularly in notable British cases, but no attempt is made to separate these from the Court reports. The

EHRLR reports a larger number of Commission decisions, and more quickly than the EHRR, but they are not in full text form. The *Yearbook of the European Convention on Human Rights* contains official reports of selected decisions on admissibility only; its coverage is patchy, however, and this book does not give references to *Yearbook* reports save where the decision is not reported elsewhere. Other unofficial sources include the *Digest of Strasbourg Case-Law* and the *Human Rights Case Digest.*

The process of obtaining transcripts of unreported cases is cumber- **5.12** some. From 1994 onwards, the Council of Europe has published the full text of all Commission decisions in chronological order either in English or in French (although the author has found the relevant volumes only in the library of the Human Rights Building in Strasbourg). Decisions prior to 1994 are held in the vaults of the Human Rights Building in Strasbourg and can only be obtained by telephoning, or visiting, the Human Rights Information Centre there. The library has a computer database of all cases which the staff can use in the event that the relevant case number is not known. Decisions of the Committee of Ministers are occasionally relevant; these are published in the *Yearbook* and, from 1996 onwards, on the Committee of Ministers' web site (www.coe.fr/cm/). A broader selection is now available on the Court's web site within the HUDOC database.

2. SECONDARY SOURCES

TEXT-BOOKS AND ENCYCLOPAEDIAS

Three recent publications have dramatically improved the range of **5.13** general texts about the Convention. *Law of the European Convention on Human Rights* by Harris, O'Boyle and Warbrick (Butterworths, 1995) is by far the most comprehensive treatment of the practice of the Commission and the Court. The first edition of *The European Convention on Human Rights* by Jacobs was a pioneering student text in this field; a second edition, written by Jacobs and White has also been published (OUP, 1996). Thirdly, the human rights/civil liberties section of *Halsburys Laws of England* has recently been revised and updated. A less recent student textbook is also worthy of mention: *Theory and Practice of the European Convention on Human Rights* by van Dijk and van Hoof (Deventer, 1990) is part exposition of the law and part prescription as to how the authors believe that the Convention should develop. The former aspect has now been overtaken by *Harris, O'Boyle and Warbrick,* but it remains a useful source of ideas with which to challenge the current limits of the law.

5.14   There are comparatively few texts on specific aspects of the Convention, and even fewer which can be recommended for use by practitioners. One exception is perhaps Clements, *European Human Rights: Taking a Case under the Convention* (Sweet and Maxwell, 1994), part of which consists of a detailed account of procedure before the Commission and the Court. It will no doubt be updated following the remodelling of the Strasbourg machinery from 1 November 1998. Another, more practical, book is Reid, *A Practical Guide to the European Convention on Human Rights* (Sweet & Maxwell, 1998).

JOURNALS

5.15   Most writing on specific Convention issues is found in legal journals and the Human Rights section of *Current Law* lists a selection of recently published articles in this field. The *European Human Rights Law Review* is a relatively new journal devoted specifically to the Convention and related issues. The Human Rights Survey of the *European Law Review* is another recent advance on journal coverage of the Convention. Both these publications carry regular notes on cases before the Commission and the Court. Three other journals, the *Yearbook of European Law*, the *British Yearbook of International Law* and the *International and Comparative Law Quarterly* contain annual surveys of Convention case-law as well as occasional more detailed articles.

3. OTHER INTERNATIONAL LEGAL MATERIALS

5.16   A variety of other international legal materials may be relevant to the construction which the Court of Human Rights would accord to provisions of the Convention. Some of the more important examples are listed below.

- Other Council of Europe Conventions are published by the Council of Europe in a series entitled *European Conventions and Agreements.*

- Resolutions of the Council of Europe's Parliamentary Assembly are published in the *Yearbook of the Council of Europe.* Some can also be found at the web site of the Directorate of Human Rights in Strasbourg (www.dhdirhr.coe.fr).
- The European Convention for the Prevention of Torture and Inhuman and Degrading Treatment, and the enforcement activities of the Committee for the Prevention of Torture, are relevant to claims under Articles 3 (inhuman and degrading treatment) and 5 (deprivation of liberty). An annual survey of practice under the Torture Convention is published in the *European Law Review's* Human Rights Survey. More detailed information can be obtained from the Committee's web-site (www.dhdirhr.coe.fr/cpt.htm). The European Prison Rules, also relevant under Article 3, are reprinted at (1987) 9 EHRR 513.
- Legal rules promulgated by the International Labour Organisation may be relevant to cases under Article 11 of the Convention on freedom of association. ILO publications and reports are difficult to get hold of, save through its Internet site (www.ilo.org). The two most important Conventions on Freedom of Association and Protection of the Right to Organise (No. 87) and Right to Organise and Collective Bargaining (No. 98) are reprinted in Ewing, *Britain and the ILO* (Institute of Employment Rights, 2nd ed., 1994).
- There are a handful of specialist texts on the interpretation and application of the European Social Charter, another Council of Europe instrument. *The European Social Charter* by Harris (University Press of Virginia, 1984) and *Law and Practice of the European Convention on Human Rights and the European Social Charter* by Gomien, Harris and Zwaak (Council of Europe Publishing 1996) are the most impressive. The ESC also has a web-site (www.dhdirhr.coe.fr/ intro/eng/GENERAL/SOC.HTM).
- The enforcement of the International Covenant on Civil and Political Rights by the UN Human Rights Committee is detailed in O'Flaherty, *Human Rights and the UN: Practice before the Treaty Bodies* (Sweet and Maxwell, 1996). A useful introduction to the law of the ICCPR is Harris and Joseph (eds) *The International Covenant on Civil and Political Rights and United Kingdom Law* (OUP, 1995).
- Research into the case-law of other national jurisdictions may also be required. *European Current Law* contains a "Human Rights" section which digests major case-law from other European states, much of which is concerned with the application of Convention rights in those countries. Practice in other Contracting States is considered relevant by the Commission and the Court, in particular when they come to

decide whether a particular measure is "necessary in a democratic society". Domestic courts will, presumably, show the same interest, Butterworths Human Rights Cases is a recent set of reports which focuses on human rights cases from around the world.

- As is explained in chapter 2, important parts of the Human Rights Act were modelled on the New Zealand Bill of Rights Act 1990, and New Zealand practice may, for that reason, be highly relevant to the interpretation of the Act. A useful commentary on the application of the New Zealand legislation is Huscroft and Rishworth, *Rights and Freedoms — the New Zealand Bill of Rights Act 1990 and the Human Rights Act 1993* (University of Wellington Press, 1995). The text of the Bill of Rights Act is available on the Internet, at www.govt.nz/bor.

Part II

EUROPEAN CONVENTION RIGHTS AND FREEDOMS

Chapter 6

GENERAL PRINCIPLES OF THE LAW OF THE ECHR

The remainder of the chapters in part II of this book analyse the substantive law of the European Convention on Human Rights in relation to each right conferred by it. This chapter sets out the general principles of application of the Convention which apply in more or less every case arising under one or other of its substantive, right-conferring provisions.[1] These principles comprise, in essence, the basic preliminary questions which must be asked in each case to ascertain whether a Convention claim is viable, and then the analytical and interpretive tools which must be employed in seeking to establish what the Convention actually means, and what effect it has, in a particular case. Some of these general principles have arisen from the case-law of the Commission and the Court of Human Rights, for example the methods of interpretation of Convention provisions and the principles of proportionality and the margin of appreciation. Others are contained in the text of the Convention itself within specific articles, but have a general application to all Convention rights, for example, the principle of non-discrimination in Article 14.

The following principles of Convention law will be examined in this chapter:

6.1

6.2

- the rules of "statutory interpretation" which apply to the Convention.
- state responsibility: for whose actions can the Government be held responsible under the Convention?
- permissible restrictions upon Convention rights: "necessary in a democratic society", "prescribed by law", proportionality and the margin of appreciation.

---

[1] The label "general principles" is that of the author, and is not one used by the Commission or the Court.

- the rule against discrimination.
- the requirement of an effective remedy for breach of Convention rights.

1. INTERPRETING THE CONVENTION

METHODS OF INTERPRETATION

6.3 British rules of statutory interpretation form a complex code — the leading texts on the subject each contain several hundred pages of rules and refinements. The Convention has its own, much shorter, interpretative code, set out in the Vienna Convention on the Law of Treaties. The Convention on Human Rights was agreed some years before the Vienna Convention and, in theory, is unaffected by the latter, which does not have retrospective effect. Nevertheless, the Court has indicated that it considers itself to be bound by the Vienna Convention.[2] The Vienna Convention is a lengthy document, but the main principles of interpretation of the Convention on Human Rights can be reduced to a handful of basic precepts, some of which are derived from the Vienna Convention and some from the case-law of the Court.

Ordinary meaning

6.4 The starting point is Article 31 of the Vienna Convention, which provides that the words of a treaty should be given their ordinary meaning.

Purposive interpretation

6.5 The Convention must be given a purposive or teleological interpretation, in accordance with its object and purpose.[3] The object and purpose of the Convention is stated in its preamble to be the "maintenance and further realisation of human rights and fundamental freedoms" on the basis of an "effective political democracy". The Court will, in general, prefer an interpretation which promotes individual protection rather than a

---

[2] *Golder* v *UK*, A/18, (1979–80) 1 EHRR 524, 532.
[3] Art. 31 of the Vienna Convention.

restrictive interpretation which would limit the obligations imposed upon the state. However, purposive interpretation is not, by any means, a panacea for applicants which will ensure that the rights of the individual triumph in every case. It will assist in some cases by providing a justification for departure from the ordinary meaning of the Convention text. It also provides an answer to the argument that the powers transferred under the Convention should be construed narrowly, as it represents an exceptional derogation from the sovereignty of states.[4] A related principle is that the Court will be concerned to give the Convention a meaning which ensures that the rights which it confers are "practical and effective" rather than "theoretical and illusory".[5] A good example of the operation of this principle is the *Soering* case, where the prohibition in Article 3 on inhuman and degrading punishment was extended so as to protect the applicant from the treatment which he was liable to receive following extradition to a non-Convention state.[6]

6.6 Purposive interpretation has become increasingly common in the domestic courts, particularly with the advent of EC law, which requires such an approach, and the ruling of the House of Lords in *Pepper* v *Hart* which permits recourse to the record of Parliamentary proceedings in Hansard in certain cases.[7] A difference in emphasis should, however, be noted. In domestic law, a purposive construction will be adopted only where there is ambiguity in the ordinary meaning of the words used; under the Convention, there is no pre-condition of ambiguity — purposive interpretation is always required in order to give the text its true meaning.

Dynamic interpretation

6.7 Next, the Convention must be given an interpretation which is dynamic or evolutive rather than static or historical. That is to say, it is to be interpreted in the light of social and political circumstances as they exist today, rather than as they existed in the early 1950s when the Convention was drafted. The clearest statement of this principle is in *Tyrer* v *UK*, a case concerning the Isle of Man practice of birching convicted criminals. The Court emphasised that "the Convention is a living instrument which ... must

---

[4] See the dissenting argument to this effect of Judge Fitzmaurice in *Golder* v *UK*, above n. 2.
[5] See, for example, *Airey* v *Ireland*, A/41, (1979) 2 EHRR 305, 314–315.
[6] *Soering* v *UK*, A/161, (1989) 11 EHRR 439.
[7] [1993] AC 593.

be interpreted in the light of present-day conditions."[8] Birching was to be judged on the basis of commonly-accepted penal standards as they had developed since the 1950s.

6.8   The dynamic or evolutive approach has been central to the decision-making of the Court in a number of important areas, including the rights of homosexuals and of illegitimate children. Another good example of its use is *Piermont* v *France,* in which a German Member of the European Parliament was expelled from French territory in the South Pacific after taking part in anti-Government demonstrations. The Court held that her status as a national of an EU Member State, and as an MEP, meant that Article 16, which permits states to impose restrictions on the political activities of aliens, could not be raised against her.[9] Neither the EU nor its predecessor the EEC, was in existence when the Convention was adopted, but its development, and the creation in the Treaty on European Union of the status of "citizen" of the EU, had to be taken into account. Dynamic interpretation does, however, have its limits. In *Johnston* v *Ireland,* for example, the applicant argued that the Convention had developed such as to confer a right to divorce, The Court held that the Convention could not evolve so as to confer a right which had deliberately not been conferred at the outset.[10] The Court's dynamic approach contrasts markedly with the standard practice of the English courts which is to attempt to discern the historical intention of Parliament when it passed the legislation in question. That practice has been reinforced by the wider use of Hansard since *Pepper* v *Hart.*[11]

Autonomous interpretation

6.9   A further important principle is that legal terms in the Convention are to be given an autonomous interpretation. Concepts such as "civil rights and obligations" and "criminal charge" in Article 6 and "possessions" in Article 1 of the First Protocol have a Convention meaning which is independent of the meaning which might be accorded to them in the domestic legal system of any one Convention state.[12]

---

[8] A/26, (1979–80) 2 EHRR 1, 10.
[9] A/314, (1995) 20 EHRR 301.
[10] A/112, (1987) 9 EHRR 203.
[11] For an isolated domestic example of the dynamic approach, see Lord Scarman, dissenting, in *Ahmad* v *ILEA* [1978] QB 36, 48.
[12] See, for example, *Van Marle* v *The Netherlands,* A/101, (1986) 8 EHRR 483, 491.

SOURCES OF LAW

When interpreting the Convention, the Commission and the Court may **6.10** rely upon a very wide range of legal sources.

Previous Convention case-law

There is no formal doctrine of precedent in the Convention system but the **6.11** Court will usually follow its previous decisions even though it is not bound to do so. Decisions taken by the Commission both on admissibility and on the merits of cases which are found to be admissible are good authority as to the meaning of the Convention, save where the Court has taken a different view of the law. In the latter case, it is the Court's view which must prevail. No distinction is drawn between the *ratio* of a decision by the Commission or the Court, and comments which are merely *obiter dicta*.

The travaux préparatoires of the Convention

Article 32 of the Vienna Convention allows the use of a treaty's pre- **6.12** paratory works as a "supplementary means of interpretation". The Court does occasionally refer to the *travaux préparatoires* of the Convention but their value is diminished by the rule that the Convention is to be interpreted in line with present day circumstances, rather than according to the intention of the draftsmen in the 1950s. In *James*, for example, the Court examined the *travaux* before rejecting the applicants' arguments that reference in Article 1 of the First Protocol to the principles of public international law required a state to compensate its own nationals on deprivation of their property rather than just foreign nationals.[13] On other occasions, the Court has investigated the *travaux* and then declined to follow the approach which they suggest.[14]

The French language text of the Convention

The French and English language versions of the Convention are equally **6.13** authentic and, on occasion, recourse will be needed to both texts in order

---

[13] *James v UK*, A/98, (1986) 8 EHRR 123, 148–151.
[14] For example, *Young, James and Webster v UK*, A/44, (1982).

to decide upon the appropriate interpretation of a particular word or phrase. In *Wiggins*, for example, the applicant complained about the system of housing licences operated on the island of Guernsey. He based his claim upon Article 8, the right to respect for the home, and Article 1 of the First Protocol, the right to peaceful enjoyment of possessions. The Government argued that Article 1/1 did not apply, since "possessions" was restricted to chattels and did not extend to real property. The Commission disagreed, noting that the French text of the Convention used the word *"biens"* which incorporates both personal and real property.[15] Where the two texts appear to differ, the correct interpretation is the one which reconciles them, so far as this is possible in line with the Convention's object and purpose.[16]

Other Council of Europe materials

6.14 The Commission and the Court may rely upon other international agreements concluded within the framework of the Council of Europe. In *Gustafsson* v *Sweden*, for example, the Court referred to the European Social Charter as evidence of the widespread international recognition of the right to collective bargaining.[17] A large number of such agreements are in existence on subjects ranging from treatment of prisoners, to data protection, to the legal rights of illegitimate children.[18] Also, regard may be had to resolutions of the Parliamentary Assembly of the Council of Europe, which cover a wide range of subjects within the Convention's field of application. In *X, Y and Z* v *UK*, a recent case concerning the rights of transsexuals, the Commission referred to a resolution of the Parliamentary Assembly recommending that Member States allow for rectification of birth registers for transsexuals to show their changed sex.[19] These Council of Europe materials may provide useful ammunition but are in no sense binding upon the Commission or the Court. In *X, Y and Z*, the Court held that English law, which had not complied with the

---

[15] *Wiggins* v *UK*, Appl. No. 7456/76, (1978) 13 D&R 40, 46.

[16] Article 33(4) of the Vienna Convention. See, for example, *Sunday Times* v *UK*, A/30, (1979–80) 2 EHRR 245, 270–271; *Brogan* v *UK*, A/145-B, (1989) 11 EHRR 117, 134.

[17] A/618, (1996) 22 EHRR 409.

[18] European Convention for the Prevention of Torture and Inhuman or Degrading Treatment or Punishment 1987 (ETS, No. 126) and the European Prison Rules 1987; Council of Europe Convention for the Protection of Individuals with regard to Automatic Processing of Personal Data 1981 (ETS, No. 108); European Convention on the Legal Status of Children Born out of Wedlock 1975 (ETS, No. 85).

[19] *X, Y and Z* v *UK*, A/753, (1997) 24 EHRR 143, 156.

recommendation of the Parliamentary assembly did not breach Article 8 of the Convention.[20]

Other international sources

Various other international sources have been relied upon by the **6.15** Strasbourg institutions, in particular other human rights treaties and conventions. In *Müller*, for example, the Court referred to Article 19(2) of the International Covenant on Civil and Political Rights in support of its view that freedom of expression in Article 10 of the Convention included also freedom of artistic expression.[21] Conversely, in *Kosiek*, the Court relied upon the specific inclusion of a right of access to the public service in the Universal Declaration of Human Rights and the International Covenant in order to bolster the significance of the absence of such a right from the Convention.[22] Reference to another human rights treaty may necessitate an examination not only of the treaty itself but also of case-law which has developed under that treaty; for example, the case-law of the UN Human Rights Committee will be relevant to the interpretation of the ICCPR. The jurisprudence of the International Labour Organisation, which has adopted a number of Conventions on employment law and industrial relations, has a particular relevance to the scope of the freedom of association under Article 11. European Union materials may also be relevant.[23]

Case-law from Convention states

Many cases have arisen in which the Commission and/or the Court have **6.16** had cause to survey a particular aspect of legal practice in the domestic law of the Convention states. For example, the right to respect for private and family life under Article 8 has been extended to give rights to homosexuals and to illegitimate children, having regard to more liberal practice in a number of states.[24] The rights of transsexuals under the same

---

[20] *Ibid.* at 168–172.
[21] *Müller* v *Switzerland*, A/133, 91991) 13 EHRR 212, 225.
[22] *Kosiek* v *Germany*, A/105, (1986) 9 EHRR 328, 340–341. See also the references to the International Convention on the Elimination of all Forms of Racial Discrimination 1965 in *Jersild* v *Denmark*, A/298, (1995) 19 EHRR 1.
[23] For example, the Court relied upon a resolution of the European Parliament in *Goodwin* v *UK*, A/610, (1966) 22 EHRR 123, 143.
[24] *Dudgeon* v *UK*, A/45, (1982) 4 EHRR 149; *Marckx* v *Belgium*, A/31, (1979–80) 2 EHRR 330.

article apparently await a more substantial consensus.[25] In general terms, it can be said that the Court is wary about extending the Convention in a manner which will cause a major change of practice in a number of states. For example, the requirement in Article 6(1) that judgments be pronounced in public would, if taken literally, cause problems in many civil law systems where courts of cassation commonly do not give judgment in open court but publish their rulings through the court registry, and indeed in common law systems where it is increasingly common for a written judgment to be handed down without being read out in full. In *Pretto*, following a survey of domestic practice, the Court gave Article 6(1) a restrictive interpretation in this regard.[26]

Case-law from other jurisdictions

6.17　The practice of non-Convention states in the human rights field may also be pertinent to a decision as to how the Convention should develop. For example, the US Supreme Court has a highly developed corpus of law on freedom of expression, to which the Court occasionally makes reference. In *James* v *UK*, the Court referred to a decision of the Supreme Court in rejecting the applicants' argument that compulsory transfer of private property could never properly be described as being in the public interest.[27] In *Chahal*, the Court criticised the British judicial procedure for dealing with sensitive matters of national security which, in essence, prevented the individual and his representatives from knowing the case against him.[28] In so doing, it referred to a Canadian procedure whereby sensitive material is examined in the absence of the individual himself, but in the presence of counsel appointed by the Court, who can make representations having seen the evidence against his client.

2. STATE RESPONSIBILITY

6.18　The European Convention is an agreement by states to secure certain rights to individuals under their jurisdiction. As such, the general rule is that it imposes obligations upon states to respect human rights and not

---

[25] See, for example, *X, Y and Z* v *UK*, above n. 19 at 169.
[26] *Pretto* v *Italy*, A/71, (1984), 6 EHRR 182.
[27] Above n. 13 at 141.
[28] *Chahal* v *UK*, A/697, (1997) 23 EHRR 413, 469.

upon private individuals or non-state bodies. For example, an individual who is assaulted by the police may have a claim under Article 3 on inhuman and degrading treatment but not if he is assaulted by a mugger. In practice, however, a variety of refinements apparent from the case-law of the Commission and the Court have the effect of broadening significantly the range of situations in which the Convention may be invoked to hold a state responsible for an infringement of fundamental rights, and of including many situations where private persons or bodies are primarily to blame. These are, in summary:

- "the state" is broadly defined.
- the state is responsible whether it is acting in a private or public law capacity.
- the state may be held responsible even where it has contributed only indirectly to a violation of the Convention.
- the state is responsible for the actions of private bodies to whom it has delegated the task of upholding Convention rights.
- the state may be held responsible for failing to prevent or to protect against the infringement of rights by individuals and private bodies.
- the state includes the courts hence the state is responsible for court orders in proceedings between two individuals or private bodies.

DEFINITION OF "THE STATE"

"The state" is to be construed broadly as referring to all emanations of the **6.19** state. In *Cosans*, an early case on corporal punishment in state schools, the Government queried whether it could be held responsible for matters arising out of the day-to-day running of individual schools. The Commission noted, however, that "the responsibility of a state under the Convention may arise for acts of all its organs, agents and servants".[29] Responsibility for the actions of teachers in Scottish state schools lay with the Secretary of State for Scotland and the regional educational authorities, and through them with the Government as a whole. Applications to Strasbourg are made against the Government of the United Kingdom, but that does not mean that only the actions of central government can be impugned. It means that central government will

---

[29] *Cosans* v *UK*, Appl. No. 7743/76, (1978) 12 D&R 140, 148–49.

be held responsible for the actions of all other branches of the state apparatus, such as local authorities, police forces, criminal courts etc.

6.20   Under s. 6 of the Human Rights Act, Convention rights may be invoked against "public authorities", a term of which only a partial definition is given. Recourse will, presumably, be had to the Strasbourg case-law in order to ascertain, as a starting point at least, whether the actions of a particular body could give rise to state responsibility before the Court. In fact, there has been little in the way of guidance from the Commission and the Court as to which bodies will qualify as state bodies or even which attributes will tend towards, and which against, characterisation as a state body. The Commission has, on occasion, been faced with borderline cases, such as the BBC and the Bar Council, but has consistently declined to reach any firm decision.[30] The decision of the Court in *Casado Coca* v *Spain* tells us that various factors support the implication that a body is a public authority subject to the Convention: that it has a public law status, that it performs functions in the public interest (including for example, the regulation of a profession) and that its decisions can be challenged in the courts. It also indicates that the confirmation of its decisions by the courts will assist in establishing state responsibility. On the basis of those various factors, the Court held the Spanish Government to be responsible for the actions of the Barcelona Bar Council in disciplining a lawyer which had disregarded its rules on professional advertising.[31] The Convention will also bind a body which is set up by private agreement but is subsequently given a statutory basis.[32]

CAPACITY

6.21   The actions of a state body give rise to state responsibility even where it is acting in a private law capacity, such as that of employer. The Court so held in the *Swedish Engine Drivers Union* case, in rejecting an argument of the Swedish Government that the Convention was intended to protect the individual against the state as holder of public power, not to influence the state in its private law relations.[33] A similar principle exists in EC law.[34]

---

[30] See *Hilton* v *UK*, Appl. No. 12015/86, (1988) 57 D&R 108 (the BBC); *X* v *UK*, Appl. No. 8295/78, (1978) 15 D&R 242 (the Bar Council).
[31] *Casado Coca* v *Spain*, A/285, (1994) 18 EHRR 1, 20–21.
[32] *X* v *The Netherlands*, Appl. No. 7669/76, (1979) 15 D&R 133.
[33] *Swedish Engine Drivers Union* v *Sweden*, A/20, (1979–80) 1 EHRR 617, 626–627.
[34] *Marshall* v *Southampton and South West AHA*, Case 152/84 [1986] ECR 723.

INDIRECT RESPONSIBILITY

A public authority can be held responsible for a violation of the Conven-   **6.22**
tion where its actions have contributed only indirectly towards it. In
López-Ostra, for example, the applicant complained that severe nuisance
from a waste treatment plant adjacent to her house amounted to an
infringement of her right to respect for private and family life and for the
home. The plant was privately owned and operated but the Spanish
Government was held responsible for its operations since the municipal
council had allowed the plant to be built on land formerly owned by it,
and had provided subsidies for the construction works. It was also
relevant that the council must have been aware of the difficulties which
the plant was causing, yet did nothing, and had opposed the applicant's
attempts to have the plant closed.[35] Another example is *Arrondelle v UK*,
in which the applicant complained of noise nuisance emanating from
traffic on the M23 motorway. The Government claimed that it could not
be held responsible for the noise of private vehicles on the motorway, but
the Commission found responsibility on the basis that the motorway had
been built by, and is operated by, public authorities.[36] A more questionable decision is *Nielsen* where the Court rejected a child's claim that his
Article 5 rights were breached when he was detained as a psychiatric
patient in a state hospital. The decision to admit him to hospital was taken
by his mother, but the authorities had facilitated his detention by making
available the hospital place and, presumably, by guarding the applicant
during his stay. The Court found, nevertheless, that the part played by the
state had been "of a limited and subsidiary nature", and that it did not
thereby assume responsibility for what was, in essence, the mother's
decision.[37]

DELEGATION OF RESPONSIBILITY

In certain circumstances, the public authorities may be held responsible   **6.23**
for the actions of a private, non-state body. In *Costello-Roberts*, a pupil at a
private school complained that corporal punishment which had been

---

[35] *López-Ostra v Spain*, A/303-C, (1995) 20 EHRR 277, 296–297.
[36] *Arrondelle v UK*, Appl. No. 7889/77, (1980) 19 D&R 186, 198.
[37] *Nielsen v Denmark*, A/144, (1989) 11 EHRR 175, 192–193.

inflicted upon him by the headmaster amounted to inhuman and degrading treatment contrary to Article 3 and a breach of his right under Article 8 to respect for his private life. The reasoning in *Cosans* did not apply since the school was not under the direct control of any state authority and the Government argued that it could not be held responsible for matters such as discipline which arose out of the day-to-day running of the school. The Court disagreed, noting that the disciplinary regime of a school fell within the ambit of the right to education which was guaranteed by Article 2 of the First Protocol to the Convention, and that the right was conferred upon all pupils equally, whether they attended state, or independent, schools. The UK Government could not absolve itself from responsibility for securing the right to education by delegating its obligations to schools in the private sector. Hence the actions of an headmaster of an independent school could engage the responsibility of the state.[38] The key to the delegation principle of state responsibility is, therefore, that the state has delegated responsibility for the securing of a Convention right to a private body. Another example is *Van der Mussele* v *Belgium*, where the Belgian Government was held responsible for the actions of the Belgian Bar Council, on whom it relied for securing the right to free legal assistance in Article 6(3)(c) of the Convention.[39] The doctrine is, potentially of great importance in this country since large scale privatisation of state functions has placed a range of private bodies in roles which involve the securing of Convention rights, notably in the penal system.

POSITIVE OBLIGATIONS

6.24   The basis of the doctrine of positive obligations is that the state can be held responsible both for oppressive actions and for culpable failure to act. Article 1 of the Convention requires state parties to "secure" certain rights to individuals under its jurisdiction. This basic obligation may give rise to negative obligations to refrain from particular action, as well as positive obligations to take steps to confer, or to facilitate the exercise of, rights. In some situations, negative and positive obligations are merely two sides of the same coin. To take the example of Article 3, the state has the negative obligation not to subject prisoners to inhuman and degrading

---

[38] *Costello-Roberts* v *UK*, A/247-C, (1995) 19 EHRR 112, 132–133
[39] *Van der Mussele* v *Belgium*, A/70, (1984) 6 EHRR 163.

prison conditions and the correlative positive obligation to take steps to provide prisons which meet the requisite standards. In other cases, positive obligations play an important role in regulating the relationship between the individual and the state, in requiring the state to put in place legal structures which will enable individuals to protect their rights against violation by the state. An example is child custody proceedings, which have been reviewed by the Court under the right to respect for family life in Article 8. The state has a negative duty not to interfere unduly with family life in taking decisions about the custody of children and also a positive duty to provide legal procedures whereby custody decisions are transparent, can be challenged by the individuals affected, and will be reviewed in the light of the principle of family life.[40]

6.25 In certain situations, positive obligations provide the basis for holding the state responsible where the exercise of Convention rights has been frustrated by the actions of private individuals. A good example is the case of *Plattform Ärtze für das Leben* v *Austria,* where an Austrian anti-abortion group complained about the disruption of its protests by counter-demonstrators. This interference with its right of assembly under Article 11 was not perpetrated by the forces of the state but by individuals opposed to the views of the group, and the Austrian Government sought to escape liability on that basis. However, the Court accepted the group's argument that the state authorities could, in principle, be held responsible on the basis that they had failed to take adequate security measures to secure the right of assembly.[41] The Court has consistently refused to espouse a general theory of positive obligations, and the law has developed on a case-by-case basis. So far, it is apparent that there may be positive obligations to protect the following rights from violation by non-state bodies.

- Freedom from inhuman and degrading treatment under Article 3: the state has a positive obligation to ensure that children are not subjected to inhuman or degrading treatment, including corporal punishment in their own homes.[42]
- Liberty and security of the person under Article 5: a dissenting judgment in *Nielsen* argued that the state should provide legal redress against decisions by parents to place restrictions upon the liberty of their children.[43]

---

[40] See, for example, *W* v *UK,* A/121, (1988) 10 EHRR 29; *Hökkanen* v *Finland,* A/299-A, (1995) 19 EHRR 139. See also *Airey* v *Ireland,* A/32, (1979–80) 2 EHRR 305.
[41] A/139, (1991) 13 EHRR 204. However, the applicant's claim was rejected on the facets.
[42] *Y* v *UK,* A/247-A, (1994) 17 EHRR 238; *A* v *UK,* A/991, decision of 23 September 1998.
[43] Above n. 37 at 199–201.

- Private and family life under Article 8: the Court first explicitly recognised positive obligations in *X and Y* v *The Netherlands*, where a victim of child abuse complained that the Dutch legal system should have made provision for her attacker to be prosecuted and so provided her with the protection of the criminal law.[44] The application of Article 8 to protect individuals from intrusion into their private lives by the press depends upon the recognition of a positive obligation to regulate press activity.[45]
- Freedom of thought, conscience and religion under Article 9: the state may be required to take positive steps to curtail freedom of expression where offence to the religious feelings of others is likely to be caused.[46]
- Freedom of expression under Article 10 and freedom of assembly under Article 11: duties to protect both of these rights from interference by individuals and private bodies may be deduced from the *Plattform Ärtze für das Leben* case.[47]

6.26   On the other hand, the Court has not definitively ruled out state responsibility pursuant to positive obligations under any other article of the Convention. There are, however, indications in certain areas, for example under Article 1 of the First Protocol, that interference with protected rights by individuals or private bodies will rarely, if ever, give rise to liability on the part of the authorities.[48]

6.27   It is important to note that it will usually prove more difficult to establish a breach of the positive obligations of the state to intervene to protect individuals against the actions of others in society. This is because the state's margin of appreciation, the area of legitimate discretion within which the Court will not intervene, is deemed to be inherently wider when it comes to making choices as to the appropriate way in which to regulate relationships between private individuals. In *Stubbings* v *UK*, for example, the applicants were victims of alleged child sex abuse whose claims for damages for personal injuries against their assailants were ruled out of time in the domestic courts.[49] The House of Lords had held that deliberately inflicted injury was subject to the standard six year time limit in s. 2 of the Limitation Act 1980 (which started to run from the applicants'

---

[44] A/91, (1986) 8 EHRR 235.
[45] The Commission indicated in *Spencer* v *UK* that such obligations could be found within Art. 8: Appl. No. 28851/95, [1998] EHRLR 348.
[46] *Otto-Preminger-Institut* v *Austria,* A/295-A, (1995) 19 EHRR 34.
[47] Above n. 41.
[48] *Gustafsson* v *Sweden,* above n. 17.
[49] A/683, (1997) 23 EHRR 213.

eighteenth birthdays), rather than the flexible limit in s. 11(1)(b) of three years from the date of knowledge of the person injured.[50] The applicants claimed, *inter alia*, that the Government had failed in its positive obligation to protect them from abuse. The Court set out the principles relating to positive obligations under Article 8 as follows:

"It is to be recalled that although the object of Article 8 is essentially that of protecting the individual against arbitrary interference by the public authorities, it does not merely compel the State to abstain from such interference: there may, in addition to this primary negative undertaking, be positive obligations inherent in an effective respect for private or family life. These obligations may involve the adoption of measures designed to secure respect for private life even in the sphere of the relations between individuals themselves. There are different ways of ensuring respect for private life and the nature of the State's obligation will depend upon the particular aspect of private life that is in issue. It follows that the choice of means calculated to secure compliance with this positive obligation in principle falls within the Contracting States' margin of appreciation."[51]

In the light of the broad discretion accorded to states in this field, the position in British law, whereby child sex abusers were subject to severe criminal penalties, even if civil claims were barred in some cases, was deemed to be sufficient protection of the applicants' rights.

COURT ORDERS IN PRIVATE PROCEEDINGS

A final principle which has the effect, in practice, of extending the reach **6.28** of the Convention beyond a narrow conception of individual-state relations is that the courts are an integral part of the state, and court orders restricting Convention rights will engage the responsibility of the state even where they are made in proceedings between private parties. In *Hoffman*, the applicant was a Jehovah's Witness who, following divorce, lost the custody of her children to their Roman Catholic father, pursuant to an order of the Austrian Supreme Court. She successfully claimed that the Court's decision had been based upon religious discrimination against Jehovah's Witnesses and so constituted an unjustified interference in her family life.[52] Judge Matscher argued in a dissenting opinion that there had been no "interference by a public authority" with

---

[50] *Stubbings* v *Webb* [1993] AC 498.
[51] Above n. 49 at 235.
[52] *Hoffman* v *Austria*, A/255-C, (1994) 17 EHRR 293.

the applicant's rights because the custody dispute was a private dispute between individuals which had merely been resolved with the help of the courts.[53] The majority of the Court disagreed, finding that the Supreme Court's decision constituted an interference with the applicant's rights contrary to Article 8(1), since it had compelled her to give up her children to their father. The fact that the Supreme Court's decision had been taken in the context of a dispute between private individuals "makes no difference in this respect."[54] It is also apparent from the *Casado Coca* case that where the actions or decisions of an individual or private body are challenged in the courts, judicial approval for them may create an actionable violation of the Convention.[55] This principle, which makes the state responsible under the Convention for the outcome of private proceedings, is potentially of wide application and certainly has the effect of broadening the effect of the Convention beyond the classic "vertical" situation.

SUMMARY: THE NATURE OF CONVENTION RIGHTS

6.29   It is important not to lose sight of the fact that, notwithstanding the various developments outlined above, Convention rights remain rights enjoyed by the individual against the state. Judicial intervention has permitted the attribution of responsibility to the state in a broader range of circumstances and notably in circumstances where one individual has suffered at the hands of another, but it has not altered the essential nature of the rights themselves. Under certain constitutional codes, fundamental rights are rights *inter omnes*, enforceable against both state and non-state bodies. Under the Convention, the state may be held responsible for the actions of private parties, and rights against the state may be enforced in the context of proceedings between private parties, but only the state, and not any individual or private body, owes a duty to secure and respect Convention rights.

---

[53] *Ibid.* at 317–318.
[54] *Ibid.* at 314.
[55] Above n. 31.

3. PERMISSIBLE RESTRICTIONS UPON CONVENTION RIGHTS

The vast majority of the rights guaranteed by the Convention are not **6.30** absolute. Some Convention rights are subject to express exceptions; Articles 8–11, for example, are each constructed on the basis of a protected right (para. (1)), followed by permitted exceptions to that right (para. (2)). Even the right to life, the most basic of human rights, is subject to three specific defences listed in Article 2(2). Other rights appear in the Convention in absolute terms but are, in practice, subject to implied exceptions which operate to restrict the circumstances in which a breach of the right will occur. The right to the peaceful enjoyment of one's possessions under Article 1 of the First Protocol to the Convention is a good example. Not all interferences with peaceful enjoyment will amount to a breach of that provision; the Court will examine whether a fair balance has been struck between the rights of the individual and the general needs of the community. A similar analysis is required in order to ascertain whether discrimination is unjustified and so contrary to Article 14. Protection from torture and inhuman and degrading treatment under Article 3 is perhaps an exception, being subject neither to express nor to implied restrictions. In substance, however, it is also restricted, by the manipulation of a threshold below which highly unpleasant treatment will not be considered inhuman or degrading.

Similar principles apply across a range of Convention provisions for the **6.31** purposes of determining whether a restriction upon a right is permissible. The express exceptions in Articles 8–11 entail an almost identical analysis, and some of the principles used, including the requirement of proportionality and the margin of appreciation of states, pervade the reasoning of the Commission and the Court under all the provisions of the Convention. It is convenient, therefore, to examine certain principles in this chapter, on a general level, although reference should also made to the chapters dealing with each specific Convention right, where further explanation is given.

PRESCRIBED BY LAW

Under para. (2) of Articles 9–11, permissible restrictions upon the free- **6.32** dom of thought, conscience and religion, freedom of expression and freedom of assembly and association must be "prescribed by law". The same phrase appears in Article 5 as a pre-condition for the deprivation of liberty under the exceptions laid down in Article 5(1). Restrictions upon the right to respect for private and family life, the home and correspondence under Article 8 must be "in accordance with the law" (Article 8(2)). There is no difference in meaning between these formulations, which are, in fact, alternative translations of a single phrase in the French text of the Convention.[56] Also, deprivation of property under Article 1 of the First Protocol must be "subject to the conditions provided for by law", a phrase which has been interpreted in the same way.[57]

6.33 The requirement that a restriction be prescribed by law comprises a three-fold test:[58]

- the restriction must have a basis in domestic law.
- the law must be accessible.
- the law must be sufficiently precise as to be foreseeable in its application.[59]

Authorised by law

6.34 "Law" is broadly defined, including both statute and common law. In the *Sunday Times* case itself, the "law" in question was the law of contempt of court which was, at that stage, a common law offence but which was put on a statutory footing shortly thereafter. Law could also include international law,[60] and, in certain circumstances, the rules of a professional association such as the Bar Council or the Law Society.[61] The need for authorisation within the domestic legal system entails that a measure which is not positively authorised by law, or which is illegal under domestic law, can never found a justified restriction upon a Convention right. In *Malone*, for example, the Court criticised the practice of "metering", whereby the police obtained from the Post Office details of the telephone numbers called by people under surveillance, on the ground that it was not governed by any legal rules at all.[62] In the English courts,

---

[56] *Silver* v *UK*, A/61, (1983) 5 EHRR 347, 371.
[57] See also Art. 12, which uses the words "according to the national laws".
[58] *Ibid.* at 372.
[59] The latter two elements were elaborated by the Court in *Sunday Times* v *UK*, A/30, (1979–80) 2 EHRR 245, 270–271.
[60] *Groppera Radio* v *Switzerland*, A/173, (1990) 12 EHRR 321, 340–341.
[61] *Barthold* v *Germany*, A/90, (1985) 7 EHRR 383, 398–399.
[62] *Malone* v *UK*, A/82, (1985) 7 EHRR 14, 46–47.

the absence of legal regulation had led to the opposite conclusion: there was no law against what the police had done and so no basis upon which a claim could be founded.[63]

Accessibility

The requirement of accessibility has, first, a physical connotation: the law **6.35** must be available to be read by the individual affected by it. In *Silver*, for example, the restrictions on prisoners' correspondence were contained in the Prison Rules, which were publicly available, together with various Orders and Instructions to prison governors, which were not. The restrictions could not, therefore, be defended as being "in accordance with the law".[64] The second facet of the accessibility requirement is that the law must be comprehensible. It is assumed that the individual will take appropriate legal advice to help him to understand the law,[65] but the extent to which the Court will accept complexity and obscurity in legal regulation may depend upon the resources available to the persons at whom the law is directed. In *Groppera Radio*, for example, the international broadcasting regulations at issue were highly technical and liable to change without obvious warning, but it was assumed that a radio station would have the facilities and resources to keep itself up to date.[66]

Foreseeability

A rule must be formulated with sufficient precision to enable the citizen to **6.36** regulate his conduct in accordance with it. The vagueness of the regime governing telephone tapping was fatal to the Government's defence in *Malone*.[67] The French rules on telephone tapping have also fallen foul of the Convention on this basis.[68] The relevant provisions of the Interception of Communications Act 1985, the new rules which were put in place after the *Malone* decision, survived a challenge on similar grounds in *Christie*.[69] The Act authorises the issue of warrants to monitor telephone

---

[63] *Malone* v *UK*, A/82, (1985) 7 EHRR 14, 46–47.
[64] Above n. 56 at 372.
[65] *Sunday Times* v *UK*, above n. 59 at 271.
[66] *Groppera Radio* v *Switzerland*, above n. 60 at 341–342.
[67] Above n. 62.
[68] See *Huvig* v *France*, A/176-B, (1990) 12 EHRR 528; *Kruslin* v *France*, A/176-A, (1990) 12 EHRR 547.
[69] *Christie* v *UK*, Appl. No. 21482/93, (1994) 78-A D&R 119.

calls on the public network on grounds of national security, detection of serious crime and the protection of the economic well-being of the UK, and the applicant complained that these were too vague. The Commission noted that the requirements of foreseeability were less stringent in the special context of national security. It is not necessary that individuals be able to foresee precisely what checks will be made upon them; they need only have an adequate indication of the basic circumstances in which, and the conditions upon which, surveillance powers will be exercised. Grounds such as "national security" were necessarily flexible and inevitably vague, and the meaning of the various terms had been fleshed out in the reports of the Interception of Communications and Security Services Commissioners.[70] The Commission's rulings were notwithstanding the consistent view of the Court that the interception of telephone calls constitutes a serious interference with private life and correspondence and, as such, has to be "based on a law that was particularly precise, especially as the technology available for use was continually becoming more sophisticated".[71]

6.37   The requirement of foreseeability has implications for discretionary powers: a widely drawn legal power will qualify as a "law" but if the exercise of discretion is unstructured, such that its limits are not clear, the application of the law may not be foreseeable. There must be "sufficient indication of the circumstances in which the discretion will be exercised" either contained within the empowering provision itself, or within supplementary regulations or guidance.[72] The interpretation of statutes and the development of the common law may also be affected: if the law takes a new and unexpected turn it can be argued that its application was not foreseeable. In *Harman*, for example, the applicant was a solicitor who had been found guilty of contempt of court after she had shown to a journalist various documents which had been disclosed in legal proceedings conducted by her and read out in court. She argued that she had been penalised by the English courts for a new species of contempt of court which had not been in existence at the time of her actions and which she could not reasonably have predicted.[73] She had, accordingly, been subjected to a criminal offence with retroactive effect, contrary to Article 7, and her freedom of expression had been restricted in a manner which was not prescribed by law. Her claim was declared admissible by the Commission but then settled out of court.[74]

---

[70] *Ibid.* at 132–135.
[71] See, most recently, *Kopp v Switzerland* A/891, decision of 25 March 1998.
[72] *Silver v UK*, above n. 56 at 00.
[73] *Harman v UK*, Appl. No. 10038/82, (1984) 38 D&R 53.
[74] (1986) 46 D&R 57.

The need for greater flexibility in the law in certain areas is a significant **6.38** fetter on the requirement of foreseeability and, in certain circumstances, may eclipse it altogether. In *Tolstoy*, the applicant complained that it was impossible for him to foresee the extent of the £1.5 m award of damages for libel made against him by the jury in his case. The jury's discretion was, at that point, unfettered by specific legal guidelines and an award could only be overturned on the unlikely grounds that it was capricious, unconscionable or irrational. While the case was pending in Strasbourg, the Court of Appeal, in *Rantzen v MGN*, expressed its own doubts as to whether the existing system of libel awards was justified under Article 10(2), as a prelude to finding that the system should be altered in significant ways.[75] The Court of Human Rights found a breach of Article 10, although not on "prescribed by law" grounds. On that issue, it reasoned that the need to cater for an unlimited range of factual situations meant that the absence of guidelines was an inherent feature of the law of damages for libel. There was, in the circumstances, no requirement that the applicant should be able to anticipate with any degree of certainty the quantum of damages which would be awarded.[76]

In general, the Court appears reluctant to find that the application of a **6.39** law is not foreseeable where, as in the UK, national practice is to refine and develop the law through judicial interpretation.[77] A more interventionist approach would make it very difficult for judges to develop or change the law, particularly the criminal law. This is in line with the Court's non-interventionist approach to retrospective criminal liability under Article 7 of the Convention.[78] Indeed, Article 7 overshadows this aspect of the "prescribed by law" test since a finding that the application of a criminal law was not foreseeable amounts, in effect, to a finding of breach of Article 7 as well.

NECESSARY IN A DEMOCRATIC SOCIETY: SUMMARY

Restrictions imposed upon the rights conferred by Articles 8-11 must, by **6.40** virtue of para. (2) of those articles, be "necessary in a democratic

---

[75] [1994] QB 670, 692–694.
[76] *Tolstoy Miloslavsky v UK*, A/323, (1995) 20 EHRR 442, 469–470.
[77] See, for example, *Sunday Times v UK*, above n. 59 at 270–273.
[78] For example, *SW v UK*, A/335-B, (1996) 21 EHRR 363.

society".[79] The burden is on the state to demonstrate that a restriction is necessary, and necessity must be "convincingly established" (at least in cases brought under Article 10),[80] which, arguably, implies a standard of proof higher than the ordinary civil burden of proof on the balance of probabilities. There is no single word or single sentence which encapsulates the meaning of "necessary". The Court has stated that "necessary" is not so high a standard that it means "indispensable" but nor is it as lax a requirement as "useful", "reasonable" or "desirable".[81] There are, in substance, four elements to the test of necessity:

- the restriction must be necessary to achieve one of the legitimate objectives set out in Articles 8–11(2);
- the restriction must serve a "pressing social need", which is a level of necessity pitched somewhere between "desirable" and "indispensable";
- the restriction must be proportionate to the aim pursued;
- the final judgment as to whether a restriction is "necessary" is subject to the margin of appreciation of states. It may be within the discretion of the state to consider a measure to be necessary, even if the Court disagrees with that assessment.

LEGITIMATE AIMS AND OBJECTIVES

6.41   The list of permissible objectives under each article is exhaustive, and the various heads under which restrictions may be justified will be narrowly interpreted, but in practice this first hurdle rarely proves difficult to overcome. Several of the permitted objectives are inherently broad, for example, the prevention of disorder,[82] and of crime, and the protection of the rights of others. Also, where the Court doubts the strength of the connection between the restriction at issue and the objective cited, it will generally rule that the restriction is disproportionate and so not necessary for the achievement of the objective rather than that the objective

---

[79] A parallel can also be drawn with the requirement in art. 5 that pre-trial detention be "lawful" and not arbitrary: see Murdoch, "Safeguarding the liberty of the person: recent Strasbourg jurisprudence" (1993) 42 ICLQ 494, 499.

[80] *Barthold* v *Germany,* above n. 61 at 403.

[81] *Handyside* v *UK,* A/24, (1979-80) 1 EHRR 737, 754.

[82] Disorder includes disruption of public order but has a wider meaning. It may cover, for example, disruption to the regulation of international telecommunications: *Autronic* v *Switzerland,* A/178, (1990) 12 EHRR 485.

attributed to the restriction is spurious. The objective relied upon may, nevertheless, be relevant to the extent of the margin of appreciation accorded to the respondent state, certain objectives implying a wider margin of appreciation than others (see below).

NECESSITY AND PRESSING SOCIAL NEED

In clear cases, the Court will rule against a measure simply on the grounds **6.42** that it was not "necessary" without relying upon the more sophisticated test of proportionality. Two particular variants of this approach should be noted.

The suitability test

A restriction will be found to be unnecessary where it is patently not **6.43** suitable to achieve its objectives. The best examples of the suitability test have arisen in the context of freedom of expression, where restrictions are often vulnerable to the charge that the damage they seek to prevent has already been done. In the *Spycatcher* cases, the Court was asked to rule upon the legality under Article 10 of injunctions which had been obtained by the Attorney-General against various newspapers, preventing them from publishing extracts from the biography of a former secret service agent, Peter Wright. The Government argued that it had been necessary to restrict freedom of expression on grounds of national security and the Court agreed, but only up to 30 July 1987, the date when the disputed book had been published in the US. After that, the sensitive information which had prompted the intervention of the Attorney-General was in the public domain, and was being imported into this country without restriction. Following the book's publication, the injunctions were "no longer necessary in a democratic society".[83] Another example is *Weber*, where the applicant had been fined under Swiss law for unauthorised disclosure of confidential information. The Court found that the penalty imposed upon him was not necessary because the information in question was already public knowledge at the date when it was disclosed by the applicant.[84]

---

[83] *The Observer and The Guardian* v *UK*, A/216, (1992) 14 EHRR 153, 194–196; *The Sunday Times* v *UK (No. 2)*, A/217, (1992) 14 EHRR 229, 242-244.
[84] *Weber* v *Switzerland*, A/177, (1990) 12 EHRR 508, 523–525.

The least restrictive alternative test

6.44   A measure must impose no greater a restriction than is absolutely necessary to achieve its desired goals. A measure will be adjudged unnecessary and unlawful if a less restrictive measure would have sufficed. This is known in the United States, although not in Strasbourg, as the principle of the least restrictive alternative. A good example is *Campbell* v *UK*, a case concerning the interception of prisoners' correspondence.[85] The applicant complained that the prison authorities had breached Article 8 when they opened and read correspondence with his solicitor, and opened letters to him from the Commission. The Government argued that it was necessary to intercept legal correspondence in order to check that it did not contain prohibited material. According to the Court, the authorities' concerns could have been met by opening letters in the presence of the prisoner; reading them was not necessary, and could only be justified in exceptional circumstances where the contents of a letter were suspected to pose a danger to prison security or the safety of the public.[86] Many would consider the least restrictive alternative principle, properly analysed, to be a component of the proportionality test.[87]

PROPORTIONALITY

6.45   The principle of proportionality requires that the restrictive effects of a measure are strictly in proportion to its legitimate aims and objectives. It plays a vital role in the validation of restrictions upon Convention rights under Articles 8–11 in particular, but is a principle of general application and there is evidence of its influence in the case-law under most if not all of the other substantive articles.[88] The vast majority of defeats suffered by states under Articles 8–11 are explained by the Court on the basis that the measure at issue is disproportionate, sometimes where it might be more obvious to find that a restriction was not in fact imposed for the reasons

---

[85] *Campbell* v *UK*, A/223, (1993) 15 EHRR 137.
[86] *Ibid.* at 161.
[87] Compare the approach of the European Court of Justice: *SPUC* v *Grogan*, Case C-159/90 [1991] ECR I-4685, 4719-20 (per Advocate-General Van Gerven). In fact, the Court of Human Rights has also adopted a least restrictive alternative test under the heading of proportionality: see para. 6.51 below.
[88] See Eissen, "The Principle of Proportionality in the Case-Law of the European Court of Human Rights" in MacDonald, Matscher and Petzold (eds), *The European System for the Protection of Human Rights* (Martinus Nijhoff, 1993).

given by the state, or that it does not serve a pressing social need. Proportionality is an inherently imprecise and malleable concept, and the Court's tendency to use it as a catch-all test of necessity only exacerbates the difficulty of formulating a precise definition. This section will analyse in more detail what is meant when it is said that a measure is disproportionate. The aim is not to provide any guide to the likely outcome of a particular case, but only to establish the analytical framework within which decisions are reached. The facts of the case and the relevant margin of appreciation must be added to the bare bones of the proportionality test before any predictions could be made.

The starting point is to appreciate that the basic principle of proportionality, that the ends must justify the means, is only the headline under which a number of separate but inter-related tests are subsumed. It is possible to identify at least five distinct tests and if a measure falls foul of any one of them, it is liable to be found to be disproportionate. **6.46**

The balancing test

A measure is disproportionate if it imposes restrictions which are not **6.47** justified in the light of the objectives which it seeks to achieve. On that basis, there is no proportionality where the objective of a measure is not sufficiently important to justify the restrictions which it imposes. In *F v Switzerland*, the Swiss Government was called upon to justify a court order which prohibited the applicant from remarrying for one year after his divorce. It argued that the restriction was designed to protect people who might wish to marry the applicant in the future, and indeed to protect the applicant from himself. The Court did not accept that the ban was designed to protect the rights of the applicant's prospective wife and, as to the second ground relied upon, found that paternalistic motivations were not of sufficient weight to justify the imposition of a restraint upon a fully competent adult.[89]

In other cases, the Court has not questioned the importance of the aims **6.48** pursued by a measure but has ruled it to be disproportionate on the basis of the serious effects which it had, or would have, on the applicant. A good example of this approach is *Nasri v France*, one of a series of cases in which the Court has examined the proportionality of immigration decisions which interfere with family life.[90] In *Nasri*, the Court relied upon "an accumulation of special circumstances", notably the fact that the

---

[89] A/128, (1988) 10 EHRR 411, 420–422.
[90] A/324, (1996) 21 EHRR 458.

applicant was deaf and dumb and dependent upon his family for his social development, in finding that it would be disproportionate to deport him.[91] Similarly, in *Dudgeon v UK*, the Government put forward various justifications for the criminalisation of homosexual acts in Northern Ireland. The Court accepted that the relevant law pursued aims which were legitimate under Article 8 but held that it was disproportionate: the justifications were outweighed by the serious detrimental effects caused to homosexuals.[92]

6.49   A third type of situation where a balancing test dictates that the means are disproportionate to the ends is that in which the objectives of a measure could have been achieved even without the restrictions which it imposes. In *Young, James and Webster*, for example, the applicants had been dismissed by British Rail for refusing to join a recognised trade union upon the introduction of a closed shop arrangement.[93] This was held to be an interference with their negative freedom of association, and the Court proceeded to examine whether or not it was a necessary interference. It reviewed the conclusions of a Royal Commission and other surveys of industrial relations practice before finding that the railway unions' objectives of striving for the protection of their members' interests would not have been hampered even in the absence of a power to compel dissenters to join them.[94]

The "relevant and sufficient reasons" test

6.50   A measure will be held disproportionate if it is not supported by "relevant and sufficient reasons". This is the formulation which the Court has preferred in recent cases on freedom of expression under Article 10. In *Goodwin*, for example, it held to be disproportionate an injunction imposed upon a journalist which required him to hand over documents which would reveal his confidential source.[95] The company which obtained the injunction had already succeeded in preventing publication of the story written by the journalist on the basis of the confidential information which he had received. Its residual reasons for pursuing the source of the information were, according to the Court, relevant but not sufficient to justify the restrictions imposed on the freedom of the press.[96]

---

[91] *Ibid*. at 475–477.
[92] A/45, (1982) 4 EHRR 149, 167.
[93] *Young, James and Webster* v *UK*, A/44, (1982) 4 EHRR 38.
[94] *Ibid*. at 57-58.
[95] *Goodwin* v *UK*, Appl. No. 17488/90, (1966) 22 EHRR 123.
[96] *Ibid*. at 145–146; see also *Vogt* v *Germany*, A/323, (1996) 21 EHRR 205.

The test of careful design

The Court will find a restriction to be disproportionate if it is over-broad **6.51** and covers a wider range of situations than is justifiable. In *Open Door Counselling*, the applicant counselling centres complained about an injunction which had been obtained in the Irish courts by the Society for the Protection of Unborn Children preventing them from disseminating information regarding the availability of abortion facilities on the English mainland and elsewhere.[97] The injunction was phrased in absolute terms, prohibiting in perpetuity the provision of information to pregnant women, regardless of their age or state of health or their reasons for seeking counselling on the termination of their pregnancy. The Irish courts had subsequently allowed an exception to the constitutional prohibition on abortion in cases where the life of the mother was in serious danger, and the injunction could not have applied in respect of women who fell within that category. In short, the injunction was "over-broad" and, on that ground alone, disproportionate.[98] Restrictions must, therefore, be carefully tailored to the circumstances and must allow for exceptions where appropriate.

The "essence of the right" test

A restriction can never be justified, and will always be disproportionate, **6.52** where it "impairs the very essence of a right". For example, the temporary ban on re-marriage in *F* v *Switzerland* was found to be disproportionate on the grounds that it impaired the very essence of the right to marry under Article 12.[99]

The evidential test

If the state is unable to produce satisfactory evidence of the pressing **6.53** social need which its restriction seeks to address, the restriction will be disproportionate. In *Kokkinakis*, for example, the applicant was a Jehovah's Witness who had been convicted and fined for proselytism after being invited into a woman's house and engaging in a religious discussion

---

[97] *Open Door Counselling and Dublin Well Woman* v *Ireland*, A/246, (1993) 15 EHRR 244.
[98] *Ibid.* at 266. The Court then also cited a range of additional factors in support of its decision.
[99] Above n. 89.

with her.[100] The Court accepted that his conviction pursued the legitimate aim of protecting the religious rights and freedoms of others but found no evidence that the applicant had exerted any improper pressure which might infringe those rights and freedoms. His conviction was, therefore, disproportionate.[101]

THE MARGIN OF APPRECIATION

6.54 Judicial review of Government decisions in English law is constrained by fundamental constitutional limitations upon the role of the courts. The most basic rule is that judicial review is not an appellate procedure and the courts are not permitted to substitute their opinions for those of the relevant decision-makers.[102] The margin of appreciation of states is the equivalent instrument used by the Court of Human Rights to delimit the boundaries of its supervisory function.[103] The state must convincingly establish that a particular measure is necessary in the interests of a legitimate objective and national decision-makers (whether executive, legislature or courts) are, in principle, in a better position to determine the necessity of a measure than is the international judge. They have a margin of appreciation, an area of discretion within which the Court will not intervene to overturn their judgment. The margin of appreciation is, in short, "the amount of latitude left to national authorities once the appropriate level of review has been decided upon by the Court".[104] Again, it is Articles 8–11 where the margin of appreciation has been most apparent in the case-law of the Court. There is also ample evidence of its application to the prohibition of arbitrary detention under Article 5, the issue of fairness of proceedings under Article 6, discrimination under Article 14, derogation from Convention rights under Article 15 and property rights under Article 1 of the First Protocol. Arguably, like proportionality, it is, in practice, a principle of general application, whether or not it is given its true label in the Court's judgments.

---

[100] *Kokkinakis* v *Greece*, A/260-A, (1994) 17 EHRR 397.

[101] *Ibid.* at 421–422. See also *Socialist Party* v *Turkey,* A/919, decision of 25 May 1998.

[102] See Irvine, "Judges and Decision-Makers: the Theory and Practice of *Wednesbury* Review" [1996] PL 59.

[103] As to the differences between the margin of appreciation doctrine and the basic principles of judicial review, see chapter 2, paras. 2.110–2.121.

[104] MacDonald, "The Margin of Appreciation" in MacDonald, Matscher and Petzold (eds), *The European System for the Protection of Human Rights* (Martinus Nijhoff, 1993), p. 85.

The breadth of the margin of appreciation determines the level of **6.55** intensity with which national decisions will be reviewed by the Court and is the single most important determinant of the prospects of success of a case under the majority of Convention provisions. It will, for that reason, be a vital issue in claims brought under the regime of the Human Rights Act.[105] It is clear that the permitted area of discretion varies from case to case: according to the Court, "the scope of the margin of appreciation is not identical in respect of each of the aims justifying restrictions of a right enshrined in the Convention"[106] and "the scope of the margin of appreciation will vary according to the circumstances, the subject matter and its background".[107] There is, in practice, a spectrum, ranging from extreme deference at one end, to strict control and a willingness to examine very carefully the strength of a given justification at the other.

Unfortunately, the Court has not expounded any coherent theory **6.56** which would enable accurate prediction of where on the spectrum any given case will fall. To some extent, the margin of appreciation is a test of justiciability, an enquiry into how well placed is the Court to second-guess judgments made at national level. Where those judgments concern universal values understood and upheld by the Convention, such as freedom of the press, the Court will be well-placed to intervene and the margin of appreciation is narrow. Conversely, if the subject matter is a moral issue upon which opinions may differ widely from place to place, the notion of a universal, international standard is much more difficult to sustain, and the margin of appreciation will be wider. That, however, is only a partial explanation of the complexities of the case-law on this issue. One of the most distinguished judges of the Court has noted that there is "no common denominator" amongst the various situations where the margin of appreciation has featured.[108] A leading English advocate has accused the Court of using the margin of appreciation as "a substitute for coherent legal analysis of the issues at stake".[109]

With those comments in mind, a general survey of the Court's practice **6.57** on this issue has only limited value. Advice on the effect of the margin of appreciation in a particular case must be based upon the Court's previous practice under the relevant article, and with reference to the particular justification which is likely to be proffered by the state. Even then, it

---

[105] See chapter 2, paras. 2.110–2.121.
[106] *Sunday Times* v *UK*, above, n. 59 at 276.
[107] *Rasmussen* v *Denmark*, A/87, (1985) 7 EHRR 352, 380.
[108] MacDonald, above, n. 104 at 122.
[109] Lord Lester QC, "The European Convention on Human Rights in the New Architecture of Europe" in *Proceedings of the 8th International Colloquy on the European Convention on Human Rights* at p. 236.

should be borne in mind that the interpretation of the Convention is liable to change over time, with changing political and social conditions, and a measure which is within the margin of appreciation in one case, may be outside it in a similar case a few years later. The following chapters on each of the substantive articles of the Convention under which the margin of appreciation has featured will contain a more detailed analysis of the factors likely to widen, or to narrow the margin in a particular case. It is, however, valuable at this stage to note certain factors which will tend to increase or to decrease the intensity with which a measure is reviewed by the Court.

A common European standard?

6.58 An important barometer of the Court's willingness to intervene in any case is the extent to which there is a European consensus on the legal approach to be adopted to the matter before it, and, if there is anything approaching a common approach, whether the restriction in question is consistent or inconsistent with it. The greater the consensus, the less the margin of appreciation which a state has to depart from it. In *Dudgeon,* for example, the Court noted that homosexual acts were not contrary to the criminal law in the vast majority of member-States of the Council of Europe. There was, accordingly, no pressing need for the criminal law to be applied in Northern Ireland.[110] Conversely, in the recent case of *Wingrove* v *UK,* the Court upheld a restriction on freedom of expression based upon the law of blasphemy, rejecting the applicant's submissions that such a law was outmoded and no longer "necessary in a democratic society". Although the application of blasphemy laws in Council of Europe states had become increasingly rare, and several states had recently repealed blasphemy laws altogether, there was insufficient common ground to warrant a finding that such laws were unnecessary in the few states which retained them.[111] Recent case-law on the treatment of transsexuals has also turned on the wide margin of appreciation to be accorded to states given the absence of any consensus on the issue within the domestic legal systems of the members of the Council of Europe.[112]

---

[110] Above n. 24 at 167.

[111] Above n. 25 at 30.

[112] *X, Y and Z* v *UK,* above n. 19. See also *Petrovic* v *Austria,* A/893, [1998] EHRLR 487 (absence of Europe-wide consensus on paternity leave payments).

Moral and religious issues

A wider margin of appreciation is generally available to the state **6.59** authorities when making decisions which are based upon moral value judgments. The Court has frequently held that there is no uniform European conception of morals and that the requirements of morality may vary from time to time and from place to place. As a result, state authorities are, in principle, in a better position than international judges to give an opinion as to the exact content of those requirements and the necessity of a restriction or penalty intended to meet them.[113] On this basis, the applicants in *Handyside* and *Müller* failed in their challenges to the application of obscenity laws to artistic works.[114] Similarly, in *Open Door Counselling*, the Irish Government was afforded a wide margin of appreciation in its handling of the abortion issue although it was found to have overstepped even that.[115] Identical reasoning has been applied in relation to restrictions which aim to protect people from attacks on their religious convictions.[116] The more generous margin of appreciation on moral issues is, however, limited where restrictions impinge upon the intimate private life of individuals. That, at any rate, is one explanation of the Court's intolerance for legal prohibitions upon homosexuality.[117]

Political expression

A great many cases under Article 10 have concerned restrictions upon **6.60** political speech or on debate of questions of public interest — freedom of the press, in broad terms. The Court is firmly convinced of the vital role played by the press in a democratic society and the margin of appreciation in this area is slight, even non-existent. The Court confirmed in *Wingrove* that there would be "little scope" for such restrictions.[118] A paradigm case is, perhaps, *Goodwin* where the Court appeared to allow the House of Lords no margin of appreciation at all when reviewing Their

---

[113] *Handyside* v *UK*, above n. 81 at 753–754; *Müller* v *Switzerland*, A/133, (1991) 13 EHRR 212, 228–229.
[114] *Ibid.*
[115] Above n. 97 at 265.
[116] For example, *Wingrove* v *UK*, above n. 25 at 30–31.
[117] *Dudgeon* v *UK*, above n. 24; *Norris* v *Ireland*, A/142, (1991) 13 EHRR 186; *Modinos* v *Cyprus*, A/259, (1994) 16 EHRR 485.
[118] Above n. 25 at 30.

Lordships decision to uphold the grant of an injunction requiring a journalist to disclose his source.[119]

National security

6.61 The measures which are required in order to safeguard the national security of a state are, in principle, within the margin of appreciation of that state. Not surprisingly, the Court will be very reluctant to overturn the view of the national authorities that a particular measure is "necessary" on those grounds.[120] It will, however, insist upon the provision of adequate safeguards against the abuse of powers exercised in the name of national security.[121]

Positive obligations

6.62 The margin of appreciation is wider where the complaint is that the state authorities have violated their positive obligations to protect individuals from interference with their Convention rights. The Court has held on a number of occasions that positive obligations can be met in a variety of ways and that the choice of means adopted is, in principle, a matter for the state concerned.[122]

Conflict between two Convention rights

6.63 The margin of appreciation is also wider where the subject matter of the complaint concerns the balance which has been struck between two competing Convention rights. For example, private life and freedom of expression come into conflict in the field of press regulation; freedom of artistic expression may impinge upon the rights of others to respect for their religious beliefs. Drawing the line between conflicting rights is always a delicate and controversial matter, the outcome of which is conditioned to a large extent by local and regional political culture. It is therefore primarily a matter for the state concerned, and the Court will be reluctant to intervene.[123]

---

[119] Above n. 23.
[120] Arts. 8–11 all contain specific exceptions on grounds of national security.
[121] See, for example, *Leander* v *Sweden,* A/116, (1987) 9 EHRR 433.
[122] See above, paras. 6.24–6.27.
[123] For example, *Winer* v *UK,* Appl. No. 10871/84, (1986) 48 D&R 154.

The area of national law at issue

The Commission and the Court have declared various areas of legal **6.64** regulation to be within the broad discretion of the national authorities. Broad choices of economic and social policy can only be challenged in Strasbourg in extreme circumstances.[124] Planning law,[125] tax law,[126] and questions of admissibility of evidence[127] are other areas in which the margin of appreciation is wide and the Court will be reluctant to intervene.

4. DISCRIMINATION AFFECTING CONVENTION RIGHTS

Discrimination, particularly on grounds of race, may be sufficiently **6.65** serious as to amount to inhuman and degrading treatment under Article 3.[128] However, Article 3 will only apply in extreme cases. The principal anti-discrimination provision of the Convention is Article 14, which provides:

"The enjoyment of the rights and freedoms set forth in this Convention shall be secured without discrimination on any ground such as sex, race, colour, language, religion, political or other opinion, national or social origin, association with a national minority, property, birth or other status."

Like the principle of effective remedy under Article 13, discrimination **6.66** under Article 14 can only be claimed in conjunction with another Convention right. It does not provide for a general right to equality but only for equal treatment in the exercise of Convention rights. Convention rights, for this purpose, include rights conferred by the Protocols to the Convention which, in the UK, means the rights to property, to education and to free elections, which are conferred by the First Protocol.[128a]

As with Article 13, a claim of discrimination under Article 14 is **6.67** dependent upon the existence of a substantive claim which is within

[124] *Powell and Rayner v UK,* A/172, (1990) 12 EHRR 355; *James v UK,* A/98, (1986) 8 EHRR 123.
[125] *ISKCON v UK,* Appl. No. 20490/92, (1994) 76-A D&R 90, 108.
[126] *National Provincial Building Society and others v UK,* A/845, (1998) 25 EHRR 127, 171.
[127] *Schenk v Switzerland,* A/140, (1991) 13 EHRR 242, 265–266.
[128] See chapter 7, para 7.19.
[128a] The Sixth Protocol on the death penalty was also included in the Human Rights Act and will be ratified in due course.

the scope of the Convention but is not dependent upon that claim for its success: for example, an applicant may bring a claim which is within the scope of Article 8 but which ultimately fails, whilst succeeding in an Article 14 claim. In *Abdullaziz, Cabales and Balkandali*,[129] the applicants were female immigrants to the UK who had been granted indefinite leave to remain and whose husbands had also sought permission to settle in the UK. They complained about the application of the Immigration Rules which made it easier for a foreign wife to join a husband in the UK than for a husband to join his wife. Their claim under Article 8 failed, on the grounds that the right to private life did not encompass a right to live in the country of one's choice, but they succeeded in a claim of sex discrimination under Article 14. Conversely, a finding of a violation under a substantive provision of the Convention does not preclude a further finding of discrimination under Article 14, although, in practice, where the basic substantive claim succeeds, the Court will, generally, not proceed to examine the claim of discrimination.[130]

6.68 Even though Article 14 does not lay down a general principle of equality, it is potentially a very significant addition to domestic discrimination law, for two reasons. First, there is no restriction upon the grounds of discrimination which it covers: certain grounds are mentioned, but Article 14 is expressly non-exhaustive, prohibiting discrimination on grounds "such as" those specified and including a catch-all category of discrimination on grounds of "other status". Domestic law, by contrast, protects against discrimination on only a limited range of grounds: sex, race,[131] disability and, in Northern Ireland, religion.[132] The fact that Article 14 is open-ended means that the grounds upon which an applicant has been discriminated against are not strictly relevant to establishing discrimination but only to assessing the strength of the justification for the difference in treatment (as to which, see below).[133] Secondly, discrimination in the exercise of Convention rights under Article 14 covers a much wider range of subject areas than domestic discrimination law which, in general, is restricted to discrimination in employment and in the provision of goods and services.

---

[129] *Abdullaziz, Cabales and Balkandali v UK,* A/94, (1985) 7 EHRR 471.
[130] For example, *Dudgeon v UK,* above n. 24.
[131] "Race" in the Race Relations Act incorporates discrimination on grounds of nationality and discrimination against certain religious groups.
[132] Directly effective provisions of EC law also prohibit discrimination on grounds of nationality and sex (which includes discrimination against transsexuals).
[133] See, for example, *Rasmussen v Denmark,* above n. 107.

THE DEFINITION OF DISCRIMINATION UNDER ARTICLE 14

Discrimination under Article 14 consists of a difference of treatment in the **6.69** exercise of a right which is within the scope of the Convention and which does not pursue a legitimate objective and/or which has effects which are disproportionate to its objectives.[134] There is a marked contrast with the definition of direct discrimination in English law; in particular, it is notable that direct discrimination is not, in principle, open to justification save where it falls within narrowly defined grounds set out in the relevant statute.[135] English and EC anti-discrimination law also catches indirect discrimination, the imposition of a condition or requirement which is phrased in neutral terms but which has, in practice, a greater adverse impact on one group than on another. Indirect discrimination is open to justification on objective grounds and, under EC law at least, objective justification incorporates a consideration of the proportionality of a measure.[136] It appears that Article 14 does encompass indirect discrimination: the Court has stated that it prohibits rules which have the object of prejudicing a particular section of the population and rules which have that result.[137] However, there has been no decision of the Court which specifically addresses the issue of indirect discrimination and it is not clear whether and to what extent the rules on justification of discrimination differ according to whether the discrimination is direct or indirect.[138]

DIFFERENTIAL TREATMENT

An applicant must show that he has been treated less favourably than **6.70** others who are in a similar or analogous situation,[139] and claims under Article 14 are frequently rejected on the grounds that the suggested

---

[134] *Belgian Linguistics Case,* A/6, (1979–80) 1 EHRR 252, 284.

[135] For example, s. 7 of the Sex Discrimination Act 1975 on genuine occupational qualification.

[136] *Bilka-Kaufhaus* v *Weber von Hartz,* Case 170/84, [1987] ICR 110.

[137] *Marckx* v *Belgium,* A/31, (1979–80) 2 EHRR 330, 346.

[138] Indirect discrimination was raised by dissenting members of the Commission in *Abdullaziz, Cabales and Balkandali* v *UK,* B/77, (1983–85) Com. Rep. 46, but not pursued by the Court.

[139] There is no express requirement that differential treatment be less favourable, rather than more favourable treatment, but in practice complaints arise from treatment which is less favourable.

comparator is not, in fact, in a "relevantly similar" situation. Comparison may be made with others who are in a different category which is analogous to that of the applicant. For example, in *Lindsay v UK*, the applicants, who were co-habitees, sought (unsuccessfully) to compare themselves with married couples.[140] Also, comparison may be made with other members of the same group as the applicant who are receiving different treatment. In *National Provincial Building Society and others v UK*, the applicant building societies, whose restitutionary claims to repayment of unlawfully levied tax were cancelled by retrospective legislation, sought to compare themselves with the Woolwich Building Society, which had won pioneering litigation to establish that the tax had been illegal, and was allowed to recovery the money which it had sought. The Court held, however, that the Woolwich was not in a relevantly similar situation because it had borne the risks and the costs of that litigation whereas the applicants had not.[141] Comparison with other members of the same group is a function of the unlimited range of grounds of discrimination which may be alleged under Article 14 and is a significant departure from the approach of domestic law which does not, in general, permit such comparisons. To take the example of sex discrimination, an employer is free to treat some female employees more favourably than other female employees; it is only male/female discrimination which must be avoided.

6.71   Treatment which differs from that afforded to the applicant's chosen comparators is undoubtedly an independent requirement of discrimination within Article 14. In practice though, this question may be glossed over by the Court at the first stage of the discrimination analysis, only to figure more strongly under the head of justification.[142] The extent to which the alleged comparators are, in truth, in a similar position to that of the applicant is an important element of the justification analysis: the lesser the similarity, the easier to justify will be the less favourable treatment. The requirement that differential treatment has caused detriment to the complainant, which is a fundamental requirement of a discrimination claim in domestic law, is not a separate requirement of Article 14. Again though, the extent to which detriment has been suffered will be relevant to justification.

---

[140] Appl. No. 11089/84, (1986) 49 D&R 181.
[141] Above n. 127 at 174–175; see also *Pine Valley Developments v Ireland*, A/222, (1991) 14 EHRR 319 (property developers).
[142] See Van Dijk and Van Hoof, *Theory and Practice of the European Convention on Human Rights* (Deventer, 1990) at 540.

WITHIN THE SCOPE OF THE CONVENTION

As noted above, discrimination under Article 14 is discrimination in the **6.72**
exercise of a right protected by the Convention. According to the Court,
"there can be no room for [the application of Article 14] unless the facts at
issue fall within the ambit of one or more of [the substantive provisions of
the Convention and the Protocols]."[143] Therefore, Article 14 does not
assist where the discrimination alleged relates to a right or privilege which
is completely outside the scope of the Convention. The two fields covered
by domestic discrimination law, access to, and treatment during employment, and provision of services, would not, in general, be covered by
Article 14 since they do not correspond to any Convention right.[144]

Article 14 may, however, have the effect of significantly extending the **6.73**
scope of state obligations under the Convention. A claim may fail on the
grounds that the state has no duty to secure the right sought by the
applicant, but succeed under Article 14 if the right has, in fact, been
provided but on a discriminatory basis. For example, Article 6 does not
guarantee a right of appeal and so does not require states to provide for
appeal mechanisms; however, Article 14 would bite if the state did, in fact,
provide for appeals, but for some and not others. Similarly, the right to
education under Article 2 of the First Protocol is notoriously restrictive in
the positive obligations which are placed upon the state. There is no duty to
create or provide any particular type of educational provision, but if steps
are taken, the outcome must be even-handed and not discriminatory.

JUSTIFICATION FOR DISCRIMINATION

The next stage of the Article 14 analysis is to ascertain whether the state **6.74**
can establish an "objective and reasonable justification" for the differential treatment. As under the substantive provisions of the Convention
(in particular, Articles 8–11), states enjoy a margin of appreciation in
assessing whether and to what extent differences between otherwise
similar or comparable situations justify a different treatment in law, a
margin which varies according to the particular circumstances of the case.

---

[143] See, for example, *Abdullaziz, Cabales and Balkandali* v *UK,* above n. 130 at 499.
[144] Although discrimination in those fields on certain grounds, for example, on grounds of sexuality,
    may impinge upon the right to respect for private life under Art. 8.

6.75   The state must show, first, that the differences in treatment are directed at a legitimate aim. Unlike para. 2 of Articles 8–11, Article 14 does not lay down an exhaustive list of acceptable aims but just as states rarely fail to establish a legitimate objective when limiting rights to private life, freedom of religion, etc. so it seems equally easy to surmount this hurdle under Article 14. An isolated instance of a claim succeeding at this stage is *Darby* v *Sweden,* where the respondent state failed to cite an objective for a taxation policy which discriminated against non-residents.[145] The real reason for the policy was administrative convenience.

6.76   The aim of redressing a pre-existing situation of inequality has been accepted as a legitimate objective of differential treatment. Therefore, positive discrimination is, in principle, permitted under Article 14. The Court recognised, in the *Belgian Linguistics* case, that not all instances of differential treatment are unacceptable and that "certain legal inequalities tend only to correct factual inequalities".[146] Therefore, for example, a protected quota of university places for members of a particular racial group could result in discrimination within the ambit of a Convention right (the right to education under Article 2 of the First Protocol) but would not, in principle, breach Article 14 if it had the objective and reasonable justification of increasing the disproportionately low percentage of members of that disadvantaged group in the university student population. However, the Court has not gone so far as to rule that Article 14 *requires* states to engage in positive discrimination in order to remedy inequality.[147]

6.77   Differential treatment which has a legitimate aim will nevertheless fall foul of Article 14 if the impact of the treatment goes beyond what is justified by the aim sought to be achieved. This is akin to the necessity test in para. 2 of Articles 8–11 and, like that test, incorporates an assessment of proportionality, and of the state's margin of appreciation. The Court will consider the type of discrimination at issue: certain forms of discrimination are treated as particularly serious and must be justified by "weighty reasons". So far, sex discrimination, race discrimination, discrimination against illegitimate children and discrimination on grounds of nationality fall within this category.[148] A related issue is the extent to which there exists a European consensus on a particular issue: the greater the

---

[145] A/187, (1994) 18 EHRR 513.
[146] Above n. 135 at 284.
[147] Compare the analogous position under the EC Equal Treatment Directive: *Marschall* v *Land Nordrhein-Westfalen,* Case C-409/95, [1997] ECR I-6363.
[148] *Schmidt* v *Germany,* A/291-B, (1994) 18 EHRR 513 (sex); *East African Asian Cases,* Appl. No. 4403/70 (1970) 13 *Yearbook* 929 (race): *Inze* v *Austria,* A/126, (1988) 10 EHRR 394 (illegitimacy); *Gaygusuz* v *Austria,* Appl. No. 17371/90, (1997) 23 EHRR 364 (nationality).

consensus, the more difficult to justify will be the differential treatment. In *Petrovic* v *Austria*, for example, the applicant complained that the refusal of the authorities to grant him a paternity leave allowance amounted to unlawful sex discrimination, since his wife was eligible for a maternity leave allowance. It was a blatant case of discrimination, and discrimination of a type which must usually be justified by weighty reasons. However, the Court rejected the claim on the grounds that there was not yet a sufficient European-wide consensus on the issue of paternity leave, and Austria was in fact one of the most progressive states in that regard.[149] The degree of hardship imposed by the differential treatment is relevant, as is the extent of the similarity between the applicant and his chosen comparators. Reference should also be made to the various factors which go to demarcate the margin of appreciation under Articles 8–11.[150]

5. THE RIGHT TO AN EFFECTIVE REMEDY

Article 13 provides: **6.78**

"Everyone whose rights and freedoms as set forth in this Convention are violated shall have an effective remedy before a national authority notwithstanding that the violation has been committed by persons acting in an official capacity."

The right to an effective remedy before a national authority reflects the basic principle underlying the Convention system, that Convention rights are intended to be given effect in national law. Individuals will then be able to vindicate their rights in domestic courts and tribunals and recourse to Strasbourg becomes a matter of last resort in exceptional cases. The Human Rights Act is, of course, intended precisely to enable claimants to give effect to their Convention rights in the domestic courts and the Government view at the time of the passage of the legislation was that the Act would in itself preclude all possible claims under Article 13. That at least was its explanation for why Article 13 was excluded from the list of Convention rights which are to be incorporated by the Human Rights Act into English law.[151]

---

[149] Above n. 112. Compare *Van Raalte* v *The Netherlands*, A/732, [1997] EHRLR 449.
[150] Above, paras 6.54–6.64.
[151] HRA s. 1(a): HC Debs., 20 May 1998, col. 979.

"REMEDY BEFORE A NATIONAL AUTHORITY"

6.79   The notion of a remedy under Article 13 is not restricted to judicial remedies but extends to any legal mechanism which might provide redress. Recourse to Parliamentary committees, members of the executive and ombudsmen could all be relied upon to show compliance with Article 13. Nor is it necessary that one single remedy satisfies the requirement of effectiveness — the Court will take account of the cumulative effect of all available avenues of recourse. The case of *Silver* v *UK*,[152] which concerned the right of a prisoner under Article 8 to respect for his correspondence, is a good illustration of the wide scope of Article 13. The Government argued that redress regarding the interception of a letter from the applicant to his legal advisor could be obtained from the Board of Visitors of the Prison, the Ombudsman, by petition to the Home Secretary and by judicial review. The Court found that the four remedies, taken together, satisfied the demands of Article 13.[153]

THE REQUIREMENT OF EFFECTIVENESS

6.80   It is well-established that Article 13 does not go so far as to require that the Convention is actually implemented into domestic law, or that national legislation is subject to judicial review on the basis of inconsistency with the Convention. Such action is, however, the most direct and obvious way of meeting the demands of Article 13. A small number of states, including the UK, which chose not to incorporate the Convention into their domestic law, have therefore given rise to the vast majority of case-law under Article 13. Where a claim is made that national law lacked an effective remedy, it is for the Government to put forward a remedy or remedies which it considers to be effective; the burden then shifts to the applicant to disprove that contention.

6.81   The Court has given a certain amount of guidance as to when a remedy will amount to an effective remedy under Article 13.

---

[152] Above n. 56.
[153] See also *Leander* v *Sweden,* above n. 121.

- Article 13 does not require that the Convention can be raised directly in opposition to a domestic measure, only that the substance of the applicant's Convention rights can be canvassed before a domestic court or tribunal. In *Soering*, the Government succeeded in persuading the Court that this could be done in judicial review proceedings, by arguing that a decision is irrational because it breaches the Convention.[154]

- The remedy or remedies put forward by the state as effective remedies must offer the possibility of a legally enforceable decision, but it is not necessary that the applicant be likely to succeed on the facts of his case.[155] In *Leander*, the Court made an exception to this rule where a non-binding recommendation only could be obtained, but such recommendations were usually followed in practice.[156]

- The body or bodies alleged to provide an effective remedy must be "sufficiently independent".[157] In *Silver*, one of the remedies put forward as open to use by an aggrieved prisoner was that of petition to the Home Secretary. The Court held that insofar as a complaint concerned the scope of prison governors' powers to intercept correspondence, the Home Secretary was not sufficiently independent because he was the author of the relevant directives. However, there would be no difficulty if the complaint was that one of his directives had been implemented incorrectly.[158]

- The demands of Article 13 will vary according to the substantive right in connection with which it is claimed. For example, remedies for infringement of privacy by the surveillance activities of the security services must necessarily be limited if the surveillance is to achieve its objectives, and cannot include prior notification of the target in order that a challenge may be brought.[159]

- The reference at the end of Article 13 to acts committed by persons acting in an official capacity appears to prevent the application of any principle of immunity from suit to prevent the consideration of claims to Convention rights.

---

[154] *Soering* v *UK*, A/161, (1989) 11 EHRR 439, 481–482; see also *Vilvarajah* v *UK*, A/215, (1992) 14 EHRR 248, 292.

[155] *Murray* v *UK*, A/300-A, (1995) 19 EHRR 193, 236; *Pine Valley Development* v *Ireland*, A/222, (1992) 14 EHRR 319, 358–359.

[156] *Leander* v *Sweden*, above n. 121.

[157] *Silver* v *UK*, above n. 56 at 381–392; see also the requirement of independence under Art. 6, chapter 8, paras. 9.58–9.60

[158] *Ibid.* at 382.

[159] *Klass* v *Germany*, A/28, (1979–80) 2 EHRR 214.

RELATIONSHIP WITH OTHER PROVISIONS OF THE CONVENTION

6.82   The relationship between Article 13 and other substantive provisions of the Convention is complex and at times rather difficult to understand. Article 13 does not, in spite of its clear wording, require an applicant to establish that he is a victim of a violation of a Convention right, but only that he has an "arguable claim" to another Convention right.[160] A claim to an effective remedy is, therefore, subsidiary to a substantive claim under, say, Article 8 or 10, but is not dependent upon that claim for its success: an applicant may bring a claim under Article 8 which is arguable but ultimately fails, whilst succeeding in an Article 13 claim. The Court has refused to expand upon the meaning of "an arguable claim" but has stated that a claim which is rejected by the Commission at the admissibility stage on the grounds that it is manifestly ill-founded cannot be considered to be arguable.[161] The converse must also be true: a claim which is declared admissible by the Commission is arguable for the purposes of Article 13.

6.83   The rule that Article 13 does not require that national legislation be subject to legal challenge means that a complaint about the lack of protection in national law for a Convention right may fall outside the scope of Article 13. In *Murray*, one of the applicants complained about the taking of her photograph without her consent whilst she was in police custody, and the retention of it on police files. The lack of recourse in domestic law to a right of privacy which might have protected her against this was characterised by the Court as a challenge to the content of national law which could only be brought under Article 8 and not Article 13.[162] However, *Murray* is difficult to reconcile with the later case of *Halford*, where the applicant's claim was equally that there was no domestic legal regulation of privacy, this time in relation to the monitoring of phone calls made on her office phone. The Court found a violation of Article 13: the absence of legal regulation meant that the applicant was unable to seek redress at national level.[163]

6.84   A successful claim under a substantive provision of the Convention may render Article 13 otiose. Article 5(4), for example, requires that persons detained be allowed to bring proceedings to challenge the lawfulness of

---

[160] *Silver v UK*, above n. 56 at 381.
[161] *Powell and Rayner v UK*, above n. 124
[162] *Murray v UK*, above n. 155.
[163] *Halford v UK*, A/773, (1997) 24 EHRR 523, 547–548.

their detention, and imposes stronger procedural obligations than Article 13. Therefore, where the Court finds a violation of Article 5(4) it will not proceed to examine whether there has been a breach of Article 13 as well.[164] Finally, there is an overlap between Article 13, on the right to an effective domestic remedy and Article 26 which requires that individuals exhaust their domestic remedies before bringing a claim. The obligation of exhaustion only applies to domestic remedies which are "effective", but caution is necessary since the notion of an effective remedy is not identical under the two provisions. For example, a judicial remedy is not effective under Article 26, and need not be exhausted, if it offers the applicant little or no prospect of success. Under Article 13, however, it is sufficient that such a remedy exists even if it would not have helped the applicant on the facts of his case.[165]

THE EFFECT OF THE HUMAN RIGHTS ACT ON ARTICLE 13 CLAIMS

The incorporation of the Convention into domestic law by the Human Rights Act ought to go a long way towards meeting the demands of Article 13. Article 13 requires only that the substance of a claim to rights under the Convention can be canvassed in a forum with the power to take binding decisions, and the Act will enable such claims to be litigated in the domestic courts. The Act's most notable limitation on the effect of Convention rights, the rule that clear statutory provisions must always prevail, should not cause a problem under Article 13 since, as noted above, the latter does not require that legislation be subject to judicial review on the grounds of conflict with Convention rights. Nevertheless, it is significant that the declaration of incompatibility the only remedy available in cases of inconsistent primary legislation has no legal effect as between the parties. It is impossible to say, however, whether the Act is a complete answer to the requirements of Article 13. The historical evidence shows that Article 13 has given rise to some claims, albeit a small minority, from states where the Convention is incorporated into domestic law. Moreover, it remains to be seen how important provisions of the Act will be interpreted and applied by English judges and so just how effective domestic law remedies will be after the Act has come into force.

6.85

---

[164] For example, *De Wilde, Ooms and Versyp* v Belgium, A/12, (1979–80) 1 EHRR 438.
[165] *Murray* v *UK,* above n. 155; *Pine Valley Developments* v *Ireland,* above n. 139.

6. EXPRESS PERMISSIONS TO LIMIT CONVENTION RIGHTS

6.86 Convention rights are subject to limitation in a variety of ways. Some have express limitations in their text;[166] the Court has found within others implied limitations;[167] others are inherently limited by virtue of a restrictive definition of their key terms.[168] This section is concerned with certain specific articles of the Convention which make express provision for Convention rights to be restricted or ignored by states in particular circumstances.

DEROGATION IN TIME OF WAR OR PUBLIC EMERGENCY

6.87 Article 15 provides:

> "1. In time of war or other public emergency threatening the life of the nation any High Contracting Party may take measures derogating from its obligations under this Convention to the extent strictly required by the exigencies of the situation, provided that such measures are not inconsistent with its other obligations under international law.

> 2. No derogation from Article 2, except in respect of deaths resulting from lawful acts of war, or from Articles 3, 4 (paragraph 1) and 7 shall be made under this provision.

> 3. Any High Contracting Party availing itself of this right of derogation shall keep the Secretary General of the Council of Europe fully informed of the measures which it has taken and the reasons therefor. It shall also inform the Secretary General of the Council of Europe when such measures have ceased to operate and the provisions of the Convention are again being fully executed."

Under this provision, certain Convention rights may be suspended in time of war or public emergency, provided that certain conditions regarding notification are complied with. The right to life (other than where it is violated by a lawful act of war) and the rights against inhuman and degrading treatment, slavery and servitude, and retrospective criminal legislation, are non-derogable. So far as the UK is concerned, the power to derogate under Article 15 has only been relevant in the context

---

[166] Arts. 2, 4, 5, 8-11 and Art. 1 of the First Protocol.
[167] Arts. 6 and 1-2 of the First Protocol.
[168] For example, Arts. 3 and 14.

of the political situation in Northern Ireland and even then only to events occurring in Northern Ireland itself, not on the mainland.[169] Counter-terrorism measures in Great Britain have, however, been upheld under other substantive provisions of the Convention.[170]

A public emergency falling within Article 15(1) is defined by the Court as "an exceptional situation of crisis or emergency which affects the whole population and constitutes a threat to the organised life of the community of which the state is composed".[171] Whether a public emergency exists is ultimately a matter for the Commission and the Court, but states are accorded a wide margin of appreciation on this point. Whilst the intensity of political violence in Northern Ireland has fluctuated dramatically in recent years, it is, in practice, very unlikely that the Government's judgment as to the existence of a public emergency there would be overturned. Derogation is only permitted "to the extent strictly required by the exigencies of the situation". This limitation involves consideration, first, of whether emergency measures are needed at all. If they are needed, they must be proportionate and the Court will examine whether less restrictive measures could have been taken instead. Again, states have a wide margin of appreciation in deciding what is necessary to meet the demands of the public emer-gency.[172] In *Brogan*, the Court found against the UK on the issue of extended periods of detention without charge or production before a magistrate which were applicable by virtue of s. 12 of the Prevention of Terrorism Act.[173] No Article 15 derogation was then in force and the detention of the applicants was found to breach Article 5 of the Conven-tion. Rather than changing the law so as to shorten the permitted period of detention, the Government notified a new derogation, the validity of which was upheld by the Court in *Brannigan and McBride*. The derogation remains in force, and specific provision for its application in the UK is made in ss. 1(2), 14 and 16 of the Human Rights Act.[174]

6.88

The reference in Article 15(3) to emergency measures being "not inconsistent with [a state's] other obligations under international law" means that Article 15 should not be taken as excusing a state from complying with other, stricter standards of justification for the introduc-tion of such measures under other treaties to which it is a party.[175] In

6.89

---

[169] See *McVeigh, O'Neill and Evans* v *UK*, Appl. No. 8022/77, (1982) 25 D&R 15.
[170] See, for example, *Brind and McLaughlin* v *UK*, Appl. No. 18714/91, (1994), 77-A D&R 42.
[171] *Lawless* v *Ireland*, A/3, (1979–80) 1 EHRR 15, 31-32.
[172] See *Brannigan and McBride* v *UK*, A/253-B, (1994) 17 EHRR 539, 569-570.
[173] *Brogan and others* v *UK*, A/145-B, (1989) 11 EHRR 117.
[174] Its text is reprinted in Part 1 of Schedule 2 to the Act (Appendix I below).
[175] See also Art. 60 of the Convention.

Brannigan and McBride, it was argued that the Government had not, in introducing its new derogation, officially proclaimed a public emergency as required by Article 4 of the International Covenant on Civil and Political Rights. The Government did not accept that Article 4 did require an official proclamation but the Court found, without presuming to resolve the dispute, that a statement by the Home Secretary to the House of Commons counted as a sufficient proclamation.[176] Pursuant to Article 15(3), states must notify the Secretary-General of the Council of Europe when they have taken measures in exercise of its right of derogation, the reasons for those measures, and when the measures have been lifted. Notification is not a pre-condition for the validity of such measures — they may have legal force even before they are notified — but measures should be notified without delay.[177]

6.90   Under the Human Rights Act, Article 5 of the Convention is to take effect within the UK subject to the terms of the current derogation. Section 1(2) of the Act provides that Convention rights are to have effect subject to designated derogations, defined by s. 14 to include the current derogation and any future derogation which is adopted in accordance with the requisite Parliamentary procedure. A renewable time-limit of five years is placed on the effect of the current derogation and of any future derogation.[178]

POLITICAL ACTIVITIES OF FOREIGNERS

6.91   Article 16 states:

"Nothing in Articles 10, 11 and 14 shall be regarded as preventing the High Contracting Parties from imposing restrictions on the political activities of aliens."

This provision is targeted specifically at the political rights conferred by the freedoms of expression and association, and the prohibition upon discrimination. It would not justify restrictions on the rights conferred by Articles 10 and 11 insofar as they are relied upon for non-political purposes. Other provisions of the Convention may permit states to adopt special rules for foreigners: Article 3 of the First Protocol, for example, may allow restrictions upon the rights of foreigners to stand and

---

[176] *Brannigan and McBride v UK,* above n. 172 at 576–577.
[177] *Lawless v Ireland,* above n. 171 at 36–37.
[178] HRA s. 16.

to vote in elections to the legislature. In general, however, discrimination on grounds of nationality will be particularly difficult to justify.[179]

Article 16 reflects an international law perception of the status of foreigners which has arguably been superseded, at least within Europe, by the political and economic integration brought about by the European Union and the European Economic Area. The Parliamentary Assembly of the Council of Europe has called for its abolition.[180] It has only been considered by the Court on one occasion, when the term "alien" was given a very narrow interpretation. In *Piermont* v *France*, a German member of the European Parliament was expelled from French territory in the South Pacific after taking part in anti-Government demonstrations. The Court held that her status as a national of an EU Member State, and as an MEP, meant that Article 16 could not be raised against her.[181] The status of "citizen" conferred upon nationals of EU states by Article 8 of the Treaty of European Union, and the Europe Agreements concluded between the EU and the countries of Eastern European will only reinforce that view, and deprive Article 16 of much of its force so far as European nationals are concerned.

6.92

ABUSE OF RIGHTS

Article 17 provides:

6.93

"Nothing in this Convention may be interpreted as implying for any state, group or person any right to engage in any activity or perform any act aimed at the destruction of any of the rights and freedoms set forth herein or at their limitation to a greater extent than is provided for in the Convention."

This provision has, principally, been invoked to justify measures taken against anti-democratic political activists which might not be justifiable under the express limitations of Articles 8–11(2). It has never been invoked by the UK. Two limitations upon the scope of Article 17 should be noted. First, it allows restrictions only upon those rights which are used in order to destroy or limit the Convention rights of others, typically rights to private life and to freedom of expression and association. It could not justify, for example, removal of due process guarantees under Articles 5 and 6

---

[179] See *Gaygusuz* v *Austria*, above n. 146.
[180] Recommendation 799 (1977) on the Political Rights and Position of Aliens, 25 January 1977.
[181] Above n. 9.

because these rights are used to protect the individual himself rather than to subvert the rights of others.[182] Secondly, any measures which are sought to be justified under Article 17 must be strictly proportionate to the perceived threat to the Convention rights of others.[182a]

ABUSE OF POWER TO RESTRICT CONVENTION RIGHTS

6.94   Article 18 states:

"The restrictions permitted under this Convention to the said rights and freedoms shall not be applied for any purpose other than those for which they have been prescribed."

This provision, which is analogous to the improper purpose ground of judicial review in English public law,[183] must be relied upon in conjunction with a substantive right under the Convention upon which limitations are permitted. It establishes that a legitimate ground of restriction cannot be used as a pretext for a measure which is really aimed at another, improper purpose. A good example of the potential application of Article 18 is that of prisoners's rights, which may be restricted under Article 8 so as to prevent disorder or crime, but may not be limited as a means of punishing the individual concerned. However, Article 18 probably adds little to the substantive provisions of the Convention: if punishment of the prisoner is the real motive there will most likely be a breach of Article 8 on its own, regardless of Article 18. No complaint under Article 18 has ever been upheld, due in large part to difficulties in gathering sufficient evidence of bad faith on the part of the authorities.

RESERVATIONS TO THE CONVENTION

6.95   Article 64(1) provides:

"1. Any State may, when signing this Convention or when depositing its instrument of ratification, make a reservation in respect of any particular provision of the Convention to

---

[182] *Lawless* v *Ireland,* above n. 171 at 22.
[182a] See, recently, *Lehideut* v *France* A/996, decision of 23 September 1998, in which the Court adopted a narrow interpretation of, and declined to apply, Art. 17.
[183] *Padfield* v *Minister of Agriculture* [1968] AC 997.

the extent that any law then in force in its territory is not in conformity with the provision. Reservations of a general character shall not be permitted under this Article.

2. Any reservation made under this Article shall contain a brief statement of the law concerned."

A distinction should be drawn between a failure to ratify the Convention or a protocol to it, and reservations in respect of those provisions which have been ratified. The UK has avoided the effect of, for example, the free movement rights conferred by the Fourth and Seventh Protocols to the Convention by refusing to ratify them. It has submitted only one, partial reservation to the provisions which it has ratified, in respect of Article 2(2) of the First Protocol on the right of parents to have their children educated in accordance with their religious and philosophical convictions. That reservation is discussed further in chapter 15. As with derogations, the Human Rights Act makes provision for the application of the UK's reservation to Article 2 of the First Protocol, for the making of reservations in the future and for the periodic review of any reservation currently in force.[184]

7. FURTHER READING

Clapham, "The *Drittwirkung* of the Convention" in MacDonald, Matscher and Petzold (eds), *The European System for the Protection of Human Rights* (Kluwer, 1993)

Klug, "The concept of an arguable claim under Article 13 of the European Convention on Human Rights" (1990) 39 ICLQ 891

Lavender, "The problem of the margin of appreciation" [1997] EHRLR 380

Mahoney, "Universality versus subsidiarity in the Strasbourg case law on free speech: explaining some recent judgments" [1997] EHRLR 364

---

[184] HRA ss. 1(2), 15 and 17.

Chapter 7

THE RIGHT TO LIFE AND PHYSICAL INTEGRITY

1. THE RIGHT TO LIFE

Article 2 of the Convention provides: **7.1**

1. Everyone's right to life shall be protected by law. No one shall be deprived of his life intentionally save in the execution of a sentence of a court following his conviction of a crime for which this penalty is provided by law.

2. Deprivation of life shall not be regarded as inflicted in contravention of this article when it results from the use of force which is no more than absolutely necessary:

   (a) in defence of any person from unlawful violence;
   (b) in order to eect a lawful arrest or to prevent the escape of a person lawfully detained;
   (c) in action lawfully taken for the purpose of quelling a riot or insurrection.

Article 2 protects the most fundamental right of all, the right to life. Its starting point is that the state must not take life intentionally, and it must protect by law the lives of its citizens. Four exceptions are laid down within Article 2 itself, the death penalty in Article 2(1) and, in Article 2(2), three instances of justified killing before arrest or trial. Most other provisions of the Convention have their own express exceptions and can, in addition, be subject to the power of derogation in time of public emergency under Article 15.[1] However, the right to life is non-derogable — no further exceptions are permitted.

---

[1] See chapter 6, paras. 6.87–6.90 on the power of derogation under Art. 15.

7.2   There is relatively little substantive case-law under Article 2. The leading cases, indeed the only cases in which it has been directly addressed by the Court of Human Rights, are *McCann, Savage and Farrell* v *UK*, concerning the killing by the British army of three IRA personnel in Gibraltar and *Osman* v *UK*, where complaint was made that the police had not taken adequate steps to protect the right to life.[2] Controversial moral and legal subjects, such as abortion and euthanasia, clearly raise important issues under Article 2 but have, as yet, only been considered by the Commission, not the Court.

2. PROTECTING THE RIGHT TO LIFE

7.3   The obligation of states under Article 2(1) is to protect by law the right to life. At the most basic level of the state's relations with its citizens, Article 2 dictates that the forces or agents of the state may not take life, whether intentionally or unintentionally,[3] save in the exceptional circumstances listed in Article 2(2). There are also procedural obligations: there must be "some form of effective official investigation" where someone has died as a result of use of force by agents of the state.[4] In *McCann*, the applicants criticised the inquest into the killings which was held in Gibraltar; the Court found, however, that the lengthy and detailed proceedings in that case were sufficient.[5]

7.4   Article 2(1) also goes further, in imposing some degree of positive obligation upon the state to take steps to safeguard the lives of its citizens. The most obvious legal step is to outlaw killing, and, as in Britain, to subject it to criminal and civil sanctions. However, two areas of controversy arise. First, who has the right to life? Article 2(1) says "everyone", but does that include, for example, foetuses and persons in a persistent vegetative state. Secondly, how broad is the state's obligation to protect life? Risk to life arises from a wide range of factors at large in society — crime, roads, disease, etc. — but does the state have to protect us against all of those things?

ABORTION

7.5   The Commission has not excluded the possibility that a foetus can be a person benefiting from the right to life under Article 2. However, if it can

---

[2] A/324, (1996) 21 EHRR 97; A/1017, decision of 28 October 1998.
[3] *Ibid.* at 160.
[4] *Ibid.* at 163.
[5] *Ibid.* at 164.

so benefit, its rights would be subject to implied limitations, for example, in the interests of the health of its mother.[6] There is, accordingly, no breach of Article 2 where an abortion is carried out after ten weeks of pregnancy and to avert the risk of injury to the health of the mother;[7] nor where the foetus is 14 weeks' old and the abortion is carried out so as to avoid placing the mother in "a difficult situation of life".[8] Conversely, there is no absolute right to an abortion.[9] The Commission has, in truth, sought to avoid laying down any principle of general application. It recognises that the regulation of foetal life is a sensitive area and that practice differs widely from state to state. It would, probably, need a case with extreme facts to prompt a finding of breach of Article 2 in the future.

EUTHANASIA

Two forms of euthanasia should be distinguished: passive euthanasia, or euthanasia by omission, where life-prolonging treatment is withheld, and active euthanasia, whereby active steps are taken to bring about the death of a person whose life was not immediately dependent on the continuation of medical treatment. The former is permitted, in certain circumstances, under English law,[10] and the Commission has held that it is no breach of Article 2 to allow death to occur in this way.[11] Active euthanasia is not permitted in England although it is generally treated with leniency by the courts. It may be contrary to Article 2 to permit active euthanasia, since there is no express exception within Article 2 for killing by consent. Given that active euthanasia is permitted and widely practised in Holland, it may be only a matter of time before the issue comes before the Commission and/or the Court.

7.6

OTHER RISK TO LIFE

The imposition of obligations upon the state to protect its citizens from other dangers to life clearly has major political implications, given scarce

7.7

---

[6] *Paton* v *UK*, Appl. No. 8416/78. (1980) 3 EHRR 408, 415.
[7] *Ibid.*
[8] *H* v *Norway*, Appl. No. 17004/90 (unreported).
[9] See *Brüggemann and Scheuten* v *Germany*, Appl. No. 6959/75, (1978) 10 D&R 100.
[10] *Airedale NHS Trust* v *Bland* [1993] AC 789.
[11] *Widmer* v *Switzerland*, Appl. No. 20527/92 (unreported).

resources and differing ideological views as to the appropriate extent of state intervention in society. The Commission is of the view that the state must take "appropriate steps to safeguard life".[12] In an early case brought by an applicant who feared that he was a target for terrorist attack, the Commission held that the state is not obliged to provide *indefinite* protection for someone who is at risk of being murdered.[13] Article 2 implies positive preventive measures but not the prevention of every possibility of violence.[14] These principles were recently applied in *Osman* v *UK*, where the applicants complained that the police failed to take adequate steps to protect their family from murderous attack. The second applicant was seriously injured and his father killed by a former teacher at his school who had given various indications of mental instability and violent intention towards him. The Court confirmed that the Convention could impose a positive obligation on the authorities to take preventive operational measures to protect an individual whose life was at risk from the criminal acts of another individual. The scope of that obligation was, however, subject to various limiting considerations, including that of prioritising scarce resources, with the result that not every claimed risk to life could trigger it. In the applicants' case, the police did not have sufficient knowledge of a real and immediate risk to life as to warrant a finding of breach of Article 2. The Court was also concerned that the police should not be encouraged to act too easily to restrict the liberty of potential criminals.[15]

7.8   Other notable Commission decisions on Article 2 include the following:

- Prison conditions giving rise to serious illness may breach Article 2.[16]
- It may breach Article 2 to permit the eviction of someone whose health may be seriously endangered as a result.[17]
- A state-run vaccination scheme which results in the death of some children does not breach Article 2 if it is carried out with appropriate safeguards.[18]

---

[12] *Association X* v *UK*, Appl. No. 7154/75, (1979) 14 D&R 31, 32.
[13] *X* v *Ireland*, Appl. No. 6040/73, (1973) 16 *Yearbook* 388.
[14] *W* v *UK*, Appl. No. 9348/81, (1983) 32 D&R 190.
[15] Above, n. 1.
[16] *Simon-Herold* v *Austria*, Appl. No. 4340/69, (1971) 14 *Yearbook* 352.
[17] *X* v *Germany*, Appl. No. 5207/71, (1971) 14 *Yearbook* 698.
[18] *Association X* v *UK*, above n. 12. See, further, O'Sullivan, "The allocation of scarce resources and the right to life under the European Convention of Human Rights" [1998] PL 389.

3. EXCEPTIONS TO THE RIGHT TO LIFE

The death penalty is of very limited relevance in the UK.[19] Article 2(1) **7.9**
permits the death penalty but is subject to the Sixth Protocol to the
Convention, which requires its abolition save in relation to certain war-
time offences. The Sixth Protocol has been included within the Human
Rights Act and will require to be ratified by the UK in due course.[20] The
three express exceptions in Article 2(2), covering the use of force in self-
defence or in the defence of others from unlawful violence, to effect a
lawful arrest or prevent the escape of a person lawfully detained and to
quell a riot or insurrection, constitute an exhaustive list and are to be
narrowly interpreted.[21] In each case, the force used by the agents of the
state must be no more than absolutely necessary in the circumstances.
This is said to be a stricter and more compelling test of necessity than the
phrase "necessary in a democratic society" which appears in Articles 8-11
of the Convention. It implies, in particular, that the force used must be
strictly proportionate to the aims and objectives of the use of force, having
regard to the nature of the aim pursued, the dangers to life and limb
inherent in the situation and the degree of risk that the force employed
might result in loss of life.[22]

Arguably, Article 2 allows little margin for error and there is a potential **7.10**
for conflict between the Convention and English law, which is much more
indulgent of the person using force. It allows "reasonable force" to be
used,[23] and attaches considerable weight to the opinion of the aggressor
that the amount of force used was reasonable.[24] Nor does Article 2 reflect
the authorisation in s. 3 of the Criminal Law Act 1967 that force may be
used in the prevention of crime, although this is, in effect, covered by the
exceptions for unlawful violence and lawful arrest.

In *McCann*, the IRA members had been confronted and killed on the **7.11**
basis that they were carrying a remote control device which could be used
instantaneously to detonate a car-bomb causing large-scale loss of life. In
fact, British intelligence was defective and there was neither a bomb nor a
remote-control device; indeed, the suspects were not even armed. The
Court found that the operation of the s. 2(2) exceptions was not precluded
altogether where a person is killed on the basis of an honest belief which

---

[19] It does still exist, for example, for some military offences committed in time of war.
[20] HRA s. 1(1)(c).
[21] *Stewart v UK*, Appl. No. 10044/82, (1984) 39 D&R 162.
[22] *Ibid.* at 169; *McCann v UK*, above n. 2 at 160–161.
[23] Section 3 of the Criminal Law Act 1967 and s. 117 of the Police and Criminal Evidence Act 1984.
[24] *Palmer v R* [1981] AC 814.

turns out to be mistaken. However, an operation such as this (designed to prevent the use of unlawful violence and to effect an arrest) must be planned so as to minimise recourse to lethal force. In particular, the use of lethal force should not be automatic and the training and instructions given to state agents should not, as was the case with the SAS troops, preclude shooting to wound.[25]

7.12   Finally, the words "lawful" and "lawfully" which appear in Articles 2(b) and (c) do not imply merely that the action taken must be in conformity with domestic law. The notion of "law" under the Convention implies also that the relevant rules are both accessible to the persons likely to be affected and foreseeable in their application.[26] The rules and guidance which govern the use of lethal force by the agents of the state must, therefore, be clearly framed, and available to the public.

4. TORTURE, INHUMAN AND DEGRADING TREATMENT AND PUNISHMENT: OVERVIEW

7.13   Article 3 provides:

"No one shall be subjected to torture or to inhuman or degrading treatment or punishment"

Article 3 protects the physical integrity of the individual. It is the Convention's equivalent of the prohibition of "cruel and unusual punishment" which appears in the US and many Commonwealth constitutions, although it has a much broader scope, protecting against "treatment" as well as "punishment". It has been given a broad interpretation by the Court, such that the treatment of prisoners and detainees, its most obvious field of application, is now only one of the potential uses to which it may be put. Unlike the other substantive rights laid down by the Convention, Article 3 appears without express exception or qualification, and the Court has refused to find any implied exceptions. In a recent case concerning mistreatment during police interrogation, the French Government argued that the behaviour of the police could be excused in the light

---

[25] Above n. 2 at 172–177.
[26] See chapter 6, paras. 6.35–6.39.
[27] *Tomasi* v *France*, A/241-A, (1993) 15 EHRR 1, 56.

of the circumstances of the fight against terrorism in Corsica. The Court, however, refused to accept any limitations on the protection to be afforded to the physical integrity of individuals.[27] Like Article 2, Article 3 cannot be the subject of a public emergency derogation under Article 15. The only mechanism by which the application of Article 3 can be limited is, therefore, that of restrictive definition of its key terms, "torture", "inhuman" and "degrading".

5. STATE RESPONSIBILITY FOR BREACH OF ARTICLE 3

Article 3 raises two particular issues of state responsibility which are **7.14** worthy of mention. The first is that of the liability of the state for unauthorised or *ultra vires* acts of its agents. This is important since acts of ill-treatment by the authorities may frequently occur upon the initiative of individual agents and in breach both of the law and of official policy or practice. A strict approach is taken: in *Ireland* v *UK*, the Court held that the state is under a duty to ensure that its agents obey the law and, accordingly, is "strictly liable" for their conduct.[28]

The second issue is to what extent the state can be held responsible for **7.15** ill-treatment meted out by non-state bodies. This issue has been high-lighted in the UK by the problem of corporal punishment, which may constitute degrading treatment, in private schools. State schools are treated as state-bodies and so bound by the Convention, in any event. In *Costello-Roberts*, the applicant sued the Government after being beaten with a slipper in a private school. The Court held that the UK had accepted, in Article 1 of the First Protocol to the Convention, a positive obligation to secure the right to education and, if it chose to delegate its responsibilities in the field of education to private institutions, it could not thereby escape responsibility for their acts in breach of the Convention.[29] Private schools may well exercise a public function, within s. 6 of the Human Rights Act, and so qualify as public authorities which are bound to respect Convention rights, at least in respect of their non-private acts.[30]

The Commission took a much broader approach in another corporal **7.16** punishment case, *Y* v *UK*, finding that "the UK has a duty under the Convention to ensure that all pupils, including pupils at private schools,

---

[28] A/25, (1979–80) 2 EHRR 25, 77–78.
[29] *Costello-Roberts* v *UK*, A/247-C, (1995) 19 EHRR 112.
[30] Chapter 2, paras. 2.19–2.30.

are not exposed to treatment contrary to Article 3 of the Convention".[31] That duty was based, in part, upon the special role of the state in regulating education, but more recently the Court has taken the Commission's views to their logical conclusion in finding that the UK had breached Article 3 in not protecting a child from corporal punishment in the home at the hands of his stepfather.[32]

6. TORTURE

7.17   Torture is defined as "deliberate inhuman treatment causing very serious and cruel suffering".[33] Torture coves not just physical abuse but also "the infliction of mental suffering by creating a state of anguish and stress by means other than bodily assault".[34] In assessing the level of suffering caused, the Court will take into account all relevant circumstances, including the duration of the treatment, its physical or mental effects and, in some cases, the sex, age and state of health of the victim. In *Ireland* v *UK*, the Irish Government complained about interrogation techniques used by the security forces in Northern Ireland, which included forcing prisoners to stand for long periods, subjecting them to continuous loud noise, sleep deprivation and restricted diet. The Commission held that these practices amounted to torture but the Court disagreed, finding that they did not inflict a sufficient level of suffering to constitute torture (although they did amount to inhuman treatment).[35] The *Greek* case, a decision of the Committee of Ministers concerning the treatment of political suspects by the Greek police, was the first and for a long time the only case in which a final finding of torture has been made.[36] The accession of Turkey to the ECHR has given rise to further findings of torture.[36a]

---

[31]   A/247-A, (1994) 17 EHRR 238, 241.
[32]   *A* v *UK*, A/991, decision of 23 September 1998.
[33]   *Ireland* v *UK*, above n. 28 at 80.
[34]   *Denmark, Norway, Sweden and The Netherlands* v *Greece* ("the *Greek* case") (1969) 12 *Yearbook* 186, 451.
[35]   Above n. 28 at 79–80.
[36]   Above n. 34.
[36a]   *Aydin* v *Turkey*, A/825 (1998) 25 EHRR 251.

7. INHUMAN AND DEGRADING TREATMENT OR PUNISHMENT

There are two differences, in principle, between torture and inhuman **7.18** treatment. First, inhuman treatment need not be deliberate: it is not necessary that pain and suffering are inflicted with the intention to cause pain and suffering. The second difference is one of degree — the level of pain and suffering inflicted by inhuman treatment is less severe than that caused by torture. Suffering must nevertheless "attain a minimum level of severity"[37] in order to found an Article 3 application and a multitude of cases have been thrown out for failing the *de minimis* test. In *Tyrer*, for example, the Court ruled that three strokes of the birch which had been administered as a judicial punishment in the Isle of Man did not cause sufficient suffering as to be an inhuman punishment (although it was degrading).[38] As with torture, it is necessary to examine a range of factors in order to ascertain whether the level of suffering is sufficient to amount to inhuman treatment or punishment.

Degrading treatment was defined in the *Greek* case as that which grossly **7.19** humiliates an individual before others or drives him to act against his will or conscience.[39] A slightly broader definition was given in the *East African Asians* case, where treatment was said to be degrading if it lowers the individual in rank, position, reputation or character, whether in his own eyes or the eyes of other people.[40] It is not confined to physical acts, and again, there is a *de minimis* rule — many applications under this heading have been rejected on the basis that the treatment alleged was not sufficiently humiliating. In *Tyrer*, the Court held that Article 3 required a particular level of humiliation and debasement which was more than that inherent in the very fact of being convicted and punished by a court. Looking at the nature and context of the punishment inflicted on the applicant, and the manner and method of its execution, the birching was, in its view, degrading. Even though the applicant had not suffered any long-term physical damage, the punishment had been an assault on his dignity and physical integrity, the protection of which was central to Article 3.[41]

The difference between treatment and punishment has not yet to be **7.20** defined in Strasbourg, but is of little significance. Whilst "punishment"

---

[37] *Ireland* v *UK*, above n. 28 at 79.
[38] *Tyrer* v *UK*, A/26, (1979–90) 2 EHRR 1.
[39] Above n. 34 at 186.
[40] *East African Asians* v *UK*, Appl. No. 4403/70 *et al*, (1981) 3 EHRR 76, 79–80.
[41] Above n. 38 at 10–11.

suggests that the individual has been convicted of an offence, a measure imposed as a punishment may also constitute "treatment" and it is extremely unlikely that measures which are unlawful as "treatment" could be lawful as "punishment", or vice versa. It should also be noted that Article 3 may be used on a *quia timet* basis, to stifle a threat or risk of mistreatment. The threat of torture may itself constitute inhuman treatment; the threat of inhuman or degrading treatment may conflict with Article 3 if it is sufficiently real and immediate.[42] Also, an applicant may use Article 3 to avoid extradition or deportation if there is "a real risk" of inhuman or degrading treatment at his proposed destination.[43]

ARREST AND INTERROGATION

7.21 The application of Article 3 to physical mistreatment in the course of arrest does not preclude the use of reasonable force to apprehend suspects, but only the use of force which is disproportionate in the circumstances.[44] Similarly, Article 3 does not prohibit the use of all physical force during interrogation, nor even the use of force in excess of that necessary to restrain a detainee. On the contrary, force can be used up to the minimum level of suffering necessary to make out a claim of inhuman treatment and the Commission and the Court have, on occasion, taken a robust view of the level of suffering actually inflicted. Regulation of interrogation of suspects under the Police and Criminal Evidence Act 1984 (PACE) offers greater protection than the Convention in this respect but there is evidence to suggest that police practice does not always match the standards laid down in PACE. In July 1997, three cases reached the High Court concerning the failure of the Director of Public Prosecutions to prosecute police officers over deaths in police custody. In two of the cases, suspects had been found by inquest juries to have been unlawfully killed; in the third, a High Court judge had awarded damages to a detainee whose treatment under interrogation was described as "nothing less than torture".[45] These cases prompted an *ad hoc* visit in September 1997 by the European Committee for the Prevention of Torture and Inhuman or Degrading Treatment or Punishment (CPT).[46] The CPT

---

[42] For example, *Campbell and Cosans* v *UK*, A/48, (1982) 4 EHRR 293 (threat of corporal punishment if children continued to attend school).
[43] Below, paras. 7.30-7.34.
[44] *Hurtado* v *Switzerland*, A/280-A (1994).
[45] In the former two cases, the DPP admitted her error; in the third, the court found her to have acted unlawfully: *R.* v *DPP ex parte Treadaway*, *The Times*, 31 October 1997.
[46] "Custody deaths provoke European inquiry", *The Guardian*, 8 September 1997.

polices the operation of the European Convention for the Prevention of Torture and Inhuman or Degrading Treatment or Punishment 1987 by visiting prisons and other places of detention in the states concerned, including the UK, and reporting thereon.[47]

PRISON CONDITIONS

Imprisonment in itself is not an inhuman treatment or punishment, even where the individual is in a poor state of health which will be aggravated by confinement.[48] However, the conditions in which a prisoner is kept clearly fall within the scope of Article 3 (which applies equally to other places of detention, such as remand centres, young offender institutions and mental hospitals). Previous Strasbourg case-law is the obvious starting point in assessing the compatibility with the Convention of a particular practice, but there are, in reality, very few practices which can be ruled categorically in or out of Article 3. Much depends on the circumstances of the case and, in particular, the reason for the adoption of the practice. Therefore, dangerous terrorists may legitimately be subjected to treatment such as intimate body searches and solitary confinement which might not justified in ordinary circumstances.[49] Reference should also be made to two further sources, the European Prison Rules 1987, a Council of Europe initiative to set minimum standards of penal policy,[50] and the reports of the CPT. In 1991, the Committee found that conditions in four overcrowded British prisons amounted to inhuman and degrading treatment. A breach of the European Prison Rules or a finding of inhuman or degrading treatment by the CPT would be highly relevant to, although not determinative of, an Article 3 claim.

7.22

Overcrowding

In *Delazarus*, the Commission found that confinement of prisoners to their overcrowded cells for 23 hours a day and the absence of proper toilet facilities could constitute inhuman treatment, although not of the

7.23

---

[47] A useful account of the visits of the Committee on the Protection of Torture to places of detention in the UK is contained in Kelly, "Preventing Ill-treatment: the Work of the European Committee for the Prevention of Torture" (1996) EHRLR 87.

[48] *Bonnechaux* v *Switzerland*, Appl. No. 8224/78, (1979) 18 D&R 100. Adequate medical care must, of course, be provided: see below.

[49] See *McFeely* v *UK*, Appl. No. 8317/77, (1981) 3 EHRR 161 (body searches) and *Ensslin, Baader and Raspe* v *Germany*, Appl. No. 7572/76, (1979) 14 D&R 64 (solitary confinement).

[50] Reprinted at (1987) 9 EHRR 513.

applicant, who was in solitary confinement.[51] The clear implication is that a claim from a prisoner directly exposed to the practices would be admissible. The detention of at least two prisoners in a small, dark cell meant for one contributed to a finding of breach of Article 3 in the *Greek* case.[52]

Hygiene

7.24 In *McFeely*, the Commission agreed that keeping prisoners in dirty and unsanitary conditions may amount to a breach of Article 3. It should be noted, however, that the conditions in that case, which concerned the so-called "Dirty Protest" at the Maze Prison in Northern Ireland, were extreme, and that the application failed because the conditions had been created by the prisoners themselves.[53] In *Reed*, the fact that the applicant's cell was infested with cockroaches was not sufficient to give rise to a breach, although this was mainly because the prison was being renovated and conditions there were exceptional.[54]

Exercise

7.25 Lack of opportunity to exercise is viewed by the Commission as raising a serious danger to the physical and mental well-being of prisoners. However, a limit of one hour per day, which is commonplace in British prisons, has been found not to amount to a breach.[55]

Assault by prison officers

7.26 Not all instances of assault upon prisoners by the prison authorities will be serious enough to amount to inhuman and degrading treatment. Reed's complaint of ill-treatment in Hull prison, where several prisoners had been systematically assaulted after they had taken part in riots, was admitted by the Commission. However, his complaint regarding his later treatment in Leeds prison, where prison officers were alleged to have continually and deliberately jostled him, was rejected.[56]

---

[51] *Delazarus* v *UK*, Appl. No. 17525/90 (unreported). The applicant had relied upon the findings of a CPT report.
[52] Above n. 34.
[53] Above n. 49.
[54] *Reed* v *UK*, Appl. No. 7630/76, (1979) 19 D&R 113.
[55] *McFeely*, above n. 49 at 55.
[56] *Reed* v *UK*, above n. 54.

Solitary confinement

Solitary confinement is not, in principle, prohibited. However, it is **7.27** "undesirable", particularly where the prisoner is only on remand,[57] and it may amount to a breach of Article 3 depending upon the particular conditions which apply, the stringency of the measure, its duration, the objective pursued and its effect on the person concerned.[58] There must be a sound, objective justification for the confinement, such as the need to maintain security or discipline, but beyond that, the authorities have a large amount of leeway in determining which conditions will apply. In *Reed*, 12 weeks of solitary confinement did not breach Article 3 because there was no evidence of a serious adverse effect upon the applicant.[59] The Government has also successfully defended several challenges to their treatment by Category A prisoners. In particular, it is clear that the Commission will not entertain a challenge to the decision of the authorities to place a prisoner in that category, which, generally, entails solitary confinement.[60] The conditions attaching to solitary confinement must, however, fall short of complete sensory isolation coupled with complete social isolation. The Commission has found that such conditions may destroy the personality and cannot be justified under any circumstances.[61]

Medical facilities

In *Hurtado* v *Switzerland*, the Commission confirmed that Article 3 **7.28** imposes upon the state "a specific positive obligation to protect the physical well-being of persons deprived of their liberty".[62] Adequate medical facilities must be provided for the treatment of sick or injured prisoners, either in the prison or elsewhere. A related point is whether forcible medical treatment amounts to inhuman treatment. In this regard, the Court draws a distinction between measures which are therapeutic within the established principles of medicine and those which are not.[63] An example within the permitted category would be the force-feeding of a prisoner who is on hunger-strike.

---

[57] *Ibid.* at 136.
[58] *Ensslin, Baader and Raspe* v *Germany*, above n. 49.
[59] Above n. 54.
[60] *X v UK*, Appl. No. 8575/79, (1979) 20 D&R 202.
[61] *Ensslin, Baader and Raspe* v *Germany*, above n. 49 at 109.
[62] Above n. 44. See also *Bonnechaux* v *Switzerland*, above n. 48.
[63] For example, *Herczegfalvy* v *Austria*, A/242-B, (1993) 15 EHRR 437.

Other aspects of prison conditions

7.29 The range of possible conditions which might breach Article 3 is limited only by the imagination of the prison authorities, and novel practices regularly come to light. The handcuffing of women prisoners during childbirth is a relatively recent British example of a practice which may fall foul of Article 3. In *Soering*, the holding of prisoners in conditions likely to give rise to distress and anguish (in that case, the "death row phenomenon" of prolonged detention in US prisons prior to execution) was found to breach Article 3.[64]

EXTRADITION AND DEPORTATION

7.30 The Convention does not contain a right of asylum as such, or any other direct protection against extradition or deportation, for individual aliens who have entered a Convention state.[65] Certain of its provisions may nevertheless have an indirect impact upon the authorities' ability to extradite or deport. Article 8 may prohibit an extradition or deportation which involves the break-up of a family, but Article 3 is perhaps of greater importance, amounting in substance, if not in name, to a right of asylum in certain cases.

7.31 The Court's reasoning is straightforward: if there is a real risk of torture or inhuman or degrading treatment or punishment in the destination country, the extradition or deportation of the applicant to that country will breach of Article 3. In *Soering*, for example, the United States sought the extradition from the UK of a German national, who had confessed to a double murder in the state of Virginia.[66] Had he been handed over, he would probably have faced the death penalty, and a wait of several years on death row. The Court held that "death-row phenomenon" amounted to inhuman punishment and that extradition to face such a punishment would, if implemented, breach Article 3. The UK could not, therefore, extradite Soering to the US, but it could send him to Germany, which had nationality jurisdiction over his crimes and had also requested his

---

[64] *Soering v UK*, A/161, (1989) 11 EHRR 439. A long period of detention on death row has been found by the Privy Council to amount to inhuman punishment under the Constitution of Jamaica: *Pratt v AG for Jamaica* [1994] 2 AC 1.

[65] Arts. 3 and 4 of the Fourth Protocol to the Convention, which does not apply in the UK, provide protection in the exceptional cases of expulsion of nationals and collective expulsion of aliens.

[66] *Soering*, above n. 64. Another British example is *Amekrane v UK*, Appl. No. 5961/72, (1973) 44 CD 101.

extradition. In the event, Soering was extradited to the US on the under-standing that he would only be proceeded against for offences which did not carry the death penalty. The upshot is that a signatory to the Convention may, in effect, be held responsible for ill-treatment committed by, or in,[67] a state which is not bound by the Convention. The Court found this novel state of affairs to be necessitated by the spirit and intent of Article 3, and despite much criticism, the principle is now well-estab-lished.

Significantly, the requirements of Article 3, following *Soering*, may **7.32** conflict directly with the powers of the Home Secretary to order deporta-tion or extradition. Under the traditional English approach, the prospect of ill-treatment of the individual in the destination country is a mandatory relevant consideration for the Home Secretary, but it is only one consideration among many. Article 3 makes it an overriding consideration which cannot be ignored in favour of other aspects of the public interest. This conflict was laid bare in *Chahal*, where the applicant, a Sikh separatist, successfully challenged the Home Secretary's decision to deport him to India.[68] The Home Secretary considered him to be a threat to national security, but Chahal argued that he was at risk of torture and possibly death at the hands of the Punjab police if he was returned to India. The Court emphasised that Article 3 contained an absolute prohibi-tion and that the applicant's activities, however undesirable or dangerous, could not be a material consideration. There was no question, under Article 3, of balancing the risk of ill-treatment against the reasons for expulsion:

"Thus, whenever substantial grounds have been shown for believing that an individual would face a real risk of being subjected to treatment contrary to Article 3 if removed to another State, the responsibility of the Contracting State to safeguard him against such treatment is engaged in the event of expulsion."[69]

The Court relied upon reports by Amnesty International, the US State Department and the Indian National Human Rights Commission in finding the applicant's fears to be well-founded.[70]

Just as the scope of Article 3 is broad when it comes to assessing ill- **7.33** treatment in the UK, so there are few limits on the types of ill-treatment

---

[67] The feared ill-treatment need not be at the hands of the authorities: *Altun* v *Germany*, Appl. No. 10308/83, (1984) 36 D&R 209, 232.
[68] *Chahal* v *UK*, A/697, (1997) 23 EHRR 413.
[69] *Ibid.* at 457.
[70] See also *Cruz Varas* v *Sweden*, A/201, (1993) 14 EHRR 248; *Ahmed* v *Austria*, A/706, (1997) 24 EHRR 278.

abroad which may prevent expulsion. The Court has recently applied the *Soering* principle in the case of a man dying from AIDS whom the British Government wished to repatriate to St Kitts.[71] Had he been deported, he would have lost the benefit of sophisticated treatment and of professional counselling which he was receiving in this country and which was not available in St Kitts. According to the Court, the conditions in St Kitts were not in themselves in breach of the standards of Article 3 but the applicant's removal there would expose him to a risk of dying under the most distressing circumstances and would amount to inhuman treatment.[72] The Court also emphasised that the absolute guarantee of Article 3 applied irrespective of the conduct of the applicant (who had been convicted and imprisoned for smuggling cocaine).[73]

7.34   In *Soering, Chahal* and *D*, Article 3 was used as a pre-emptive remedy, which can prevent an extradition/deportation going ahead and not merely as an *ex post facto* ground for complaint. Under the regime of the Human Rights Act, a putative breach of Article 3 could found an injunction against the Home Secretary preventing action until the point is decided. If no remedy is forthcoming in the English courts and it is necessary to apply to Strasbourg, the Court should be notified of the urgency of an application and of the need for pre-emptive action. It is assumed that the Court will continue the former practice of the Commission which, in the ordinary case, would request that the Home Secretary take no action until the matter has been determined in Strasbourg.[74] Where, however, the applicant has already been returned to the destination he sought to avoid, the Court will take into account the circumstances which were known to the state at the time it took the decision to extradite/deport. This is only logical but can lead to the somewhat bizarre result that no breach of Article 3 is found even where the applicant has actually been subjected to torture or inhuman treatment on his return.[75]

CORPORAL PUNISHMENT

7.35   It is clear that the prohibition of degrading treatment and punishment in Article 3 has major implications for the practice of corporal punishment in schools, albeit that the Court has not yet found a breach of Article 3 in

---

[71] *D v UK*, A/758, (1997) 24 EHRR 423.
[72] *Ibid.* at 448.
[73] *Ibid.* at 447.
[74] See chapter 4, paras. 4.15–4.17.
[75] See *Vilvarajah v UK*, A/215, (1993) 14 EHRR 248.

any school corporal punishment case decided by it. In *Campbell and Cosans*, the pupils were not actually subjected to the punishment and whilst a risk of subjection in the future might be humiliating, in breach of Article 3, this was not so in Scotland where corporal punishment met with wide approval. However, the applicants won on the alternative basis of a breach of the right to education under Article 2 of the First Protocol.[76] In *Costello-Roberts*, the Court found that the punishment was not, in the circumstances, sufficiently damaging to amount to degrading treatment.[77] Important factors to be taken into account in assessing the compatibility of corporal punishment with Article 3 include the severity of the injury inflicted by the punishment, the length of time between the notification and the infliction of the punishment (a significant wait can cause unnecessary anguish), the manner of infliction of the punishment (whether it is administered in front of others, whether it requires the removal of clothing, etc.) and, generally, the long-term psychological effects, if any, which it causes. The Court noted, however, that corporal punishment which was not severe enough to breach Article 3 might nevertheless interfere with the right to respect for private life under Article 8.[78]

7.36 In principal then, corporal punishment in schools may breach Article 3, and the Government has settled other cases where the Commission had found just such a breach, thus preventing them from coming before the Court.[79] Each of the decisions in *Campbell and Cosans* and *Costello-Roberts* prompted a change in domestic law on corporal punishment in schools. The Article 3 prohibition has now been transcribed into ss. 47(1A) and (1B) of the Education (No. 2) Act 1986 such that corporal punishment by a teacher cannot be justified if the punishment is inhuman or degrading. The factors to which the Court adverted in *Costello-Roberts* are to be taken into account in determining whether or not any given punishment is inhuman or degrading.

7.37 The Court has recently found a breach of Article 3 in a case of corporal punishment in the home. In *A v UK*, it held that the Government could be held liable for inhuman treatment inflicted on a child by its parent or guardian.[80] The child in question had been severely beaten with a garden cane but a criminal prosecution of his stepfather failed when a jury accepted the defence that the assault had been a reasonable and moderate physical punishment. The Court adopted the views of the

[76] Above n. 42.
[77] Above n. 29.
[78] *Ibid.* at 133–135.
[79] For example, *Y v UK*, above n. 31; *Warwick v UK*, Appl. No. 9471/81, (1986) 60 D&R 5.
[80] Above n. 32.

Commission to the effect that whilst criminal sanctions were available in English law, the burden on the prosecution of proving that punishment was not reasonable or moderate in the circumstances unacceptably reduced the level of protection for children.

DISCRIMINATION

7.38 Discrimination on grounds such as sex, race, religion is prohibited under Article 14 of the Convention, but only insofar as it relates to the enjoyment of the rights and freedoms set out in the Convention. The consequence is that discrimination per se, or in respect of a matter which is not protected under the Convention, is not expressly unlawful. However, this lacuna has been filled to some extent by the interpretation of Article 3 so as to prohibit discrimination which amounts to degrading treatment.

7.39 The major impact of Article 3 as an anti-discrimination rule has been upon race discrimination in immigration rules. The leading example is the *East African Asians* case, in which the Commission found the UK to be guilty of discrimination amounting to degrading treatment when it refused to admit to the country people of Asian origin with British nationality who had been expelled from countries in East Africa.[81] There is no reason why the prohibition upon discrimination as degrading treatment should be restricted to immigration rules, nor indeed why race discrimination only could qualify as degrading treatment. However, the difficulties faced in mounting an Article 3 challenge to discrimination were illustrated in another British case, *Abdulaziz, Cabales and Balkandali.*[82] The applicants were three immigrant women whose husbands had been refused permission to remain with them in the UK; had the position been reversed, the Immigration Rules would have permitted them to join their husbands. They won their claim for breach of Article 8, taken together with the prohibition upon sex discrimination under Article 14 but their claim under Article 3 failed. The Court held that the rules were intended to achieve legitimate immigration objectives and did not evidence any contempt or lack of respect for the applicants. They were not designed to, and did not, humiliate or debase and so were not degrading.[83]

---

[81] Above n. 40.
[82] *Abdulaziz, Cabales and Balkandali*, A/94, (1985) 7 EHRR 471.
[83] *Ibid.* at 506.

OTHER EXAMPLES OF INHUMAN AND DEGRADING TREATMENT

Since breaches of Article 3 are defined only in terms of the physical or **7.40**
mental effects of "treatment" upon the individual applicant, there is no
obvious restriction upon the range of circumstances in which it could
apply. The case of *Van Volsem* raised the prospect of Article 3 applying
to regulate the social and economic conditions in which people live.[84]
The applicant in that case was dependent upon social security and lived
in poor quality local authority accommodation. She complained to the
Commission about her electricity supply being cut off shortly before
Christmas, when she found herself unable to pay the electricity bill. The
Commission rejected her claim on the basis that her treatment did not
reach the level of suffering, humiliation or debasement needed for there
to be inhuman or degrading treatment. There is no reason, in principle,
why a more extreme case of social hardship could not engage Article 3
although the Court would be wary of imposing wide-ranging obligations
upon Governments to maintain the "quality of life" of their citizens.
Another area in which Article 3 may apply is suffering caused by
environmental pollution, although the circumstances would have to be
extreme.[85]

8. PROVING ARTICLE 3 CLAIMS

Whilst the Court has been relatively liberal in its interpretation of what **7.41**
actually constitutes inhuman and degrading treatment, it requires a high
standard of proof that such treatment has actually occurred, conscious
perhaps of the political implications of an Article 3 finding against the
respondent state. In *Ireland* v *UK*, the Court adopted the criminal
standard of proof beyond reasonable doubt.[86]

Difficulties of proof frequently arise where an applicant complains of **7.42**
ill-treatment by the police or other security forces, since there may be
no independent witnesses, particularly where the ill-treatment occurs in

---

[84] *Van Volsem* v *Belgium*, Appl. No. 14641/89 (unreported); see Cassese, "Can the Notion of
Inhuman Degrading Treatment be Applied to Socio-Economic Conditions?" (1991) 2 *European
Journal of Int'l Law* 141.
[85] Cf *López Ostra* v *Spain*, A/303-C, (1995) 20 EHRR 277, 297.
[86] Above n. 28 at 79.

custody. There is no general principle that the burden of proof should fall upon the authorities to establish that the applicant's suffering was not caused by their actions. However, where the applicant has suffered injuries whilst in custody and no sufficient explanation is offered by the authorities as to how these might have occurred other than through ill-treatment by state agents, the Court will infer that ill-treatment did occur,[87] even if this involves departing from findings of fact made in the national courts.

9. FURTHER READING

Ermacora, "The Application of the ECHR in Asylum Cases" in Lawson and Blois (eds), *The Dynamics of the Protection of Human Rights in Europe* (Kluwer, 1994)

Kelly, "Preventing Ill-treatment: the Work of the European Committee for the Prevention of Torture" (1996) EHRLR 87

Warbrick, "State responsibility for damage sustained in another state: Article 3" (1989) 9 YEL 387

---

[87] See *Tomasi* v *France*, above n. 27.

Chapter 8

PERSONAL LIBERTY

The protection of the liberty of the individual is clearly one of the most **8.1**
important aspects of any human rights regime. The European Convention
addresses the issue of personal liberty in Article 4, which prohibits slavery
and forced labour, and Article 5, which guarantees personal liberty and
security, and specifies the conditions under which persons may be
deprived of their liberty. Article 5 has particular relevance to the issue
of detention before trial, since it regulates both the circumstances which
justify such detention and the rights of persons so detained. It has also
been used extensively to ensure that persons detained after conviction
have some redress against decisions affecting their sentence, and the
relevant UK law has been found wanting on a number of occasions.
Overall, it is a vital means of protection for some of the least popular
groups in society, including prisoners, mental patients, vagrants and drug
addicts. The Fourth Protocol to the Convention adds a number of rights to
the Article 5 guarantee, including a right to freedom of movement, a right
of nationals not to be expelled from their home state and a freedom from
imprisonment for inability to pay a contractual debt. The Protocol has
been signed by the UK but not ratified, so it has no application in the UK.[1]
It may be relevant, nevertheless, for the purposes of interpreting those
aspects of Article 5 which do apply here.

1. THE SCHEME OF ARTICLE 5

Article 5 provides: **8.2**

"1. Everyone has the right to liberty and security of the person. No one shall be
deprived of his liberty save in the following cases and in accordance with a procedure
prescribed by law:

---

[1] There are no proposals for its ratification in the near future: see *Bringing Rights Home*, Cm. 3782,
paras. 4.14–4.16.

(a) the lawful detention of a person after conviction by a competent court;
(b) the lawful arrest or detention of a person for non-compliance with the lawful order of a court or in order to secure the fulfilment of any obligation prescribed by law;
(c) the lawful arrest or detention of a person effected for the purpose of bringing him before the competent legal authority on reasonable suspicion of having committed an offence or when it is reasonably considered necessary to prevent his committing an offence or fleeing after having done so;
(d) the detention of a minor for the purpose of educational supervision or his lawful detention for the purpose of bringing him before the competent legal authority;
(e) the lawful detention of persons for the prevention of the spreading of infectious diseases, of persons of unsound mind, alcoholics or drug addicts or vagrants;
(f) the lawful arrest or detention of a person to prevent his effecting an unauthorised entry into the country or of a person against whom action is being taken with a view to deportation or extradition.

2. Everyone who is arrested shall be informed promptly, in a language which he understands, of the reasons for his arrest and of any charge against him.

3. Everyone arrested or detained in accordance with the provisions of paragraph (1)(c) of this article shall be brought promptly before a judge or other officer authorised by law to exercise judicial power and shall be entitled to trial within a reasonable time or to release pending trial. Release may be conditioned by guarantees to appear for trial.

4. Everyone who is deprived of his liberty by arrest or detention shall be entitled to take proceedings by which the lawfulness of his detention shall be decided speedily by a court and his release ordered if the detention is not lawful.

5. Everyone who has been the victim of arrest or detention in contravention of the provisions of this article shall have an enforceable right to compensation."

8.3 Article 5(1) lays down a basic right to personal liberty and security and then sets out a list of circumstances in which an individual may be deprived of his liberty. The most important of these are detention before trial and after conviction (Article 5(1)(c) and (a)) but provision is also made for the special circumstances of particular groups in society — immigrants (Article 5(1)(f)), children (Article 5(1)(d)), vagrants, alcoholics, drug addicts and the mentally ill (5(1)(e)). These exceptions are exhaustive and must be narrowly interpreted.[2] They are not mutually exclusive.[3] The remainder of Article 5 is then concerned with the basic rights which must be afforded to people who have been deprived of their liberty in accordance with the provisions of Article 5(1). Paragraphs 5(2) and 5(3) are directed at specific types of detention, namely arrest and pre-trial detention. Paragraphs 5(4) and 5(5) are general requirements which apply whichever of the Article 5(1) grounds for detention is invoked.

---

[2] *Winterwerp* v *The Netherlands*, A/33, (1979–80) 2 EHRR 387, 402–403.
[3] *McVeigh, O'Neill and Evans* v *UK*, Appl. No. 8022/77, (1982) 25 D&R 15, 36.

2. THE SCOPE OF ARTICLE 5

Article 5 is concerned with physical liberty. It provides for a right to both **8.4**
liberty and security, but it is well-established that the term "security" adds
nothing. It is simply the other side of the same coin: a person is secure
from having his liberty taken away in circumstances other than those
permitted by Article 5. The right to security does not mean, for example,
that a person should be protected from attack by others.[4] Also, Article 5 is
concerned with the fact of detention, not with the conditions in which a
person is detained, a subject which comes within Article 3, the prohibition
upon inhuman and degrading treatment and punishment.[5]

The scope of the protection afforded by Article 5, both within and **8.5**
outside the context of the criminal law, is determined by the interpretation
of the concept of deprivation of liberty. The basic distinction to be drawn
is between a deprivation of liberty and a mere restriction upon freedom of
movement (which would fall within Article 2 of the Fourth Protocol). This
is clearly a matter of degree, and it will be necessary to take into account
the type, duration, effects and manner of implementation of the detention
in seeking to draw the line.[6] The "type" of detention refers primarily to
the purpose behind it: for example, a schoolgirl who was kept in a police-
station for two hours without being locked up was not deprived of her
liberty because the aim of the police had been to question rather than to
arrest her.[7] Article 5 applies equally where a person has voluntarily given
themselves up for detention.[8] The duration of detention is only one
relevant factor and, provided that there is a real restriction on the
individual's freedom to leave, even very short periods of detention may
amount to a deprivation of liberty. A good example of the Court's
approach, focusing on the effects and manner of implementation of
detention, is *Engel*, where Article 5 was found not to apply to the status
of light arrest in the Dutch army, whereby soldiers were confined only
during off-duty hours, but did apply to strict arrest under which they were
held in a locked cell.[9]

Once a person who has been deprived of liberty pending trial is **8.6**
released, Article 5 ceases to apply and Article 6, the right to a fair trial,

---

[4] *X v Ireland*, Appl. No. 6040/73, (1973) 16 *Yearbook* 388.
[5] See *Ashingdane v UK*, A/93, (1985) 7 EHRR 528, a complaint about confinement at Broadmoor
secure mental hospital.
[6] *Guzzardi v Italy*, A/39, (1981) 3 EHRR 333.
[7] *X v Germany*, Appl. No. 8819/79, (1981) 24 D&R 158.
[8] *De Wilde, Ooms and Versyp v Belgium*, A/12, (1979–80) 1 EHRR 373.
[9] *Engel v Netherlands*, A/22, (1979–80) 1 EHRR 647. See also *W v Sweden*, Appl. No. 12778/87, (1989)
59 D&R 158.

takes over. However, if a person who has been detained is released and then taken back into detention, the second period of detention cannot be justified simply as a continuation of the first period, but must be separately validated under Article 5. In *Weeks*, it was established that this rule applied to the English penal practice of releasing prisoners on licence which may be revoked if they re-offend. Although an offender released on licence does not, as a matter of English law, regain his right to liberty, his freedom outside prison is a sufficient state of liberty for Article 5 purposes, such that he is deprived of his liberty on being recalled to prison.[10]

3. GENERAL CONDITIONS FOR DETENTION IN ACCORDANCE WITH ARTICLE 5

8.7   As well as falling within one of the six grounds enumerated in Article 5(1), detention must fulfil two general conditions if it is to be authorised under the Convention. According to the second sentence of Article 5(1), detention must be "in accordance with a procedure prescribed by law". There is a considerable overlap with the second requirement, stated in each of the subparagraphs of Article 5(1), which is that detention must be "lawful". Most of the relevant authority focuses upon the ambit and consequences of the latter requirement.

PRESCRIBED BY LAW

8.8   Clearly, detention "in accordance with a procedure prescribed by law" requires that there is a procedure laid down in domestic law for the particular type of detention, and that it is followed.[11] According to the Court, it also requires that the domestic law procedures are in conformity with the Convention.[12] By analogy with Articles 8-11 of the Convention, the phrase "prescribed by law" has further connotations, requiring that

---

[10] *Weeks* v *UK*, A/114, (1988) 10 EHRR 293.
[11] See, for example, *Van der Leer* v *The Netherlands*, A/170, (1990) 12 EHRR 567.
[12] *Winterwerp* v *The Netherlands* above n. 2 at 405.

law be accessible by those affected by it, and sufficiently precise that the manner of its application can reasonably be foreseen.[13]

LAWFULNESS

The requirement of lawfulness is also primarily a reference to domestic **8.9** law and covers both the procedure preceding the decision to detain (hence the overlap with the first requirement) and the substantive grounds which are relied upon as justifying detention. In *Zamir*, the Commission applied the Court's Article 10 case-law on the meaning of "prescribed by law" to the word "lawful" in Article 5(1)(f).[14] The applicant had been detained as an "illegal entrant" to the UK, and complained that his detention was not lawful because the meaning of that term had not been foreseeable to him. When he entered the country, illegal entrants were those who had entered clandestinely; in his case, the House of Lords then extended the meaning to immigrants, like the applicant, who had entered openly but on a fraudulent basis.[15] The Commission found, however, that the extension of the law, whilst novel, was reasonably foreseeable and detention was, accordingly, lawful. It is important to note that the reversal on appeal of a decision resulting in detention does not imply that the detention was unlawful for the purposes of Article 5. Where detention has been ordered by magistrates, the Court adopts the English law distinction between errors which are within the magistrates' jurisdiction, and errors which amount to an excess of jurisdiction and render their decision null and void. Only in the latter case is detention unlawful.[16] A lawful arrest or detention also implies one which is not "arbitrary".[17]

Both of these general requirements oblige the Court to review the way **8.10** in which domestic courts have applied domestic law. It is usually reluctant to act as a court of appeal on the application of domestic law and will permit national courts a broad discretion to find the facts in any case and then to apply the law to those facts. Provided that a person has been detained on a ground which is a legitimate ground under national law (and is not itself contrary to the Convention), the Court will intervene only

---

[13] See chapter 6, paras. 6.35–6.39. The test was recently applied in *Steel and Others* v *UK*, A/992, decision of 23 September 1998.
[14] *Zamir* v *UK*, Appl. No. 9174/80, (1985) 40 D&R 42.
[15] *R.* v *Home Secretary ex parte Zamir* [1980] AC 930.
[16] *Benham* v *UK*, A/631, (1996) 22 EHRR 293, 320–321.
[17] See, for example, *Kemmache* v *France*, A/296-C, (1995) 19 EHRR 349, 365.

in cases of bad faith or arbitrariness. A blatant failure to follow domestic procedures will suffice,[18] as will the use of detention for an improper purpose.[19]

4. ARTICLE 5(1)(a):
DETENTION FOLLOWING CONVICTION

8.11   Article 5(1)(a) allows lawful detention following conviction by a competent court. Save that the convicting court must be competent in the sense of having jurisdiction to try the case, the requirement of lawfulness relates to the detention and not to the decision to convict or to sentence. This means, as noted above, that it is no breach of Article 5 if an individual is detained pursuant to a conviction which is overturned on appeal. It also means, more generally, that Article 5 cannot be used as a means of challenging a conviction or sentence.[20] The exception to the latter rule is where a sentence is discriminatory, in which case a challenge can be made to it under Article 5 taken together with Article 14.[21]

8.12   Conviction by a competent court is, generally, conviction of a criminal offence by a criminal court. However, the relevant terms are defined broadly enough to encompass other forms of proceedings resulting in detention, notably those of military tribunals.[22] It is the initial conviction by the trial court with which Article 5(1)(a) is concerned. Detention pending appeal is, therefore, within (a) rather than (c), the exception for detention pending trial.[23] The court may be in another state, so permitting the transfer of prisoners convicted abroad to prisons in their home country.[24] Prisoners detained following such a transfer might, however, complain of breach of Article 5(1) if there has been a "flagrant denial of justice" in the foreign courts.[25]

8.13   There must be a sufficient causal connection between conviction and detention. Usually, the detention will follow automatically from the

---

[18] For example, *Van der Leer v The Netherlands*, above n. 11.
[19] See *Bozano v France*, A/111 (1987) 9 EHRR 297. Under Art. 18 of the Convention, permitted restrictions upon Convention rights may not be relied upon for purposes other than those for which they were prescribed.
[20] *Kryzycki v Germany*, Appl. No. 7629/76, (1978) 13 D&R 57; *Weeks v UK*, above n. 10 at 312.
[21] *RM v UK*, Appl. No. 22761/93, (1994) 77-A D&R 98. See also *Nelson v UK*, Appl. No. 11077/84, (1986) 49 D&R 170.
[22] See *Engel v The Netherlands*, above n. 9.
[23] *Wemhoff v Germany*, A/7, (1979–80) 1 EHRR 55.
[24] *Drozd and Janousek v France and Spain*, A/240, (1992) 14 EHRR 745.
[25] *Ibid.* at 793.

conviction, but there are circumstances in which the link is broken by an intervening decision, such as a decision to recall into custody a prisoner who has been released on licence. The important factors are the relationship between the detention and the original sentence and also the justification for the additional detention. The causal connection between conviction and detention will be broken if a period of detention is not justified according to the objectives of the judicial sentence or the legislation underlying it. In *Weeks*, the applicant had received a discretionary life sentence for robbery. He was released on licence and a year later recalled into custody after further, minor offences. The Court held that there was a sufficient causal connection: the later period of detention was authorised by the original sentence and was intended to achieve the same purposes of rehabilitation and protection of society.[26] It was reluctant to question the motives of the Home Secretary in recalling the applicant to prison and relied upon the margin of appreciation doctrine, emphasising that the national authorities were in a better position to assess what was required.

5. ARTICLE 5(1)(b): DETENTION FOR NON-COMPLIANCE WITH A COURT ORDER OR AN OBLIGATION PRESCRIBED BY LAW

8.14 Article 5(1)(b) is primarily concerned with detention in the civil law sphere. However, it may permit detention for purposes which are connected with the enforcement of the criminal law, such as the completion of security checks, but which do not come within Article 5(1)(c) on detention pending trial. The first limb of Article 5(1)(b) authorises detention for failure to comply with an order of the court, whether the detention aims to secure compliance or simply to punish the individual concerned. Committal to prison for civil contempt of court for failing to abide by the terms of an injunction is a good example.

8.15 Under the second limb of Article 5(1)(b), a person may be detained where this is necessary to secure compliance with an obligation prescribed by law (which, by implication, need not arise from a court order). Aside from the general requirements of Article 5(1) — "lawful" and

---

[26] Above n. 10 at 312. See also *Monnell and Morris* v *UK*, A/115, (1988) 10 EHRR 205.

"pursuant to a procedure prescribed by law" — three conditions must be met.

- The obligation must be "specific and concrete" — to undergo a blood test, complete a security check, etc. This requirement excludes blanket justifications, such as the needs of public order or the security of the state, which could be used as a pretext for abuses.[27] In *B* v *France*, the Commission accepted that the obligation to prove one's identity to the police could justify detention, as could the rather more general obligation "not to hinder the police in their work".[28]
- The obligation must not conflict with other provisions of the Convention.[29] The right to respect for private and family life (Article 8) and freedom of expression (Article 10) are perhaps the most likely candidates.
- The purpose of the detention must be to secure compliance with the obligation rather than to punish the individual for non-compliance. The reason is that if punishment were permitted, the guarantees surrounding punishment contained in Article 5(1)(a) would be undermined.[30]

8.16   This limb of Article 5(1)(b) is, primarily, intended to cover the case of detention as a coercive measure to induce a person to perform a specific obligation which he has wilfully or negligently failed to perform hitherto. In limited circumstances, however, a person may be detained in order to fulfil an obligation which has not previously been imposed, and which he has not previously failed to fulfil. The requisite circumstances were deemed to have arisen in *McVeigh, O'Neill and Evans*, where the applicants complained unsuccessfully about being detained for 45 hours for the purposes of anti-terrorist security checks at Liverpool, their point of entry from Ireland into the UK. They had not previously been asked, and declined, to comply with a check but the urgency of the obligation, the lack of alternative ways in which compliance might be secured and the length of detention required enabled the Government to justify itself under Article 5(1)(b).[31]

---

[27] *Engel* v *The Netherlands*, above n. 9 at 672–673.
[28] Appl. No. 10179/82, (1987) 52 D&R 111, 126.
[29] *McVeigh, O'Neill and Evans* v *UK*, above n. 3.
[30] *Engel* v *The Netherlands*, above n. 9 at 672–673.
[31] Above n. 3 at 38.

6. ARTICLE 5(1)(c): DETENTION ON REMAND

Article 5(1)(c) authorises, by rather convoluted language, detention **8.17** pending trial for a criminal offence. Lawful arrest or detention for the purposes of bringing someone before the competent legal authority is permitted, in three situations:

- where he is reasonably suspected of having committed an offence;
- where arrest or detention is reasonably considered necessary to prevent him from committing an offence;
- where arrest or detention is reasonably considered necessary to prevent him from absconding after having committed an offence.

Aside from the need for detention to be "lawful" under domestic law, **8.18** the basic requirements of Article 5(1)(c) are that a person be detained in connection with an offence, and that detention be for the purpose of bringing him before "the competent legal authority". The term "offence" should be given a broad interpretation, by analogy with the term "criminal charge" in Article 6, which incorporates certain military, disciplinary or regulatory offences which are not classified as criminal under domestic law. Hence in *Steel*, the Commission held that detention pending proceedings for breach of the peace, which are civil proceedings under English law, was covered by Article 5(1)(c).[32] The "competent legal authority" is the "judge or other officer authorised by law to exercise judicial power" who must review the legality of detention under Article 5(3).[33] The requirement that arrest or detention be for the purposes of bringing the individual before the competent legal authority applies to all three limbs of Article 5(1)(c), and rules out preventive detention, whereby someone is detained with no intention of charging him or bringing him to trial.[34] Given that, the second situation — arrest or detention to prevent someone from committing an offence — is significantly restricted.[35] Provided that a person is detained with the initial intention of taking action against him, there is no breach of Article 5 if, following further enquiries, he is ultimately released without charge.[36] However, arrests for the purpose of merely gathering information are not permitted.[37]

---

[32] Appl. No. 24838/94, *Steel and others v UK*, above n. 13.
[33] *Schiesser v Switzerland*, A/34, (1979–80) 2 EHRR 417, 425.
[34] *Lawless v Ireland*, A/3, (1979–80) 1 EHRR 15.
[35] See, for example, *Letellier v France*, A/207, (1992) 14 EHRR 83.
[36] For example, *Murray v UK*, A/300-A, (1995) 19 EHRR 193.
[37] Cf *Mohammed-Holgate v Duke* [1984] AC 437, 444–445.

8.19   Reasonable suspicion of having committed an offence, the first limb of Article 5(1)(c), connotes the existence of facts or information which would satisfy an objective observer that the person concerned may have committed the offence.[38] This requirement is broadly reflected in ss. 24-25 of the Police and Criminal Act 1984 (PACE) which govern the powers of the police to arrest without a warrant. However, the issue for the Court is not whether domestic legislation complies with Article 5(1)(c) (although that is a relevant consideration), but whether a particular arrest is justified on reasonable grounds. It has decided two cases where arrests were made under provisions of Northern Ireland emergency legislation (now repealed) which permitted arrest on the basis of a subjective, honest and genuine suspicion. In *Fox, Campbell and Hartley*, the Court noted that the subjective standard was capable of authorising detention in breach of Article 5(1)(c) but held that the grounds relied upon for arrest in that case — essentially, that the applicants had been convicted in the past of terrorist offences — were not sufficient.[39] Conversely, in *Murray*, the applicant was arrested under similarly worded legislation, but the Court was satisfied that arrest was justified to an objective standard. It deferred to the findings of fact made by the Northern Irish courts, and relied upon the "special exigencies of fighting terrorist crime".[40]

8.20   The second limb of Article 5(1)(c), arrest to prevent the commission of an offence, is more generous to the authorities than the equivalent PACE provisions, which require the arrestee to be in the course of committing or attempting to commit an offence (both of which are offences in their own right). The third limb — arrest or detention to prevent abscondment — appears not to cover any person who could not be arrested and detained under the first limb. Arguably, it only has independent significance in delimiting the circumstances in which an individual can be detained after having been brought before the competent legal authority, and before trial. Such detention would then be permitted only where the detainee is reasonably suspected of having committed an offence and further detention is necessary to prevent commission of a criminal offence or to prevent abscondment. Additional grounds for refusing bail have, however, been recognised under Article 5(3).

---

[38] *Fox, Campbell and Hartley* v *UK*, A/182, (1991) 13 EHRR 157.
[39] *Ibid.*
[40] *Murray* v *UK*, above n. 31 at 223–227.

7. ARTICLE 5(1)(d): DETENTION OF MINORS

Article 5(1)(d) authorises the detention of a minor by lawful order for the **8.21** purpose of educational supervision, and lawful detention for the purpose of bringing him before a competent legal authority. It caters for certain special features of the treatment of children but does not exclude the application of the other grounds for detention under Article 5(1). Therefore, the case of a minor who has been detained pending trial on a criminal offence would fall within Article 5(1)(c). Other aspects of the "detention" of minors are authorised under Article 5 because they are deemed not even to constitute a deprivation of liberty.[41] An example is the placing of a child in a children's home, which was said by the Commission to impose no more onerous restrictions on liberty than were a normal incident of bringing up children.[42] There is no common rule stating the age at which a person ceases to be a minor for the purposes of the Convention and the British approach, deeming the age of majority to be 18, is unexceptionable.

The first limb of Article 5(1)(d) caters for the particular need to secure **8.22** attendance at school, and for orders of a court or administrative authority which compel attendance.[43] *A fortiori*, a general obligation placed upon parents that children attend school, which falls short of a compulsory order, would be permitted.[44] The second limb of Article 5(1)(d) caters not for the detention of minors pending criminal trial, which falls under Article 5(1)(c), but for detention pending the possibility of their "removal from harmful surroundings".[45] This would apply in only limited circumstances, for example, the detention of a child whilst care proceedings are completed.[46]

---

[41] See *Nielsen* v *Denmark*, A/144, (1989) 11 EHRR 175, 191.
[42] *Family T* v *Austria*, Appl. No. 14013/88, (1989) 64 D&R 176, 180.
[43] In domestic law, see Chapter II of Part VI of the Education Act 1996.
[44] See s. 7 of the Education Act 1996.
[45] See Fawcett, *The Application of the European Convention on Human Rights* (Clarendon Press, 2nd ed., 1987) at 90.
[46] Harris, O'Boyle and Warbrick, *Law of the European Convention on Human Rights* (Butterworths, 1995) at 121.

8. ARTICLE 5(1)(e): DETENTION OF THE MENTALLY ILL, VAGRANTS, ETC.

8.23   Article 5(1)(e) deals with certain categories of person who may have to be detained for their own protection or for the protection of the public — persons with infectious diseases, persons of unsound mind, alcoholics, drug addicts and vagrants. Each of these terms has a meaning under the Convention which is autonomous of their meaning under national law, and national law must be validated accordingly. In practice, however, the Court has been reluctant to lay down firm definitions. As to vagrants, the Court has noted that a Belgian legal definition of vagrants as "persons who have no fixed abode, no means of subsistence and no regular trade or profession" was acceptable since it was not irreconcilable with the usual meaning of the term.[47] The Court has held that no definitive interpretation can be given of the term "persons of unsound mind" since medical understanding advances constantly but that , as a minimum, a person may not be detained simply because his views or behaviour deviate from the prevailing norms.[48] A case currently pending in Strasbourg raises the issue of whether a person is of unsound mind for the purposes of Article 5(1)(e) who is diagnosed by the Mental Health Tribunal as suffering from a mental illness which is not serious enough to require him to be detained in hospital.[49]

8.24   It is only in respect of the mentally ill that the Court has gone into detail on the safeguards necessary to justify detention, but the required approach, would, arguably apply by analogy to the other categories within Article 5(1)(e). Objective medical evidence must reliably show that the individual is of unsound mind and the mental illness so established must be of a kind or degree as to justify detention both initially, and on a continuing basis.[50] The Court will review the medical and other evidence but is reluctant to challenge the assessment of the national authorities, who have a margin of appreciation in assessing the need for detention.

8.25   Despite this, English law has recently been found wanting in two important respects. In *Kay* v *UK*, the applicant successfully challenged the power of the Home Secretary to recall to hospital a restricted patient who has been conditionally discharged, which does not need to be

---

[47] *De Wilde, Ooms and Versyp* v *Belgium*, above n. 8 at 404.
[48] *Winterwerp* v *The Netherlands*, above n. 2 at 401–402.
[49] *Roux* v *UK*, Appl. No. 25601/94, [1997] EHRLR 102.
[50] *Ibid.* at 403.

backed up by any medical evidence.[51] In *Johnson*, the applicant was found by a Mental Health Review Tribunal to be no longer suffering from a mental disorder in June 1989, but was granted only a deferred conditional discharge, contingent upon a hostel place being found for him. No hostel place was found and he was not released until January 1993. The Court held that there was no automatic entitlement to release once the criterion of mental disorder ceases to be met — the authorities may be justified in ordering a deferred, or phased, discharge in the interests of the individual himself, or of the community as a whole. However, the imposition of the hostel requirement had led to a breach of Article 5 since neither the Tribunal nor the mental health authorities had the power to order that a place be made available.[52]

In "emergency cases" the usual safeguards do not apply and there is no **8.26** need for objective medical evidence showing mental illness before detention.[53] In *X* v *UK*, a case of emergency, the Court upheld the powers of the Home Secretary under what is now s. 42 of the Mental Health Act 1983 to recall into detention at any time a patient subject to a restriction order, even if there is no recent medical evidence before him.[54] Safeguards are imposed at the later stage of review of that decision, by which time there will be appropriate medical evidence available. Another British case, *Ashingdane*, gives rise to a further requirement of Article 5(1)(e): detention of a person of unsound mind is only "lawful" if effected in a hospital, clinic or other appropriate institution authorised for that purpose.[55]

9. ARTICLE 5(1)(f): DETENTION PENDING DEPORTATION OR EXTRADITION

The Convention does not directly regulate immigration, deportation or **8.27** extradition, but several provisions have an indirect bearing upon those areas, notably the right to family life under Article 8 and Article 3, which prohibits the extradition or deportation of a person to a country where there is a real risk of him being subjected to inhuman or degrading treatment or punishment.[56] Art. 5(1)(f) permits lawful detention in order

---

[51] *Kay* v *UK*, Appl. No. 17821/91, unreported decision of 1 March 1994.
[52] *Johnson* v *UK*, A/846, [1998] EHRLR 224.
[53] *Winterwerp* v *The Netherlands*, above n. 2 at 403.
[54] A/46, (1982) 4 EHRR 188; cf *Kay* v *UK*, above n. 51.
[55] *Ashingdane* v *UK*, above n. 5 at 543.
[56] *Soering* v *UK*, A/161, (1989) 11 EHRR 439.

to prevent a person effecting an unauthorised entry into the country and also of persons against whom action is being taken with a view to deportation or extradition. It also covers the situation where an individual who is originally detained with a view to deportation challenges the decision to deport him and is detained pending the outcome of the challenge.

8.28   Article 5(1)(f) cannot be used as a general basis of challenge to the legality of the decision to detain or to deport an immigrant. This is so even where lawfulness under domestic law of the decision to detain an immigrant is conditioned by the legality of the decision to deport him. This situation occurred in *Zamir*, where the applicant was detained and then deported on the same basis, that he was an illegal entrant: if there was no basis for his deportation, then his detention was also unlawful. The Commission held, however, that it could only consider whether there was a legal basis for the detention and whether the decision of the domestic courts on the issue of legality under domestic law was arbitrary.[57] The Convention will also assist where the authorities have acted for an improper purpose or in bad faith.[58] The reason why Article 5(1)(f) is of so little use in challenging the substance of decisions to detain and/or to deport is that it authorises detention "with a view to deportation". Detention is with a view to deportation even if it precedes a deportation order which is unlawful, or if no such order is actually made. The Court noted in *Chahal* that it is, therefore, immaterial for the purposes of Article 5(1)(f) whether the underlying decision to expel the applicant was justified under national or Convention law.[59]

8.29   The Court will, however, review the duration of the period of detention with a view to deportation. Article 5(1)(f) will cease to avail the authorities if deportation proceedings are not conducted with "due diligence",[60] a test which turns very much on the facts of the individual case. In *Chahal*, detention between August 1990 and March 1994 did not indicate a lack of diligence, having regard to the detailed and careful consideration required to determine his request for political asylum. Conversely, the Court found a breach in *Quinn v France*, where the applicant was detained pending extradition for a shorter period, from August 1989 to July 1991. The part played by the applicant in causing delay is a relevant factor in the analysis. In the recent case of *Khan*, the Commission rejected a claim for lack of diligence in prosecuting a

---

[57] Above n. 14 at 55.
[58] See, for example, *Bozano v France*, above n. 19.
[59] *Chahal v UK*, A/697, (1997) 23 EHRR 413, 465. See also *Caprino v UK*, Appl. No. 6871/75, (1982) 4 EHRR 97.
[60] *Chahal, ibid.* at 465; *Quinn v France*, A/311 (1996) 21 EHRR 529, 550–551.

deportation in part because the applicant had been to blame for bringing *habeas corpus* and appeal proceedings consecutively rather than simultaneously, as he had been entitled to do.[61]

10. ARTICLE 5(2): THE RIGHT TO BE INFORMED OF THE REASONS FOR DETENTION

Everyone who is arrested has the right to be informed promptly, in a language he understands, of the reasons for his arrest and of any charge against him. Only Articles 5(1)(b), (c) and (f) make reference to arrest in addition to detention, but the requirements of Article 5(2) are, nevertheless, general, and apply whichever limb of Article 5(1) is used to justify detention.[62] The guarantee has two purposes: to enable a person to deny any offence for which he has been detained and so obtain his release,[63] or to challenge the lawfulness of his detention before a court, pursuant to Article 5(4).[64] The information provided to him must include the essential factual and legal grounds for arrest, and otherwise be sufficiently detailed to allow for these purposes to be fulfilled. There is a useful contrast with the right to be notified of criminal charges under Article 6(3)(a), where the purpose is to enable a person adequately to prepare his defence, and information must, accordingly, be more detailed. **8.30**

The requirements of Article 5(2) have been applied very loosely by the Court. Whether information has been given "promptly" will be assessed according to the circumstances of each case. Promptness does not require that information is given at the moment of arrest but only within "a sufficient period" thereafter. In *Fox, Campbell and Hartley* and *Murray*, there was no breach of Article 5(2) even though a period of hours had passed between the arrest of the applicants and notification to them of the reasons for their arrest.[65] The information does not have to be given all at once but can be divulged in stages. In certain cases, the detainee need not be directly informed at all, if, for example, the reasons for arrest are apparent to him from all the surrounding circumstances, including the **8.31**

---

[61] *Khan v UK*, Appl. No. 28021/95, [1996] EHRLR 161. See also *Kolompar v Belgium*, A/235-C, (1993) 16 EHRR 197.

[62] See, for example, *Van der Leer v The Netherlands*, above n. 11, a case under Art. 5(1)(e).

[63] *X v Germany*, Appl. No. 8010/77, (1979) 16 D&R 101, 114.

[64] *Fox, Campbell and Hartley v UK*, above n. 38 at 170.

[65] *Ibid.*; *Murray v UK*, above n. 36.

questions which are being put to him.[66] The requirement that the Article 5(2) information be given in a language which the detainee understands may place an obligation upon the authorities to translate it into his mother tongue. Otherwise, the information does not have to be conveyed in any particular form.

11. ARTICLE 5(3): SPECIAL RIGHTS FOR PERSONS DETAINED ON REMAND

8.32   Article 5(3) guarantees three further rights to persons who are detained on remand pending trial on a criminal charge: the right to be brought promptly before a judge or other authorised officer, the right to be released on bail and the right to be tried within a reasonable time.

THE RIGHT TO BE BROUGHT PROMPTLY BEFORE A JUDGE

8.33   A detainee must be brought promptly before a judge or other authorised judicial officer who will assess the justification for continuing detention and who has the power to take a binding decision to release if necessary. The requirement of promptness is, as under Article 5(2), to be assessed according to the special circumstances of each case. It implies a longer period than promptness in giving information under Article 5(2) given the greater logistics involved in arranging a hearing. In *Brogan*, the Court emphasised that judicial control of interferences by the state with the fundamental right to liberty of the individual was an essential feature of the Article 5 guarantee. The equivalent word in the French text of Article 5(3) is *aussitôt* meaning immediately, and the Court concluded that the notion of promptness had, accordingly, limited flexibility. The applicants had been detained under s. 12 of the Prevention of Terrorism (Temporary Provisions) Act 1984 and held for lengthy periods, the shortest of which was four days and six hours, before being charged or brought before a magistrate. Under the Act, they could have been so detained for up to seven days. The Court found that even the shortest period did not comply

---

[66] *Murray v UK, ibid.*, at 231.

with the requirements of Article 5(3).[67] The Government responded not by amending s. 12 (which is now contained in s. 14 of the Prevention of Terrorism (Temporary Provisions) Act 1989) but by submitting a public emergency derogation from Article 5(3). The validity of the derogation was upheld by the Court in the later case of *Brannigan and McBride*.[68]

8.34 For non-terrorist offences, ss. 40-44 of PACE lay down a detailed system of controls on continued detention. However, detention for up to 36 hours without charge can be authorised by police officers of varying rank, who do not satisfy the judicial requirements of Article 5(3). It is only after 36 hours that detention need be approved by a magistrate and it is that period which must satisfy the requirement of promptness within Article 5(3).

THE RIGHT TO RELEASE ON BAIL

8.35 A literal reading of Article 5(3) would suggest that the authorities have a free choice either to release a person pending trial or else to try him within a reasonable time. This "purely grammatical interpretation" has been rejected by the Court,[69] with the result that Article 5(3) creates a presumption that a person will be released pending trial. The key to understanding the justifications for continued detention under Article 5(3), which rebut the presumption, is the relationship between that provision and Article 5(1)(c), the general authorisation for pre-trial detention.

- The first limb of Article 5(1)(c), a suspicion that the detainee has committed an offence, is a pre-requisite for continuing detention but it is not sufficient in itself; the authorities must have an additional public interest justification.[70] The additional justification given by the court for refusing bail will be reviewed in Strasbourg, both as to whether it might in principle be sufficient and as to whether it is sufficient on the facts of the case.
- The third limb of Article 5(1)(c), the risk of the individual absconding before trial, is the principal justification for refusing bail. As under the Bail Act 1976, the court must consider a range of factors in assessing

---

[67] *Brogan* v *UK*, A/145-B, (1989) 11 EHRR 117.
[68] *Brannigan and McBride* v *UK*, A/253-B, (1994) 17 EHRR 539.
[69] *Wemhoff* v *Germany*, A/7, above n. 23.
[70] *Stögmüller* v *Austria*, A/9, (1979–80) 12 EHRR 155, 190–191.

that risk, including the individual's various ties in the community, and not merely the severity of the sentence which he is likely to receive.[71] The court must order release where the risk of absconding can be abated by financial guarantees, or other bail conditions,[72] a requirement which is also reflected in the Bail Act.

- The second limb of Article 5(1)(c), the possibility of the detainee committing a further offence, can be invoked only where two requirements are met: there must be plausible evidence of a danger of repetition of a serious offence, and detention must be appropriate in the light of the detainee's history and personality.[73] Arguably, these criteria should be strictly applied since this is, in effect, preventive detention which is inconsistent with the presumption of innocence. Schedule 1 to the Bail Act (Part I, para. 2) permits continued detention if there are substantial grounds for believing that the defendant will commit an offence on bail but no distinction is drawn between "serious" and non-serious offences. Section 25 of the Criminal Justice and Public Order Act 1994 went even further in establishing a rule that bail cannot be granted to a defendant charged with or convicted of homicide or rape where he has previously been convicted of such an offence, regardless of the danger of re-offending. It has now been modified.[74]

- The three limbs of Article 5(1)(c) are not, however, exhaustive of the justifications for continued detention. Various justifications relating to the preservation of the integrity of the criminal process have been accepted. For example, detainees who were considered likely to destroy evidence or to threaten potential witnesses if released could be held, but the risk to the criminal process must be assessed on a continuing basis.[75] Public disquiet giving rise to a genuine risk to public order if the detainee is released may also justify refusing bail.[76]

8.36 Article 5(3) specifically provides that conditions may be attached to an order for release and, as under the Bail Act, such conditions might comprise a financial guarantee, or direct restrictions on the individual's movements — reporting to a police station, surrender of his passport, etc. However, any conditions must be directed strictly at ensuring that he

[71] *Neumeister* v *Austria*, A/8, (1979–80) 1 EHRR 91, 127–128.
[72] *Wemhoff* v *Germany*, above n. 23.
[73] *Clooth* v *Belgium*, A/225, (1992) 14 EHRR 717, 734.
[74] See *BH* v *UK*, Appl. No. 30307/96, (1998) 29 EHRR CD 136; *CC* v *UK*, Appl. No. 32819/96, [1998] EHRLR 335.
[75] For example, *Wemhoff* v *Germany*, above n. 23 at 76–77.
[76] *Tomasi* v *France*, A/241-A, (1993) 15 EHRR 1, 50–51.

appears for trial, so, for example, a financial condition must be set with reference to the accused, his assets and his relationship with any persons who are to provide the security for him.[77] The Bail Act may go rather further in permitting restrictions to be imposed which are directed not only at preventing abscondment but also at ensuring that the accused does not commit an offence while on bail or interfere with witnesses or otherwise obstruct the course of justice.[78]

TRIAL WITHIN A REASONABLE TIME

If a detainee is held in custody and not released pending trial, he must be tried within a reasonable time. This right is parallel to that contained in Article 6(1) which guarantees a hearing to determine criminal charges within a reasonable time, and applies where an accused has been released from custody. The relevant period, for the purposes of Article 5(3), runs from initial arrest or detention to conviction by the trial court. If the accused is released and later taken back into custody, the relevant period is the aggregate period of detention.[79] **8.37**

As under Article 6(1), in assessing whether a period is "reasonable", the Court will take into account the complexity of the case, whether the accused has contributed towards the lengthening of proceedings and, in particular, whether there have been any unjustified delays on the part of the judicial authorities. There is, nevertheless, an important contrast with Article 6; the fact that an individual is in detention pending trial requires "special diligence" and particular urgency in prosecuting his case.[80] The need for special diligence does not, however, imply any upper limit on time in custody, or preclude very long periods of detention in an appropriate case. In *Di Stefano* v *UK*, for example, there was no breach of Article 5(3) where the applicant had been detained for over 19 months pending trial on complex fraud charges.[81] In another fraud case, the Court found that four years of pre-trial detention was justified.[82] A recent example of a successful claim under Article 5(3) is *Scott* v *Spain*, where the applicant had been detained for two years and four months **8.38**

---

[77] *Neumeister* v *Austria*, above n. 31 at 128–129.
[78] Para. 8 of Part I of Schedule 1 to the Act.
[79] *Kemmache* v *France*, above n. 17.
[80] *Stögmüller* v *Germany*, above n. 70 at 191.
[81] Appl. No. 12391/86, (1989) 60 D&R 182.
[82] *W* v *Switzerland*, A/254-A, (1994) 17 EHRR 60.

pending trial on rape charges (of which he was acquitted).[83] The Court rejected the argument of the Spanish Government that the difficulties of liaising with the alleged victim, who lived in Finland, could justify the delay.

12. ARTICLE 5(4): THE RIGHT TO CHALLENGE THE LAWFULNESS OF DETENTION

8.39 Article 5(4), the Convention equivalent of *habeas corpus*, guarantees to everyone deprived of his liberty the right to take proceedings by which the lawfulness of his detention shall be decided speedily by a court and his release ordered if necessary. The emphasis on obtaining release if appropriate dictates that it is not sufficient that the lawfulness of detention can be reviewed after release, for example, by an action for damages for false imprisonment.[84]

WHEN DOES ARTICLE 5(4) APPLY?

8.40 Where detention has been authorised by a court, such as pursuant to a sentence following conviction for a criminal offence, the requirements of Article 5(4) are deemed already to have been satisfied.[85] Article 5(4) has, therefore, two principal applications. First, to guarantee a right of challenge before a court by those individuals who have been detained other than by order of a court. Secondly, to provide for a periodic right of challenge to detention, even where authorised by a court, if the justification for detention is based upon circumstances which may change over time.[86] In the ordinary case of a fixed penal sentence imposed upon conviction, the circumstances justifying detention, namely the commission of the crime, cannot change.[87] Conversely,

---

[83] A/711, (1997) 24 EHRR 391.
[84] *Caprino* v *UK*, above n. 59 at 100–101.
[85] *De Wilde, Ooms and Versyp* v *Belgium*, above n. 8 at 407: detention of vagrants under Art. 5(1)(e) ordered by a court.
[86] See, for example, *X* v *UK*, above n. 54.
[87] See *Wynne* v *UK*, A/294, (1995) 19 EHRR 333. Arguably, the discovery of new evidence which casts light upon the soundness of a conviction could justify a review of the lawfulness of detention.

circumstances may change, and periodic review may be required in the following situations.

Refusal of bail

Refusal of bail to a person detained on remand must be reviewed at short **8.41** intervals. This is not only because the circumstances justifying the refusal of bail may change over a relatively short period but also because the Convention assumes that detention on remand will be of strictly limited duration. In *Bezicheri*, the Court applied these principles in finding that the facility of applying for a re-consideration of bail after a period of four weeks from first refusal was not unreasonable, but there was a breach of Article 5(4) because it had taken the judge a further four and a half months to decide the application.[88]

Life sentences

English law draws a distinction between mandatory and discretionary life **8.42** sentences. The difference, in theory, is that discretionary life sentences are imposed not because of the inherent gravity of the offence, but because of the presence of factors which are susceptible to the passage of time, namely mental instability and dangerousness. Accordingly, they consist of a tariff, a compulsory period of detention, followed by a further discretionary period, determined according to the danger to society which is posed by the offender. The Court has ruled that Article 5(4) entitles discretionary lifers to periodic review of their detention during the discretionary period.[89] There must also be a review where the individual is released on licence and then recalled into custody.[90] Mandatory lifers are not entitled to periodic review, since the Court views the mandatory life sentence as essentially punitive in nature (a constant rather than a fluid factor). This view has been maintained notwithstanding the fact that a notional tariff period is also established for mandatory lifers in order to determine their eligibility for release on licence, and comments in the English courts that mandatory and discretionary life sentences are converging.[91]

---

[88] *Bezicheri* v *Italy*, A/164, (1990) 12 EHRR 210.
[89] *Thynne, Wilson and Gunnell* v *UK*, A/190-A, (1991) 13 EHRR 666.
[90] *Weeks* v *UK*, above n. 10.
[91] *Wynne* v *UK*, above n. 87. The Court noted the decision of the House of Lords in *R.* v *Home Secretary ex parte Doody* [1994] 1 AC 531.

Children detained "at Her Majesty's Pleasure"

8.43　In *Hussein and Singh*, the Court decided that the detention of child offenders "at Her Majesty's Pleasure" was analogous to a discretionary, rather than to a mandatory life sentence, and was therefore subject to a right of periodic review under Article 5(4).[92] Detention "at Her Majesty's Pleasure" is a mandatory penalty in the sense that it is the only sentence which may be imposed upon a minor who is convicted of murder. However, the Court held that it could only be justified by considerations based upon the need to protect the public, which must necessarily take account of development in the young offender's personality and character over the years. If no account was taken of personal development, the young offender would have forfeited his liberty for the rest of his life, which might be contrary to Article 3's prohibition on inhuman punishment.[93] In *Venables and Thompson*, the House of Lords found that the Home Secretary was required by domestic law to keep under review the detention of children detained at Her Majesty's Pleasure and had erred in setting for the applicants a fixed minimum tariff of 15 years.[94]

The mentally ill

8.44　Article 5(4) confers a right of periodic review upon the mentally ill who are compulsorily confined in a psychiatric institution for an indefinite or lengthy period.[95] This function is performed in England and Wales by the Mental Health Review Tribunals, although access to the MHRT system is not yet universal. In *Lines* v *UK*, for example, the applicant has challenged the validity of detention pursuant to an application for admission for treatment under s. 3 of the Mental Health Act 1983, which does not allow any right of challenge before the Mental Health Tribunal.[96]

---

[92] *Hussein and Singh* v UK, A/599, (1996) 22 EHRR 1.
[93] *Ibid.* at 24–25.
[94] *R.* v *Home Secretary ex parte Venables and Thompson* [1997] 3 WLR 23. Applications by Venables and Thompson (Nos. 24724/94 and 24888/94) have been declared admissible by the Commission: [1998] EHRLR 484.
[95] *X* v *UK*, above n. 54 at 207.
[96] Appl. No. 24519/94, (1997) 23 EHRR CD59. See also *Benjamin and Wilson* v *UK*, Appl. No. 28212/95, [1998] EHRLR 226.

CHARACTERISTICS OF A COURT

A "court" does not have to be court of law which is integrated into the **8.45**
standard judicial machinery, but must be a body with a "judicial character". That implies, as a bare minimum, independence from the executive, impartiality between the parties, the power to take binding decisions
and the existence of certain procedural guarantees. In *X v UK*, for
example, the Court reviewed the procedure surrounding the detention
of a mental patient and found that neither the Responsible Medical
Officer, who was not independent, nor the Mental Health Tribunal,
which could only make non-binding recommendations, satisfied the
requirements of a court.[97] Mental Health Tribunals have since been
empowered to take binding decisions to discharge patients.[98]

In *Weeks*, the Court found that the Parole Board satisfied the conditions **8.46**
of independence and impartiality, but had an inadequate, advisory role
when reviewing the possible release on licence of discretionary lifers.[99]
The Government only took remedial legislative action to provide for the
review of detention of discretionary lifers four years later after the Court
rejected its argument that *Weeks* was confined to its special facts.[100]
Section 34 of the Criminal Justice 1991 now provides that the trial judge
can and should set the punitive, tariff period of the discretionary life
sentence in open court after conviction. After the tariff has expired, the
prisoner may require the Home Secretary to refer his case to the Parole
Board, which has the power to order release if it is satisfied that detention
is no longer necessary for the protection of the public. The 1991 Act also
restricts the power of the Home Secretary to recall prisoners into custody
without the approval of the Parole Board, but the Home Secretary retains
the power to decide upon the continued detention of mandatory lifers.

As for procedural requirements, the "court" must, at the very least, offer **8.47**
an adversarial procedure, which allows the detained person to challenge
the evidence put forward in support of his detention. This requirement
was also breached in *Weeks* since the prisoner was not allowed access to
all of the documents which were used by the Parole Board in assessing his
case.[101] Further procedural requirements are very much dependent upon
the circumstances of the case and reference should be made to fair

---

[97] Above n. 54 at 210.
[98] See ss. 72-74 of the Mental Health Act 1983.
[99] *Weeks* v *UK*, above n. 10 at 317.
[100] See *Thynne, Wilson and Gunnell* v *UK*, above n. 90.
[101] Above n. 10 at 317–318. See also *Lamy* v *Belgium*, A/151, (1989) 11 EHRR 529.

hearing principles under Article 6. The more serious the consequences of a hearing for the detainee, the greater the safeguards which must be offered. For example, the court need not necessarily proceed by way of oral hearing, but an oral hearing, with full examination and cross-examination of witnesses, is required where a substantial term of imprisonment could result and the personality and/or maturity of the detainee will be at issue.[102] Article 5(4) may also require legal aid to be made available to the detainee.[103]

THE NATURE OF REVIEW

8.48   A remedy to challenge the lawfulness of a decision to detain requires a review not only of the procedure which has been followed but also whether detention complies with the substantive requirements of domestic law, and the general principles of the law of the Convention. The Court will examine the whole range of remedies available to a detainee, on the basis that shortcomings in one procedure may be remedied by safeguards available in other procedures.[104] The remedy of judicial review has been deemed to be insufficient by the Court because it does not allow a full examination of the merits of a decision — a decision of the Home Secretary can, generally, be overturned on its merits only if it is irrational.[105] The English law remedy of *habeas corpus* has also been found wanting, in certain circumstances, as a means of challenging the legality of detention under Article 5(4). In *habeas corpus* proceedings, the court will set aside a decision where it has been taken *ultra vires* or in bad faith. However, this does not assist where the detention is *intra vires* the governing statute but the statute itself is incompatible with Convention principles.[106] Nor does *habeas corpus* allow for review on specific Convention principles such as necessity or proportionality.[107]

---

[102] *Hussein and Singh* v *UK*, above n. 93 at 26.
[103] See, *Zamir* v *UK*, above n. 14 at 60 (immigrant with limited command of English); *Megyeri* v *Germany*, A/237-A, (1993) 15 EHRR 584, 593 (person of unsound mind).
[104] *X* v *UK*, above n. 54 at 210.
[105] See *Weeks* v *UK*, above n. 10 at 318–319; *Thynne, Wilson and Gunnell* v *UK*, above n. 90 at 695.
[106] *X* v *UK*, above n. 54 at 201–210.
[107] *Caprino* v *UK*, above n. 59 at 102.

THE SPEED OF REVIEW

Finally, the requirement that the lawfulness of detention be determined **8.49**
speedily incorporates consideration both of the period of time which
elapses before a detainee is permitted access to the procedure for
challenge and the time taken to reach a decision on his challenge. The
relevant period will include, therefore, any compulsory delay before
proceedings can be brought and ends when a final determination is
made. The factors to be considered are essentially the same as under the
"reasonable time" guarantee of Article 5(3) and Article 6(1). In *Zamir*, the
applicant had applied for *habeas corpus* three weeks after being arrested
and was detained for a further seven weeks, mainly due to delays in
obtaining legal aid approval. The initial delay did not count, being due to
the applicant himself, but the Commission found that the further seven
week delay breached the temporal requirement.[108] In *ex parte Norney*,
the Divisional Court found that the Home Secretary had acted in breach of
Article 5(4) in his handling of the new review procedures for discretionary
lifers in s. 34 of the Criminal Justice Act.[108a] He had been advised that the
tariff periods of the applicants were approaching expiry and asked to
refer their cases to the Parole Board (since the normal Parole Board
timetable took 23 weeks). He did not do so, however, until after the tariff
had expired, and the applicants' cases were not considered for at least a
further 23 weeks. Dyson J relied upon *E* v *Norway*, in which the Court
of Human Rights had found that an eight week delay in hearing a
substantive challenge to the merits of continuing detention, was contrary
to Article 5(4).[109]

13. ARTICLE 5(5): THE RIGHT TO COMPENSATION FOR UNLAWFUL DETENTION

Any applicant who establishes a breach of the Convention is entitled, **8.50**
under Article 50, to "just satisfaction" from the state in breach, which
frequently necessitates an award of compensation. In addition, Article 13
requires contracting states to provide effective remedies for the enforce-

---

[108] *Zamir* v *UK*, above n. 14 at 58–60.
[108a] *R* v *Home Secretary ex parte Norney* (1995) *Admin LR* 861.
[109] A/181, (1994) 17 EHRR 30.

ment of Convention rights. Article 5(5) is unique in the Convention system in going further than the general remedies provisions and requiring an enforceable right to compensation *in domestic law* for anyone who is detained in breach of Article 5. It is not, therefore, sufficient merely to release someone who has been unlawfully held; a right to compensation must also be available. In English law, the appropriate remedy is an action for damages for wrongful arrest and/or false imprisonment. These actions will only lie where arrest or detention is unlawful as a matter of domestic law and the UK has, in the past, been found to have breached Article 5(5) where detention was in accordance with domestic law but in breach of Article 5.[110] The Commission has recently ruled against s. 108 Courts and Legal Services Act 1990 whereby magistrates can only be sued for, *inter alia*, false imprisonment where they have acted in bad faith.[110a] Following incorporation of the Convention, many more incidents of detention which are in breach of Article 5 will also be in breach of domestic law and therefore found a claim for damages.[111] Certain breaches of Article 5 will, however, continue to be lawful as a matter of domestic law, and not compensable, because they are clearly authorised by a domestic statute.

8.51   The requirements of Article 5(5) as to the quantum of compensation for unlawful arrest and/or detention is a live issue, both at home and in Strasbourg. In *Cumber*, the applicant was awarded £350 damages after she had been wrongfully detained for five hours. The Commission declared her claim under Article 5(5) to be inadmissible, since, in its view, the compensation was low but not negligible.[112] The Court of Appeal has recently laid down guidance for awards of damages against the police in actions including wrongful arrest and false imprisonment.[113] Its judgment indicates that damages awards for persons in Ms Comber's situation should be significantly higher.

14. SLAVERY AND FORCED LABOUR

8.52   Article 4 provides:

"1. No one shall be held in slavery or servitude.

2. No one shall be required to perform forced or compulsory labour.

3. For the purposes of this Article the term "forced or compulsory labour shall not include:

---

[110]   *Fox, Campbell and Hartley* v *UK* and *Brogan* v *UK*, above n. 38 and 67.
[110a]   *Santa Cruz Ruiz* v *UK*, Appl. No. 26109/95, decision of 1 July 1998.
[111]   Special provision is made within HRA s. 9 for Art. 5(5) claims for damages.
[112]   *Cumber* v *UK*, Appl. No. 28779/95, [1997] EHRLR 191.
[113]   *Thompson* v *Commissioner of Police of the Metropolis*]1997] 3 WLR 403.

(a) any work required to be done in the ordinary course of detention imposed according to the provisions of Article 5 of this Convention or during conditional release from such detention;
(b) any service of a military character or, in the case of conscientious objectors in countries where they are recognised, service exacted instead of compulsory military service;
(c) any service exacted in case of an emergency or calamity threatening the life or well-being of the community;
(d) any work or service which forms part of normal civic obligation."

Article 4 incorporates another basic feature of human rights in a democratic society, so basic, indeed, that no breach of its terms has ever been found.

SLAVERY AND SERVITUDE

8.53   Slavery and servitude are matters of status. A slave is a person in the legal ownership of another. In *Van Droogenbroeck*, the Commission noted that "in addition to the obligation to provide another with certain services, the concept of servitude includes the obligation on the part of the 'serf' to live on another's property and the impossibility of changing his condition".[114] Just as an individual who gives himself up voluntarily for detention does not thereby waive his rights under Article 5, so it is likely that a person may not waive the protection of Article 4 by voluntarily assuming the status of slave or serf.

8.54   It is scarcely conceivable that the British authorities would themselves be holding people in slavery or servitude, but there may be implications for Government regulation of private employment practices. For example, there is considerable anecdotal evidence that large numbers of non-national domestic servants in this country are "employed" in conditions little short of servitude. Whilst such people might not have any remedy under the Convention against their (non-state) employers, it must be at least arguable that the Government has positive obligations under Article 4 to ensure that conditions of private employment in this country do not deteriorate to such an extent as to constitute servitude. A better documented issue is that of specific performance of employment contracts which has the effect of forcing an employee to remain with his employer. The general rule is that specific performance is not available, precisely

---

[114] *Van Droogenbroeck*, B/44 (1980) at 30 (Commission Report).

because it would amount to slavery. In practice, however, employers can and do obtain "garden leave" injunctions which hold employees to part or all of lengthy notice periods, so preventing them from taking up employment with a competitor in the meantime. The Commission's view that servitude involves living on the employer's property would, of course, be a significant obstacle to employees relying on Article 4 in the latter case.

15. FORCED OR COMPULSORY LABOUR

8.55   The term "forced or compulsory labour" is derived from two Conventions of the International Labour Organisation.[115] The ILO defines it as "all work or service which is exacted from any person under the menace of any penalty and for which the said person has not offered himself voluntarily",[116] and this has been adopted as the starting point for the Convention definition. The leading case is *Van Der Mussele*, in which a trainee Belgian *avocat* challenged regulations which required him, as part of his training, to provide free legal representation.[117] The Court noted that forced labour implies physical or mental constraint, and that compulsory labour does not cover all forms of legal compulsion or obligation, such as work to be carried out in pursuance of a freely negotiated contract. It endorsed the ILO definition and held that the essential elements of Article 4(2) are that the work is performed involuntarily and under the menace of a penalty (defined broadly). There was a sufficient penalty in this case, since the applicant risked being refused entry to the profession.[118] As for the criterion of voluntariness, it was not conclusive that the applicant had consented in advance to the work. The issue was whether there the work imposed a burden which was excessive or disproportionate when compared with the advantages which an individual would gain through consenting to it: here, it was not.[119] The Court rejected Commission jurisprudence to the effect that Article 4(2) also required that the obligation to perform work must be unjust or oppressive.[120]

---

[115] ILO Convention, No. 29 (1930) and No. 105 (1957).
[116] Article 2(1) of Convention No. 29.
[117] *Van Der Mussele* v *Belgium*, A/70, (1984) 6 EHRR 163.
[118] *Ibid.* at 173–174.
[119] *Ibid.* at 178.
[120] *Ibid.* at 175.

One potential application of Article 4(2) in the UK is the policy of **8.56** depriving an unemployed person of social security benefits if he refuses to take a suitable job or undergo training. The Commission has rejected just this argument in a case about an analogous Dutch rule, drawing a distinction between the imposition of a penalty and the withdrawal of a benefit.[121] However, its view may have to be reconsidered in the light of the rather broader approach advocated by the Court in *Van Der Mussele*.

Article 4(3) lists four types of compulsory labour which are not to be **8.57** regarded as falling within the prohibition of Article 4(2). The first is work done in the ordinary course of detention imposed according to Article 5 and work during conditional release from such detention (Article 4(3)(a)). Detention, according to Article 5, is detention which falls within one of the limbs of Article 5(1); the fact that there has been a breach of another aspect of Article 5, for example, on the right to challenge the unlawfulness of the decision to detain, does not render work required of a detainee contrary to Article 4.[122] The most obvious application of Article 4(3)(a) is to prison work, the burdens of which will be measured against "ordinary" European standards.[123] The payment of nominal wages, the omission to pay national insurance in respect of prison employment and the obligation to work for a private firm, rather than the state as such, have all been validated under this provision.[124] Article 4(3)(a) may also have to be relied upon to justify the imposition, as a penal sentence, of Community Service Orders. These may well constitute compulsory labour, performed under the menace of a custodial sentence. They are not performed as part of "normal civic obligation" within Article 4(3)(d) and the only possible way in which they could be saved is by viewing them as requiring labour during conditional release from detention. This analysis is not without its problems, but the Court would undoubtedly be reluctant to rule out such a progressive form of punishment.

16. FURTHER READING

Klug, Starmer and Weir, *The Three Pillars of Liberty* (Routledge, 1996), chapter 13

---

[121] *X* v *The Netherlands*, Appl. No. 7602/76, (1976) 7 D&R 161.
[122] *De Wilde, Ooms and Versyp* v *Belgium*, above n. 9 at 411.
[123] See the European Prison Rules, reprinted at (1987) 9 EHRR 513.
[124] *Twenty One Detained Persons* v *Germany*, Appl. No. 3134/67, (1968) 11 *Yearbook* 528.

Murdoch, "Safeguarding the liberty of the person: recent Strasbourg jurisprudence" (1993) 42 ICLQ 494

Murdoch, "A Survey of Recent Case Law under Article 5 ECHR" (1998) 23 EC Rev. HRC 31.

Thorold, "Implications of the European Convention on Human Rights for United Kingdom Mental Health Legislation" [1996] EHRLR 619

Chapter 9
DUE PROCESS OF LAW

The European Convention contains a number of safeguards which **9.1**
contribute towards ensuring the due process of law, or fair administration
of justice, in national legal systems. The right to a fair trial under Article 6 is
by far the most popular of all the Convention rights in terms of the number
of applications submitted. The vast majority of applicants to Strasbourg
have gone through some sort of judicial process in their domestic legal
system, and most can think of some way in which Article 6 might apply in
their case, even if only as an afterthought. Article 7, which prohibits
retrospective penal legislation, is also important in setting minimum
standards for the criminal process. The Seventh Protocol to the Convention adds four other rights which are relevant to the issue of due process
— no expulsion without due process of law, protection from double
jeopardy (that is, from being tried more than once for the same offence),
the right to an appeal, and to compensation for miscarriages of justice.
However, because the Protocol has not been signed by the UK, those
additional rights have no force in this country.

1. ARTICLE 6: THE RIGHT TO A FAIR TRIAL

Article 6 provides: **9.2**

"1. In the determination of his civil rights and obligations or of any criminal charge
against him, everyone is entitled to a fair and public hearing within a reasonable time by
an independent and impartial tribunal established by law. Judgment shall be pronounced
publicly but the press and public may be excluded from all or part of the trial in the interest
of morals, public order or national security in a democratic society, where the interests of
juveniles or the protection of the private life of the parties so require or to the extent strictly
necessary in the opinion of the court in special circumstances where publicity would
prejudice the interests of justice.

2. Everyone charged with a criminal offence shall be presumed innocent until proved
guilty according to law.

3. Everyone charged with a criminal offence has the following minimum rights:

   (a) to be informed promptly, in a language which he understands and in detail, of the nature and cause of the accusation against him;

   (b) to have adequate time and facilities for the preparation of his defence;

   (c) to defend himself in person or through legal assistance of his own choosing or, if he has not sufficient means to pay for legal assistance, to be given it free when the interests of justice so require;

   (d) to examine or have examined witnesses against him and to obtain the attendance and examination of witnesses on his behalf under the same conditions as witnesses against him;

   (e) to have the free assistance of an interpreter if he cannot understand or speak the language used in the court."

In its first paragraph, Article 6 lays down a general right to a fair hearing which applies in both criminal and civil spheres. Then, in Articles 6(2) and 6(3), it enumerates a number of specific requirements which must be met in criminal proceedings. These requirements are minimum rights, and even if they are observed, there is no guarantee that the proceedings will be held to be fair within the meaning of Article 6(1). Although they are expressly confined to the criminal sphere, they are also relevant as a yardstick for determining what is fair in the context of a civil trial. All of the rights conferred by Article 6 are to be given a broad interpretation: the Court has frequently stated that the right to a fair administration of justice holds such a prominent place in a democratic society that a restrictive interpretation would not conform to the aim and purpose of Article 6.[1]

9.3   The analysis of Article 6 in this chapter will commence by examining the scope of Article 6(1) with reference to the defining terms "civil rights and obligations" and "criminal charge". It will then summarise the fundamental components of the right to a fair hearing guaranteed by Article 6(1), followed by the specific components of fair criminal proceedings set out in Articles 6(2) and (3).

2. THE SCOPE OF ARTICLE 6(1): CIVIL PROCEEDINGS

9.4   The pre-conditions for the application of Article 6(1) to civil proceedings are threefold: the civil rights and obligations of the applicant must be at issue, there must be a dispute in respect of those civil rights and

---

[1] See, for example, *Delcourt v Belgium*, A/11, (1979–80) 1 EHRR 355, 366–367.

obligations and the proceedings under challenge must be determinative of them.

CIVIL RIGHTS AND OBLIGATIONS

The term "civil rights and obligations" has an autonomous, Convention **9.5** meaning. The way in which it is interpreted in any national legal system is relevant, since the Convention has developed with reference to the principles of law applicable in the various contracting states, but not determinative. The Convention meaning is flexible in that the Court has consistently declined to give a generic definition of the term "civil rights and obligations". In each case, various indicators, both for and against that classification, must be weighed up.

Civil rights and obligations are rights and obligations in private (as **9.6** opposed to public) law. Clearly, this takes in rights and obligations at issue in ordinary civil proceedings between private parties — tort, contract, family law, employment law, personal and real property, etc. Rights in the nature of constitutional rights, such as the right not to be discriminated against on grounds of religion, are also "civil rights".[2] The main area of controversy in the civil sphere is the extent to which Article 6(1) covers "public law proceedings", which may be determinative of private law rights and obligations. The extent to which the proceedings are, in fact, determinative of civil rights and obligations is the starting point for ascertaining whether Article 6 applies in any particular case.

Certain categories of decision which have certain public law character- **9.7** istics have been held to fall within the scope of Article 6(1).

- Decisions of the state which affect individual property rights, whether real property (for example, in respect of the sale, expropriation, confiscation, consolidation or use of land) or personal property (for example, bankruptcy proceedings).[3] The first case in which Article 6(1) was applied to a public law decision was *Ringeisen*, where the applicant complained about proceedings before a land tribunal which had refused him permission to receive a transfer of land. The administrative decision of the tribunal was decisive

---

[2] *Süßmann v Germany*, A/656, (1998) 25 EHRR 64; *Tinnelly and McElduff v UK*, A/935, decision of 10 July 1998 (where it was significant that the right in question had a specific pecuniary value).
[3] *Ringeisen v Austria*, A/13, (1979–80) 1 EHRR 455; *Anca v Belgium*, Appl. No. 10259/83, (1984) 40 D&R 170.

of Mr Ringeisen's civil law rights since it prevented him from completing a contract to purchase the land which he had entered into.[4]

- Licensing decisions, which affect the right of an individual to carry on a commercial activity. In *Pudas* v *Sweden*, for example, the Court held that Article 6(1) applied to administrative proceedings whereby the applicant challenged the revocation of his taxi licence.[5] Another example is professional disciplinary proceedings, which may result in the individual being deprived of the right to practise his profession.[6]
- Decisions which affect the right of an individual to compensation for loss caused by unlawful government decisions, for example, in the course of contract or tort claims against a state body.[7] In *National Provincial Building Society and others* v *UK*, the Court held that Article 6 applied to action taken by the Government which determined the outcome in proceedings brought for restitution of unlawfully levied taxes.[8]
- Decisions affecting rights to social security benefits.[9]
- Child custody and access decisions, and others which impinge upon family life.[10]

9.8   Conversely, various types of public law decision have been held to fall outside Article 6(1).

- In *Schouten and Meldrum*, the Court ruled that pecuniary obligations to pay criminal fines, to pay taxes and otherwise to discharge "normal civic duties in a democratic society" belonged exclusively to the realm of public law and so fell outside Article 6(1).[11] Contrast decisions which affect recovery in respect of unlawful state action, which are included. Hence, proceedings in which a company claimed damages in respect of the refusal of the authorities to grant it a tax exemption did fall within Article 6.[12]
- Certain types of public sector employment dispute are also deemed to concern rights and obligations in public law alone, namely

---

[4] *Ibid.* at 489–490.
[5] A/125, (1988) 10 EHRR 380.
[6] *H* v *Belgium*, A/127, (1988) 10 EHRR 339.
[7] *Stran Greek Refineries* v *Greece*, A/301-B, (1995) 19 EHRR 293.
[8] A/845, (1998) 25 EHRR 127.
[9] *Schuler-Zgraggen* v *Switzerland*, A/263, (1993) 16 EHRR 405.
[10] See, for example, *W* v *UK*, A/121, (1988) 10 EHRR 29.
[11] *Schouten and Meldrum* v *The Netherlands*, A/304, (1995) 19 EHRR 432, 455.
[12] *Editions Périscope* v *France*, A/234-B, (1992) 14 EHRR 597; *National Provincial Building Society and others* v *UK*, above n. 8.

disputes concerning recruitment, career progression and termination of service.[13] Other public sector employment issues, relating, for example, to conditions of service or pensions, do involve civil rights and obligations and are protected by Article 6(1).[14] As for civil servants in this country, the distinction, so far as employment rights are concerned, between office holders and employees, which has effectively been abandoned by the English courts, persists in the Strasbourg case-law.[15]

- Immigration and nationality decisions.[16]
- Decisions regarding the provision to an individual of state education. This was the decision of the Commission in *Simpson* v *UK*, in which a dyslexic child complained about the failure of a Local Educational Authority to educate him at a special school.[17] The Commission held that the right not to be denied education was not a "civil right or obligation" within Article 6(1) and its decision would extend to cases of refusal to admit to, or exclusion from, state schools.
- Decisions on the granting or refusal of civil legal aid.[18]
- Decisions concerning the operation and validity of public elections (which affect political rather than civil rights).[19]

Where a case arises which may engage Article 6(1), the first step is to **9.9** look for analogies in the Court's previous case-law. In borderline cases, which do not fall easily into any established category, the approach of the Court is to balance the public and private law features of a decision. The classification of a particular decision in domestic law as public or private is relevant to this analysis but not determinative. A good example of the Court's approach is *Feldbrugge* v *The Netherlands*, in which it held that the decision of a Dutch social security tribunal to withdraw sickness benefits, a purely public law matter under Dutch law, was determinative of civil rights and obligations.[20] The private law elements which influenced the Court's decision were that state sickness benefit was analogous

---

[13] *Neigel* v *France*, A/738, [1997] EHRLR 424; *Balfour* v *UK*, Appl. No. 30976/96, [1997] EHRLR 665; *Maillard* v *France*, A/925, decision of 9 June 1998.

[14] See, for example, *Lombardo* v *Italy*, A/249-B, (1996) 21 EHRR 188 (dispute over judge's pension).

[15] *X* v *UK*, Appl. No. 8496/79, (1980) 21 D&R 168 (police officer) cf *C* v *UK*, Appl. No. 11882/85 (1987) 54 D&R 162 (assistant janitor in a state school).

[16] *Agee* v *UK*, Appl. No. 7729/76, (1976) 7 D&R 164 (immigration); *S* v *Switzerland*, Appl. No. 13325/87, (1988) 59 D&R 256 (nationality).

[17] Appl. No. 14688/89, (1989) 64 D&R 188.

[18] *X* v *Germany*, Appl. No. 3925/69, (1970) 32 CD 56.

[19] *IZ* v *Greece*, Appl. No. 18997/91, (1994) 76-A D&R 65.

[20] A/99, (1986) 8 EHRR 425. It is now well-established that Art. 6(1) applies, in principle, to all decisions to grant or withhold social security benefits: see *Schuler-Zgraggen* v *Switzerland*, above n. 9.

to private sector sickness insurance, was funded (in part) by employee contributions, was otherwise closely connected with a private contract of employment (being a substitute for salary paid under the contract) and had important social and economic consequences for the claimant. These outweighed the various public law elements.

THE REQUIREMENT OF A DISPUTE

9.10 The requirement of a dispute arises from the use of the word "*contestation*" in the French text of Article 6(1), which has no direct counterpart in the English version. The term should be given "a substantive rather than a formal meaning". A dispute can relate to the existence of a right, or to its scope or the manner of its exercise but it must be genuine (rather than hypothetical) and of a serious nature. The result of the proceedings must be directly decisive for the rights and obligations at issue.[21] A further requirement, laid down in *Van Marle*, is that the dispute must be justiciable, that is, susceptible to judicial resolution.[22] The applicants were accountants who had failed to prove their competence to practise pursuant to a new system of registration. The Court noted that there would have been a dispute within the meaning of Article 6(1) if they had been complaining that the decision of the Board of Appeal was arbitrary or *ultra vires* or tainted by procedural irregularities, or indeed if there was a question of interpretation of the statutory conditions for registration. However, their complaint was, essentially, that the Board of Appeal had assessed their competence incorrectly. That assessment was akin to a school or university exam and so far removed from the normal judicial function that it fell outside Article 6.[23]

9.11 Finally, there will be no "dispute" where the rights claimed by the applicant are clearly not recognised in domestic law.[24] This is because Article 6 is intended to regulate the form and conduct of legal remedies which have been established in a state, not to require a state to provide legal remedies in order to protect particular rights (although other articles of the Convention may do just that). For example, a complaint based upon the failure of English law to protect landowners from nuisance by aircraft noise had to be brought under Article 8 (the right to respect for

---

[21] These requirements are listed *Van Marle* v *The Netherlands*, A/101, (1986) 8 EHRR 483.
[22] *Ibid.*
[23] *Ibid.* at 489–490.
[24] *H* v *Belgium*, above n. 6 at 346.

private life and the home) or Article 1 of the First Protocol (the right to peaceful enjoyment of possessions). It could not be brought under Article 6 precisely because English law did not protect the rights claimed.[25] Article 6 may, however, apply where a right is recognised in national law but its enforcement is hampered by immunities or procedural obstacles.[26]

9.12 The distinction between a situation of "no right" and a situation where there is a right in domestic law, but its enforcement is barred by a procedural rule, privilege or immunity is frequently difficult to draw. The current trend, however, is towards the latter conclusion. In *Osman*, for example, the applicants' claim for negligence against the police was struck out on public policy grounds, following *Hill* v *Chief Constable of West Yorkshire*.[27] The Court did not accept the Government's argument that the applicants had no right in domestic law to sue the police for negligence in the investigation of crime, preferring to view police immunity as a bar on to the enforcement of pre-existing rights in negligence.[28]

DETERMINATION OF RIGHTS AND OBLIGATIONS

9.13 The proceedings under attack must be determinative of civil rights and obligations either directly or where the determination of rights and obligations is not the object of the proceedings, but will follow as an inevitable consequence. The latter will often be the case in public law proceedings which bear upon civil rights and obligations: in *Ringeisen*, for example, the land tribunal did not expressly forbid the applicant from completing his contract to transfer land, but that was the practical result of its decision.[29] The requirement of "determination" excludes, however, proceedings which are preliminary, or incidental to, the determination of civil rights and obligations. In *Fayed*, for example, the applicant's complaints about a highly critical report written by Inspectors appointed by the Department of Trade and Industry was rejected on the basis that

---

[25] For example, *Powell and Rayner* v *UK*, A/172, (1990) 12 EHRR 355.
[26] See *Fayed* v *UK*, A/294-B, (1994) 18 EHRR 393, 429–431 (applicant's claim for defamation excluded by the defence of qualified privilege). *Fayed* supersedes the approach taken by the Commission in *Dyer* v *UK*, Appl. No. 10475/83, (1984) 39 D&R 246.
[27] [1989] AC 53.
[28] *Osman* v *UK*, A/1017, decision of 28 October 1998. See also *Tinnelly and McElduff* v *UK*, above n. 2.
[29] Above n. 3.

the report did not determine any of the applicant's rights, including his right to an unsullied reputation.[30]

9.14 Applications for interim relief are not determinative of civil rights and obligations, but only regulate the position pending the outcome of the main proceedings.[31] A more questionable decision is *Porter* v *UK*, where the Commission ruled that the rejection by the House of Lords of a petition for leave to appeal falls outside Article 6(1) as not being determinative.[32] In *Robins* v *UK*, the Court rejected the view of the Commission that costs proceedings fall outside Article 6(1) as not determinative of civil rights and obligations. It held that the issue of costs, even if determined separately, must be seen as determinative because it is a continuation of the substantive litigation.[33]

THE SCOPE OF ARTICLE 6(1):
CRIMINAL PROCEEDINGS

9.15 The treatment of an offence as criminal under domestic law is conclusive of it being a criminal charge under Article 6(1). However, "criminal charge" has an independent Convention meaning, such that charges which are not labelled as criminal in domestic law may fall within Article 6(1) by virtue of their criminal characteristics.[34] The Court will consider the nature of the offence and the severity of the penalty which attaches to it. An offence which only applies to a defined group of people and is not of general application is more likely to be classified as disciplinary.[35] A penalty which is intended to be deterrent and/or punitive and which consists of fines or deprivation of liberty is a strong indication of the criminal nature of a charge.

9.16 Applying these factors, the Court has found that military disciplinary charges may be criminal charges within Article 6(1), provided that the penalty is serious enough.[36] Prisoners' disciplinary proceedings before a Board of Visitors were also held to involve a criminal charge, primarily

---

[30] Above n. 26 at 427–428.
[31] *X* v *UK*, Appl. No. 7990/77, (1981) 24 D&R 57.
[32] Appl. No. 12972/87, (1987) 54 D&R 207.
[33] A/822, (1998) 26 EHRR 527.
[34] *Engel* v *The Netherlands*, A/22, (1979–80) 1 EHRR 647, 677–680.
[35] See the analysis in *Weber* v *Switzerland*, A/177, (1990) 12 EHRR 508, 519–520. Hence, professional disciplinary charges are not criminal charges: for example, *Wickramsinghe* v *UK*, Appl. No. 31503/96, [1998] EHRLR 338.
[36] *Engel* v *The Netherlands*, above n. 34.

because they resulted in substantial loss of remission and so a deprivation of liberty.[37] However, in a subsequent case, the Commission ruled that a sanction of 18 days' loss of remission was not severe enough to warrant the classification of the offence as a criminal one.[38] The severity of the potential penalty (three months' imprisonment) was also prominent in *Benham*, where the Court decided that civil enforcement proceedings for non-payment of the poll tax were criminal in nature.[39] Administrative or regulatory offences may also be covered.[40] As in the civil sphere, the application of Article 6(1) is premised upon a "determination" of criminal charges. Decisions in the criminal process which are ancillary to the determination of a charge, such as the granting or refusal of bail, are thereby excluded.[41] This may also be the basis for the exclusion from the scope of Article 6 of extradition proceedings.[42]

3. WHEN DOES THE PROTECTION OF ARTICLE 6 BEGIN AND END?

In the civil sphere, the operation of Article 6 begins when proceedings are instituted, and ends when the rights and obligations are finally determined, including any appeal from, or judicial review of, a decision. However, where an applicant is required to exhaust other remedies before he can commence proceedings before a court, the guarantee of a hearing within a reasonable time will take account of the preliminary stages.[43]   **9.17**

In the criminal sphere, protection begins with the charge, defined as "the official notification given to an individual by the competent authority of an allegation that he has committed a criminal offence".[44] This is a matter of substance rather than form, and notification is deemed to have been given whenever the applicant is "substantially affected" by the steps taken against him which have the implication of an allegation.[45] That point may occur well before a formal charge is laid, on arrest or even   **9.18**

---

[37] *Campbell and Fell* v *UK*, A/80, (1985) 7 EHRR 165.
[38] *Pelle* v *France*, Appl. No. 11691/85, (1986) 50 D&R 263.
[39] *Benham* v *UK*, A/631, (1996) 22 EHRR 293.
[40] See, for example, *Öztürk* v *Germany*, A/73, (1984) 6 EHRR 409 (minor motoring offence); *Bendenoun* v *France*, A/284, (1994) 18 EHRR 54 (customs, exchange control and tax offences).
[41] *Neumeister* v *Austria*, A/8, (1979–80) 1 EHRR 91.
[42] *Farmakopoulos* v *Belgium*, Appl. No. 11683/85, (1990) 64 D&R 52.
[43] *König* v *Germany*, A/27, (1979–80) 2 EHRR 170.
[44] *Eckle* v *Germany*, A/51, (1983) 5 EHRR 1, 27.
[45] *Ibid*.

during preliminary investigations.[46] The protection of Article 6(1) spans the proceedings which determine conviction, sentence, leave to appeal and appeal against conviction and/or sentence.[47] In a case brought by the Birmingham Six, the Commission decided that the referral of a case by the Home Secretary to the Court of Appeal under s. 17 of the Criminal Appeal Act 1988, which may occur many years after conviction and sentence have been finalised, should be treated as an appeal because it has the effect of determining or re-determining the charges against the accused.[48] The same would, presumably, apply to referrals by the Criminal Cases Review Commission. Other proceedings which take place after conviction and sentence have been definitively fixed are not covered, for example, an application for release on probation or parole or the implementation of a suspended sentence.[49] However, where a person is sentenced to probation, or to community service, and is accused of breaching the terms of his/her order, so that the court may substitute a full sentence for the original crime, that will count independently as the determination of a criminal charge.[50]

4. THE SUBSTANTIVE REQUIREMENTS OF ARTICLE 6(1): SUMMARY

9.19 Article 6(1) can be broken down into a fivefold guarantee, to a hearing, which is fair, in public, within a reasonable time, by an independent and impartial tribunal. Article 6 applies to a wide range of different types of judicial process and, whilst the same guarantees are common throughout, the strictness of its requirements does vary considerably according to the nature of the proceedings. A higher standard operates in respect of criminal proceedings than civil,[51] a lower standard in respect of professional and other disciplinary tribunals than the ordinary courts, and the following account should be read accordingly.

---

[46] See, for example, *X* v *UK*, Appl. No. 6728/74, (1978) 14 D&R 26.
[47] *Eckle* v *Germany*, above n. 44 at 28–29.
[48] *Callaghan* v *UK*, Appl. No. 14739/89, (1989) 60 D&R 296.
[49] *X* v *UK*, Appl. 4133/69, (1970) 13 *Yearbook* 780, 790 (parole hearing); *X* v *Germany*, Appl. 2428/65, (1967) 25 CD 1 (suspended sentence).
[50] *X* v *UK*, Appl. No. 4036/69, (1970) 32 CD 73.
[51] *Dombo Beheer* v *The Netherlands*, A/274, (1994) 18 EHRR 213, 229.

5. THE RIGHT TO A HEARING

THE PRINCIPLE OF EFFECTIVE ACCESS TO A COURT

Article 6(1) does not operate only in respect of those actions which have **9.20** already been initiated, but contains a guaranteed right of access to a court. This is not expressly stated in the text but, in the landmark *Golder* case, the Court reasoned that it was inconceivable that Article 6(1) should have detailed procedural guarantees for civil cases without first having protected the basis right of access.[52] In that case, a prisoner's rights under Article 6(1) were found to have been breached when he was refused permission to consult a solicitor for the purposes of instituting legal proceedings. Another leading example is *Keegan v Ireland*, in which the father of a child who had been given up for adoption by its mother successfully challenged the omission of Irish law to give fathers any standing in the adoption procedure.[53] Moreover, access to a court must be possible not only as a matter of law, it must also be effective. Whereas Articles 6(2) and (3) lay down specific components of effective justice in the criminal sphere, there is no such list for civil cases. The general principle of effective access under Article 6(1) must, therefore, be used to challenge obstacles to claims in the civil sphere.

LIMITATIONS ON ACCESS TO A COURT

The right of access to a court is not absolute, but is subject to implied **9.21** limitations.[54] According to the Court, any restrictions placed upon the right must not impair its very essence, must have a legitimate aim and must be proportionate to its objectives. The state has a margin of appreciation in assessing which limitations are appropriate.[55] Access to a court is, in practice, subject to a wide variety of limitations, and various restrictions have been challenged in Strasbourg, with a conspicuous lack of success.

---

[52] *Golder v UK*, A/18, (1979–80) 1 EHRR 524, 535–536.
[53] A/290, (1994) 18 EHRR 342.
[54] *Golder v UK*, above n. 52 at 536–537.
[55] See chapter 6, paras. 6.54–6.64.

Time limits

9.22   Time limits are intended precisely to limit access to the courts, in the interests of legal certainty. Reasonable time limits upon the bringing of claims are not, in principle, contrary to Article 6(1), but there may be circumstances in which a time limit deprives the right of access of all substance. In *Stubbings* v *UK*, the Court rejected a challenge to English time limits for personal injury claims, as they operated in the cases of victims of childhood sexual abuse.[56] The applicants had commenced proceedings after receiving psychological treatment as adults, arguing that under s. 11(1)(b) of the Limitation Act 1980, the time limit for their claim should be three years from the point when they realised the connection between the abuse they had suffered and their continuing mental problems. The House of Lords ruled, however, that s. 33 did not cover intentionally inflicted injury and that the time limit, under s. 2 of the Act, was six years from their eighteenth birthdays.[57] The actions were, therefore, time-barred. The Court held that the English rules did not impair the very essence of the right of access to a court. The time limit of six years was not unduly short and a criminal prosecution could be brought at any time, and may result in a compensation order. The time limits pursued the legitimate aim of ensuring legal certainty and preventing stale claims, and were proportionate to their aims.[58] Clearly then, the mere fact that a claim cannot be brought because it is time-barred does not mean that there has been a breach of the right of access to a court. A useful contrast can be drawn between *Stubbings* and *Perez de Rada Cavanilles* in which the Court found a breach of Article 6(1) where a time limit had been subjected to "particularly rigorous application".[58a]

Security for costs

9.23   The applicant in *Tolstoy Miloslavsky* v *UK* had been prevented from appealing an excessive award of libel damages against him by an order for security for costs made by the Court of Appeal.[59] He was required to pay £124,900 within 14 days, on the grounds that he was unlikely to be able to afford to pay the respondent's costs if he failed in his appeal. When he was unable to provide the security, his appeal was dismissed.

---

[56] A/683, (1997) 23 EHRR 213.
[57] *Stubbings* v *Webb* [1993] AC 498.
[58] *Stubbings* v *UK*, above n. 56 at 233–234.
[58a] *Perez de Rada Cavanilles* v *Spain*, A/1019, decision of 28 October 1998.
[59] A/323, (1995) 20 EHRR 442.

Again, this was a clear instance of a bar being placed in the way of a legal action, but the Court found no breach of the right of access to a court. The security for costs order fulfilled the legitimate aim of ensuring that the respondent was not faced with an irrecoverable bill for costs if the appeal were to fail, and its terms were proportionate to that aim. Whilst the grant of a security for costs order on the grounds of impecuniosity was likely to bar access to the court, it was significant that the Court of Appeal was required to take account of the prospects of success of the appeal (and had found them to be minimal in this case). The Court also noted that the applicant had had a full hearing in the High Court.[60]

Privilege and immunity from suit

The granting of immunities in or from the judicial process has the effect of   **9.24**
barring access to the courts and must be considered under Article 6(1). As noted above, there is an important distinction between rules which bar a right and those which bar a remedy for infringement of a right. Only the latter fall within the scope of Article 6(1). Once it is established that Article 6(1) can apply, the next step is to examine the privilege or immunity according to the standard criteria of impairing the essence of the right of access, legitimate aim, proportionality and margin of appreciation. In *Fayed*, the Court approved the defence of qualified privilege in defamation actions, which had applied so as to bar the applicant's claim for defamation in respect of comments made in a report by DTi inspectors.[61] In *Osman*, the Court ruled against police immunity from suit for negligent investigation of crime. It found the immunity to be disproportionate in a case where there was undeniably a close proximity between the police and the victims of the crime in question, and rejected the justifications put forward by the Government, which focused on the allegedly detrimental effect on operational policing decisions of potential liability in negligence, and on cost.[62]

A more extreme situation which may fall within Article 6(1) is where the   **9.25**
state legislates in such a way as to determine the outcome in legal proceedings to which it is a party. Hence, in *Stran Greek Refineries*, the Greek Government acted in breach of Article 6(1) when it legislated so as to render invalid an arbitral award in favour of the applicant.[63] However,

---

[60] *Ibid.* at 475–478. Contrast *Aït-Mouhoub* v *France*, A/1018, decision of 28 October 1998.
[61] Above n. 26.
[62] Above n. 28; see also *TP* v *UK*, Appl. 28945/95 and *KL* v *UK*, Appl. No. 29392/95, decisions of 26 May 1998.
[63] Above n. 8. See also *Pressos Compania Naviera* v *Belgium*, A/332, (1996) 21 EHRR 301.

self-serving legislative intervention in legal proceedings will not always breach Article 6. In *National Provincial Building Society and others v UK*, the applicants complained about legislation which had retrospectively validated tax regulations which were otherwise unlawful and so had the effect of stifling claims for restitution of taxes levied pursuant to those regulations. The Court rejected the argument that the tax legislation unlawfully barred access to the courts, relying upon its view that the legislation had not specifically been directed at stifling the applicants' legal proceedings and that those proceedings were a deliberate strategy to frustrate the original intention of Parliament, an intention which had itself been defeated on technical grounds alone.[64]

Qualifying periods of employment for Industrial Tribunal claims

9.26 One special category of restriction worthy of mention is the issue of qualification to bring claims for unfair dismissal and for redundancy payments in the Industrial Tribunal. At present, an employee must have two years of continuous employment before he can bring all but exceptional claims for unfair dismissal, or apply for a redundancy payment. In *Stedman* v *UK*, the Commission ruled that the two year period qualifying period was not contrary to Article 6(1) since it served the legitimate aim of protecting employers from undue burdens, was not arbitrary and did not impair the essence of the right of access to the tribunal.[65]

Categories of litigant

9.27 There are various categories of person for whom the state may wish to ration access to the courts, and the Court has approved restrictions in respect of, for example, vexatious litigants,[66] bankrupts,[67] and the mentally ill.[68]

---

[64] Above n. 8 at 177–182.
[65] Appl. No. 29107/95, (1997) 23 EHRR CD168.
[66] *H* v *UK*, Appl. No. 11559/85, (1985) 45 D&R 281.
[67] *M* v *UK*, Appl. No. 12040/86, (1987) 52 D&R 269.
[68] *Ashingdane* v *UK*, A/93, (1985) 7 EHRR 528.

Legal aid

The extent of the state's duty to facilitate civil claims by providing legal **9.28** aid is a matter of some controversy. State duties to provide legal aid in criminal cases are set out in Article 6(3)(c); comparable obligations in the civil sphere must be found in Article 6(1). There is no obligation to provide legal aid in every civil case,[69] and the Commission has recognised that, given limited resources, all legal aid systems must select cases on the basis of their prospects of success, and may require financial contributions from assisted persons.[70] In *Stewart-Brady* v *UK*, the applicant complained that the failure to provide legal aid for an appeal against the striking out of a civil action brought by him amounted to a breach of Article 6(1). Legal aid had been refused on the basis of there being no reasonable prospects of success and the costs of the litigation being disproportionate to the amount of damages likely to be recovered, grounds which, according to the Commission, were not arbitrary. There was, accordingly, no denial of access to a court, contrary to Article 6(1).[71]

However, the case of *Airey* v *Ireland*, provides some basis for arguing **9.29** that legal aid should be provided in certain civil cases.[72] In that case, the Court found that the right of effective access to a court had been breached where a woman was refused legal aid to seek a decree of judicial separation from her husband. It relied upon the complexity of procedure in the Irish High Court, the fact that the litigation was likely to involve complicated points of law and possibly expert witnesses, and also that the applicant had an emotional involvement with the case which was incompatible with the objectivity required for forensic advocacy. In the circumstances, it was not acceptable that the applicant be required to represent herself.[73] The point, it seems, is that the absence of legal aid can only be criticised where legal representation is essential to the success of a case, and cannot be obtained without legal aid. This situation may also arise where a claim is brought by someone under a legal disability (for example, a mental patient) who is required by law to be represented in any proceedings.[74]

---

[69] *Airey* v *Ireland*, A/32, (1979–80) 2 EHRR 305, 317.
[70] *X* v *UK*, Appl. No. 8158/78, (1981) 21 D&R 95, 101.
[71] Appl. No. 27436/95, (1997) 24 EHRR CD38.
[72] Above n. 69.
[73] See also the approach of the Commission in *Webb* v *UK*, Appl. No. 9353/81, (1983) 33 D&R 133, 140.
[74] See *Stewart-Brady* v *UK*, above n. 71.

RIGHTS ON APPEAL

9.30   Article 6 does not guarantee any right to an appeal. The right of access to a court refers to access to a first instance court. However, if an appeal mechanism is provided, it must comply with minimum standards of due process.[75] If appeal proceedings are available, the appellate court may rectify breaches of the requirements of Article 6(1) at first instance. In *Edwards*, for example, the fairness of the applicant's trial had been prejudiced by the failure of the police to disclose relevant evidence to the defence. However, an appeal had been heard by the Court of Appeal when this omission came to light and the conviction was not overturned. The appellate process was sufficient to cure the initial breach of Article 6(1).[76]

THE SUFFICIENCY OF JUDICIAL REVIEW

9.31   Since Article 6(1) has been extended into the sphere of decisions taken by public authorities, the issue arises as to whether the principle of effective access is satisfied by the availability of judicial review for error of law, or whether it requires that the reviewing tribunal has full appellate jurisdiction to consider the factual merits of decisions, as well as their legality. The basic rule is that appeals against the decisions of administrative bodies (including professional regulatory bodies) which themselves do not comply with the requirements of Article 6 will only be consistent with Article 6(1) if they are conducted before "judicial bodies which have full jurisdiction".[77] In *W v UK*, the Court found that the remedy of judicial review against the decision of a local authority regarding the applicant's access to his child, who was in care, was too limited in scope to comply with Article 6(1).[78]

9.32   However, in more recent cases, the Court has retrenched, perhaps mindful of the drastic consequences which a general principle to this effect would have for administrative law in the UK, amongst others. Now, its favoured approach will produce results which vary dramatically according to the particular facts of the case. In *Bryan v UK*, the remedy

---

[75] *Delcourt v Belgium*, A/11, (1979–80) 1 EHRR 355, 366.
[76] *Edwards v UK*, A/247-B (1993) 15 EHRR 417, 431–432.
[77] *Albert and Le Compte v Belgium*, A/58, (1983) 5 EHRR 533, 541–542; *Wickramsinghe v UK*, above n. 35.
[78] A/121, (1988) 10 EHRR 29.

at issue was that of appeal to the High Court on a point of law against the decision of a planning inspector, which is identical in scope to judicial review.[79] The Court noted that the High Court could not substitute its decision on the merits for that of the Inspector and that its jurisdiction over the facts of the case was limited. However, in assessing the sufficiency of the review process, it was necessary to take account not only of the powers of the reviewing body but also the circumstances surrounding the decision which is appealed against — its subject matter, the manner in which it was arrived at and the content of the dispute, including the desired and actual grounds of appeal.[80] Having considered those matters, the Court held that, overall, there was no breach of the requirements of Article 6(1).

9.33 Three factors appeared to be of particular importance to the Court. First, whilst the Inspector did not himself satisfy all of the requirements of Article 6(1) (in particular, since he was not completely independent of the executive), his decision-making was subject to important safeguards, including a quasi-judicial process and a commitment on the part of the Inspectorate to openness, fairness and impartiality. Secondly, the High Court had been able to address all of the grounds of appeal actually put before it (although, to be fair, this was because the applicant had thought better of appealing certain findings of fact with which he took issue). Thirdly, the limited powers of review of the High Court on issues of fact were typical of appeal tribunals operating in specialised areas of law.[81] Following *Bryan*, the issue of sufficiency of review of planning decisions is probably settled,[82] but judicial review in other circumstances does not, by any means, have a clean bill of health. Much will depend upon the safeguards which surrounded the taking of the administrative decision which is under challenge.[82a]

CRIMINAL HEARINGS

9.34 The right to a hearing, naturally, applies also in respect of criminal charges. The right may be waived by the accused, in circumstances

---

[79] A/335-A, (1996) 21 EHRR 342.
[80] *Ibid.* at 360.
[81] *Ibid.* at 361. See also *Zumtobel v Austria*, A/268-A, (1994) 17 EHRR 116.
[82] The Court's position is also supported by the views of the Commission in *ISKCON v UK*, Appl. No. 20490/92, (1994) 76-A D&R 90.
[82a] See also *X v UK*, Appl. 28530/95, (1998) 25 EHRR CD 88 (procedure to bar appointment as chief executive of insurance company).

akin to a plea bargain, but the Court will scrutinise carefully the nature of the pressure which has been brought to bear upon him.[83] There would, for example, be no breach of Article 6(1) where a motorist summoned to appear in court on a speeding offence is offered, and accepts, the option of paying a fine instead.

6. A FAIR HEARING

9.35 The guarantee of a fair hearing is inherently general and open-ended in nature. The Court of Human Rights has spelled out of it a number of more precise principles, but fairness is a malleable concept and established categories of infringement can offer only guidance. It is important to note that the Court, generally, does not take a technical approach to breach of the fair hearing requirements but attempts to ascertain whether, overall, the irregularity had a material effect upon the fairness of the proceedings. Having said that, there are certain types of breach which are treated *per se* as depriving the applicant of a fair trial, for example, unjustified failure to allow for a personal appearance by the accused.

9.36   The fair hearing guarantee, arguably, has four essential components — personal appearance, procedural equality, an adversarial process and a reasoned decision. The analysis below will summarise first these basic components, and then analyse in more detail the rules of evidence which may be derived from Article 6(1). Under the regime of the Human Rights Act, these are likely to be of considerable importance in the domestic courts.

BASIC REQUIREMENTS

9.37 An accused in a criminal trial has a right to be present at the hearing subject to limitation where, for example, this is necessary to protect witnesses,[84] or the accused has deliberately disrupted the proceedings. The right to be present can also be waived by the accused provided that he does so unequivocally, and there are minimum safeguards surrounding the circumstances of waiver.[85] English law is rather stricter in this

---

[83] See *Deweer* v *Belgium*, A/35, (1979–80) 2 EHRR 439.
[84] *X* v *Denmark*, Appl. No. 8395/78 (1981) 27 D&R 50 cf *R.* v *Smellie*, 14 Cr. App. R 128.
[85] *Poitrimol* v *France*, A/277-A, (1994) 18 EHRR 130, 145.

respect.[86] The accused has no right to be present at an application for leave to appeal,[87] but may be required at the hearing of a full appeal.[88] The right to be present at civil hearings applies only where the conduct or "personal character and manner of life" of the individual is at issue, for example, in child custody or access cases.[89]

A fair trial implies procedural equality, referred to by the Court as **9.38** "equality of arms": everyone shall have a reasonable opportunity of presenting his case to the court under conditions which do not place him under a substantial disadvantage *vis-à-vis* his opponent. In the criminal sphere, the general principle of equality of arms is closely related to the specific guarantees contained in Article 6(3), although it goes further in some respects. In *Bönisch*, for example, an expert appointed by the court had been treated more favourably than the expert proffered by the defence. Article 6(3)(d) deals specifically with witnesses but does not cover court-appointees; nevertheless, the Court found a breach of Article 6(1).[90]

In the civil sphere, the requirement of procedural equality can be used **9.39** to challenge a wide variety of procedural or evidential features of the proceedings. A good example is *Dombo Beheer*, in which a Dutch rule of civil procedure, that a party to a case may not give evidence in it, was held to have caused a breach of the guarantee of procedural equality. The case in question was a dispute between the applicant company and a bank as to the existence of an oral agreement allegedly made between the managing director of the company and a branch manager of the bank. The managing director was not permitted to give evidence, even though he was no longer employed by the company; the bank manager was, however, considered not to be a party to the case, and his evidence was heard. According to the Court, the Dutch authorities enjoyed a greater latitude in civil than criminal cases, but the company had been placed at a substantial disadvantage *vis-à-vis* the bank and Article 6(1) had been breached.[91]

A related principle underlying Article 6(1) is that a fair trial is an **9.40** adversarial trial. An individual must have the opportunity to comment upon and criticise all the evidence put forward by the opposing side. In *McMichael*, for example, the Court found a breach of the adversarial

---

[86] See *R. v Lee Kun* [1916] 1 KB 337, 341.
[87] *Monnell and Morris v UK*, A/115, (1988) 10 EHRR 205.
[88] See *Ekbatani v Sweden*, A/134, (1991) 13 EHRR 504.
[89] *X v Sweden*, Appl. No. 434/58, (1958–59) 2 *Yearbook* 354; *Muyldermans v Belgium*, A/214-B, (1993) 15 EHRR 204, 215.
[90] *Bönisch v Austria*, A/92, (1984) 9 EHRR 191.
[91] *Dombo Beheer v The Netherlands*, above n. 51.

principle in care proceedings before a Scottish childrens' panel and the Sheriff Court. Both tribunals placed considerable reliance upon social reports about a child, copies of which had not been disclosed to his mother.[92] The right to cross-examine opposing witnesses applies both to criminal trials, pursuant to Article 6(3)(d), and to civil actions.[93]

9.41   Finally, Article 6(1) implies a right to a reasoned decision. A person is entitled to know the grounds of a decision which affects his interests, not least to enable him to exercise an effective right of appeal. However, national courts have a wide discretion as to the form and content of their judgments and a claim under this head can only succeed if it the court has failed to address a key point which could be decisive of the case.[94]

RULES OF EVIDENCE

9.42   Article 6 does not prescribe specific rules of evidence and issues of the admissibility and probative value to be attached to evidence are, in principle, a matter for the domestic courts. Nevertheless, the way in which evidence is admitted and weighed against an individual may prejudice the fairness of the hearing and this aspect of the Article 6 guarantee has proved a fertile ground for legal challenges. The key to the Court's approach is that it will examine the issue of fairness in the light of the proceedings as a whole. A breach of Convention rules, or other unfairness, will not lead to a finding of breach of Article 6 if, viewed in their entirety, the proceedings were nevertheless fair to the applicant.[95]

Illegally obtained evidence

9.43   Under English law, evidence is admissible if it is relevant and relevant evidence remains admissible even if it has been obtained illegally.[96] Admissible evidence may, however, be excluded at the discretion of the trial judge if it would have an unacceptably adverse effect on the fairness of the proceedings.[97] The Convention proceeds on a broadly similar basis. There is no general rule that illegally obtained evidence should

---

[92] *McMichael* v *UK*, A/308, (1995) 20 EHRR 205. See also *Ruiz-Mateos* v *Spain*, A/262, (1993) 16 EHRR 505.
[93] *X* v *Austria*, Appl. No. 5362/72, (1972) 42 CD145.
[94] *Hiro Balani* v *Spain*, A/303-B, (1995) 19 EHRR 566.
[95] A recent example is *Miailhe* v *France (No. 2)*, A/659, (1997) 23 EHRR 491.
[96] *R.* v *Khan (Sultan)* [1997] AC 558.
[97] Section 78 of the Police and Criminal Evidence Act 1984 (PACE).

be excluded and it makes no difference that the illegality amounts to a breach of a Convention right, such as the right to respect for private life and the home under Article 8. This was the case in *Schenk v Switzerland*, where the applicant had been convicted of attempted incitement to murder on the basis of a telephone conversation which had been recorded unlawfully (in breach of Swiss rules on telephone tapping).[98] The Court noted that Article 6 does not lay down any rules on the admissibility of evidence as such, which is therefore primarily a matter for regulation under national law. It could not, therefore, rule in the abstract as to whether an unlawfully obtained recording should be treated as admissible or inadmissible but could only decide whether the applicant's trial as a whole was fair. The Court concluded that the use of the recording had not deprived him of a fair trial. Two factors were of particular importance in reaching this conclusion. First, the applicant had had a full opportunity to challenge the authenticity of the recording and to oppose its use against him. The fact that he failed in his attempts to exclude it was irrelevant. Secondly, the recording was by no means the only evidence against the applicant; the trial court relied on a number of other matters.[99] Whilst neither the domestic courts nor the Court of Human Rights said so expressly, it appears that the applicant would most likely have been convicted even if the recording had been excluded.

In *R. v Khan*, the House of Lords relied upon *Schenk* in deciding that a   **9.44** trial judge was correct in refusing to exclude evidence against the defendant which had been obtained with the aid of an electronic listening device, the use of which had involved the police in invasion of privacy (almost certainly contrary to Article 8 of the Convention), trespass and, arguably, criminal damage.[100] Their Lordships weighed up the extent of the trespass and damage caused against the gravity of the conduct being investigated and concluded that the public interest in the detection of crime should take precedence.[101] The police bugging which took place in *Khan* is now subject to Part III of the Police Act 1997 and to a Code of Practice issued by the Home Office. The Code does not prohibit the use of evidence obtained in breach of its terms, and it will continue to be up to the courts to decide in the particular case whether fairness demands that the evidence be excluded. In this and other areas, the interface between s. 78 of PACE and the requirements of Article 6(1) will be of great importance.

---

[98] A/140, (1991) 13 EHRR 242.
[99] *Ibid.* at 265–267.
[100] Above n. 96.
[101] *Ibid.* at 175–176. See Carter, "Evidence Obtained by Use of a Covert Listening Device" (1997) 113 LQR 468.

9.45 *Schenk* is an important guide for criminal courts when assessing the requirements of Article 6(1), but, like most Court judgments, it is particular to its own facts. In a different case, where, for example, the unlawfully obtained evidence is the principal or the only evidence against an accused, the outcome might well be different. It is certainly arguable that the House of Lords in *Khan*, where the evidence at issue was of central importance to the case against the defendant, failed to take account of this feature of the Court's reasoning. It should also be noted that, as under s. 78, the way in which the evidence has been obtained, and the nature of the illegality involved, is of considerable importance to the issue of fairness under Article 6(1). In *Saunders*, for example, evidence had been obtained from the applicant by DTi inspectors in breach of the rule against self-incrimination.[102] The fundamental nature of this rule meant that the use of the evidence against the applicant at trial led more or less directly to a breach of Article 6, without the need to take account of factors such as the strength of the other evidence against him.

Confession evidence

9.46 The use of confessions obtained by maltreatment is not permitted under Article 6,[103] and there must be adequate safeguards in place to test the validity of confession evidence.[104] The Commission approved the safeguards contained in the Judges' Rules and the common law, which preceded s. 76 of PACE.[105]

Accomplice evidence

9.47 Evidence from an accomplice of the accused who has been granted immunity from prosecution, or other privilege, may be admitted provided that the jury are fully appraised of the situation.[106]

Hearsay evidence

9.48 In principle, witnesses for the prosecution must appear in court so that their evidence can be tested, and there may be a breach of Article 6 where

---

[102] *Saunders* v *UK*, A/702, (1997) 23 EHRR 313.
[103] *Austria* v *Italy* (1963) 6 *Yearbook* 740.
[104] *G* v *UK*, Appl. No. 9370/81, (1983) 35 D&R 75.
[105] *Ibid*. at 80.
[106] *X* v *UK*, Appl. No. 7306/75, (1976) 7 D&R 115.

the evidence of a person who does not appear has played a primary role in the conviction of the accused.[107] In *Blastland* v *UK*, the Commission held that the English rules of hearsay comply, in principle, with Article 6(1), although that case was perhaps not typical in that the rules had operated to exclude evidence for the accused (rather than failing to operate to exclude evidence against him).[108]

Circumstantial evidence

There is no breach of Article 6(1) where an accused is convicted solely on the basis of circumstantial evidence.[109] **9.49**

Disclosure of evidence by the prosecution

Article 6(1) imposes a duty upon the prosecution to disclose all evidence **9.50** helpful to the defence and overlaps, in this respect, with the right of an accused under Article 6(3)(b) to have adequate facilities for the preparation of his defence. The duty of disclosure extends to all facts and documents which could be used by the accused for the purposes of his defence "that have been or could be collected by the competent authorities".[110] A failure to disclose may, however, be remedied by consideration of the relevant evidence on appeal.[111] In English law, the right to fair disclosure is regarded as an inseparable part of the accused's right to a fair trial,[112] and is now regulated by the Criminal Procedure and Investigations Act 1996. The prosecution must disclose material which, in the opinion of the prosecutor, might undermine the case for the prosecution, and then, after the defence has disclosed its evidence, all material which might reasonably be expected to assist the accused's defence. One area of potential conflict with Article 6(1) lies in the failure of the 1996 Act to impose a duty in respect of evidence which has not actually been collected by the prosecution, but which could have been collected.

Another limitation upon prosecution disclosure which is expressly **9.51** preserved by the 1996 Act is public interest immunity (PII). This was a

---

[107] *Unterpertinger* v *Austria*, A/110, (1991) 13 EHRR 175; *Lüdi* v *Switzerland*, A/238, (1993) 15 EHRR 173.
[108] Appl. No. 12045/86, (1987) 52 D&R 273. See Osborne, "Hearsay and the European Court of Human Rights" [1993] Crim LR 255.
[109] *Alberti* v *Italy*, Appl. No. 12013/86, (1989) 59 D&R 100.
[110] *Jespers* v *Belgium*, Appl. No. 8403/78, (1982) 27 D&R 61, 88.
[111] *Edwards* v *UK*, above n. 76.
[112] R. v *Winston Brown* (1995) 1 Cr. App. Rep 191, 198.

feature of the *Edwards* case, although the Court did not consider it because counsel for the defendant had failed to ask for disclosure of the report which had been withheld.[113] However, one of the dissenting judges of the Court questioned the compatibility with Article 6(1) of the use of PII certificates in criminal trials.[114] In *Cannon*, the Commission rejected a claim under Article 6(1) in circumstances where information relevant to the defence — that the two main prosecution witnesses were police informants — had not been disclosed on grounds of PII.[115] It relied upon the fact that the disputed evidence had been considered by both the trial judge and the Court of Appeal. The *ex parte* procedure whereby the prosecution can obtain permission not to disclose on grounds of PII without informing the defence is also under challenge in Strasbourg.[116]

Use of agents provocateurs

9.52 In a recent case, the Court found a breach of Article 6 where *agents provocateurs* were used to obtain evidence against the applicant. It drew a distinction between police acting merely as undercover agents and investigating criminal activity "in an essentially passive manner", which was acceptable, and cases where police agents exercise an influence such as to incite the commission of an offence. In the instant case, the police had instigated the offence with which the applicant had been charged and there was nothing to suggest that it would have been committed without their intervention. The activities of the *agents provocateurs*, and reliance upon them in subsequent criminal proceedings meant that, right from the outset, the applicant was definitely deprived of a fair trial.[117]

The rule against self-incrimination

9.53 Another important component of the evidential rules of Article 6 is the rule against self-incrimination. A person under investigation cannot be

---

[113] Above n. 76 at 432.
[114] *Ibid.* at 434–435.
[115] *Cannon v UK*, Appl. No. 29335/95, [1997] EHRLR 280.
[116] *R. v Davis, Johnson and Rowe* [1993] 1 WLR 281; *Rowe and Davis v UK*, Appl. No. 28910/95, (1998) 25 EHRR CD 118.
[117] *Teixeira de Castro v Portugal*, A/930, decision of 9 June 1998. Compare *Lüdi v Switzerland*, above n. 107, where the role of the police did not go beyond that of undercover agent and *Shadzad and KL v UK*, Appl. No. 34225/96, [1998] EHRLR 210 where the applicants had committed an offence even before the intervention of the *agent provocateur*. For the position under English law, see *R. v Smurthwaite and Gill* [1994] 1 ALL ER 896.

forced to produce incriminating documents,[118] or to answer questions which may incriminate him. The rule does not extend, however, to other aspects of the investigatory process, such as breathalyser and blood tests.[119] The rule against self-incrimination is embodied in the English common law,[120] but has on occasion been overridden by statute. A notable example to come before the Court was s. 436 of the Companies Act 1985, which required persons questioned by DTi company inspectors to answer questions and produce documents on pain of being held in contempt of court.[121] In *Funke*, the Court held that anyone charged with a criminal offence has the right "to remain silent and not to contribute to incriminating himself".[122] The rule against self-incrimination clearly has important implications for the right to silence in criminal cases, which is the right to remain silent and not to be taken to have incriminated oneself by so doing. That right, which was curtailed in English law by ss. 34-39 of the Criminal Justice and Public Order Act 1995, is considered further below under the heading of the presumption of innocence.

7. A PUBLIC HEARING

The right to a public hearing under Article 6(1), which aims, above all, to **9.54** maintain public confidence in the judicial system, is subject to a list of permitted limitations, in the interests of morals, public order, national security, juveniles, the protection of the private life of the parties or justice generally. A decision to hold a hearing in private must be necessary to achieve one of the permitted aims, and must be a proportionate response to the needs which it seeks to meet. In *Campbell and Fell*, for example, the Commission had held that the holding of prison disciplinary proceedings before a Board of Visitors behind closed doors was a breach of the public hearing requirement. The Court disagreed, accepting the potential difficulties involved in admitting the public to the precincts of a prison or of transporting prisoners if the proceedings were held outside. To hold the hearings in public would impose a disproportionate burden upon the state authorities.[123]

---

[118] *Funke* v *France*, A/256-A, (1993) 16 EHRR 297.
[119] For example, *X* v *Netherlands*, Appl. No. 8239/78, (1978) 16 D&R 184.
[120] *In re O* [1991] 2 WLR 475, 480.
[121] *Saunders* v *UK*, above n. 102.
[122] Above n. 118 at 326.
[123] *Campbell and Fell* v *UK*, A/80, (1985) 7 EHRR 165, 201.

9.55   Again, Article 6 requires an examination of the entirety of the particular judicial process. It may be permissible for hearings to be held in private where the individual has the option of an appeal which will be held in public. Applications for leave to appeal to the Court of Appeal in a criminal case (which, if rejected, may be renewed in open court), and civil interlocutory proceedings before a Master, which are held in private but which may be appealed ultimately into open court before the Court of Appeal, are two English examples which have been endorsed in Strasbourg.[124] Conversely, where a first instance hearing has taken place in public, it may not be necessary for an appeal also to be in public, particularly where issues of fact are not addressed on appeal.[125] The right to a public hearing may legitimately be waived by the individual, provided that the waiver is clear and unequivocal and there is no important public interest which weighs against it.[126] Article 6(1) further guarantees, without express limitation, that judgment will be publicly pronounced. That does not mean, however, that judgment must always be read out in open court; often, it will be sufficient for judgments to be made available to the public through the court registry.[127] There would, in principle, be no difficulty with the handing down to the parties of written judgments, which has become increasingly common in the English courts.

8. WITHIN A REASONABLE TIME

9.56   Article 6(1) guarantees a hearing, and a determination, within a reasonable time, in order to protect individuals from excessive procedural delays. It is this provision which has guaranteed the position of Italy at the top of the league table of states defaulting on their Convention obligations and, in general, excessive delay in the judicial process is a problem which has tended to afflict Continental legal systems to a greater extent than our own. Nevertheless, the UK has been found by the Court to be in breach of the temporal guarantee of Article 6 on three occasions. In *H v UK*, care proceedings lasting two years and seven months were held to be unreasonably lengthy.[128] In *Darnell v UK*, a consultant microbiologist was dismissed from his post in August 1984 and had his claim for unfair

---

[124] *Monnell and Morris v UK*, above n. 87; *X v UK*, Appl. No. 3860/68, (1970) 30 CD70.
[125] *Axen v Germany*, A/72, (1984) 6 EHRR 195.
[126] *Håkonsson v Sweden*, A/171, (1991) 13 EHRR 1.
[127] *Pretto v Italy*, A/71 (1984) 6 EHRR 182, 188–189.
[128] A/120, (1988) 10 EHRR 95.

dismissal finally rejected in April 1993.[129] In *Robins*, a breach of Article 6(1) arose out of costs proceedings which took more than four years to settle.[130]

9.57 The first step in assessing compliance with the reasonable time guarantee is to identify the beginning and end of the relevant period (see the discussion above on the beginning and the end of the protection afforded by Article 6(1)).[131] Next, a variety of factors are relevant in determining whether the period is reasonable, including the complexity of the case in fact and law, the importance of the interest which is at stake for the applicant and the part played by both the applicant and the judicial authorities in delaying matters. Matters must proceed all the faster where the interest is particularly important, as in criminal cases, and if the accused is being detained pending trial, the state must be especially diligent to progress the case without delay.[132] The Court has drawn an analogy with the Article 5(3) guarantee to trial of detainees within a reasonable time, although it should be noted that Article 6 covers also the period between conviction and the final determination of an appeal. Certain interests in the civil sphere have also been recognised as being of particular importance including employment status and access to children.[133]

9.58 No complaint can be made about delays which are caused by the applicant's own conduct and a difficult distinction has frequently to be drawn between the legitimate exercise of procedural rights and unnecessary or deliberate obstruction. In criminal cases, the accused has no duty actively to cooperate with the authorities.[134] In civil cases, the parties must show diligence in carrying out the procedural steps available to them, refrain from using delaying tactics and avail themselves of any means provided for shortening proceedings.[135] Even though the conduct of civil proceedings is primarily in the hands of the parties, the state retains ultimate responsibility for the length of civil cases.[136] On the other hand, an applicant may legitimately complain of delays which have been caused by the prosecuting authorities or the courts. States have a positive duty to organise their legal systems in such a way as to deliver justice within a reasonable time. For that reason, a backlog of other cases before

---

[129] A/272, (1994) 18 EHRR 205.
[130] Above n. 33.
[131] Paras. 9.17–9.18.
[132] *Abdoella* v *The Netherlands*, A/248-A, (1995) 20 EHRR 585, 598.
[133] See, for example, *H* v *UK*, above n. 66 at 111; *Buchholz* v *Germany*, A/42, (1981) 3 EHRR 597, 608–609.
[134] *Eckle* v *Germany*, above n. 44 at 30.
[135] *Unión Alimentaria Sanders* v *Spain*, A/157, (1990) 12 EHRR 24, 31.
[136] *Buchholz* v *Germany*, above n. 133 at 608.

the courts is, in principle, no excuse for delay but the Court will be sympathetic towards unexpected, temporary difficulties provided that the state has shown willing by taking remedial action.[137]

9. AN INDEPENDENT AND IMPARTIAL TRIBUNAL ESTABLISHED BY LAW

9.59 A tribunal is a body with a judicial function, which implies, in essence, that it has the capacity to take decisions which are legally binding,[138] even if it also acts in other capacities. The tribunal must be independent of the other branches of government and of the parties, subject, as are other components of Article 6(1), to the possibility of waiver in appropriate circumstances.[139] In *Campbell and Fell*, the Court laid down four basic criteria to be used in assessing the independence of a tribunal:[140]

- The manner of appointment of the members of the tribunal. Appointment by the executive is normal and does not in itself imply lack of independence.
- The duration of members' term of office. Even a relatively short, fixed term may be acceptable if there is a good reason for it. In *Campbell and Fell*, the three year tenure of the members of prison Boards of Visitors was explained by the fact that the position was unpaid.
- The existence of guarantees against outside pressures, which are particularly important where civil servants serve on tribunals. It is crucial that the executive does not retain the power to remove tribunal members during their term of office, save for exceptional reasons (such as misconduct, impropriety, etc.). In *Bryan*, the power of the Secretary of State for the Environment to revoke at any time the power of a planning Inspector to decide a planning appeal was central to the Court's conclusion that he was not independent and impartial within Article 6(1). It was irrelevant that the power was, in practice, exercised only very occasionally, and that there was no question of its exercise in the instant case.[141]

---

[137] *Ibid.*
[138] *Van de Hurk* v *The Netherlands*, A/288, (1994) 18 EHRR 481, 498.
[139] *Pfeifel and Plankl* v *Austria*, A/27, (1992) 14 EHRR 692.
[140] *Campbell and Fell* v *UK*, above n. 37 at 198–199.
[141] Above n. 79 at 358–359.

- Whether the tribunal presents an appearance of independence. This is an objective test, similar to that applied in respect of the requirement of impartiality (see below). In *Findlay* v *UK*, for example, the Court found that the system of court-martials within the armed forces breached the independence and impartiality requirements of Article 6(1).[142] The convening officer, who was the prosecuting authority, had appointed the members of the court-martial, all of whom were subordinate officers in units commanded by him. He also acted as the confirming officer, who ratified the decision of the court-martial.

9.60   The issue of the impartiality of a tribunal is hard to distinguish from its independence from the parties, and these labels are interchangeable in many cases. A tribunal must be impartial in the subjective sense that the personal convictions of its members are not biased, but also in the objective sense that it offers guarantees sufficient to exclude any legitimate doubt as to its partiality.[143] The approach of the Convention closely mirrors that of the English rule of bias, which also demands that justice must be seen to be done.[144]

9.61   The need for impartiality impinges also upon the jury system but the Convention will only assist in clear cases of bias. In *Holm*, for example, there was a breach of Article 6(1) where the majority of the jury in a libel case were active members of a political party with whom the defendants were closely connected, and against the interests of which the plaintiff had been accused of acting.[145] The difficulties of impugning the impartiality of a jury are more typically illustrated by the recent case of *Gregory* v *UK*.[146] In that case, the jury had broken off from their deliberations to pass a note to the judge saying that members had been showing signs of being racially prejudiced against the defendant. The judge consulted with both counsel and decided merely to direct the jury to ignore any prejudice in reaching their decision. The defendant was convicted, and complained that the jury should have been discharged or at the very least asked if they were capable of continuing. The Court dismissed the application, emphasising the importance of the rule protecting the secrecy of jury

---

[142] A/734, (1997) 23 EHRR 221; see also *Coyne* v *UK*, A/824, [1998] EHRLR 91.
[143] See, for example, *Langborger* v *Sweden*, A/155, (1990) 12 EHRR 416; *Gautrin* v *France*, A/913, decision of 20 May 1998.
[144] *R.* v *Gough* [1993] AC 646.
[145] *Holm* v *Sweden*, A/279-A, (1994) 18 EHRR 79.
[146] A/735, (1998) 25 EHRR 577.

deliberations and noting that both counsel had been consulted and that the defendant's counsel had not pressed for the jury to be discharged.[147]

10. ARTICLE 6(2): THE PRESUMPTION OF INNOCENCE

9.62 The presumption of innocence, enshrined in Article 6(2), is a fundamental principle of the English criminal law. There is a certain amount of overlap between the presumption of innocence, the requirement of a fair hearing under Article 6(1) and the specific guarantees listed in Article 6(3): matters such as the ability of an accused to challenge prosecution evidence, the disclosure of an accused's previous convictions, the admissibility of confession evidence and the right to silence, which are discussed above under Article 6(1), must be examined also under Article 6(2). Many imaginative arguments on the application of Article 6(2) have been rejected by the Commission and the Court. This section will focus on three issues of particular importance in the English criminal law, the right to silence, the use of presumptions and the effect of prejudicial publicity.

THE RIGHT TO SILENCE

9.63 According to the Court, "the right to remain silent under police questioning, and the privilege against self-incrimination are generally recognised international standards which lie at the heart of the notion of fair procedure under Article 6".[148] It has been argued that the provisions of the Criminal Justice and Public Order Act 1994, which allow inferences to be drawn from the failure of the accused to answer police questions or to testify at trial, create a very real risk that an accused will feel compelled to forfeit his right to silence, and to give potentially incriminating evidence. This compulsion may have the effect of shifting the burden of proof from the prosecution to the accused, contrary to Article 6(2). As such, the provisions of the Act have caused concern amongst defence lawyers

---

[147] Contrast *Remli* v *France*, A/612, (1996) 22 EHRR 253, where the domestic court had refused to take formal note of a racist remark attributed to a juror. In the civil sphere, see *Reid* v *UK*, Appl. 32350/96, [1998] EHRLR 41.
[148] *Murray (John)* v *UK*, A/593, (1996) 22 EHRR 29, 60.

and given rise to applications which are currently pending before the Commission.[149] In *Murray*, the Court has recently ruled, by a majority, in favour of the Government in proceedings concerning the Northern Ireland Order upon which the provisions of the 1994 Act were based.[150] Its decision is highly relevant to future challenges asserting the right to silence.

9.64 The applicant in *Murray* had been convicted of aiding and abetting false imprisonment after he had been arrested in a house in which a suspected police informer was being held captive by the IRA. He had declined to answer police questions, or to give evidence at trial, and so offered no explanation for his presence in the house. The trial court had, pursuant to the Criminal Evidence (Northern Ireland) Order 1988, drawn adverse inferences from his silence. According to the Court, the parameters of the right to silence under Article 6 are two-fold. On the one hand, it would be a breach of Article 6 to base a conviction "solely or mainly on an accused's silence or on a refusal to answer questions or to give evidence himself". On the other hand, the accused's silence may be taken into account "in situations which clearly call for an explanation from him." The line must be drawn somewhere in the middle, according to "the situations where inferences may be drawn, the weight attached to them by the national courts in their assessment of the evidence and the degree of compulsion inherent in the situation". Each case must be judged on its particular facts.

9.65 The important factors in *Murray* tending to the conclusion that Article 6 had not been breached were that the consequences of remaining silent had been clearly explained to the applicant, the prosecution case against him was "formidable" and there were various restrictions within the Order as to when inferences might be drawn. Also, it being a Northern Ireland case, the trier of fact was an experienced judge rather than a jury, who gave detailed reasons for his decision which were subject to review on appeal. In the circumstances, and having regard to the weight of evidence against the applicant, the drawing of inferences from his failure to account for his presence in the house was "a matter of common sense" and could not be regarded as unfair or unreasonable.[151] Five judges dissented, arguing that the drawing of inferences from silence amounted to the imposition of a penalty upon the accused by reason of his relying upon a right protected by the Convention.[152] The decision of the majority

---

[149] For example, *Quinn* v *UK*, Appl. No. 23496, (1997) 23 EHRR CD41; *Condron* v *UK*, Appl. No. 35718/97.
[150] Above n. 148.
[151] *Ibid.* at 61–63.
[152] *Ibid.* at 73–75.

clearly does not rule out future challenges to the restrictions upon the right to silence.[153] In English cases, the trier of fact will be a jury not a judge, and one of the major factors relied upon the Court will be absent. Also, much appears to depend upon the strength of the prosecution case. The 1994 Act allows a judge to direct that inferences from silence may be drawn regardless of the strength or weakness of the prosecution case, but it is not clear that this would be permitted under Article 6 where the prosecution case is less than "formidable".

THE USE OF PRESUMPTIONS

9.66   The presumption of innocence does not, in principle, preclude presumptions of law or fact by which proof of certain facts establishes a presumption which the accused then has the burden of rebutting. There are a number of these presumptions in the English criminal law, for example, the presumption that a man who lives habitually in the company of prostitutes is knowingly living on the earning of prostitutes, and the presumption that a person importing more than a certain amount of alcohol is doing so for business purposes. According to the Court, such presumptions must be maintained within reasonable limits having regard to the importance of what is at stake for the accused, and the rights of defence.[154] The Commission has stated that a presumption must not be so widely or unreasonably worded as to amount to a presumption of guilt.[155]

9.67   Neither of these formulations is of great use in predicting whether the operation of a particular presumption is in breach of Article 6(2). To add to the difficulty, it is clear that the answer depends very much on the facts of each case: a presumption which operates within reasonable limits in the case of one defendant, may breach Article 6(2) in the case of another. In *Salabiaku* v *France*, the defendant had been found by customs officers to be in possession of cannabis and, under French law, was presumed to be guilty of the offence of smuggling, subject to a limited range of extenuating circumstances.[156] The Court found no breach of Article 6(2), for two reasons. The French courts were careful to avoid resorting automatically to the presumption but diligently assessed all of the evidence before them and, secondly, they had concluded from

---

[153] See Munday, "Inferences from Silence and European Human Rights Law" [1996] Crim LR 370.
[154] *Salabiaku* v *France*, A/141-A, (1991) 13 EHRR 379, 388.
[155] *X* v *UK*, Appl. No. 5124/71, (1972) 42 CD135.
[156] Above n. 154.

the evidence that, regardless of the presumption, the applicant knew what was contained in his luggage.[157] It is apparent from the Court's judgment that the same provisions of French law could have operated in breach of Article 6(2) given a weaker case against the accused, and so a greater need to rely upon the presumption.

9.68 The presumption of innocence does not rule out offences of strict liability, which require only the proof of an *actus reus* and not a *mens rea*. The definition of the elements of an offence is a matter for national law; the important point is that the prosecution retains the burden of proving that the *actus reus* has been committed.[158]

PREJUDICIAL PUBLICITY

9.69 The presumption of innocence may be prejudiced by publicity surrounding a trial. Article 6(2) will be most easily breached where prejudicial statements are made by the investigating authorities. In *Allenet de Ribemont*, for example, a senior police officer stated at a press conference that the applicant had been the instigator of a murder, although formal charges had not yet been brought.[159] It is permissible, however, to indicate that a named individual is suspected of having committed an offence.[160] A more widespread problem is that of prejudicial comments in the media, given ever more intrusive press coverage of the judicial process. In one British case, the trial of which had been surrounded by substantial publicity, the Commission relied heavily on the fact that the trial judge had directed the jury in unambiguous terms that they should eliminate any prejudice from their minds.[161] This may be a requirement of Article 6. Also, it is probably sufficient that the matter of prejudicial publicity can be aired on appeal.[162]

---

[157] *Ibid.* at 390–391.
[158] *Bates v UK*, Appl. No. 26280/95, [1996] EHRLR 312.
[159] *Allenet de Ribemont v France*, A/308, (1995) 20 EHRR 557. Compare *Hall v UK*, Appl. No. 28772/95, [1998] EHRLR 215.
[160] *Krause v Switzerland*, Appl. No. 7986/77, (1978) 13 D&R 73.
[161] *X v UK*, Appl. 7542/76, 2 *Digest* 688.
[162] *Adolf v Austria*, A/49, (1982) 4 EHRR 313.

11. ARTICLE 6(3): MINIMUM GUARANTEES FOR CRIMINAL TRIALS

9.70 Article 6(3) lays down a series of minimum rights for persons charged with a criminal offence. "Charge" is to be interpreted in the same way as under Article 6(1) and certain of the rights may be capable of application during the pre-trial stages of the criminal process. Arguments based on a failure to comply with one of the specific guarantees set out in Article 6(3) tend to be examined also under Article 6(1) on the basis that they are all aspects of the right to a fair trial in criminal proceedings.

NOTIFICATION OF CHARGES

9.71 Under Article 6(3)(a), an accused must be notified promptly, in a language he understands, of the "nature and cause" of the charges against him, in order that he may have the basic information necessary for the preparation of his defence. In *Brozicek* v *Italy*, the Court found that a notification was sufficient for the purposes of Article 6(3)(a) which identified the offences alleged, the place and date when they were alleged to have been committed, the relevant laws breached and the name of the victim. There was a breach of this provision, however, because the notification was in Italian, which the accused did not understand.[163] An accused cannot complain, however, if it is his own fault that he has not learned of the full details of the charges against him, because, for example, he declined to attend a hearing.[164] There is also a suggestion in *Brozicek* that the accused is responsible for telling the authorities that he does not understand the language in which they have sought to communicate.[165]

PREPARATION OF THE DEFENCE

9.72 Under Article 6(3)(b), an accused must have adequate time and facilities for the preparation of his defence, and his appeal, if a right of appeal is

[163] A/167, (1990) 12 EHRR 371.
[164] *Campbell and Fell* v *UK*, above n. 37 at 203.
[165] Above n. 163 at 381.

provided.[166] A complainant must show that lack of time and/or facilities has caused actual prejudice to the fairness of his trial and, whilst there is considerable overlap between Article 6(3)(b) and other provisions of the Convention (in particular, Articles 6(1), 6(3)(c) and 8), successful applications under this heading are comparatively rare. The duration of an "adequate time" will clearly depend upon the circumstances, notably the complexity of the case and the logistics of appointing a defence lawyer. In the English courts, accused persons frequently meet their legal aid barrister for the first time only minutes before their trial, but the Commission has decided that this is not a breach of Article 6(3)(b) unless the applicant can show "prejudice to his representation during the proceedings".[167] It was significant in that case, however, that there had been a delay of several months before the applicant's trial came on for hearing in which he was able to contemplate his defence. Also, it appears that the more recent Court decision in *Twalib* v *Greece* adopts a more rigorous approach to this issue.[168]

9.73 As to facilities, the accused must be allowed to consult with his lawyer for the purposes of preparing his defence. This issue really only arises in the context of prisoners, and it is well-established that restrictions upon contact between prisoners and their legal advisors may be imposed for legitimate security or other public interest reasons.[169] Article 6(3)(b) also has implications for the disclosure by the prosecution of information and evidence which is likely to be useful to the defence.[170]

LEGAL ASSISTANCE

9.74 Under Article 6(3)(c), an accused has the right to defend himself, in person, or with the aid of effective legal assistance of his own choosing, which must be free if he lacks the means to pay for it and the interests of justice so require. There is an overlap between this provision and the right to adequate time and facilities under Article 6(3)(b), which focuses in particular on preparation for trial. Both provisions may be invoked, for example, to complain that private access to a lawyer has been frustrated by the authorities.[171]

---

[166] *Hadjianastassiou* v *Greece*, A/252, (1993) 16 EHRR 219.
[167] *X* v *UK*, Appl. No. 4042/69, (1970) 13 *Yearbook* 690, 696.
[168] A/929, decision of 9 June 1998.
[169] For example, *Campbell and Fell* v *UK*, above n. 37.
[170] See above, paras. 9.50–9.51.
[171] See *Can* v *Austria*, A/96 (1985); *S* v *Switzerland*, A/220, (1992) 14 EHRR 670.

9.75   The right of the accused to defend himself in person is not absolute: it is permissible for the state to require that a defendant has legal assistance in certain circumstances.[172] If the defendant does choose to represent himself, he cannot complain of any difficulties which result from his own failure to show the care which could reasonably be expected of him in the conduct of his defence.[173] If the accused does not wish to represent himself, he must have legal assistance. The accused's right to choose his legal representation is also not absolute but is subject to the standard domestic rules on professional qualifications and professional conduct, and to logistical difficulties — there will be no breach if the accused's preferred counsel cannot accept the brief because he is unavailable. The number of lawyers appointed by the accused may also be restricted provided that he is not thereby put at a disadvantage *vis-à-vis* the prosecution.[174]

9.76   The mere appointment of a legal aid lawyer is not sufficient to discharge the Government's obligations: states are also obliged to ensure that legal assistance for accused persons is effective. This means that there will be a breach of Article 6(3)(c) if official action has frustrated the ability of the lawyer to represent his client, such as the failure of the court to inform him of the date of a hearing.[175] It also means that whilst the authorities are not taken to guarantee the competence of legal aid lawyers and will not be responsible for any shortcomings in the accused's defence which are the fault of his lawyer, they must take action if the lawyer is manifestly ineffective, or if his shortcomings have otherwise been brought to their attention.[176] In contrast with other provisions of Article 6, an applicant does not need to show that he has suffered actual prejudice as a result of the failure of the state to secure legal assistance for him. The standard is much lower — the Court will ask merely whether it is plausible that a lawyer would have been of assistance.[177]

At what stage is legal assistance required?

9.77   The right of access to a lawyer applies also at the stage of preliminary investigations by the police.[178] It is not an absolute right at the preliminary

---

[172] For example, *Croissant v Germany*, A/237-B, (1993) 16 EHRR 135.
[173] See, for example, *Melin v France*, A/261-A, (1994) 17 EHRR 1, where the defendant was formerly a practising lawyer.
[174] *Ensslin, Baader and Raspe v Germany*, Appl. No. 7572/76, (1978) 14 D&R 64.
[175] *Goddi v Italy*, A/76, (1984) 6 EHRR 457.
[176] *Kamasinski v Austria*, A/168, (1991) 13 EHRR 36, 62.
[177] *Artico v Italy*, A/37, (1981) 3 EHRR 1, 14–15.
[178] *Imbrioscia v Switzerland*, A/275, (1994) 17 EHRR 441.

stage, but it must be respected where a failure to grant access might seriously prejudice the fairness of the trial. This was the case in *Murray*, where the accused had been denied access to a lawyer for 48 hours under s. 15 of the Northern Ireland (Emergency Provisions) Act 1987. The fact that, pursuant to restrictions upon his right to silence, inferences could be drawn at trial from his attitude to police questioning, meant that, without the benefit of legal advice at the earliest opportunity, his right to a fair trial could be irretrievably prejudiced.[179] Section 58 of PACE provides for the right to consult a solicitor before being questioned by the police, a right which is subject to various grounds of delay. It may be that the advent in England and Wales of restrictions upon the right to silence similar to those which concerned the Court in *Murray* will affect the propriety of delaying access to a lawyer under s. 58.

Legal aid rules

9.78 Legal aid must be given where the accused lacks sufficient means to pay (a criterion which has not been developed in the Strasbourg case-law), and the interests of justice so require. The complexity of the case, the ability of the accused to conduct or contribute to his own defence and the seriousness of the charges and potential penalty are all relevant to the assessment of what justice requires. Of these factors, the potential penalty is the most important: where the accused faces being deprived of his liberty, the interests of justice in principle require that free legal representation is provided.[180] It should not matter that the accused has little prospect of success on appeal.[181] Any decision to refuse legal aid should be periodically reviewed to examine whether circumstances have changed and the interests of justice require a different decision.[182]

9.79 Various reforms have been proposed to the legal aid system in England and Wales with the aim of reducing the overall cost to the taxpayer, but it is unlikely that financial considerations could justify depriving an accused of legal assistance, and of a fair trial. Whilst the Commission has recognised the issue of cost in the context of limiting the amount of contact between an accused and his legal aid counsel,[183] it is submitted that legal aid must be made available where this is necessary to guarantee a fair hearing, regardless of the cost to the state. That view accords with

---

[179] Above n. 148 at 66–67.
[180] *Benham v UK*, above n. 39 at 324.
[181] *Boner v UK*, A/300-B, (1995) 19 EHRR 246.
[182] *Granger v UK*, A/174, (1990) 12 EHRR 469.
[183] *M v UK*, Appl. No. 9728/82 (1983) 36 D&R 155, 158.

the approach adopted by the Court in the civil sphere.[184] One way of reducing the cost to the public purse which does not breach Article 6(3)(c) is by requiring beneficiaries of legal aid to pay back the costs at a later date (provided, of course, that they have sufficient means to pay).[185]

WITNESSES

9.80 Under Article 6(3)(d), the accused has the right, first, to cross-examine witnesses against him. The application of the fair hearing guarantee to witness evidence, and in particular the primacy of oral evidence and the hearsay rule has been noted above, under Article 6(1). Article 6(3)(d), in principle, requires that the accused is present when witnesses against him are being questioned but is subject to exceptions in the interests of justice, for example, where it is necessary to protect the witness from intimidation.[186] On this basis, it is unlikely that English law rules which permit evidence to be given by video link in, for example, child abuse cases, would contravene the Convention.

9.81 Secondly, the accused has the right to obtain the attendance and examination-in-chief of witnesses on his behalf under the same conditions as witnesses against him. Violations of this guarantee are unlikely to occur under the common law system whereby the parties are responsible for calling their own witnesses. Most complaints arise as a result of the decisions of defence lawyers, and it is well-established that the failure of a defence lawyer to call an important witness cannot be imputed to the state.[187]

FREE ASSISTANCE OF INTERPRETERS

9.82 Once he has been charged, an accused has the unqualified right under Article 6(3)(e) to the free assistance of an interpreter if he cannot understand or speak the language of the investigatory and judicial system. The right is a once and for all exemption from interpretation costs which,

---

[184] *Airey* v *Ireland*, above n. 69.
[185] *X* v *Germany*, Appl. No. 9365/81, (1982) 28 D&R 229.
[186] *Kurup* v *Denmark*, Appl. No. 11219/84, (1985) 42 D&R 287.
[187] *F* v *UK*, Appl. No. 18123/91, (1993) 15 EHRR CD32.

unlike the general right to legal assistance under Article 6(3)(d), applies regardless of whether or not the accused has sufficient means to pay.[188] It extends to the translation of all documents or statements which it is essential that the accused understand if he is to have a fair trial.[189]

12. RETROSPECTIVE CRIMINAL OFFENCES

Article 7 provides: **9.83**

"1. No one shall be held guilty of any criminal offence on account of any act or omission which did not constitute a criminal offence under national or international law at the time when it was committed. Nor shall a heavier penalty be imposed than the one that was applicable at the time the criminal offence was committed.

2. This article shall not prejudice the trial and punishment of any person for any act or omission which, at the time when it was committed, was criminal according to the general principles of law recognised by civilised nations."

The principle that a person should not be penalised for an act or omission which was not clearly illegal at the time that it was done is a fundamental aspect of the rule of law. Article 7 applies the principle to conviction for "criminal offences", which should be given the same interpretation as "criminal charge" in Article 6(1).[190] It may, therefore, include charges which are classified as civil under national law, such as civil contempt of court.[191] Article 7 does not, however, apply to other aspects of the criminal process which do not involve conviction for an offence charged, such as a decision to detain.[192] Nor does it apply to retrospective laws which are properly characterised as civil in character, although such laws are vulnerable to challenge under Article 1 of the First Protocol which confers the right to the peaceful enjoyment of possessions. A good example of a successful challenge to a retroactive civil law is *Pressos Compania Naviera and others* v *Belgium*, in which the Belgian Government had legislated with retrospective effect so as to deprive the

---

[188] *Lüdicke, Belkacem and Koç* v *Germany*, A/29, (1979–80) 2 EHRR 149, 160–161.
[189] *Ibid.* at 164.
[190] Harris, O'Boyle and Warbrick, *Law of the European Convention on Human Rights* (Butterworths, 1995) at 276.
[191] *Harman* v *UK*, Appl. No. 10038/82, (1984) 38 D&R 53.
[192] *De Wilde, Ooms and Versyp* v *Belgium*, A/12, (1979–80) 1 EHRR 373, 411.

applicants of accrued causes of action in negligence (which qualified as "possessions" within Article 1).[193]

9.84   The first and most obvious application of Article 7 is to retrospective criminal legislation.[194] In interpreting both civil and criminal legislation, English courts apply a presumption that statutory rules are not intended to have retroactive effect, which can only be displaced by clear wording to the contrary.[195] However, despite the opinion of Lord Reid that it is "scarcely credible that any government department would promote or that Parliament would pass retrospective criminal legislation", British legislation has been successfully challenged under Article 7.[196] In *Welch*, a convicted drug dealer complained of an order made pursuant to the Drug Trafficking Offences Act 1986 which confiscated the proceeds of his crimes.[197] He had been arrested in November 1986, but the Act had not come into force until January 1987. The Court rejected the Government's arguments that the Act, whilst admittedly having retroactive effect, did not impose a "penalty" within Article 7. "Penalty", like "criminal" has a specific Convention meaning and, having regard to the nature and purpose of the order, the procedures involved in making and implementing it, and its severity, the applicant had suffered "a more far-reaching detriment" than was lawful at the time he committed the offences.[198]

9.85   A less obvious but equally unlawful type of retroactive effect occurs where a statutory or common law rule is extended through judicial interpretation so as to apply to acts which were not foreseeably criminal at the time they were committed.[199] The elements of an offence may be clarified and adapted to new circumstances but they may not be fundamentally changed. A good example of this distinction is the English law offence of marital rape, which was "created" by the House of Lords in *R* v *R* when it finally abrogated the common law principle that a man could not rape his wife.[200] In *SW and CR* v *UK*,[201] two men whose offences took place before *R* v *R* but who were nevertheless convicted of marital rape, challenged their convictions as contrary to Article 7. The Court held that the new offence of marital rape was merely an example of

---

[193] Above n. 63.
[194] Note the same rule in European Community law: *R* v *Kirk*, Case 63/68 [1984] ECR 2689.
[195] See Bennion, *Statutory Interpretation* (Butterworths, 3rd ed., 1997) at 623; *Waddington* v *Miah* [1974] 1 WLR 693. See also the judgment of Lord Steyn in *R.* v *Home Secretary ex parte Pierson* [1997] 3 WLR 492.
[196] And under EC law: *R.* v *Kirk*, above n. 194.
[197] *Welch* v *UK*, A/307-A, (1995) 20 EHRR 247.
[198] *Ibid.* at 262–263. Contrast *Curran* v *UK*, Appl. No. 36987/97, [1998] EHRLR 507.
[199] See the analogous rule in EC law: *Kolpinghuis Nijmegen* Case 80/86 [1987] ECR 3969.
[200] [1992] 1 AC 599.
[201] A/355-B/C, (1996) 21 EHRR 363, 401–2.

the gradual clarification of the rules of criminal liability through judicial interpretation, a clarification which could reasonably have been foreseen. In *Choudhury*, the Divisional Court relied in part on Article 7 when refusing to extend the application of the common law offence of blasphemy to religions other than Christianity.[202]

9.86 International law rules are mentioned in both Article 7(1) and (2). According to Article 7(1), a person may be convicted of an offence which was not contrary to national law at the time it was committed but was contrary to international law. This allows certain offences, such as hijacking, drug trafficking and torture, which are recognised as criminal under international law to be prosecuted in any jurisdiction, regardless of whether there is an appropriate prohibition under national law. It does not allow the criminal law of one jurisdiction to be enforced in the courts of another. Article 7(2) makes specific provision for war crimes trials, which generally involve the prosecution of offences which were not criminal under domestic law at the time they were committed. As a result of these exceptions to the general rule, s. 1 of the War Crimes Act 1991, which allows the prosecution in the UK of crimes committed on foreign soil during the Second World War, would not contravene Article 7.

---

[202] *R. v Chief Metropolitan Stipendiary Magistrate ex parte Choudhury* [1991] 1 QB 429.

Chapter 10
PRIVACY AND FAMILY LIFE

10.1

Article 8 provides:

"1. Everyone has the right to respect for his private and family life, his home and his correspondence.

2. There shall be no interference by a public authority with the exercise of this right except such as is in accordance with the law and is necessary in a democratic society in the interests of national security, public safety or the economic well-being of the country, for the prevention of disorder or crime, for the protection of health or morals, or for the protection of the rights and freedoms of others."

Article 8 is one of the most frequently-invoked Convention articles and has given rise to some of the most far-reaching decisions of the Court of Human Rights. Contrary to what has occurred in relation to other of the Convention's key provisions, including freedom of expression and the right to a fair trial, the English courts have never indicated that the provisions of Article 8 are already reflected in the common law. Indeed, there are a number of authoritative judicial statements to precisely the opposite effect, that English law does not recognise a right to privacy.[1] For that reason, the advent in domestic law of the right to privacy and family life has been one of the most eagerly awaited aspects of the passage of the Human Rights Act.

10.2

Article 8 is one of the four central provisions of the Convention to lay down a right, or a series of rights (Article 8(1)) and then immediately provide for various limitations upon it (Article 8(2)). The express limitations contained in Article 8(2) mean that establishing an interference with private life, etc. is only the first stage towards showing a violation of the Convention. As the scope of Article 8 has developed, a growing proportion of complaints are found, without difficulty, to fall within Article 8(1); the focus then shifts to Article 8(2), to the validity of the justification cited

---

[1] Notably *Kaye* v *Robertson* [1991] FSR 62, 71 and *R.* v *Broadcasting Complaints Commission ex parte Barclay* [1997] EMLR 62, 69.

by the authorities for the interference in question. A great number of cases turn on the criterion of whether the interference is "necessary in a democratic society", and to the application of the principle of proportionality which is inherent in that test. The Commission and the Court are then engaged in what is, essentially, a fact-specific exercise of determining whether a particular measure went further than was necessary in order to achieve its objectives.

10.3   This chapter will, first, sketch out in broad terms the scope of the interests which are protected by Article 8 — private and family life, the home and correspondence — and then analyse the central components of the requirement that a state "respect" those interests. It will then proceed to outline the principal case-law under Article 8 under a series of different subject headings. These headings are not exhaustive: it is not possible in a work of this nature to cover even the existing, voluminous case-law, and further categories of claim will undoubtedly arise in the future.

1. THE SCOPE OF ARTICLE 8

10.4   Article 8 incorporates the right to respect for four distinct interests: private life, family life, the home and correspondence. There is considerable overlap between these four interests and the Commission and the Court have frequently not descended to specifics as to which of the four they felt to be at issue in a particular case. The scope of private life is the broadest of the four, and in many situations, the obligation to respect private life takes effect as the boundaries of the obligation to respect one of the other interests are reached: for example, a personal relationship which is not covered by the notion of family life may require respect under the broader heading of private life.

PRIVATE LIFE

10.5   The Court has repeatedly stated that the notion of private life is a broad one and is not susceptible to exhaustive definition.[2] In general, it encompasses, firstly, the idea of an "inner circle", in which the individual

---

[2] See, for example, *Costello-Roberts v UK*, A/247-C, (1995) 19 EHRR 112, 135.

may live his own personal life as he chooses and from which he may exclude the outside world. It also comprises to a certain degree the right to move outside the inner circle and to establish and develop relationships with other human beings.[3] Various specific aspects of the right to private life can be identified.

Privacy

The English law notion of private life tends to focus upon privacy in the sense of excluding the outside world from the individual's personal space. This is the starting point for Article 8(1), and has implications for intrusions by the forces of the state and by private bodies such as newspapers, both in the home, and outside. Intrusions contrary to Article 8(1) may be physical, as where an individual is placed under surveillance, or his home or office is searched, or rather more abstract, such as where personal records are compiled and kept by the state.[4]   **10.6**

Identity

Private life includes the right to choose a name as a means of personal identification.[5] More fundamentally perhaps, it protects the individual's choice of sexual identity, and the Court has decided a number of cases on the rights of homosexuals and transsexuals. In *Gaskin*, the applicant complained about the refusal of a local authority to disclose files concerning his childhood spent with various foster parents. The Court held that Article 8 was engaged since the files contained information concerning highly personal aspects of his childhood, development and history, and were his principal source of information about those formative years.[6] The applicant's very identity was at issue.   **10.7**

---

[3] *Niemietz v Germany*, A/251-B, (1993) 16 EHRR 97, 111. Private life does not extend to relationships with animals, so the keeping of a pet is not an aspect of its owner's private life: for example, *Bates v UK*, Appl. 26280/95, [1996] EHRLR 312.
[4] For example, *Leander v Sweden*, A/116, (1987) 9 EHRR 433; *Murray v UK*, A/300-A, (1995) 19 EHRR 193.
[5] For example, *Stjerna v Finland*, A/299-B, (1996) 24 EHRR 195.
[6] *Gaskin v UK*, A/160, (1990) 12 EHRR 36, 45.

Physical integrity

10.8   The "inner circle", obviously, includes the physical integrity of the individual, and, subject to a *de minimis* test, any interference with the body might fall within Article 8(1). Physical abuse, including corporal punishment, is covered,[7] as is, for example, the obligation to take a blood test.[8]

Moral integrity

10.9   This is also an extremely broad concept which takes in both the individual's moral and philosophical preferences, and the expression of those preferences in relationships with others. State regulation of sexual preferences has been an important area of concern for the Court, which has taken several decisions on the legal treatment of homosexuals.[9] Personal political or religious convictions also fall within the private sphere but the Court tends to deal with them under Article 10 (freedom of expression) or, occasionally, Article 9 (freedom of thought, conscience and religion).[10]

FAMILY LIFE

10.10   The right to family life is, in essence, the right to live in proximity as a family such that family ties can develop normally.[11] Protection is afforded to the family ties which the individual has already established. There is no right under Article 8 to establish a family or to break up a family, for example, by way of divorce.[12] Article 12 goes some way towards a right to establish a family, but only for married persons.[13]

10.11   The central "family" relationships envisaged in Article 8 are those between spouses and between parents and their children. In reality, however, the types of relationships which may count as family ties under

---

[7] See *Costello-Roberts v UK*, above n. 2 at 135.
[8] *X v Austria*, Appl. No. 8278/78, (1979) 18 D&R 154, 156.
[9] For example, *Dudgeon v UK*, A/45, (1982) 4 EHRR 149.
[10] See, for example, *Vogt v Germany*, A/323, (1996) 21 EHRR 205; *Kokkinakis v Greece*, A/269-A, (1994) 17 EHRR 397.
[11] See generally Liddy, "The Concept of Family Life under the ECHR" [1998] EHRLR 15.
[12] *Johnston v Ireland*, A/112, (1987) 9 EHRR 203.
[13] See, for example, *Rees v UK*, A/106, (1987) 9 EHRR 56, 68.

Article 8 extend much further. A *de facto* relationship between a man and a woman short of marriage may constitute family life, depending on the strength of the ties between them. According to the Court, important indicators are "whether the couple live together, the length of their relationship and whether they have demonstrated their commitment to each other by having children or by any other means."[14] Adopting this analysis, it found that there were family ties between a female to male transsexual, his partner with whom he had lived for almost 20 years and their child, conceived through artificial insemination. Another prominent example is *Kroon v The Netherlands* in which the Court stated that, as a rule, it is necessary that the man and woman live together but, exceptionally, other factors may demonstrate that their relationship has sufficient constancy to create *de facto* family ties.[15] In that case, Article 8 did protect a man and woman who were not married and did not co-habit, but had four children.

The ambit of the protected parent-child relationship extends to illegitimate children,[16] and to adopted children,[17] but it will not cover the relationship between an adult child and his parents without evidence of "further elements of dependency involving more than the normal emotional ties".[18] In a British case, the father of an unborn child which was aborted by its mother without the father's consent complained of an interference with the family ties between himself and the foetus. The Commission appeared to accept that family life under Article 8 could extend to the relationship between parent and foetus, but the absence of procedural rights for the father did not amount to a failure to respect his family life, having regard to the rights of the pregnant mother.[19] "Family" ties may also exist between brothers and sisters,[20] between uncle and nephew,[21] and between grandparents and grandchildren.[22] **10.12**

Establishing that a particular relationship falls within the scope of family life involves a twofold enquiry: first, is the relationship is of a type which has been recognised in the past as giving rise to family ties and second, how close is the actual relationship between the individuals concerned. The second enquiry is necessary since a family tie, such as that between husband and wife which is, in principle, firmly within Article 8 can be **10.13**

---

[14] *X, Y and Z v UK,* A/753, (1997) 24 EHRR 143, 166.
[15] A/297-C, (1995) 19 EHRR 263, 283.
[16] *Marckx v Belgium,* A/31, (1979-80) 2 EHRR 330.
[17] *X v France,* Appl. No. 9993/82, (1982) 31 D&R 241.
[18] *Pathan v UK,* Appl. No. 26292/95, unreported decision of 16 January 1996.
[19] *X v UK,* Appl. No. 8416/78, (1980) 19 D&R 244, 254.
[20] For example, *Boughanemi v France,* A/613, (1996) 22 EHRR 228.
[21] *Boyle v UK,* A/282-B, (1995) 19 EHRR 179.
[22] *Price v UK,* Appl. No. 12402/86, (1988) 55 D&R 224.

found to have been broken by subsequent events. For example, the fact that a married couple have had a lengthy voluntary separation will count against them; co-habitation, or enforced separation may count in their favour. The strength of the ties revealed by this enquiry serves not only to indicate whether a relationship is within Article 8(1) but also affects the strength of the justification which a state will need to establish under Article 8(2) if it is to interfere with it. Where a particular relationship falls outside the recognised bounds of family life, it may nevertheless acquire protection as an aspect of private life.[23]

THE HOME

10.14   The home is a stable place of residence. In *Buckley*, one of a number of recent challenges by gypsies to British planning legislation which restricts their itinerant lifestyle, the applicant had been refused planning permission for her caravan on the land which she owned, and had been subject to enforcement proceedings. The Court rejected the Government's argument that only a "home" which was legally established could fall within Article 8(1). It noted that the applicant had bought the land to establish her residence there, had lived there continuously for several years and that it had not been suggested that she had established, or intended to establish, another residence elsewhere.[24] A more difficult question is whether the home includes a place where one does not actually live but wishes to live. In *Gillow*, the applicants sought to return to live in a house in Guernsey which had once been their home. The Court found that they had retained sufficient connection with the house for it to merit that description but it was notable that the applicants did not have a home anywhere else.[25] More recently, however, the Court has ruled that a woman who had been deprived of access to land upon which she wished to build a new residence could not rely upon Article 8's protection for the home.[26] In *Niemietz*, the Court decided that the home also covers business premises, in that case the offices of a lawyer. It would have been difficult to draw a firm distinction since, as the Court pointed out,

---

[23] For example, *Wakefield* v *UK*, Appl. No. 15817/89, (1990) 66 D&R 251, 255 (engagement); *B* v *UK*, Appl. No. 16106/90, (1990) 64 D&R 278 (stable homosexual relationship).

[24] *Buckley* v *UK*, A/658, (1997) 23 EHRR 101, 124-125. See also, on gypsies, planning law and the right to respect for the home, *Turner* v *UK*, Appl. No. 30294/96, (1997) 23 EHRR CD181; *Smith* v *UK*, Appl. No. 26666/95 (1998) 25 EHRR CD 52 (and others there reported).

[25] *Gillow* v *UK*, A/109, (1989) 11 EHRR 335.

[26] *Loizidou* v *Turkey*, A/707, (1997) 23 EHRR 513, 533–534.

professional or business activities might well be carried out from a private residence and non-commercial activities from business premises. It indicated, however, that business premises would be less deserving of protection from state interference than an individual's place of residence.[27]

As with the right to family life, Article 8 does not confer a right to a **10.15** home, only a right to respect for the home which one already has. This aspect of Article 8 must be viewed in conjunction with Article 1 of the First Protocol, the right to peaceful enjoyment of possessions, which extends to real property. Whereas Article 1 protects the property right in a home, and so its financial value, Article 8 protects the right to occupy it peacefully and to enjoy its comforts.

CORRESPONDENCE

"Correspondence" has its ordinary meaning — letters, telephone calls, **10.16** presumably also faxes, e-mails, etc. The right to respect for correspondence is a right that the *medium* of correspondence is not monitored, censored or otherwise restricted. Complaints about censorship or restriction of the *content* of correspondence fall more easily under Article 10 on freedom of expression.

2. THE MEANING OF "RESPECT" FOR PRIVATE LIFE, ETC.

The rights contained in Article 8(1) are not laid down in absolute terms. **10.17** There is no right to privacy as such, only a right that the state respect your privacy and the notion of "respect" has important implications for the extent of the protection afforded by Article 8.

THE DE MINIMIS TEST

The requirement of respect for private life incorporates a *de minimis* test: **10.18** not every interference in the private sphere of an individual will constitute

---

[27] Above n. 3 at 112.

a failure to respect his private life. The *Costello-Roberts* case, for example, raised the issue of corporal punishment, which is undoubtedly a violation of a child's physical integrity. However, the Court found that the incident of corporal punishment at school which was complained of did not have sufficient adverse physical and psychological effects on the child to fall within Article 8, having regard to the fact that sending a child to school was in itself an interference with his private life.[28]

POSITIVE OBLIGATIONS

10.19 The duty to respect private life entails, as a starting point, that the state should not take active measures which interfere with the private lives of its citizens. The enactment of penal legislation to prohibit certain personal, moral choices, or the undertaking of surveillance activities by the police or the security services are examples of active steps which infringe the negative obligation to respect private life. It is well-established, however, that, in ensuring respect for private life, Article 8 also imposes positive obligations upon states, that is, obligations to take positive steps to facilitate and protect the essential features of private life.

10.20   These positive obligations fall into two categories. The first category comprises the state's obligations to take positive steps to respect private life in its relationship with its citizens. In *Gaskin*, for example, the applicant's complaint was that Liverpool City Council had failed to disclose to him vital information about his childhood and personal development. The case was not, therefore, about a measure taken by the Council which infringed the right to private life but about the Council's omission to act, and to take the necessary steps to ensure respect for private life. The Court found, accordingly, that there had been a breach of the positive obligations imposed by Article 8.[29] Another prominent example is that the state has a positive obligation to provide adequate legal procedures and remedies which may be invoked where private and family life is endangered. Therefore, where the state seeks to interfere with family life by taking children into care, it must ensure that those affected have sufficient opportunity to influence and to challenge the relevant decisions.[30]

---

[28] Above n. 2 at 134–135.
[29] Above n. 6.
[30] See, for example, *B v UK*, A/121, (1988) 10 EHRR 87.

The second category of positive obligations are state obligations to **10.21**
regulate relationships between its citizens so as to protect an individual's
private life from interference by other individuals. There are innumerable
ways in which it may be argued that the state ought to intervene in
relations between individuals in the interests of private life. In one early
example, the Court held that the Dutch Government had a positive duty
to protect mentally handicapped minors from sexual assault by, in that
case, enabling their parents to file criminal complaints in respect of
assaults upon them.[31] Those persons who would seek to use Article 8
to curb the intrusive activities of the mass media must base their claims
upon the positive obligation of the state to provide laws which protect
their private life from interference by other individuals in society.
Recently, in *Botta* v *Italy*, the Court indicated that it would only find a
breach of positive obligations under Article 8 where there is "a direct and
immediate link between the measures sought by an applicant and the
latter's private and/or family life". The applicant had complained about
inactivity on the part of Italian authorities in enforcing a law which
required operators of private beach facilities to make them accessible
to disabled people. The Court held, however, that the right asserted
concerned interpersonal relations of such broad and indeterminate scope
that no conceivable direct link could exist.[32]

The nature and scope of positive obligations under the Convention are **10.22**
further discussed in chapter 6; they are particularly important under
Article 8 since, in modern society, the greatest threat to private life is
frequently posed not by the state but by private bodies, such as the press.
However, whilst the recognition of positive obligations within Article 8(1)
has the effect of significantly extending the range of potential uses to
which Article 8 can be put, it is not easy to establish a breach of the
Convention on this basis. Where it is argued that the state has failed to
take reasonable and appropriate (positive) measures to secure rights
guaranteed by Article 8(1), Article 8(2), with its list of permitted interferences, is not engaged. However, the Court also permits a wide margin
of appreciation to states in deciding which positive steps are required by
the need to respect private life and the process of balancing the rights of
the individual against the needs of society under Article 8(1) is ultimately
very similar to the analysis required under Article 8(2).

---

[31] *X and Y* v *The Netherlands*, A/91, (1986) 8 EHRR 235. See also *Stubbings* v *UK*, A/683, (1997) 23
EHRR 213.
[32] A/880, decision of 24 February 1998.

PROCEDURAL OBLIGATIONS

10.23 The notion of "respect" for private life, etc. encompasses an obligation not only of substance, to refrain from unjustified interference, but also of procedure. As noted above, states must provide for appropriate procedures for determining, as a matter of domestic law, whether a particular interference is warranted. The procedures in the UK for determining issues of custody, care or adoption of children have been called into question a number of times in Strasbourg. In *B* v *UK*, for example, a mother successfully complained that she had been excluded from important stages of the procedure leading to the adoption of her child.[33] Insofar as it imposes procedural obligations, Article 8 may overlap with the right to a fair hearing under Article 6, but whereas the latter requires, in essence, access to a court, Article 8 can found claims relating to earlier stages of the proceedings.

DISCRIMINATION

10.24 Article 8 is frequently more potent where it can be coupled with a claim of discrimination under Article 14. Many of the successful claims brought by applicants claiming legal recognition of, or legal protection for their gender, their sexuality or their sexual morality have incorporated a claim of discrimination under Article 14.[34] Also, once a state has taken a positive step to promote or protect private or family life it must, in principles extend the benefits to all without discrimination.[35]

3. JUSTIFYING A FAILURE TO RESPECT PRIVATE LIFE

INTERFERENCE BY A PUBLIC AUTHORITY

10.25 Where there has been interference with private life by legislation, or otherwise through the actions of a public authority, the authority will

---

[33] Above n. 30.

[34] See, for example, *Abdulaziz, Cabales and Balkandali*, A/94, (1985) 7 EHRR 471.

[35] See, however, *Petrovic* v *Austria*, A/893, [1998] EHRLR 487 (discrimination in providing maternity but not paternity leave payments was justified).

attempt to justify itself under Article 8(2). In practice, the majority of claims under Article 8 founder at this stage. A more detailed discussion of the justification test, which is, for all intents and purposes, identical to that employed under Articles 9-11, is contained in chapter 6 and the following is intended as a summary only. Any interference must be "in accordance with the law", a phrase which has the same meaning as "prescribed by law" in Articles 9-11.[36] It implies that the interference must be sanctioned by legal rules which are accessible to potential victims and that the application of those rules is foreseeable. Interference with privacy by the state security forces, for example, by surveillance or telephone-tapping, has fallen foul of these requirements because it has lacked formal legal sanction, or because the rules regulating it were vague and open-ended.[37]

10.26   Interferences which are in accordance with the law must be directed at one of the legitimate aims set out in Article 8(2). These are broadly worded and, save in rare cases of bad faith, the state authority will usually be able to make out a case that one or more of the permitted aims are at issue. The interference must be "necessary" to achieve its desired aim. This implies, first, that it must be intended to meet a "pressing social need".[38] Secondly, and more important, it implies that the restrictive effects of a measure must be proportionate to the objective(s) which it seeks to achieve. Put another way, the interference must go no further than is strictly necessary to achieve its aims, and the state has a margin of appreciation in deciding whether this is so. For example, it is disproportionate to intercept, open and read prisoners' correspondence for the purposes of checking whether it includes unauthorised enclosures; opening it in the presence of the prisoner would be sufficient to meet the needs of the situation.[39] Again, depending upon his individual circumstances, it may be disproportionate and unnecessary to deport an immigrant who is found guilty of a criminal offence. An example is *Nasri* v *France*, where the Algerian applicant, whom the French Government had proposed to deport, was a deaf-mute who was dependent upon his family and friends in France.[40] The breadth of the state's margin of appreciation will determine how prepared are the courts to intervene and substitute their judgment of what is necessary for that of the public authority. It varies from case to case according to a variety of factors, including the particular

---

[36] See *Silver* v *UK*, A/61, (1983) 5 EHRR 347, 371.
[37] For example, *Malone* v *UK*, A/82, (1985) 7 EHRR 14.
[38] *Handyside* v *UK*, A/24, (1979–90) EHRR 737, 753–754.
[39] See *Campbell* v *UK*, A/223, (1993) 15 EHRR 137, 161.
[40] A/324, (1996) 21 EHRR 458.

facet of private life which is at issue, and the harmful effects of the interference upon the applicant.[41]

JUSTIFYING A FAILURE TO ACT TO PROTECT PRIVATE LIFE

10.27   Where the allegation is that the state is in breach of its positive obligations under Article 8 by failing to take active steps to protect private life, there is no question of any "interference by a public authority" which requires justification under Article 8(2). Therefore, the claim must be determined under Article 8(1) alone. This does not mean, however, that a failure to take steps to safeguard private life cannot be justified. Rather, the Court has imported into Article 8(1) a justification test akin to that which applies under Article 8(2).[42] Two factors should be considered. The first is that justification will be easier where the current state of the law can be shown to pursue one of the legitimate objectives enumerated in Article 8(2).[43] For example, a failure to prohibit press intrusion into private life might be justified on the basis of safeguarding the rights of others to freedom of expression.

10.28   The second factor is the state's margin of appreciation, which is wider where positive obligations are concerned. According to the Court, the choice of means calculated to secure respect for private life falls, in principle, within the margin of appreciation, and a claim will only succeed where some facet of private life has been left completely unprotected. In *Stubbings*, for example, the complaint was that English law time limits governing claims for intentionally-inflicted personal injuries left private life unprotected, because they precluded claims by victims of childhood sexual abuse who had not appreciated the nature of their injuries until years after the abuse was inflicted.[44] The claim raised the issue of the positive steps which the Government should take to protect the physical and moral integrity of individuals from invasions by others. It was rejected by the Court, essentially because criminal sanctions were available against the wrongdoers, hence private life was not wholly unprotected.[45]

---

[41] See further, chapter 6, paras. 6.54-6.64.
[42] See *Powell and Rayner* v *UK*, A/172, (1990) 12 EHRR 355, 368; *López-Ostra* v *Spain*, A/303-C, (1995) 20 EHRR 277, 295.
[43] *Ibid.*
[44] *Stubbings* v *UK*, above n. 31.
[45] *Ibid.* at 235–236.

Similar reasoning was employed by the Commission in *Winer*, where the applicant claimed a breach of Article 8 because he had no legal remedy against intrusive (but true) statements about his relationship with his former wife which had been published in a book. He had recovered some money by way of a settlement of libel proceedings in respect of passages which were not true and, on that basis, the Commission held that no positive obligation to respect private life had been breached: a partial remedy was sufficient.[46]

4. IMMIGRATION AND DEPORTATION

In theory, the Convention itself does not regulate immigration,[47] and the Court is frequently at pains to stress that the Convention does not, in principle, prevent Contracting States from regulating the entry and length of stay of immigrants.[48] However, creative interpretation of certain articles of the Convention has meant that, in practice, the discretion to regulate immigration has been restricted to a very real extent. The scope of Article 3 is now wide enough that deportation of an alien may amount to inhuman and degrading treatment.[49] Article 8 is of more widespread importance, since it requires states to consider and to account for the family life of all persons whom they refuse to admit to their territory or whom they propose to deport.

10.29

INTERFERENCE WITH FAMILY LIFE CONTRARY TO ARTICLE 8(1)

The methodology used by the Commission and the Court in adjudicating upon the two types of case — where an alien has been refused admission to the country, and where an alien resident of a country is required to leave — is not wholly consistent, but in most cases, the following stages

10.30

---

[46] *Winer* v *UK*, Appl. No. 10871/84, (1986) 48 D&R 154.
[47] Arts. 2–4 of the Fourth Protocol to the Convention ensure freedom of movement within a state and freedom to leave a state, and prohibit expulsion by a state of its own nationals and the collective expulsion of aliens. These provisions clearly impinge upon immigration policy but the Protocol has not been signed by the UK and has no force in this country.
[48] See, for example, *Berrehab* v *The Netherlands*, A/138, (1988) 11 EHRR 322, 331.
[49] For example, *Chahal* v *UK*, A/697, (1997) 23 EHRR 413; see chapter 7, paras. 7.30–7.34.

are now apparent. First, one must consider whether the applicant has a family life to be respected; as noted above, this involves a consideration of the formal relationship between the applicant and the family members relied upon (who may also, of course, be applicants), and also the actual closeness of the relationship between them. Next, it is important to note that the Convention guarantees only that family life should continue, not that it must continue in a particular place. Therefore, for example, Article 8 does not impose upon a state a general duty to respect the choice by married couples of the country of their matrimonial residence and states will frequently argue that there is no breach of Article 8(1) because family life might just as easily be carried on in the country where the alien is currently residing, or to where he is to be deported. As the Court has recently noted, Article 8 does not guarantee a right to choose the most suitable place to develop family life.[50]

10.31   In addressing the argument that family life might continue elsewhere, the Commission and the Court will examine to what extent it is possible, and realistic, that other family members should join the applicant in his country of origin, and what the practical effect of such a move would be on them. It may be that the family cannot be reunited in the country of origin because one or more family members would not be entitled to entry or residence there; more often, it is argued to be unrealistic or unfair to suppose that the family could live together in the country of origin because certain of its members would suffer social disadvantage there — perhaps they cannot speak the language of the country, or cannot obtain necessary medical treatment. In *Abdulaziz, Cabales and Balkandali*, for example, the Court accepted the argument of the UK that three British residents seeking a right of entry and residence for their husbands had not shown special reasons why they could not set up home with their husbands in their own, or their husbands', countries of origin. The wives' application succeeded, however, on the grounds that the Immigration Rules discriminated as between men and women.[51]

10.32   Where a child has been brought up in the country of origin and/or still lives there, the Court will be much more willing to find that family life can be sustained in the country of origin than where the child has been born and/or brought up in the host country and/or still lives there. This was the distinction drawn by the Court between *Berrehab*, where the deportation of a father amounted to a breach of Article 8, and *Gül*, where the refusal to allow the applicant's sons to join him from Turkey, did not amount to a

---

[50] *Ahmut v The Netherlands*, A/701, (1997) 24 EHRR 62, 80.
[51] Above n. 34 at 503.

failure to respect their family life.[52] Emphasis is also placed on how adaptable a child will be to the circumstances of its proposed new home. In *Sorabjee*, for example, the Commission rejected the claim of a child who was subject to constructive deportation, the situation where the parent with custody of a child who is a British citizen is deported so that the child must either go into local authority care or leave the country as well.[53] It was submitted that the three year old child should not be made to return to Kenya because she would be deprived of British health, education and welfare benefits, would be unable to obtain adequate treatment in Kenya for a medical condition and would lose the opportunity to form a bond with her estranged father later in life. The Commission held that the obstacles to her going to Kenya were not insurmountable, since she was of an age where she could adapt to her new circumstances.

Finally, if it is determined that family life cannot be continued in another country, the authority may still argue that the separation of the family does not, in any event, put family ties at risk. In *Berrehab*, for example, the Dutch Government submitted that the father whom it proposed to deport to Morocco, could nevertheless travel to The Netherlands on a temporary visa to visit his daughter. The Court was not persuaded: it concluded that, given the very young age of the child, far more regular contact was necessary in order to maintain family ties.[54] Therefore, deportation of the father breached Article 8(1). **10.33**

JUSTIFICATION UNDER ARTICLE 8(2)

If an applicant can establish that family life has been, or will be, prejudiced by an immigration decision, it is then necessary to examine the state's justification for the interference, under Article 8(2). Where an applicant is subject to deportation after having committed a crime, the state's justification will be the prevention of disorder and/or crime, and the Court has given due weight to the concern of states to maintain public order by exercising their rights to control the entry and residence of aliens.[55] Where the applicant is not subject to deportation following criminal conviction but is refused permission to enter or remain on other grounds, the state will usually rely upon its desire to protect "the **10.34**

---

[52] *Berrehab* v *The Netherlands*, above n. 48; *Gül* v *Switzerland*, A/596, (1996) 22 EHRR 93, 115.
[53] *Sorabjee* v *UK*, Appl. No. 23938/94, [1996] EHRLR 216.
[54] Above n. 48 at 329.
[55] See, for example, *Moustaquim* v *Belgium*, A/193, (1991) 13 EHRR 802, 814.

economic well-being of the country" (by minimising the burden on the social security system, regulating the labour market in favour of nationals of the state, etc.).[56]

10.35   The real issue in most cases is whether the state can establish that the interference with family life is "necessary in a democratic society" — that it corresponds to a pressing social need, and has effects which are proportionate to its aims and objectives. The Court will weigh up all the circumstances to ascertain whether the state has struck "a fair balance" between the applicant's right to respect for private and family life and the prevention of crime or disorder or the economic well-being of the country, as appropriate. Three factors, in particular, are of importance. First, the strength of the justification in the individual case: if the prevention of crime or disorder is at issue, the Court will consider the seriousness of the offences of which the applicant has been convicted. Hence, in *Moustaquim*, the Court found a breach of Article 8 having relied heavily upon the fact that the applicant's offences had been committed when he was a minor, and that there was a long interval between the last offence for which he was convicted and the date of the deportation order.[57] Subsequently, in *Beldjoudi*, the Court compared the applicant's criminal record with that of M. Moustaquim. It was much worse, but this was outweighed by other matters.[58]

10.36   The second important factor is the effect which the immigration decision will have upon the applicant himself, of which the crucial component is the extent of the affinity felt by him towards the destination country. This was one of the determinative factors in *Beldjoudi*: the applicant was born and brought up in France, and only lacked French citizenship because of an error by his Algerian parents. At the time of the deportation order against him, he had lived and worked nowhere else but France, and had married a French woman. Conversely, in three recent cases, the Court has relied upon the applicant having maintained ties with his country of birth in finding that a deportation order was proportionate and not in breach of Article 8.[59] In *Boughanemi*, for example, the French Government's successful defence was based upon the applicant, who was Tunisian by birth, never having sought French nationality, maintaining ties in Tunisia, moving in Tunisian circles in France and having an adequate command of spoken Arabic.[60] The Court has drawn a general

---

[56] *Berrehab* v *The Netherlands*, above n. 48 at 330.
[57] *Moustaquim* v *Belgium*, above n. 55 at 815.
[58] *Beldjoudi* v *France*, A/234-A, (1992) 14 EHRR 801, 833–834.
[59] *Boughanemi* v *France*, above n. 20; *C* v *Belgium*, A/647, [1997] EHRLR 98; *Bouchelkia* v *France*, A/727, (1998) 25 EHRR 686.
[60] *Ibid* [1997].

distinction between individuals who reached the host country at a relatively advanced age, and those who were born there or arrived as young children.[61] Similar principles have been applied in cases of attempted family reunification.[62]

Thirdly, the Court will consider the effect of the immigration decision **10.37** upon the applicant's family life. The obstacles in the way of family life continuing in the proposed destination country, which is important in deciding whether there is any breach of Article 8(1) requiring justification, is again relevant. The greater the difficulties which will be encountered by the family in the destination country, the stronger the justification which must be advanced by the state. It was significant in *Beldjoudi* that the deportee's wife was French and had no knowledge of Algeria or of the Algerian language.[63] Similarly, in *Boughanemi*, it was unrealistic to suppose that the applicant could continue family life with his child and its mother after deportation, but he had been found guilty of serious offences warranting 4 years' imprisonment. That along with other previous convictions counted heavily against him. Overall, the attitude of the Court has appeared to become less stringent in the very recent past, and the run of applicant successes in the late 1980s and early 1990s has petered out. However, it would be simplistic to assume that there has been any major change of approach. Each case will turn upon its own facts and it could certainly be argued that recent applicant defeats such as *Boughanemi* and *Bouchelkia* are distinguishable on the basis of the seriousness of the criminal offences committed, or the strength of the ties between the applicant and the destination country.

PRACTICE IN THE ENGLISH COURTS

In the period prior to its incorporation into domestic law, the Convention **10.38** was relied upon more often in immigration cases than in any other type of case. A major factor contributing towards this trend was the disclosure of Home Office policy document DP 2/93 which specifically mentioned the right to family life under Article 8 as a relevant consideration in immigration and deportation decisions. A succession of cases sought to clarify the role to be played by Article 8 in immigration decisions affected by DP 2/93 and to challenge the way in which it was interpreted and applied by the

---

[61] *C* v *Belgium*, above n. 59.
[62] See, for example, *Ahmut* v *The Netherlands*, above n. 50.
[63] Above n. 58; see also *Nasri* v *France*, above n. 40.

Secretary of State.[64] Its replacement, DP 3/96, is more circumspect in its reliance upon Article 8 but will no doubt have to be revised following incorporation of the Convention.

5. SEXUALITY AND SEXUAL MORALITY

10.39   The right of an individual to choose his sexual partners, and his sexual practices, is a most intimate aspect of private life and is firmly within the scope of Article 8(1). The Court has, accordingly, struck down legislation criminalising homosexual conduct in private in both Northern Ireland and the Irish Republic.[65] In both cases, the detrimental effects upon the personal life of the individuals concerned were said to outweigh the justifications advanced by the respondent Governments (mainly based upon public morality and the protection of young people in society). An important general principle to arise out of these cases is that the mere existence of legislation can constitute an interference with private life even if it is not actually enforced against the individual. Neither applicant had actually been prosecuted, although the applicant from Northern Ireland had been subjected to a heavy-handed police investigation of his sexual conduct.[66]

10.40   The extent to which a state may lawfully prohibit sexual activity between consenting adults in private has also been raised in the context of sado-masochistic sexual practices, which are liable to prosecution as assault and trespass to the person under English law. In *Laskey, Jaggard and Brown* v *UK*, the applicants were convicted of assault occasioning actual bodily harm and unlawful wounding after the police discovered video-tapes of sado-masochistic activities over a ten year period.[67] The House of Lords had decided that consent could not be a defence to the charges.[68] The Court expressed some doubt as to whether the activities of the applicants did fall within the scope of private life. This was because a considerable number of people were involved, a succession of new "members" were recruited to take part and videos were distributed amongst those taking part.[69] However, the Government had conceded

---

[64] For example, *R.* v *Home Secretary ex parte Urmaza*, *The Times*, 23 July 1996; *R.* v *Home Secretary ex parte Mirza* [1996] Imm AR 314.

[65] *Dudgeon* v *UK*, above n. 9; *Norris* v *Ireland*, A/142, (1991) 13 EHRR 186. See also *Modinos* v *Cyprus*, A/259, (1994) 16 EHRR 485.

[66] See, further, *Sutherland* v *UK*, Appl. No. 25186/94, (1997) 24 EHRR CD22 (discrimination against homosexuals).

[67] A/730, (1997) 24 EHRR 39.

[68] *R.* v *Brown (Anthony)* [1994] 1 AC 212.

[69] Above n. 67 at 56–57.

that Article 8(1) was engaged. Instead, the Court found that the inter-ference with private life was justified under Article 8(2) on the grounds of the protection of public health. The crucial difference between this case and previous cases on homosexual conduct was that the applicant's activities involved a significant degree of injury or wounding, and it was within the UK's margin of appreciation to treat them as worthy of prosecution. The Court rejected the applicants' claim that they had been discriminated against on account of their homosexuality.[70]

6. TRANSSEXUALS

Whilst the Court has been eager to keep in step with a developing social **10.41** consensus on the issue of homosexuality, it has relied upon the absence of a similar consensus regarding the legal status of transsexuals in rejecting a series of claims brought under Article 8. British post-operative transsexuals have for some years sought formal legal recognition of their changed sex, in the form of a right to have the Register of Births altered and to obtain a new birth certificate. A new birth certificate would in turn allow a transsexual to obtain a new passport and to marry, since it is treated as conclusive proof of a person's sex. However, the Register is treated as a record of historical fact and it cannot be altered, save in cases where alteration is necessary to rectify a genuine mistake. The Court has accepted the Government's argument that an exception for transsexuals would require a major reassessment of the system for registering births, which the UK may legitimately decline to undertake.[71] However, the Court also indicated its willingness to review the situation, having regard to scientific developments and any developing consensus amongst the Convention states.[72] Nor do transsexuals have the right to marry under Article 12, which is restricted to the "traditional" marriage between persons of the opposite biological sex and does not, therefore, include transsexuals.[73]

In *B* v *France*, however, the Court ruled in favour of a transsexual on **10.42** the basis that the lack of recognition accorded by the French legal system to transsexuals constituted a rather more serious interference with private life.[74] Transsexuals in France, unlike in the UK, were not permitted to

---

[70] *Ibid.* at 59–60.
[71] *Rees* v *UK*, above n. 13.
[72] *Cossey* v *UK*, A/184, (1991) 13 EHRR 622.
[73] *Rees* v *UK*, above n. 13 at 68.
[74] A/232-C, (1994) 16 EHRR 1.

change their name for official purposes. Also, documents such as identity cards which would carry the registered name of the individual and so reveal his or her transsexual status were required to be produced and used rather more frequently in France than equivalent documents (such as a passport) in the UK. Any hopes that this decision would mark a turning point in the Court's approach to the legal treatment of transsexuals were dashed in a recent British case where it rejected a complaint regarding the lack of legal recognition of the paternity of a female to male transsexual, whose partner had given birth to a child following artificial insemination.[75] Two other British claims, in which the Court was invited to reconsider its earlier case-law on legal recognition of transsexuals in the light of a developing social consensus have recently failed.[76]

7. THE RIGHT TO MARRY AND FOUND A FAMILY

10.43   Article 12 provides:

"Men and women of marriageable age shall have the right to marry and found a family, according to the national laws governing the exercise of this right."

According to the Court, Article 12 is concerned with protecting marriage as the basis of the family.[77] It appears to confer a single right, to marry and found a family but has, in fact, been interpreted as protecting the right to marry even where there is no intention or possibility to found a family.[78] The converse does not also hold good — it appears from the case-law on transsexuals that there can be no right to found a family without marriage (although the rights of unmarried persons in that regard may be protected as family life under Article 8).[79] The application of Article 12 is confined to the so-called traditional marriage, between persons of opposite biological sex. It cannot be relied upon to promote the legal validity of homosexual unions,[80] or to assist transsexuals seeking

---

[75] *X, Y and Z v UK*, A/753, (1997) 24 EHRR 143.
[76] *Sheffield* and *Horsham* v *UK*, A/946, decision of 30 July 1998.
[77] *Rees* v *UK*, above n. 13 at 68.
[78] *Hamer* v *UK*, Appl. No. 7114/75, (1982) 4 EHRR 139.
[79] *Rees* v *UK*, above n. 13 at 68.
[80] *W* v *UK*, Appl. No. 11095/84, (1989) 63 D&R 34.

to marry in states, such as the UK, which do not legally recognise their post-operative gender.[81]

10.44 The right is to marry and found a family "according to the national laws governing the exercise of the right". That qualification is, at first sight, much more generous to states than the specific grounds for derogation allowed under Article 8(2), but various important restrictions have been read into it by the Court. First, national laws must be sufficiently clear and accessible to qualify under the Convention definition of "law".[82] National law may, in principle, regulate, and impose limitations upon, the right to marry but those limitations must not be arbitrary, or discriminatory (under Article 14), or disproportionate,[83] or deprive the right to marry of all substance. The latter requirement covers rules which appear merely to delay marriage rather than prevent it altogether.[84] The Court of Appeal has interpreted Article 12 as conferring a right to marry "only where circumstances permit", and so rejected the claim of an illegal immigrant detained with a view to deportation that the authorities should provide facilities for him to marry at a local registry office.[85] The right to marry does not include a right to divorce, and that must be seen as an exception to, or derogation from, the general approach of Article 12, since persons who may not divorce are thereby prevented from marrying again.[86]

10.45 The scope of Article 12 is limited, and the Strasbourg institutions have not been susceptible to more imaginative arguments seeking to extend its application.[87] Article 5 of Protocol No. 7 to the Convention supplements Article 12 in providing for equality of rights and responsibilities between spouses during marriage and upon the dissolution of marriage. The Protocol has not yet been signed by the UK, but the Government has indicated an intention to sign it in the near future, once appropriate adjustments to domestic law have been made.[88]

8. STATE SURVEILLANCE

10.46 Secret surveillance by the state may entail a number of different activities which infringe Article 8(1). Visual surveillance or the use of listening

---

[81] *Rees* v *UK*, above n. 13; *Cossey* v *UK*, above n. 72.
[82] See chapter 6, paras. 6.32–6.39.
[83] *F* v *Switzerland*, A/128, (1988) 10 EHRR 411.
[84] *Ibid.*
[85] *R.* v *Home Secretary ex parte Bhajan Singh* [1976] QB 198.
[86] *Johnston* v *Ireland*, above n. 12.
[87] See, for example, *Lindsay and Lindsay* v *UK*, Appl. 11089/84, (1986) 49 D&R 181 (taxation of married couples).
[88] *Bringing Rights Home*, Cm. 3782, paras. 4.14–4.16.

devices may interfere with private life and with the home; interception of telephone conversations, mail or other communications may interfere with private life, the home and with correspondence. The Court has also ruled that the production to the police of records obtained from telephone metering, the recording by telephone companies of the destination and duration of phone calls, is an interference with Article 8 rights.[89] The most serious obstacle to bringing a claim within Article 8 is probably that of evidence, since the complainant may well be unable to prove that he has, in fact, been subject to surveillance. The Court has alleviated the difficulties of proof in such cases by permitting claims by persons who can establish that they are liable to be put under surveillance.[90] In *Malone*, for example, it was deemed sufficient that, as a suspected receiver of stolen goods, the applicant belonged to a class of persons against whom measures of postal and telephone interception were liable to be employed.[91]

10.47   Consequently, the cases, generally, turn on whether surveillance is "in accordance with the law" and/or "necessary in a democratic society" in the interests of national security and/or the prevention of disorder and crime. As noted above, the "in accordance with the law" requirement denotes a threefold test. First, the conditions governing surveillance must be incorporated into legal rules, whether statutory or judge-made, rather than existing as a matter of administrative practice. In *Malone*, the Court held that telephone tapping and the disclosure of metering records by a telephone company to the police, which were lawful in England, were not in accordance with the law under Article 8(2). Telephone tapping was not subject to any overall statutory code and there was disagreement as to which, if any, legal provisions did have a bearing upon the powers of the police. The law was, according to the Court, "somewhat obscure and open to differing interpretations",[92] whilst the discretion of the police to request access to metering records was not subject to any legal regulation at all.[93] Given formal legal rules, any surveillance activities must be in conformity with them.[94]

10.48   Secondly, the law must be accessible to individuals, in that the conditions under which surveillance will be carried out are made

[89] *Malone* v *UK*, above n. 37, *Matthews* v *UK*, Appl. No. 28576/95, [1997] EHRLR 187 (anti-nuclear campaigner).
[90] *Klass* v *Germany*, A/28, (1979–80) 2 EHRR 214, 229.
[91] Above n. 37 at 38–39.
[92] *Ibid.* at 44.
[93] *Ibid.* at 47.
[94] See, for example, *A* v *France*, A/277-B, (1994) 17 EHRR 462; *HWK* v *Switzerland*, Appl. No. 23224/94, [1997] EHRLR 300.

public. Thirdly, the operation of the law must be foreseeable to those who may be affected by it. This does not mean that individuals should be able to foresee when the authorities are likely to place them under surveillance and so adapt their conduct accordingly, but rather that "the law must be sufficiently clear in its terms to give citizens an adequate indication as to the circumstances in which and the conditions on which public authorities are empowered to resort to this secret and potentially dangerous interference with the right to respect for private life and correspondence".[95] There is a considerable overlap between this principle and the requirement that surveillance be "necessary in a democratic society" which entails that the regulatory framework contains adequate and effective guarantees against abuse. Necessity requires that such safeguards exist, foreseeability that they are codified in the appropriate form. Taken together, there must be precise rules governing, for example, the categories of persons liable to come under surveillance, the types of suspected offences which will trigger surveillance, the duration of surveillance and the safeguards attaching to records obtained through surveillance.[96] It is also desirable, in principle, that overall supervision be exercised by a judge, although this is not necessary where the designated supervisory bodies are sufficiently independent to give an objective ruling.[97]

TELEPHONE TAPPING

Following *Malone*, the Interception of Communications Act 1985 was **10.49** enacted to regulate telephone tapping on the public telephone system by the police, Customs and Excise and the security and intelligence services. It establishes a formal regulatory framework, requiring the issue of a warrant by the Home Secretary, authorising the grant of warrants in only limited circumstances and imposing a duty upon the Home Secretary to control strictly the retention and disclosure of information collected, and to ensure the destruction of information whose retention is no longer necessary. A measure of independent scrutiny is provided by the Interception of Communications Tribunal, and by a Commissioner, who is a sitting or retired senior judge, and who oversees the regulatory system and reports annually.

---

[95] *Malone* v *UK*, above n. 37 at 40–41.
[96] *Huvig* v *France*, A/176-B, (1990) 12 EHRR 528, 545; *Kruslin* v *France*, A/176-B, (1990) 12 EHRR 547, 564–565.
[97] *Klass* v *Germany*, above n. 90 at 234–235.

10.50   Concerns have been expressed about the limited powers of review of the Tribunal, which will intervene only if no reasonable Home Secretary could have considered the issue of a warrant to be necessary, and whose decisions are not open to judicial review. The Tribunal has never, in fact, upheld a complaint against telephone tapping. The vagueness of the grounds justifying the issue of warrants (national security, detection of serious crime and the protection of the economic well-being of the UK) has been attacked, as have the restrictions upon publication of the reasons for Tribunal decisions. However, a direct challenge to the new system raising all of these complaints failed in *Christie*, in which the Commission held the safeguards provided to be consistent with the requirements of Article 8(2).[98]

10.51   There are, however, gaps in the coverage of the 1985 Act, which extends only to the public telephone network. In *Effik*, the House of Lords confirmed that the Act does not cover the monitoring of mobile phones, which continues on the pre-*Malone* footing.[99] Nor does it cover the monitoring of telephone calls made on an internal telephone system. Hence, in *Halford*, the Court found a violation of Article 8 in the case of a former senior police officer who, at the relevant time, was suing her employer for sex discrimination, and whose telephone calls on the office system were monitored.[100] Further, the 1985 Act has no application to the production of telephone metering records, which remains unregulated despite the *Malone* ruling.

POLICE SURVEILLANCE

10.52   The 1985 Act made no attempt either to regulate the use of listening devices by the police other than those attached to the public phone system, a matter which was until recently regulated only by Home Office guidelines.[101] Part III of the Police Act 1997 will formally allow the police to enter into homes, hotel bedrooms and office premises for the purposes of planting listening devices on the approval of a Commissioner who, as under the 1985 Act, must be a serving or retired senior judge. Approval must also be sought where surveillance could result in the acquisition of information which is legally privileged, or is confidential personal information or journalistic material. No approval need be sought where

---

[98] *Christie* v *UK*, Appl. No. 21482/93, (1993) 78-A D&R 119.
[99] *R.* v *Effik* [1995] 1 AC 583.
[100] *Halford* v *UK*, A/773, (1997) 24 EHRR 523.
[101] See, hence, *Govell* v *UK*, Appl. No. 27237/95, [1997] EHRLR 438.

the police consider the need for surveillance to be urgent. Other surveillance activities, notably those which do not involve trespass on private property or interference with wireless telegraphy remain effectively unregulated, and are subject only to the limited jurisdiction of the Police Complaints Authority.

Complaints about intrusions into privacy caused by the surveillance **10.53** activities of the police frequently arise in criminal trials where the prosecution seeks to adduce evidence which has been obtained as a result of such activities. It is important to note that evidence which has been obtained in breach of Article 8 is not *per se* inadmissible either under English law or under Article 6 of the Convention, the right to a fair trial.[102] However, both s. 78 of the Police and Criminal Evidence Act, and Article 6 may require the exclusion of such evidence where this evidence would seriously prejudice the fairness of the proceedings.

SURVEILLANCE BY THE SECURITY SERVICES

Another Convention case, *Harman and Hewitt* v *UK*, prompted the **10.54** Government to place the activities of the security and intelligence services, MI5, MI6 and GCHQ, on a statutory footing.[103] Now, warrants must be issued by the relevant Secretary of State to authorise activities which would otherwise be unlawful, and the Security Service and Intelligence Services Commissioners and Tribunals provide a degree of independent oversight (although their decisions may not be challenged through the courts). Again, it is arguable that the limited powers of these bodies, and the conditions of secrecy under which they operate, are inconsistent with the requirements of Article 8(2), but the Commission has rejected challenges made on that basis.[104]

9. POWERS OF ENTRY AND SEARCH

The right to respect for the home clearly raises issues regarding the **10.55** exercise of legal powers to enter and search the home, which, as noted above, may extend to both residential and business premises. The

---

[102] See *Schenk* v *Switzerland*, A/140, (1991) 13 EHRR 242; *R. Khan (Sultan)* [1997] AC 558.
[103] Appl. No. 12175/86, (1989) 67 D&R 88; see now the Security Service Act 1989 and the Intelligence Services Act 1994.
[104] See *Esbester* v *UK*, Appl. No. 18601/91, (1994) 18 EHRR CD72; *Christie* v *UK*, above n. 98.

conditions governing the exercise of entry and search powers must be clearly laid down by law, and subject to appropriate safeguards. In *Funke*, the Court endorsed the practice of French customs officials of searching premises and seizing documents in order to obtain evidence of exchange control offences.[105] However, the absence of appropriate safeguards on the exercise of their powers rendered the search of the applicant's home in breach of Article 8. The customs authorities had exclusive competence to assess the expediency, number, length and scale of searches and the Court relied, in particular, upon the absence of any requirement of a judicial warrant authorising a search of the home. Concerns have been expressed about the powers of the Home Secretary to authorise the Security Services (MI5) to enter the home in pursuit of its functions, which now include the prevention and detection of serious crime.[106] There is no requirement of prior *judicial* authorisation of searches and nor is the exercise of the administrative power to issue warrants subject to judicial review. The dangers for public authorities in entering the home without specific judicial authorisation were emphasised in the recent case of *McLeod*, where the police had entered the applicant's home, ostensibly so as to avert a potential breach of the peace, on the occasion of the removal of property by her former husband pursuant to a court order in matrimonial proceedings. The Court found a breach of Article 8 on the basis that the police had failed even to read the court order: had they read it they would have realised that the ex-husband had no power to enter the applicant's home at all (since the order specified that she deliver the property to him).[107]

10.56   Even where the pre-condition of a judicial warrant is satisfied, the Court will proceed to examine whether the warrant was drawn in sufficiently narrow terms. In *Niemietz*, for example, a warrant authorising the German police to search a lawyer's office was found to be disproportionate and so unlawful because it was broadly phrased and lacked special safeguards, such as the presence of an independent observer, and other measures to protect professional secrecy.[108] The Court has also examined, and approved, the execution of an *Anton Piller* order, which allows the entry and search of premises of an opponent in civil litigation. In *Chappell*, the interference with privacy and the home caused by such an order was held to be necessary for the protection of the rights of others

---

[105] *Funke v France*, A/256-A, (1993) 16 EHRR 297.
[106] Sections 1–2 of the Security Service Act 1996. See Duffy and Hunt, "The Security Service Act 1996" [1997] EHRLR 11.
[107] *McLeod v UK*, Appl. No. 24755/94, [1997] EHRLR 682.
[108] *Niemietz v Germany*, above n. 3 at 113–114.

and to be circumscribed by appropriate safeguards, such as the presence of the Plaintiff's solicitor.[109]

10. LANDLORD AND TENANT LAW

Another area which, potentially, raises issues regarding the integrity of the home is that of landlord and tenant relations, and, in particular, the circumstances in which a landlord may claim repossession of a property, thus evicting tenants from their home, and perhaps gaining a home for himself. The leading authority is *Velosa Barreto* v *Portugal*, in which the applicant, who lived with his parents-in-law sought to gain possession of a house which he had inherited from his parents.[110] The Court refused to accept that Article 8 conferred on each family a right to a home for themselves alone. Nor did it oblige the state to give landlords the right to recover a rented house on request — the protection of the rights of tenants was a legitimate policy goal. What was required was the striking of a fair balance between the general interest and the interests of the people concerned and, since the applicant had not demonstrated to the Portuguese courts a sufficient need to recover the property, there was no violation of Article 8.[111] Consequently, Article 8 may be of little further assistance to landlords in gaining possession of their properties, but it may require that the interests of the tenant are considered in all cases. This does not always occur under English law.[112] Interference with the property rights of a landlord may also give rise to a claim under Article 1 of the First Protocol to the Convention.

10.57

11. ENVIRONMENTAL LAW

There is undoubtedly some scope within Article 8 for enforcing environmental standards, where emissions cause a nuisance to individuals. Noxious emissions may cause a risk to health, and so amount to an interference with private life; also, regardless of health risk, they may deprive a person of the possibility of enjoying the amenities of their

10.58

---

[109] *Chappell* v *UK*, A/152, (1993) 16 EHRR 97.
[110] A/334, [1996] EHRLR 214.
[111] A/334 at 11–12.
[112] See, for example, the position of a tenant on expiry of an assured shorthold tenancy under s. 21 of the Housing Act 1988.

home. The leading case is *López Ostra* v *Spain*, in which the applicant and her family had suffered nuisance, and health problems, from a waste treatment plant next door to her house.[113] Her efforts to have the plant closed down had dragged on for some years, and, when the case came before the Court, were still unresolved. The Court noted that "severe environmental pollution" may affect individuals' well-being and prevent them from enjoying their homes, in breach of Article 8(1). It recognised that the state has "a certain margin of appreciation" in striking a fair balance between the rights of the individual and the needs of the local economy.[114] However, the living conditions of the applicant and her family had been unbearable, and they had suffered serious health problems. In the circumstances, the margin of appreciation had been exceeded.[115] More recently, in *Guerra* v *Italy*, the Court went further and found a breach of Article 8 in the case of applicants who had not been directly affected by environmental pollution but who lived close to a dangerous chemical factory and ran the risk of injury in the event of accidental pollution. The fault of the Italian authorities lay in not communicating essential information regarding the safety of the factory which would have enabled the applicants to make an informed judgment as to risks of continuing to live in its vicinity.[116]

10.59   The English law of nuisance does attempt to strike a balance between the competing interests of individuals and of the community as a whole, but its arcane origins and piecemeal development give rise to situations where individuals cannot gain redress regardless of the extent of the inconvenience or discomfort which they have suffered. A recent example is *Hunter* v *Canary Wharf*, in which the House of Lords confirmed that the right to sue in nuisance was confined to persons who have a legal interest in the land affected.[117] Mere licensees, such as members of the family of the person who owns the property, may not sue. Only one of the judges, Lord Cooke, referred to the Convention, noting, in his dissenting judgment, that the appellants had a right to respect for their home, whether or not they had property rights in it.[118]

10.60   Nevertheless, the difficulties of translating a failed nuisance claim into a breach of Article 8 should not be under-estimated. A good example is *Powell and Rayner*, in which the Court rejected claims arising out of

---

[113] Above n. 42.
[114] *Ibid.* at 295. This is to be compared with the "wide margin of appreciation" which was allowed in the earlier environmental case of *Powell and Rayner* v *UK*, A/172, above n. 42.
[115] *Ibid.* at 297.
[116] A/875, (1998) 26 EHRR 357.
[117] [1997] 2 WLR 684.
[118] *Ibid.* at 715. The Appellants in *Hunter* have submitted an application to the Commission.

the long-running saga of noise nuisance from Heathrow airport.[119] The applicants lived under a flight path and had suffered considerable disturbance from aircraft noise. However, they were unable to sue the British Airports Authority in nuisance because of a statutory bar to such claims in s. 76(1) of the Civil Aviation Act 1982. Their claims for breach of Article 8(1) were rejected by the Commission as manifestly ill-founded but their alternative claim for lack of an effective remedy under Article 13 was examined by the Court, and necessitated consideration of the scope of Article 8. The Court found that the Government was perfectly entitled to tackle aircraft noise by means of regulatory measures whilst excluding the possibility of private litigation. There was, in the circumstances, no arguable claim under Article 8.[120]

12. PRIVACY AND PRESS FREEDOM

The right to exclude the outside world, including the mass media, from the private sphere is the most basic and widely accepted aspect of respect for private life. Indeed, the impact of Article 8 on the freedom of the press to intrude into personal privacy is the feature of the Human Rights Act which has attracted most public attention. The absence of any right to privacy in English law has been noted in a succession of cases of media intrusion, the most notorious of which was perhaps *Kaye* v *Robertson*, where the *Sunday Sport* newspaper photographed and "interviewed" an actor lying comatose in his hospital bed after a car accident.[121] The key question is whether the enactment of the right to respect for private life in domestic law will act as a curb on the excesses of media intrusion. **10.61**

In fact, English law does regulate intrusion into privacy by the media, not directly, by a right of privacy as such, but by way of a variety of legal remedies which cover some, although by no means all, of the potential areas of concern. The law of defamation protects individuals from untrue statements which damage their reputation. Breach of confidence may provide a remedy where the intrusion into privacy consists of the publication, or proposed publication of confidential information. One judge has suggested, *obiter*, that breach of confidence might also be extended to cover the situation of a *paparazzo* photographer taking an unauthorised picture of someone engaged in a private act.[122] The **10.62**

---

[119] Above n. 42.
[120] *Ibid.* at 368–370.
[121] Above n. 1.
[122] Per Laws J in *Hellewell* v *Chief Constable of Derbyshire* [1995] 1 WLR 804, 807.

Protection from Harassment Act 1997, which was enacted ostensibly to protect the public from "stalkers", also has the potential to protect individuals from direct and personal intrusion by employees of media organisations. There are, nevertheless, many situations where existing causes of action cannot be stretched or refined to provide a remedy against media intrusion and, so far as the press is concerned, the only remedy for the individual is a complaint to the Press Complaints Commission, a self-regulatory body which has no powers to fine newspapers or award damages to individuals in cases where its Code of Practice has been contravened.[123]

10.63   Following the enactment of the Human Rights Act, individuals may seek to protect their privacy, or win compensation for intrusion into their privacy, by relying directly upon Article 8. However, the question of whether Article 8 requires that the reach of English law be extended to provide further redress against media intrusion, and if so in which circumstances, is not susceptible to a straightforward answer. On the one hand, two particular features of Article 8 claims to protection from media intrusion cause serious problems for applicants. The first is that intrusion into private life by a newspaper or television company is not "interference by a public authority" within Article 8(2) (save perhaps in the case of the BBC), so any claims must be based upon the positive obligations of the state to protect private life from interference by other individuals or non-state bodies. The margin of appreciation of states is all the wider in such cases. Therefore, whereas certain activities, such as the taking of photographs without the consent of the subject, would be contrary to Article 8(1) if carried out by a state body,[124] it may be a different matter if the perpetrator is a journalist. Secondly, almost any restriction upon the freedom of the press to intrude into private life inevitably raises a conflict with the right to freedom of expression under Article 10 of the Convention. It is not necessarily a breach of Article 10 to impose restrictions upon the press in the interests of privacy. In *Neves* v *Portugal,* for example, the Commission rejected a challenge to a conviction under Portuguese privacy laws in circumstances where a magazine had published, without consent, photographs of a well-known businessman engaging in private (sexual) activities. The severe sanction imposed upon the magazine's publisher — a prison sentence, a fine, and an order to compensate the businessman — was held to have been necessary for

---

[123] A statutory tribunal, the Broadcasting Complaints Commission, regulates intrusion into privacy by television companies.

[124] This point was conceded in *Murray* v *UK*, A/300-A, (1995) 19 EHRR 193.

the protection of "the rights of others".[125] However, to say that Article 10 permits privacy laws is one matter, to say that Article 8 requires them is quite another, and the difficulties involved in reconciling the rights to privacy and freedom of expression have also been held to justify a wide margin of appreciation for the authorities seeking to strike a balance.[126]

Hence in *Winer* v *UK*, the Commission declined to find that the **10.64** absence of a right to privacy in English law was a breach of Article 8.[127] The applicant complained that he had been unable to gain redress in respect of intrusive statements about himself and his former wife which had been published in a book about the South African security services. He had commenced libel proceedings in respect of certain of the material which was defamatory and untrue, which were settled for £5,000. His complaint to the Commission was that he had no legal remedy against those statements which were true but which nevertheless intruded upon his privacy. The Commission accepted that Article 8 could give rise to positive obligations to interfere with others' freedom of expression but held that the way in which a state meets those obligations is "largely within its discretion". The Commission then relied upon two factors in deciding that there was no breach of Article 8 in this case. The first was the ongoing public debate in the UK as to whether the law of privacy ought to be reformed, and, in particular, the conclusions of the Report of the Younger Committee on Privacy which had expressed general satisfaction with the state of the law.[128] The second factor which counted against the applicant was the settlement which he had received in his defamation proceedings. This illustrated to the Commission that his right to privacy was not wholly unprotected.

However, in the recent case of *Spencer* v *UK*, the Commission **10.65** indicated that the absence of a right to privacy in English law could indeed constitute a breach of Article 8.[129] Earl Spencer and his former wife had complained about a series of tabloid press reports regarding the admission of Countess Spencer to a clinic where she was being treated for alcoholism and an eating disorder. The reports included a photograph of Countess Spencer walking in the grounds of the clinic which had been taken by a *paparazzo* photographer from an adjoining public road, without her knowledge or consent. Earl Spencer protested to the Press Complaints Commission, which rejected the arguments of the newspapers that there was a public interest in publication of the story. This

---

[125] Appl. No. 20683/92, decision of 20 February 1995.
[126] See also *N* v *Sweden*, Appl. No. 11366/85, (1986) 50 D&R 173, 175.
[127] Appl. No. 10871/84, (1996) 48 D&R 154.
[128] Cmnd. 5012 (1972).
[129] Appl. No. 28851/95, (1998) 25 EHRR CD105.

did not, however, amount to a legal remedy and, accordingly, applications were lodged in Strasbourg.

10.66   The Commission rejected the claims on the grounds that the applicants had not exhausted their remedies in domestic law: it said that they should have brought a claim for breach of confidence against the newspapers. However, it stated that if there were no "actionable remedy" which could provide redress for the invasion of privacy which the applicants had suffered (if, say, an action for breach of confidence against the newspapers were to fail), that could give rise to a breach of the UK's positive obligations under Article 8. Significantly, it emphasised not the right to freedom of expression but the "duties and responsibilities" which, according to Article 10, go hand in hand with it and noted that states have an obligation to provide a measure of protection to the right of privacy of an individual affected by others' exercise of their freedom of expression.

10.67   Two important qualifications should be made. First, if a complaint is to be made that there is no actionable remedy to protect privacy, it must be proven that the relevant factual situation falls outside the legal scope of existing remedies. It is not sufficient that a remedy is available in principle but the applicant's case would fail on its facts, or would produce no financial award. Hence, in *Stewart-Brady* v *UK*, the applicant, the Moors Murderer Ian Brady, complained about the publication of a newspaper article containing false allegations that he had assaulted its author during a visit to the secure mental institution where he is held. He had, in theory, causes of action in domestic law for defamation and malicious falsehood, but an action for defamation had not been brought on the grounds that he had no reputation to protect, and a claim for malicious falsehood was struck out because he could show no financial loss. The Commission held that the fact that Brady could not succeed in establishing either cause of action in the particular circumstances of his case did not cast doubt on the effectiveness of those remedies in providing protection for private life.[130] Secondly, it is important to remember that the decisions of the Strasbourg institutions are always specific to their own facts. The absence of a remedy in privacy may, potentially, breach Article 8 in the Spencers' case — a gross intrusion into privacy which was unsupported by any public interest justification — but not in other cases, where the intrusion is less serious, the justification for publication stronger or, as in *Winer*, where some other remedy is available.

---

[130] *Stewart-Brady* v *UK*, Appl. No. 27436/95, (1997) 24 EHRR CD38.

Nevertheless, it is certainly true that the decision in *Winer* is somewhat **10.68** outdated. The public debate in the UK, one of the factors relied upon by the Commission in that case, has moved on considerably since the Younger Report. Various committees, notably the Calcutt Committee on Privacy and Related Matters, have reported since Younger, and have come out in favour of tighter regulation of media intrusion into privacy.[131] It remains to be seen whether that factor, together with the Commission's dictum in *Spencer*, will lead to privacy claims being upheld by the English courts, or the Court of Human Rights.

The Human Rights Act makes special provision, in s. 12, to assuage the **10.69** concerns of media organisations that Article 8 claims to privacy will place material restrictions on their freedom to publish. The Government's position was that s. 12 is consistent with the Convention and serves merely to clarify the effect of the case-law of the Commission and the Court under Article 8. Section 12 has two principal features. Firstly, it seeks to make it difficult to obtain prior restraint injunctions on the publication of material which intrudes into private life. There is no conflict with Article 8 on that count: at most, it requires that a *remedy* is available under domestic law, and not that that remedy is by way of prior restraint. Secondly, s. 12 emphasises the importance of the right of freedom of expression and requires the courts to take into account, in particular, the public interest in the publication of private material. Again, that is no more nor less than the Convention would require in any event.

13. DISCLOSURE AND USE OF PRIVATE INFORMATION

Two issues arise under this heading: freedom of information, in the sense **10.70** of a right of access to information held by public authorities which might otherwise not be forthcoming, and the right to prevent the use of private information collected for one purpose from being put to other uses. The Convention does not expressly confer a right to freedom of information. It is now well-established that the most obvious source of such a right, Article 10, which mentions "the right to receive and impart information and ideas", will not found a duty upon the state to disclose information.[132] Whilst the Court has not declared a general right of access to personal

---

[131] See the Calcutt Report, Cmnd. 1102 (1990); the Calcutt Review, Cmnd. 2135 (1993).
[132] See, for example, *Gaskin* v *UK*, above n. 6.
[133] See *Wilsher* v *UK*, Appl. No. 31024/96, (1997) 23 EHRR CD188.

data under Article 8,[133] the right to respect for private and family life may, in certain circumstances, assist in compelling disclosure of personal information.

10.71   In *Gaskin*, the applicant successfully claimed a right of access to local authority child care records which Liverpool City Council had refused to disclose in the absence of the consent of their authors. He had sought access partly in order to learn about his own past and so resolve psychological problems he was having, and partly in order to prosecute a legal action for negligence against the local authority. The Court accepted the importance of maintaining the confidentiality of public records, so as to ensure objective and reliable information, and, in some cases, to protect third parties. In principle, a system which made access dependent upon the consent of the author did comply with Article 8, but it could only be proportionate, consistent with Article 8(2), if there was an independent authority to decide whether access should be granted in the absence of consent.[134] The *Gaskin* case prompted the enactment of the Access to Health Records Act 1990, which applies to records made after November 1991.

10.72   Doubts have been cast upon the scope of the principle laid down in *Gaskin* by the decision of the Commission in the recent case of *Martin* v *UK*.[135] The applicant had sought access to his medical records in order to gain a greater knowledge of his childhood and development. The relevant authorities ultimately agreed to disclose them to a medical advisor of the applicant's choosing, who would decide whether or not their disclosure would be harmful either to the applicant or to third parties. The Court of Appeal upheld this position, distinguishing *Gaskin* on the basis that the records sought were not required for medical purposes or in connection with any dispute or projected litigation.[136] The Commission too drew this distinction, and also noted that there had been no blanket refusal to disclose, and that the records were less important for the applicant than they had been for Gaskin (they related to a much shorter period of his life, and to his adult life rather than his childhood). Nor had it been demonstrated that the records were the only source of the information sought.

10.73   Following *Martin*, it appears that, as a minimum, the information sought must be necessary either for medical purposes or for litigation regarding some aspect of private life. This is borne out by two other British cases on freedom of information under Article 8 which have arisen

---

[134] *Ibid.* at 50.
[135] Appl. No. 27533/95, (1996) 21 EHRR CD112.
[136] *R.* v *Mid-Glamorgan HSA ex parte Martin* [1995] 1 WLR 110, 119.

in the context of litigation, and are closely related to the right of access to a court under Article 6. In *McMichael*, the Court upheld a complaint regarding the failure of a local authority to disclose important documents in care proceedings.[137] In *McGinley and Egan*, the Court found that the Government had a positive obligation to facilitate the disclosure of relevant documents in the cases of two former service personnel who had participated in nuclear tests in the South Pacific and who sought access to their service medical records in order to pursue claims for a disablement pension. Article 8 required that an effective and accessible procedure be established, but on the facts, there was no violation of the Convention because such a procedure had been available to the applicants.[138] Other important factors to be considered include the intimacy of the contents of the records, whether or not the information is available elsewhere and whether disclosure is refused outright, or is subject to conditions.

A related issue is that of using private information which has been collected and stored for one purpose, for other, extraneous and unauthorised, purposes. The Court has recently ruled on this issue for the first time, upholding the claim of a woman suffering from HIV whose identity and medical condition were revealed in the course of criminal proceedings against her husband.[139] It is clear, following this case, that publication or disclosure by the authorities of personal information must be justified under Article 8(2). In particular, it must pursue an important public interest, and be accompanied by adequate and effective safeguards against abuse.[140] In *MS* v *Sweden*, the Court examined the important issue of the communication of personal information by one government department or agency to another.[141] The applicant had complained about the transmission of information from a hospital, where she had been treated for a back ailment, to the social security authorities, after she had made a claim for state industrial injury compensation. The Court held that the communication of the information was for the legitimate aim of protecting the economic well-being of the country since it helped to ensure that public funds were allocated to deserving claimants only. It had been essential to enable the applicant's social security claim to be determined and was surrounded by appropriate safeguards. In particular, information could only be released to the social security authorities pursuant to a statutory request and public employees at both ends were bound by a duty of confidentiality which was backed

10.74

---

[137] *McMichael* v *UK*, A/307-B, (1995) 20 EHRR 205.
[138] *McGinley and Egan* v *UK*, A/927, decision of 9 June 1998.
[139] *Z* v *Finland*, A/736, (1998) 25 EHRR 371.
[140] See also *TV* v *Finland*, Appl. No. 21780/93, (1994) 18 EHRR CD179.
[141] A/798, [1998] EHRLR 115.

up by civil and criminal sanctions. In the circumstances, there was no breach of Article 8.[142]

10.75   The Council of Europe has also acted on the political level to address some of the legal problems in this field, by adopting the Council of Europe Convention for the Protection of Individuals with regard to the Automatic Processing of Personal Data, an international agreement which seeks to lay down common standards for the collection, storage and use of personal information. The Convention is not to be enforced via the Commission and the Court, but through its own dedicated Consultative Committee, although it is likely that the Court would seek to give effect to the principles which it embodies in cases coming before it.[143] The protection of personal information has adopted an increasing importance in the UK in recent years, with the growth in the use of computer databases for a variety of business and other purposes. The Data Protection Act 1984 is the main statutory control; further rules have been added in order to implement a recent EC Directive on data protection.[144]

14. PRISONERS' RIGHTS

10.76   Article 8 has had a significant impact upon the rights of prisoners, particularly with regard to their correspondence, which may be intercepted, opened, read and stopped or censored by the prison authorities. Prisoners have the same rights as everyone else under Article 8(1), but the Article 8(2) exceptions (usually, in this context, public safety and prevention of disorder or crime) will be applied against the background of the ordinary and reasonable requirements of imprisonment. Interference with correspondence must not exceed what is required by the particular aim pursued and the Court has in practice adopted a strict view of the test of necessity as applied to prisoners.

10.77   Practice in British prisons has been significantly modified as a result of the Court's interpretation of Article 8. Under rule 33(3) of the Prison Rules 1964, a prison governor has the right to intercept and read all correspondence to and from a prisoner and to stop correspondence if its contents are objectionable or of inordinate length. Following the ruling of the Court in *Golder*,[145] a qualification was introduced excepting

---

[142] See also *Andersson v Sweden*, A/797, (1998) 25 EHRR 722.
[143] See Michael, *Privacy and Human Rights* (Dartmouth, 1996), pp. 35–40.
[144] EC Directive 95/46 on the protection of individuals with regard to the processing of personal data and on the free movement of such data, 1996 *Official Journal* L281/31; Data Protection Act 1998.
[145] *Golder v UK*, A/18, (1979–80) 1 EHRR 524.

correspondence between a prisoner and his legal advisor relating to pending legal proceedings but subject to the so-called "prior ventilation" rule, which required complaints about ill-treatment to be investigated first using internal procedures. The prior ventilation rule was declared to be contrary to Article 8 in *Silver*,[146] although it had already been replaced by a rule of simultaneous ventilation. *Silver* also emphasised the importance of ensuring that powers to interfere with prisoners' correspondence are clearly set out in published rules and are not supplemented or amended by unpublished circulars or informal instructions.[147]

10.78 The simultaneous ventilation rule was, in turn, struck down by the Divisional Court in *ex parte Anderson*, not because it was contrary to the Convention but because it violated the common law principle of free access to the court.[148] Then, in *Campbell*, the Court of Human Rights condemned the distinction drawn in the Prison Rules between correspondence relating to pending legal proceedings and other correspondence with a legal advisor including that relating to prospective or contemplated proceedings.[149] Following *Campbell*, the position is that communications between a prisoner and his legal advisors are regarded as privileged, both under domestic law and under Article 8, and the authorities must have a genuine and reasonable suspicion that this privilege is being abused in order to justify opening and reading such letters. It appears from subsequent applications to the Commission that practice in British prisons may not yet live up to these standards.[150]

10.79 Two specific types of prisoners' correspondence are accorded special protection by the Convention and require greater justification if they are to be interfered with. The first is correspondence with defence lawyers in criminal proceedings, which falls within the guarantee of Article 6(3)(b) that adequate facilities will be afforded for the preparation of a defence.[151] The second is correspondence with the Commission, and, following its abolition, the Court, which is given further protection by Article 34 of the Convention by which states commit themselves not to hinder the right of individual petition, and by the European Agreement relating to persons participating in proceedings of the European Commission and Court of Human Rights. The latter agreement accepts that prison authorities may read outgoing letters to the Commission (now the Court), since this may result in grievances being rectified without the necessity

---

[146] *Silver v UK*, above n. 36.
[147] *Ibid.* at 372.
[148] *R. v Home Secretary ex parte Anderson* [1984] QB 778.
[149] Above n. 39 at 161. The Court of Appeal made a similar finding, based upon the common law right of access to a court, in *R. v Home Secretary ex parte Leech* [1994] QB 198.
[150] *Gerrard v UK*, Appl. No. 21451/93, [1996] EHRLR 221.
[151] See, for example, *Schönenberger and Durmaz v Switzerland*, A/137, (1989) 11 EHRR 202.

of an application to Strasbourg. However, since the risk of forgery of Commission correspondence is negligible, opening of incoming letters from the Commission cannot be considered to be necessary in a democratic society.[152]

10.80   Article 8 may also operate to improve the family circumstances of prisoners, whose contact with their family will necessarily be limited. Restrictions upon visiting by family and physical contacts between partners are, *prima facie*, easily justified under Article 8(2), but the Court will examine penal practice across Europe,[153] and as attitudes to these matters change, so states which lag behind may find justification to be less straightforward. Article 12 of the Convention has been responsible for reforms which enable prisoners in the UK to marry, initially on temporary release, and now in prison itself.[154] It should also be noted that Article 18 of the Convention prevents interference with family contacts (and with correspondence) being imposed as a punishment, rather than as a genuine attempt to meet the objectives enumerated in Article 8(2).

15. CHILD WARDSHIP, CUSTODY AND ACCESS PROCEEDINGS

10.81   One of the attributes of the right to family life under Article 8(1) is the mutual enjoyment by parent and child of each other's company,[155] and states are bound to act in a way which is calculated to achieve that goal. There is, *prima facie*, a breach of Article 8(1) where custody of a child and/ or access to a child is granted to only one parent following the breakdown of a marriage and where children are removed from one or both parents by the state and placed in care. However, the Convention recognises, through Article 8(2), that there are a wide range of circumstances in which it may be appropriate to disrupt the normal pattern of parent-child relationships. One of the grounds justifying interference with family life is the protection of the rights and freedoms of others, which encompasses the rights of children; the protection of health and morals may also be relevant. Given the possibility of justification, in principle, the key issue is how readily the Court will intervene in the substantive and procedural aspects of the decisions of national authorities on these matters.

---

[152] *Campbell* v *UK*, above n. 39 at 164.
[153] See, for example, *X* v *Germany*, Appl. No. 3603/68, (1970) 31 CD48; *ELH & PBH* v *UK*, Appl. No. 32094/96, (1998) 25 EHRR CD158.
[154] *Hamer* v *UK*, above n. 78; the Marriage Act 1983.
[155] *Andersson* v *Sweden*, A/226, (1992) 14 EHRR 615, 643.

Article 8 does impose significant restrictions upon the discretion of **10.82**
the relevant authorities (which, in the UK, would be local authorities).
The conditions under which children will be separated from one or both
parents must be laid down in law (rather than being based upon
administrative practice) with sufficient precision that their application is
foreseeable. The authorities must have "relevant and sufficient reasons"
for their decision, having regard to the overall national policy on the
parent/child relationship. In *Olsson*, for example, the Court noted that the
aim of the Swedish policy on taking children into care was, ultimately, to
reunite the family, and that a care decision which involved separating the
children and locating them at great distances from their parents, was
contrary to this aim and so to Article 8.[156] Further, any decision which
entails separation of parent from child must be proportionate to a
legitimate aim under Article 8(2), going no further than is absolutely
necessary to achieve that aim.

It is, nevertheless, no easy matter to rely upon Article 8 to challenge **10.83**
the decision of a local authority to take a child into care. According to the
House of Lords, there is no fundamental conflict between the emphasis
upon family life in Article 8 and the paramount importance in English law
of the welfare of the child.[157] Any difference in approach is "purely
semantic".[158] It is also significant that the Court, generally, does not hear
oral evidence and defers to the national courts on issues of fact. The
English courts in turn defer to the fact-finding jurisdiction of the local
authority. There may, however, be some scope for challenging the
conditions attached to decisions that a child should be removed into
local authority care, particularly insofar as they relate to parental access.
Such conditions will be subject to stricter scrutiny than the basic care
decision. A recent example of a successful challenge is *Johansen* v
Norway, where the applicant's daughter had been placed in a foster
home with a view to adoption, and the applicant had been deprived of
any right of access to her.[159] The Court refused to accept the arguments of
the Norwegian authorities that deprivation of parental access had been in
the best interests of the child.[160]

It is often more fruitful to concentrate on the procedures which have **10.84**
been adopted in reaching the decision under challenge, since the Court
has placed great emphasis on the duty of states to provide procedural

---

[156] *Olsson v Sweden (No. 1)*, A/130, (1989) 11 EHRR 259.
[157] *Re KD (A Minor) (Ward: Termination of Access)* [1988] AC 806.
[158] *Ibid.* at 828. Subsequent Court decisions serve to strengthen this view: see *Johansen v Norway*, A/650, (1997) 23 EHRR 33, 72.
[159] *Johansen v Norway, ibid.*, at 67–68.
[160] *Ibid.* at 72–74. Compare *Whitear v UK*, Appl. No. 28625/95, [1997] EHRLR 291.

safeguards against arbitrary treatment. The more dramatic the consequences of a decision for the long-term relationship between parent and
child, the greater the need for open and inclusive procedures.[161] In a
series of cases decided in 1987, the Court criticised the procedures
adopted by British local authorities in taking care decisions, ruling that
the decision-making process must be such as to ensure that the views and
interests of both parents were made known to the local authority and
were taken into account by it.[162] Legislative reforms followed in the
Children Act 1989.[163] Excessive delay in child access proceedings must
also be avoided, particularly since lapse of time may itself be a relevant
factor against reuniting a family.[164] Another recent example of child
custody procedures in breach of Article 8 is *McMichael* v *UK*, where
the applicants were refused access to important documents submitted by
the local authority in care proceedings.[165]

10.85   A more ambitious attempt to use Article 8 to assist parental rights of
access failed in *Logan* v *UK*, where the applicant, who, following his
divorce, had only limited rights of access to his children, argued that the
high level of maintenance payments set by the Child Support Agency
prevented him from travelling to see his children and so affected family
life.[166] The Commission held that the child support legislation, which
sought to regulate the assessment of maintenance payments, did not by
its very nature affect family life. In any event, there had, on the facts, been
no failure to respect family life (presumably because the Commission
regarded the applicant's complaints to be exaggerated).

16. FURTHER READING

Klug, Starmer and Weir, *The Three Pillars of Liberty* (Routledge, 1996),
chapter 12

Michael, *Privacy and Human Rights* (Dartmouth, 1996)

Sands, "Human Rights, Environment and the *López Ostra* Case: Context
and Consequences" [1996] EHRLR 597

Warbrick, "The Structure of Article 8" [1998] EHRLR 32

---

[161] See, for example, *W* v *UK*, A/121, (1988) 10 EHRR 29, 49–50.
[162] *Ibid.*; *O* v *UK*, A/120, (1988) 10 EHRR 82; *H* v *UK*, A/120, (1988) 10 EHRR 95; *R* v *UK*, A/121, (1988) 10 EHRR 74; *B* v *UK*, above n. 30.
[163] See, in particular, s. 34, which allows for applications for access rights to be made to the court.
[164] *W* v *UK*, above n. 161 at 50.
[165] Above n. 137.
[166] Appl. No. 24875/94, [1997] EHRLR 83.

Chapter 11

FREEDOM OF THOUGHT, CONSCIENCE AND RELIGION

Freedom of thought, conscience and religion is protected by Article 9 of **11.1** the Convention:

1. "Everyone has the right to freedom of thought, conscience and religion; this right includes freedom to change his religion and belief and freedom, either alone or in community with others and in public or private, to manifest his religion or belief, in worship, teaching, practice and observance.

2. Freedom to manifest one's religion or beliefs shall be subject only to such limitations as are prescribed by law and are necessary in a democratic society in the interests of public safety, for the protection of public order, health or morals, or for the protection of the rights and freedoms of others."

There is a considerable overlap between the rights protected by Article 9 and the right to respect for private life and to freedom of expression under Articles 8 and 10. Religious or secular beliefs are an important aspect of personal identity and so within the ambit of private life, whilst the manifestation of religious or other beliefs generally constitutes a form of expression or communication within Article 10. The latter may also raise issues of freedom of association under Article 11. The thorny subject of religious education is dealt with under a separate provision, Article 2 of the First Protocol to the Convention.[1] Article 9 may also conflict with other provisions of the Convention, particularly Articles 8, 10 and 11. The paradigm situation is where one individual or group expresses ideas or views which are offensive to the beliefs of another individual or group. Where this occurs, recent case-law indicates that Article 9 rights may well take

---

[1] See chapter 15.

precedence.[2] The scope of Article 9 is, potentially, very broad but the Commission and the Court have, in practice, tended to give it a narrow interpretation, and, where possible, to resolve issues of substance under other provisions of the Convention.

1. THE RIGHTS PROTECTED BY ARTICLE 9

11.2 No case, so far, has turned on the controversial issue of what amounts to a religion or a religious belief. Neither the Commission nor the Court has questioned the right of any cult, sect or religious grouping to call itself a religion, and there has been no judicial definition of the term.[3] An applicant will, however, have to show conclusively that the conduct for which he seeks protection is necessitated by his religious beliefs. In the recent case of *Valsamis* v *Greece*, the Court adopted a sceptical attitude in this respect, rejecting the Article 9 claim of Jehovah's Witnesses who had argued that the obligation placed upon their daughter to participate in a parade held to commemorate Greek National Day conflicted with their pacifist beliefs.[4] The Court refused to accept that the parade was militaristic in character and so found no breach of Article 9 on that point.[5]

11.3 Article 9 applications usually involve alleged restrictions upon the *manifestation* of religion or belief and the key to the scope of Article 9 is perhaps the term "belief" which could apply to a whole spectrum of ideas and programmes, from those of the ancient religions to those of political parties and pressure groups. Certainly, Article 9 is not limited to religious beliefs: in *Arrowsmith*, the Commission accepted that pacifism was a belief within Article 9, on the basis that pacifism is a philosophy.[6] In a subsequent case, however, the Commission rejected the Article 9 claim of a Dutch prisoners' support group, noting that the goals of the group, whilst idealistic, did not fall within the sphere of personal beliefs and religious creeds.[7] It appears that a distinction is drawn between a

---

[2] See *Otto-Preminger-Institut* v *Austria*, A/295-A, (1995) 19 EHRR 34; *Wingrove* v *UK*, A/699 (1997) 24 EHRR 1; cf *Dubowska and Skup* v *Poland*, Appl. 33490/96, (1997) 24 EHRR CD75.

[3] *X and Church of Scientology* v *Sweden*, Appl. No. 7805/77, (1979) 16 D&R; *Chappell* v *UK*, Appl. No. 12587/86, (1987) 53 D&R 241 (pagan Druid).

[4] A/709, (1997) 24 EHRR 294.

[5] See also *X* v *UK*, Appl. 5442/72, (1975) 1 D&R 41.

[6] *Arrowsmith* v *UK*, Appl. No. 7050/75, (1980) 19 D&R 5, 19.

[7] *Vereninging Rechtwinkels Utrecht* v *The Netherlands*, Appl. No. 11308/84, (1986) 46 D&R 200, 202.

philosophy and a social or political manifesto, perhaps for the reason that beliefs of a purely political nature fall more naturally within the "freedom to hold opinions" which is protected under Article 10. Where the beliefs at issue and alleged to be under threat are those of a church or other organised group, that body will have standing as a "victim" of a Convention violation to bring a challenge in its own right.[8]

There are three other important limitations on the scope of rights under Article 9(1) which relate to the concept of "freedom" to hold and to manifest beliefs. First, an important distinction is drawn between conduct which manifests belief in the sense that it directly expresses belief and conduct which is merely motivated by, or pursuant to, belief. In *Arrowsmith*, for example, the Commission held that the distribution of pacifist leaflets was only motivated by the pacifist philosophy and was not a direct manifestation of it (although issues of freedom of expression may be raised in such a case).[9] Similarly, an advert for a religious artefact promulgated by the Church of Scientology was held to be a manifestation of a desire to market goods rather than a manifestation of belief.[10]

11.4

The second important limitation is that the Commission and the Court have been reluctant to permit individuals to object, on grounds of conscience or belief, to being subjected to laws which are of general application. Accordingly, Article 9 does not prohibit laws which are passed pursuant to the public interest but whose application incidentally offends against the conscience, or restricts the religious activities, of groups of individuals who are affected by it. It is, in truth, difficult to formulate a precise rule, in part because this result can be achieved both under Article 9(1) and (2). It is perhaps easier to predict those situations of political delicacy in which the Commission will refuse to intervene. In *C v UK*, for example, the Commission rejected the application of a Quaker who objected on religious grounds to state expenditure on defence and wished to have the relevant proportion of his taxes directed to other purposes.[11] Similarly, in *ISKCON v UK*, the Krishna consciousness movement complained about the rejection of a planning application which prevented the use of an estate owned by it for the purposes of public religious worship.[12] The Commission held that sufficient weight had been given to religious freedom in the planning process and that Article 9 could not be used to circumvent planning laws of general application.

11.5

[8] *X and Church Scientology v Sweden*, above n. 3 at 70.
[9] *Arrowsmith v UK*, above n. 6 at 19-20.
[10] *X and the Church of Scientology v Sweden*, above n. 3 at 72.
[11] Appl. No. 10358/83, (1983) 37 D&R 142; see also *Omakaranda and Divine Light Zentrum v Switzerland*, Appl. No. 8118/77 (1981) 25 D&R 105.
[12] Appl. No. 20490/92, (1994) 76-A D&R 90.

11.6   Thirdly, the scope of the freedom to manifest religion may be limited by the individual circumstances of the person claiming it. For example, the rights of prisoners will be more limited, by virtue of their detention. Contractual obligations freely entered into are another limiting factor. In *Ahmad* v *UK*, the applicant was a Moslem school teacher who had been refused permission to absent himself from school on Friday afternoons in order to attend mosque.[13] He resigned, and ultimately lost a claim for constructive dismissal before the Court of Appeal.[14] The Commission held that the applicant's employer was entitled to rely upon its contractual rights, and had discharged its duties by offering him a part-time contract which excluded Friday afternoons. It adopted an even more restrictive view in *Stedman*, where the applicant had lost her job after refusing, for religious reasons, to sign a new contract which required her to work on a Sunday. Here, the applicant had never agreed to Sunday work, but the Commission found that there had been no interference with her freedom of religion because she was free to resign and so carry on manifesting her beliefs on a Sunday.[15]

2. STATE OBLIGATIONS UNDER ARTICLE 9

11.7   Article 9 is one of the provisions of the Convention which gives rise to positive obligations. Clearly, a state must abstain from itself interfering with religious freedom, etc., by penalising or otherwise restricting protected behaviour. However, it must also take certain steps to secure religious freedom to its citizens, including protecting the holders of religious beliefs from offence at the hands of others. In *Otto-Preminger-Institut* v *Austria*, the applicant association claimed that its freedom of expression under Article 10 had been restricted when a satirical film which it was due to show was confiscated by the authorities. The film had already been shown elsewhere in Austria, and admission to screenings was strictly controlled, but it was argued that confiscation was necessary in order to protect the religious sensibilities of the local population.[16]

11.8   The Court relied heavily on the respondent state's margin of appreciation in finding that it had been entitled to restrict freedom of expression in

---

[13] *Ahmad* v *UK*, Appl. No. 8160/78, (1982) 4 EHRR 125.
[14] *Ahmad* v *ILEA* [1978] QB 36.
[15] *Stedman* v *UK*, Appl. No. 29107/95, (1997) EHRR CD168.
[16] *Otto-Preminger-Institut* v *Austria*, above n. 2.

defence of the "rights of others" under Article 9.[17] Strictly speaking, the case is authority only for the proposition that the state *may* act to protect Article 9 rights even where to do so involves a restriction upon freedom of expression. However, the terminology of the Court was much stronger than that. It noted that the state has a responsibility to ensure the peaceful enjoyment of Article 9 rights and that particular methods of criticism or opposition to religious beliefs may inhibit those who hold such beliefs from exercising their freedom to hold and express them.[18] This implies that the state *must* act in such circumstances if it is not be in breach of Article 9.

The Court's ruling in *Otto-Preminger-Institut* calls into question the **11.9** earlier decision of the Commission in *Choudhury v UK*, an application which challenged the restriction of the English law of blasphemy to offence against the Christian religion.[19] The applicant had sought the issue of summonses for blasphemy against the author and publishers of *The Satanic Verses*, failing on the basis that the criminal law did not prohibit anti-Islamic, but only anti-Christian, literature.[20] The Commission held that Article 9 did not guarantee the right to bring any particular form of proceedings against persons who cause religious offence. Since Article 9 did not apply, a claim of discrimination under Article 14 also failed. Whatever the merits of the Commission's reasoning, it was content to leave unprotected the religious sensibilities of a significant minority religion. Arguably, the only way in which *Choudhury* can be reconciled with *Otto-Preminger-Institut* is on the perhaps unlikely basis that states need only protect the religious rights and freedoms of the majority, or of the established church. Whilst it is not unlawful in principle to have an established church,[21] that surely does not mean that only the established church is worthy of protection.

The Court was also confronted with the English law of blasphemy in **11.10** the recent case of *Wingrove*, where the applicant director's film had been refused a certificate on the grounds that it infringed the criminal law of blasphemy.[22] The Court rejected the argument that the offence of blasphemy against the Christian religion was itself unnecessary in a democratic society and so incompatible with the Convention. Blasphemy legislation was still in force in various European countries and although its application had become increasingly rare, there was not as yet sufficient

---

[17] *Ibid.* at 59-50.
[18] *Ibid.* at 56.
[19] Appl. No. 17439/90 (1991) 12 *Human Rights LJ* 172.
[20] *R.* v *Chief Metropolitan Stipendiary magistrate ex parte Choudhury* [1991] 1 QB 429.
[21] *Darby* v *Sweden*, A/187, (1991) 13 EHRR 774.
[22] Above n. 2.

common ground throughout the Council of Europe states to enable the Court to conclude that blasphemy legislation was contrary to Article 10.[23] The Court declined to address the argument that the law of blasphemy could not be said to be directed at a legitimate aim under Article 10(2) because it was itself discriminatory against non-Christian faiths.[24]

3. RESTRICTIONS ON ARTICLE 9 RIGHTS

11.11 The vast majority of cases brought under Article 9 have been ruled to be outside of scope of Article 9(1), so there is comparatively little case-law concerning restrictions which are permitted under Article 9(2). Article 9(2) follows a similar pattern to the exceptions to Articles 8, 10 and 11 but is narrow in scope in two important respects. Only one aspect of the rights protected by Article 9(1), the right to manifest one's religion or beliefs, can be limited under Article 9(2) — there can be no justification for restricting the freedom to hold beliefs. Also, the list of legitimate objectives to which limitations can be directed is relatively short.

11.12 It appears that states have very little room for manoeuvre when seeking to justify restrictions on Article 9 rights. Religious pluralism is viewed by the Court as an important ingredient of a democratic society and it will subject to "very strict scrutiny" any measure which detracts from this goal.[25] In *Manoussakis*, the applicant Jehovah's Witnesses were convicted under a Greek law prohibiting the operation of a place of worship without prior ministerial approval. They had first applied for approval in 1984 and by the time of the Court's decision in 1996 they had still not received a definitive reply. The Court found that the law had been used by the authorities in order to restrict the activities of non-Orthodox faiths and, not surprisingly, that Article 9 had been breached.[26] Similarly, in *Kokkinakis*, the Court found a breach of the principle of proportionality where the applicant Jehovah's Witness had been convicted for proselytising.[27] The relevant law went beyond the legitimate aim of protecting the rights of others because it failed to draw a distinction between legitimate proselytism and proselytism by improper means.

---

[23] *Ibid.* at 30-31.
[24] *Ibid.* at 28.
[25] *Manoussakis* v *Greece*, A/660, (1997) 23 EHRR 387, 407.
[26] *Ibid.*
[27] *Kokkinakis* v *Greece*, A/260-A, (1994) 17 EHRR 397.

Several applications which have failed at the hurdle of Article 9(2), **11.13** notably from the UK, have concerned the extent to which prison rules must make provision for prisoners to practice minority religions. Complaints about restrictions upon letter-writing (from a Buddhist), a rule that prisoners clean the floor of their cell (from a Sikh) and a refusal of access to a religious book containing instruction on martial arts (from a Taoist), have all been held, without difficulty, to be justified under Article 9(2).[28]

4. RELIGIOUS DISCRIMINATION

Article 14, which precludes discrimination, *inter alia*, on grounds of **11.14** religion, has an important role to play in protecting freedom of religion. Discrimination claims cannot be freestanding — they must be brought in conjunction with another substantive right protected by the Convention. However, a state act which is held not to infringe Article 9 because of the relatively narrow interpretation accorded to that provision may nevertheless fall foul of Article 9 or of other provisions of the Convention, taken together with Article 14, if it is based upon religious discrimination. In *Hoffman* v *Austria*, the applicant complained that she had been discriminated against in custody proceedings which had been determined in favour of her husband.[29] The Austrian Supreme Court had relied on her beliefs as a Jehovah's Witness, ruling that her children would become social outcasts if they were brought up as Jehovah's Witnesses and that they risked physical danger by reason of her refusal to countenance blood transfusions. This was, according to the Court of Human Rights, a difference in treatment based solely on religious grounds and was contrary to Article 8 taken together with Article 14.

5. FURTHER READING

Cullen, "The Emerging Scope of Freedom of Conscience" (1997) 22 EL Rev HRC 32

Ghandi and James, "The English Law of Blasphemy and the European Convention on Human Rights" [1998] EHRLR 430

---

[28] *X* v *UK*, above n. 5; *X* v *UK*, Appl. No. 8231/78, (1982) 28 D&R 5; *X* v *UK*, Appl. No. 6886/75, (1976) 5 D&R 100.
[29] A/255-C, (1994) 17 EHRR 293.

Chapter 12

FREEDOM OF EXPRESSION

Article 10 of the Convention provides: **12.1**

"1. Everyone has the right to freedom of expression. This right shall include freedom to hold opinions and to receive and impart information and ideas without interference by public authority and regardless of frontiers. This Article shall not prevent States from requiring the licensing of broadcasting, television or cinema enterprises.

2. The exercise of these freedoms, since it carries with it duties and responsibilities, may be subject to such formalities, conditions, restrictions or penalties as are prescribed by law and are necessary in a democratic society, in the interests of national security, territorial integrity or public safety, for the prevention of disorder or crime, for the protection of the reputation or rights of others, for preventing the disclosure of information received in confidence, or for maintaining the authority and impartiality of the judiciary."

According to the European Court of Human Rights, freedom of expression is one of the essential foundations of a democratic society. The Court has repeatedly emphasised that Article 10 protects not only information and ideas which are received favourably or with indifference, but also those which shock, offend or disturb.[1] Hence, freedom of expression has been used to promote ideals of pluralism, tolerance and broad-mindedness which the Court sees as central to the democratic process and to the personal development of individuals.

Article 10 follows the scheme of Articles 8, 9 and 11 in setting out a   **12.2** basic right and then specifying the circumstances in which it may be limited, although the wording of Article 10(2) is broader in important respects than the equivalent provisions in those articles. As well as the limitations of Article 10(2), there are other provisions of the Convention which may be relied upon to restrict freedom of expression. Article 6(1) allows restrictions upon the reporting of judicial proceedings, Article 16 permits restrictions on the political activities of foreigners and Article 17 prohibits reliance upon Convention rights where the aim is to subvert or

---

[1] See, for example, *Handyside* v *UK*, A/24, (1979–80) 1 EHRR 737, 754.

destroy the freedoms which the Convention seeks to secure.[2] The latter may be relevant to the degree of freedom of expression accorded to Neo-Nazis and other extremist political groupings, although the Court has tended to view it as a provision of last-resort only.[2a]

12.3   Such is the wide-ranging nature of the right to freedom of expression that overlap and conflict with other rights and freedoms is inevitable. The activities of newspapers may interfere with the right to respect for private life, artistic expression may offend against the peaceful enjoyment of freedom of religion and so on. The questions arising for determination under Article 10, particularly in these situations of conflict, are among the thorniest and most controversial to come before the Court.

1. THE SCOPE OF ARTICLE 10 RIGHTS

THE MEANING OF "EXPRESSION"

12.4   Article 10(1) is extremely broad. Speech and other forms of expression are protected no matter how offensive or valueless is their content (although the value of their content may be relevant to justification under Article 10(2)). The Convention case-law can be roughly categorised under the headings of political, commercial and artistic expression, and it will be examined on that basis below, but this is not to imply any limitation upon the subject matter of expression protected by Article 10. Nor is Article 10(1) limited according to the medium by which opinions, information or ideas are conveyed and new forms of communication will fall within Article 10 as they are developed. Article 10(1) encompasses also the right not to express oneself, and to remain silent, perhaps through fear of self-incrimination, and overlaps in this respect with Article 6(1), which contains a rule against self-incrimination in the course of criminal proceedings.[3]

FREEDOM TO HOLD AND EXPRESS OPINIONS

12.5   Article 10(1) mentions, first, the freedom to hold opinions, which, implicitly includes the freedom to express those opinions to others.

---

[2] See chapter 6 para. 6.93.
[2a] See, recently, *Lebideux v France*, A/996, decision of 23 September 1998.
[3] See, for example, *Saunders v UK*, A/702, (1996) 23 EHRR 313 cf *Goodwin v UK*, A/610, (1996) 22 EHRR 123; Naismith, "Self-incrimination — Fairness or Freedom" [1997] EHRLR 229.

This freedom is related to the right to hold, and to manifest, beliefs under Article 9 which appears to be restricted to religious and philosophical convictions as opposed to social and political views.[4] The borderline between the two may be difficult to pinpoint in principle, but the Commission and the Court have tended to rule borderline cases outside Article 9 but within Article 10. Just as under Article 9 there can be no justification for restrictions being placed upon the freedom to hold beliefs, so the Court is extremely reluctant to uphold any measure which, in effect, penalises individuals merely for the opinions which they hold. In *Lingens*, for example, the applicant had been convicted under the Austrian offence of defamation, which afforded a defence only to those who could prove the truth of their statements. There was no provision for fair comment, thereby penalising statements containing value judgments which were incapable of factual proof.[5] The Court held that the freedom to hold opinions had been infringed in a way which was not necessary for the protection of the reputation of others in society.[6]

INFORMATION AND IDEAS

No limit is placed on the definition of "information and ideas". The freedom to receive information was invoked in *Autronic v Switzerland*, where the Court agreed that Article 10 protected the right of the applicant company to receive information from available sources and consequently the right to receive television programmes intended for the general public which were re-transmitted by a telecommunications satellite.[7] However, the freedom to receive information and ideas does not confer any right to freedom of information which would require the state to disclose information held by it. In *Gaskin*, for example, the applicant sought disclosure of records held by a local authority which related to his childhood spent in care and with foster parents.[8] The Court held that the right to receive information in Article 10(1) prohibits restrictions upon a person receiving information that others wish or may be willing to impart to him, but did not oblige the local authority to disclose information against its

12.6

---

[4] *Arrowsmith v UK*, Appl. No. 7050/75, (1980) 19 D&R 5 cf *Vereniging Rechtwinkels Utrecht v The Netherlands*, Appl. No. 11308/84, (1986) 46 D&R 200.
[5] *Lingens v Austria*, A/103, (1986) 8 EHRR 407.
[6] *Ibid.* at 420–421.
[7] A/178, (1990) 12 EHRR 485.
[8] *Gaskin v UK*, A/160, (1990) 12 EHRR 36.

will.[9] The applicant was, however, entitled to receive the documentation he sought pursuant to Article 8, since it was essential to his personal identity and so to his private life. A right of access to information held by the authorities may also be found in Article 6(3)(b), which guarantees adequate facilities for the preparation of a criminal defence.

LICENSING OF BROADCASTING, TELEVISION AND CINEMA

12.7 The third and final sentence of Article 10(1) apparently intends to exempt from the scrutiny of Article 10 the power of states to licence broadcasting, television and cinema. It would suggest that licensing decisions are entirely outwith the scope of Article 10(1) and that challenges to such decisions should fall at the first hurdle. However, the Court has adopted rather a different interpretation: it is now well-established that the third sentence of Article 10(1) intends only to make it clear that states are permitted to control by a licensing system the way in which broadcasting is organised in their territories, but that licensing measures still fall to be justified under Article 10(2).[10] The grant of broadcast licenses may be made conditional on technical or other considerations including the nature and objectives of the proposed broadcaster, its potential audience at national, regional and local level, the rights and needs of a specific audience and international broadcasting treaty obligations. Hence, the only effect of the third sentence of Article 10(1) is to allow interferences with freedom of expression in pursuit of legitimate aims which are not specifically listed in Article 10(2).[11]

2. STATE OBLIGATIONS TO PROTECT FREEDOM OF EXPRESSION

12.8 According to Article 10(1), freedom of expression is to be enjoyed without interference by public authority. Article 10(2) appears to define in more

---

[9] *Ibid.* at 50–51. See also *Geillustreerde Pers* v *The Netherlands*, Appl. No. 5178/71, (1976) 8 D&R 5, 13.

[10] *Groppera Radio AG* v *Switzerland*, A/173, (1990) 12 EHRR 321, 338–339.

[11] *Informationsverein Lentia* v *Austria*, A/276, (1994) 17 EHRR 93, 112. See also *Radio ABC* v *Austria*, A/840, (1998) 25 EHRR 185.

detail the types of forbidden interference in that it permits, under certain circumstances, "formalities, conditions, restrictions or penalties". The clear implication is that all these are in breach of Article 10 unless they fall within the limits of Article 10(2). The case-law confirms that Article 10 strikes not only at censorship — prior restrictions upon the dissemination of material — but also at penalties imposed following its dissemination, whether by way of criminal sanction or civil action, which are likely to induce self-censorship in the future.[12]

12.9　One exception should be noted: it appears that an individual or body may contract-out of Article 10 so that a restriction or penalty upon free expression will not amount to an interference within Article 10(1). In *Vereniging Rechtswinkels Utrecht*, the applicant was a prisoners' support group which had been granted access to a prison on certain conditions, pursuant to an agreement with the prison governors.[13] It broke the terms of its agreement by going to the newspapers about the suicide of an inmate without first informing the prison authorities, and its rights of access were withdrawn. This was undoubtedly a "penalty", but the Commission held that there was no interference within Article 10(1) since the termination of the agreement did not restrict the group's ability to impart information any further than it had accepted when entering into the agreement in the first place.[14] Similarly, in *Rommelfanger*, the Commission held that the Convention permits contractual obligations which are aimed at restricting freedom of expression, provided that they are freely entered into by the person concerned. If the obligations are breached, and, in the employment context, dismissal or other disciplinary sanction results, there will be no interference by a public authority, even if the courts are involved in upholding the sanctions.[15]

12.10　It was arguable until relatively recently that a threat of disciplinary action, including dismissal, by a state employer as a consequence of self-expression was not an interference within Article 10(1), but only a condition attaching to employment which could be avoided by giving up the job. In 1986, the Court rejected complaints from a German secondary school teacher (a Communist) and a university research assistant (a fascist) who had been dismissed from their posts because of their "unconstitutional" political activities.[16] In a more recent case, however, the Court explained that the sole basis for these decisions

---

[12] See, for example, *Handyside* v *UK*, above n. 1 (criminal law of obscenity) and *Tolstoy Miloslavsky* v *UK*, A/323, (1995) 20 EHRR 442 (civil law of libel).
[13] Above n. 4.
[14] *Ibid.* at 202–203.
[15] *Rommelfanger* v *Germany*, Appl. No. 12242/86, (1989) 62 D&R 151.
[16] *Glaseknapp* v *Germany*, A/104, (1986) 9 EHRR 25; *Kosiek* v *Germany*, A/105, (1986) 9 EHRR 328.

was the applicants' status as probationary civil servants. The Convention does not confer a right of access to the civil service and the German authorities had simply decided that the applicants were not suitable candidates for full appointment to civil service posts. In *Vogt*, the applicant had also been dismissed because of her activities on behalf of the Communist party, but she had already been appointed to a tenured position. Therefore, disciplinary action against her did amount to an interference with her freedom of expression.[17] The Court's conclusions are consistent with the view of the Commission that the state must protect private sector employees against certain forms of compulsion by their employers in matters of freedom of expression.[18]

12.11   "Interference by a public authority" within Article 10(2) also covers the situation where restrictions upon freedom of expression are imposed by a private body which is exercising functions on behalf of the state. In *Wingrove*, for example, the distribution of the applicant's film was restricted, in the first instance, by the British Board of Film Classification, which refused to grant a certificate to it.[19] The BBFC is formally a private body, but is designated under s. 4 of the Video Recordings Act 1984 as the authority responsible for the issue of certificates to video works. It is, accordingly, a public authority within Article 10(1). Various other regulatory bodies would also fall within Article 10(1) on this basis, for example, the Advertising Standards Authority and perhaps also the Press Complaints Commission.

12.12   Even though Article 10(1) mentions only interference by a public authority, there are indications that it may impose positive obligations upon the state to prevent or control interferences with freedom of expression by private parties. In *Rommelfanger*, the Commission was faced with a complaint from a doctor who had been dismissed from his post in a hospital run by the Catholic Church after speaking out in favour of abortion. His legal claims for wrongful termination of his employment were rejected by the German courts. The Commission rejected the applicant's argument that the Catholic Church should be considered to be a state authority, and so considered his claim as made on the basis that the German courts had failed to protect his freedom of expression against the sanction of dismissal by a private employer. It assumed that such positive obligations did exist, but found that German law was sufficient to protect the applicant from unreasonable demands of loyalty on the part of his employer. In this instance, the Church's demands had not been

---

[17] *Vogt* v *Germany*, A/653, (1996) 21 EHRR 205, 231–232.
[18] *Rommelfanger* v *Germany*, above n. 15; see below, para. 12.12.
[19] *Wingrove* v *UK*, A/699, (1997) 24 EHRR 1.

unreasonable given the importance to it of the abortion issue. This case has clear implications for the protection of employees who speak out against their employer in breach of their contractual obligations of loyalty and/or confidentiality.[20]

The Court has yet to rule on the important issue of positive obligations under Article 10. However, certain of its decisions under Article 11 on freedom of assembly and association are clearly applicable by analogy. The Commission in *Rommelfanger* relied upon *Young, James and Webster*, in which the Court upheld the Article 11 claims of three employees who had been dismissed for refusing to join a trade union in breach of a "closed shop" agreement.[21] The later case of *Plattform Ärtze für das Leben* v *Austria* is also highly relevant: there, the Court found that the Austrian authorities had positive obligations to protect the rights of demonstrators to protest without interference from counter-demonstrators who had succeeded in disrupting their march (although, in the circumstances, those obligations had been discharged).[22] The case was dealt with as an issue of effective remedy for breach of the right to freedom of assembly, but the rights of the applicant might just as easily have been characterised as going to freedom of expression. Indeed, in *Steel*, the Commission has recently relied upon *Plattform Ärtze für das Leben* to support a finding of breach of Article 10 where the police had removed and detained pacifist demonstrators, so preventing them from airing their views.[23]

12.13

3. LIMITING FREEDOM OF EXPRESSION: GENERAL CONSIDERATIONS

The breadth of the interpretation accorded to Article 10(1) means that the vast majority of applications succeed in establishing an interference with freedom of expression and so fall to be determined under Article 10(2). In recent cases, the Court has recited a series of basic principles concerning Article 10 which have been distilled from its previous judgments. Before examining the various facets of Article 10(2) in more detail it is convenient to set out these principles.[24]

12.14

---

[20] See Bowers and Lewis, "Whistleblowing: Freedom of Expression in the Workplace" [1996] EHRLR 637; of the Public Interest Disclosure Act 1998.

[21] *Young, James and Webster* v *UK*, A/44, (1982) 4 EHRR 38.

[22] A/139, (1991) 13 EHRR 204.

[23] *Steel and others* v *UK*, Appl. No. 24838/94, [1997] EHRLR 687. The Court's reasoning was, however, different: A/992, decision of 23 September 1998.

[24] This summary is taken from *Vogt*, above n. 17 at 235.

- Freedom of expression constitutes one of the essential foundations of a democratic society and one of the basic conditions for its progress and each individual's self-fulfilment. Subject to Article 10(2), it is applicable not only to "information" or "ideas" that are favourably received or regarded as inoffensive or as a matter of indifference, but also to those that offend, shock or disturb; such are the demands of that pluralism, tolerance and broad-mindedness without which there is no "democratic society". Freedom of expression, as enshrined in Article 10, is subject to a number of exceptions which, however, must be narrowly interpreted and the necessity for any restrictions must be convincingly established.
- The adjective "necessary", within the meaning of Article 10(2), implies the existence of a "pressing social need". The Contracting States have a certain margin of appreciation in assessing whether such a need exists, but it goes hand in hand with a European supervision, embracing both the law and the decisions applying it, even those given by independent courts. The Court is therefore empowered to give the final ruling on whether a "restriction" is reconcilable with freedom of expression as protected by Article 10.
- The Court's task, in exercising its supervisory jurisdiction, is not to take the place of the competent national authorities but rather to review under Article 10 the decisions they delivered pursuant to their power of appreciation. This does not mean that the supervision is limited to ascertaining whether the respondent State exercised its discretion reasonably, carefully and in good faith; what the Court has to do is to look at the interference complained of in the light of the case as a whole and determine whether it was "proportionate to the legitimate aim pursued" and whether the reasons adduced by the national authorities to justify it were "relevant and sufficient". In so doing, the Court has to satisfy itself that the national authorities applied standards which were in conformity with the principles embodied in Article 10 and, moreover, that they based their decisions on an acceptable assessment of the relevant facts.

12.15　　The Article 10(2) analysis proceeds in a number of stages. First, the Court will examine the preliminary issue of whether an interference has a sufficient legal basis to be "prescribed by law". It will then ascertain whether the interference can fairly be said to be directed towards one of the legitimate aims set out in Article 10(2). The third and usually determinative stage is whether the interference with freedom of expression is "necessary in a democratic society". This requires an analysis of the reasoning behind the interference and of whether it has restrictive effects which go further than are justified by that reasoning. It also raises the crucial issue of the extent of the margin of appreciation which will be allowed to the state authorities to make their own choices in this area.

The extent of the margin of appreciation allowed to public authorities **12.16** in restricting freedom of expression varies dramatically from case to case, and each case must be examined very much on is own facts. Unfortunately, the reasoning adopted by the Court in deciding whether a measure is "necessary in a democratic society" is frequently unsatisfactory. Usually, it will merely list a series of factors which it considers to be significant before indicating its conclusion. It rarely spells out in detail which aspects of the case are decisive and why. For this reason, the outcome of Article 10 cases is very often difficult to predict with any measure of certainty, as evidenced by the significant number of cases in which the Commission and the Court have reached wildly differing conclusions.[25]

4. DUTIES AND RESPONSIBILITIES

Article 10(2) commences by noting that the exercise of the freedom of **12.17** expression carries with it "duties and responsibilities". This phrase is usually relied upon by respondent states in order to justify limitations upon the rights of certain categories of person, for example, civil servants and soldiers, whose freedom of expression they are particularly concerned to curb. In *Vogt*, for example, the German Government argued, and the Court accepted, that civil servants had special duties and responsibilities having regard to the German notion of the civil service as the guarantor of the Constitution and of democracy. The discretion of the German authorities to interfere with the freedom of expression of civil servants was, accordingly, broader.[26] The British Government put forward a similar argument in *Ahmed*, a challenge to restrictions imposed upon the political activities of local government officers.[27] Recently, however, the Court has appeared keen to play down the significance of this aspect of Article 10(2). It has emphasised that whatever their status

---

[25] See, recently, *Wingrove v UK*, above n. 19; *Otto-Preminger-Institut v Austria*, A/295-A, (1995) 19 EHRR 34.
[26] *Vogt v Germany*, above n. 17 at 235.
[27] *Ahmed v UK*, A/966, decision of 2 September 1998.

and role in society may be, civil servants and soldiers are nevertheless "individuals" who benefit from the full protection of the Convention.[28] Nevertheless, even if whole groups of potential applicants may not be excluded from the protection of Article 10 on this basis, it is well-established that the duties and responsibilities undertaken by a particular individual, notably those arising from a contract of employment, may warrant restrictions upon his or her freedom of expression. For example, the Commission has found that civil servants are subject to "a duty of moderation" arising out of their employment status, and has upheld various restrictions upon the freedom of expression of civil servants.[29]

12.18   Special duties and responsibilities may also work to the advantage of applicants: journalists and publishers, amongst others, benefit from enhanced protection because of their responsibilities within a democratic society.[30] In practice, reference to the "duties and responsibilities" of a category of persons to which the applicant belongs will not be determinative but will serve only to focus attention on factors which are significant in determining the scope of the margin of appreciation where freedom of expression has been limited.

5. FORMALITIES, CONDITIONS, RESTRICTIONS OR PENALTIES

12.19   The range of conditions, restrictions, etc. which constitute an interference with freedom of expression within Article 10(1) has been addressed above.[30a] It is difficult to see how there could be a dispute over this clause of Article 10(2): the applicant will have established a condition, restriction etc. in order to demonstrate that there has been an "interference" with freedom of expression within the meaning of Article 10(1) and, in theory, the respondent state must accept that the measure in question constitutes a condition, restriction, etc. in order to justify it under Article 10(2).

---

[28] *Vogt* v *Germany*, above n. 17 at 235; *Vereinigung Demokratischer Soldaten Österreichs and Gubi* v *Austria*, A/302, (1995) 20 EHRR 55, 83.
[29] For example, *Morissens* v *Belgium*, Appl. No. 11389/85, (1988) 56 D&R 127.
[30] See, for example, *Goodwin* v *UK*, above n. 3 (journalists); *Observer and Guardian* v *UK*, A/216, (1992) 14 EHRR 153 (publishers).
[30a] Paras 12.8–12.13.

6. PRESCRIBED BY LAW

The requirement that a restriction upon freedom of expression must be **12.20** prescribed by law involves a three-stage test.[31] First, the restriction must have a foundation in law, whether statute or the common law,[32] or even international law.[33] Secondly, the law must be accessible, in the sense that it is publicly available and comprehensible, such that the citizen has an adequate indication of the rules applicable in his case. It is assumed, for these purposes, that people act with the benefit of appropriate legal advice and even highly technical and complex regulatory laws may be deemed to be sufficiently comprehensible.[34]

Thirdly, the application of the law must be foreseeable: a rule must be **12.21** formulated with sufficient precision to enable the citizen to regulate his conduct in accordance with it. There is no breach of this requirement merely because a legal provision is ambiguous, or where a restriction is based upon a discretionary power, provided that there is sufficient indication of the circumstances in which the discretion will be exercised. Indeed, given the culture of judicial law-making in the English common law system, the Court is unlikely to find a breach of the foreseeability requirement in English cases, save in extreme circumstances. A good example of its reluctance is *Goodwin*, in which a journalist who had been ordered to hand over documents which would reveal his confidential source pursuant to s. 10 of the Contempt of Court Act 1981 complained that the application of s. 10 did not satisfy the foreseeability requirement.[35] Section 10 provides that disclosure of a journalist's source may be ordered where, *inter alia*, it is necessary in the interests of justice and the House of Lords in Goodwin's case had rejected a previous dictum of Lord Diplock to the effect that "justice" was used in the narrow, technical sense of the administration of justice in the course of legal proceedings.[36] Instead, a rather broader approach was adopted, with the judge being required to weigh up the importance of "justice" being attained, in the general sense, and whether or not legal proceedings were on foot, against the importance of protecting a source.[37] The Court of Human Rights

---

[31] *Sunday Times* v *UK*, A/30, (1979–80) 2 EHRR 245, 270–271.
[32] *Ibid.* at 270.
[33] See *Groppera Radio* v *Switzerland*, above n. 10 at 340–341, in which the Swiss Government successfully relied upon rules of international telecommunications law.
[34] *Ibid.* at 341–342.
[35] Above n. 3.
[36] *Secretary of State for Defence* v *Guardian Newspapers* [1985] AC 339, 350.
[37] *X Ltd* v *Morgan-Grampian Ltd* [1991] 1 AC 1, 43 and 53–54.

rejected the applicant's submission that the law had been revised in an unexpected manner and was now wholly subjective and unpredictable. It found that judicial discretion was limited, that another earlier House of Lords decision could have alerted the applicant to the true position, and that a degree of flexibility in the formulation of laws may be desirable to enable the law to be developed by national courts.[38]

7. LEGITIMATE AIMS AND OBJECTIVES

12.22 Once a respondent state has established that a particular restriction upon freedom of expression is prescribed by law, it must go on to show that the restriction is aimed at one of the list of legitimate aims and objectives contained in Article 10(2). According to the Court, the list is exhaustive, and the various heads under which restrictions may be justified will be narrowly interpreted. In practice, however, this hurdle rarely proves difficult to surmount. Several of the justifications are inherently broad, for example, the prevention of disorder, and of crime, and the protection of the rights of others and, despite its protestations to the contrary, the Court has not always given them a narrow interpretation. For example, the prevention of disorder, narrowly construed, might be limited to prevention of disruption to public order but in *Groppera Radio*, the Court accepted that it could cover disruption to the regulation of international telecommunications, a much broader use of the phrase.[39] Where the Court doubts the strength of the connection between the restriction at issue and the aim cited, it will generally rule that the restriction is not "necessary" for the achievement of the aim rather than that the aim attributed to the restriction is spurious. The aim relied upon may, nevertheless, be relevant to the extent of the margin of appreciation accorded to the state authorities (see below).

8. NECESSARY IN A DEMOCRATIC SOCIETY

12.23 The vast majority of cases under Article 10 turn on whether a restriction upon freedom of expression satisfies the requirement of being necessary

---

[38] Above n. 3 at 140–141; see also *Sunday Times* v *UK*, above n. 31 at 271–273 and *Steel* v *UK*, above n. 23.
[39] Above n. 10 at 342.

in a democratic society. The broad parameters of the necessity test are firmly established and are routinely recited by the Court.

- A restriction which is "necessary" is one which corresponds to a "pressing social need".
- The necessity of any restriction must be "convincingly established".
- A measure must be no more restrictive than is necessary to achieve its aims (the proportionality test).

As noted above, states have a margin of appreciation in making these judgments and the outcome of a case will most often depend on the breadth of discretion which the Court is prepared to permit in the circumstances. In any case which appears to raise issues of freedom of expression, the first step is to search for closely analogous situations in the case-law of the Commission and the Court. Frequently, however, there will be no case directly on point and it becomes necessary to identify various factors which, in previous cases, have influenced the Commission and the Court to adopt a more or less interventionist approach, and to ascertain which of those factors applies in the instant case. The remainder of this chapter is devoted to an analysis of the most important of the factors going to the breadth of the margin of appreciation.

THE TYPE OF EXPRESSION

Expression can be broadly subdivided into three categories, political, commercial and artistic expression. **12.24**

Political expression

Political speech is given special protection by the Court, which views it as **12.25** an essential component of a democratic and pluralist society, and allows to state authorities little if any room for manoeuvre in restricting it. It is a broad category, which is not restricted to "high politics" but extends to discussion of all matters of public concern. Issues as disparate as the personal character of a politician, the conduct of the police, the commercial prospects of a company and the provision of emergency veterinary services all fall under the rubric of political expression,[40] and the high level of protection will be warranted even where there are also elements of commercial or artistic expression present.[41]

12.26   The Commission and the Court have been particularly concerned to safeguard the freedom of the press, which is viewed as playing a vital role of "public watchdog", and the margin of appreciation can be virtually non-existent where restrictions upon the press have been imposed. In *Goodwin*, for example, the Court stressed the sanctity of the journalist's freedom to protect his sources, which was, in its view, one of the basic conditions for press freedom.[42] Orders to disclose sources, such as had been made against the applicant, could only be justified by an overriding requirement of the public interest, which had not been demonstrated to the Court's satisfaction.[43] The English courts, including the House of Lords, had, in Goodwin's case, applied s. 10 of the Contempt of Court Act 1981, which required them to weigh up journalistic privilege against the interests of justice, a balancing test analogous to that proposed by the Court.[44] However, the Court appeared to make no allowance at all for the margin of appreciation of the national courts to reach their own conclusions on what the public interest required, noting merely that the margin of appreciation was circumscribed by the interest of society in ensuring and maintaining a free press.[45]

12.27   Another recent example of the importance attached by the Court to freedom of the press is *Jersild v Denmark*, where the applicant television journalist had been fined over a documentary film in which racist youths were invited to give voice to their views. The youths themselves were convicted of making racial insults, the applicant for aiding and abetting them.[46] The Court held that the punishment of a journalist for assisting in the dissemination of statements made by another person in an interview would seriously hamper the contribution of the press to discussion of matters of public interest and could only be justified where there were "particularly strong reasons".[47] No such reasons had been demonstrated: the interviews had a true documentary purpose and neither the film nor

[40] See *Lingens v Austria*, above n. 5, *Thorgierson v Iceland*, A/239, (1992) 14 EHRR 843; *Goodwin v UK*, above n. 3; *Barthold v Germany*, A/90, (1985) 7 EHRR 383.
[41] *Barthold v Germany*, *ibid.* (political and commercial speech).
[42] Above n. 3 at 143.
[43] *Ibid.* at 145–146.
[44] *X v Morgan-Grampian Ltd*, above n. 37.
[45] Above n. 3 at 143–144.
[46] A/298, (1995) 19 EHRR 1.
[47] *Ibid.* at 28.

the programme within which it was broadcast had expressed any support or approval for the views portrayed.[48]

In *Goodwin* and *Jersild*, the Court was concerned with restrictions upon the dissemination of factual material. It has been equally concerned to safeguard the right to publish allegations which may be true,[49] and to express views and value judgments which are not susceptible to positive proof either way.[50] It has recognised that a degree of exaggeration and even of provocation are tools of the journalist's trade and so important facets of journalistic freedom.[51] Hence, in *Oberschlick (No. 2)*, it found a breach of Article 10 where a journalist had been fined for describing a leading right wing politician as an "idiot".[52]   **12.28**

Article 10 may also interact with Article 3 of the First Protocol to the Convention, which seeks to "ensure the free expression of the opinion of the people in the choice of the legislature". The Court has emphasised that freedom of political speech is particularly important in the period preceding an election. In *Bowman*, it found that a restriction in UK electoral law on the amount of money which could be spent on campaigning by persons other than the candidates themselves, was in breach of Art. 10.[53]   **12.29**

Commercial expression

Commercial expression is seen as less fundamental to the functioning of a democratic society than political speech and so less deserving of protection. Hence, the Court has been more reluctant to overturn the judgment of the national authorities in this area. The case-law on commercial speech has, generally, concerned restrictions upon advertising, or upon the publication of true statements which have the effect of damaging or undermining the commercial interests of others. Restrictions upon the publication of true statements are unlikely to be justifiable where political speech is concerned, but the Court has adopted a much less interventionist approach to restrictions upon commercial speech, citing the need to respect the privacy of others and to respect the confidentiality of certain commercial information. This is surprising, not least because it is not clear whether Article 10(2) contains a suitable exception: protecting the rights   **12.30**

---

[48] *Ibid.* at 28.
[49] See, for example, *Castells v Spain*, A/236, (1992) 14 EHRR 445; *Barthold v Germany*, above n. 40.
[50] See *Lingens v Austria*, above n. 5; *Thorgierson v Iceland*, above n. 40.
[51] See, recently, *De Haes and Gijsels v Belgium*, A/733, (1998) 25 EHRR 1.
[52] *Oberschlick v Austria (No. 2)*, A/783, [1997] EHRLR 676.
[53] *Bowman v UK*, A/874, (1998) 26 EHRR 1.

and reputation of others is not quite the same as protecting their commercial interests against well-founded criticism.

12.31   In two cases concerning the German law of unfair competition, *Markt Intern* and *Jacubowski*, the Court has emphasised that the margin of appreciation of states is essential in commercial matters.[54] In both cases, this non-interventionist starting point translated into a refusal to criticise restrictions upon publication which had been imposed by the German courts. In *Markt Intern*, Court upheld an injunction on the publication of criticism of a mail order company which had failed to deal promptly with a complaint about its products.[55] In *Jacubowski*, the applicant was prevented from distributing a circular which criticised his former employer and sought to persuade its customers to switch to the applicant's own new enterprise.[56] The Court's reasoning in these cases is notably unsupportive of the fundamental importance of freedom of expression which has featured so prominently in political speech cases. There is no mention of pressing social need, or of the need to convincingly justify a restriction upon freedom of expression and the Court merely balances freedom of expression against a competing interest, apparently equally important, of protecting commercial reputation.[57] Restrictions on commercial speech may raise issues of European Community law, in particular under Article 59 of the EC Treaty, which guarantees free movement of services between Member States, and given the approach of the Strasbourg Court to commercial speech, this may be a more fruitful avenue of challenge to restrictions.[58]

Artistic expression

12.32   The Court appears even more reluctant to intervene against restrictions upon artistic expression, allowing to state authorities an even wider margin of appreciation. In *Wingrove*, the applicant had written and directed a video which featured erotic scenes involving a nun and the body of Christ.[59] The video was refused a certificate, so preventing its distribution, on the grounds that it infringed the criminal law of

---

[54] *Market Intern Verlag* v *Germany*, A/165, (1990) 12 EHRR 161, 174; *Jacubowski* v *Germany*, A/219-A, (1995) 19 EHRR 64, 77.
[55] *Ibid.*
[56] Above n. 54.
[57] See also *Casado Coca* v *Spain*, A/285, (1994) 18 EHRR 1. Contrast *Hertel* v *Switzerland*, A/962, decision of 25 August 1998.
[58] *GB-INNO-BM* v *Confédération du Commerce Luxembourgeoise*, Case 362/88 [1990] ECR I-667; *SPUC* v *Grogan*, Case C-159/90 [1991] ECR I-4685.
[59] Above n. 19.

blasphemy. The applicant argued that he had suffered an unjustifiable interference with his freedom of expression, principally because the law of blasphemy was out-dated, discriminatory (in that it protects only the Christian religion) and unnecessary in a democratic society. The Court drew a firm distinction between restrictions on political speech, for which there was little scope under Article 10(2), and regulation of freedom of expression in relation to matters liable to offend moral or religious convictions, where a wider margin of appreciation would generally be available. There was no uniform conception of the requirements of the protection of morals, or of the rights of others to be free from attacks upon their religious convictions. What would be likely to cause substantial offence varied significantly from time to time and place to place, and the national authorities were much better placed to make this judgment.[60]

In judging cases of artistic expression, the Court will examine the same **12.33** sort of considerations as an English court would in applying the law of obscenity: the intended audience for the artistic work, the extent to which the audience is warned about what it is to witness, the steps taken to prevent dissemination of the expression to an unsuitable, or unprepared, audience and so on. However, these factors, ultimately, seem to count for very little where national authorities act in the name of protecting religious or moral feelings. In *Otto-Preminger-Institut v Austria*, for example, the Court upheld the seizure and forfeiture of a film said to be likely to offend religious sensibilities even though it was to be shown only in private, to members of a film club, who had been fully appraised of its theme. It is also notable that the Court did not criticise the banning of the film throughout Austria, even though the authorities relied only upon its potential to affect religious feeling in the mainly Catholic region where it was first to be shown.[61]

THE CONTENT OF THE EXPRESSION

It has been noted above that the concept of "expression" in Article 10 is **12.34** extremely broad, and does not depend upon the content of the expression in question, no matter how offensive it is. The Court has also refrained from relying upon Article 17 of the Convention (which ensures that the Convention is not relied upon for the purpose of subverting the

---

[60] *Ibid.* at 30–31.
[61] Above n. 25; see also *Müller v Switzerland*, A/133, (1991) 13 EHRR 212 where the applicant was less discerning about the potential audience for his works.

rights which it seeks to guarantee) in order to exclude altogether reliance upon Article 10.[61a] However, the content of the information, ideas or opinions which are conveyed will be relevant to the analysis under Article 10(2). Little or no protection will be accorded to racist discourse: hence, in *Jersild*, the Court noted that the youths whose racist opinions had been promulgated could not benefit from the protection of Article 10, even if the documentary reporting of their views was protected.[62] *Wingrove* and *Otto-Preminger-Institut* demonstrate that material which is likely to offend the moral or religious convictions of others will carry equally little weight with the Court.[63] Another important issue to be considered under this heading is whether the expression or communication upon which a restriction has been imposed is a statement of fact, and if so whether it is true or false, or an expression of opinion. Clearly, a stronger justification must be shown to warrant a restriction upon the expression of true fact and, as noted above, the Court is reluctant to permit restrictions upon the mere statement of opinion.

THE MEDIUM OF EXPRESSION

12.35 The importance of the means by which information and ideas are conveyed is illustrated by the special provision made in Article 10(1) for the licensing of broadcasting, television and cinema; it is also relevant to the Article 10(2) analysis. The more extensive the potential dissemination of material (for example, by television or radio), the easier it will be for a state to justify a restriction imposed on grounds of offence to others, since it is more likely to reach an audience which is not prepared for it. In *Wingrove*, the Court considered the medium of the intended expression (on video cassette) and noted how difficult it was to control the distribution of, and so the audience for, video films once they are put into circulation.[64] Understandably, Article 10 will be more forgiving of restrictions imposed on the distribution of offensive material where it is contained in a children's book, as in the *Handyside* case,[65] than where it is broadcast as part of a serious news program intended for a well-informed audience.[66]

[61a] See *Lehideux* v *France*, above n. 2a.
[62] Above n. 46 at 28; see also *Glimmerveen and Hagenbeek* v *The Netherlands*, Appl. No. 8384/78, (1979) 18 D&R 187.
[63] Above n. 19 and 25.
[64] Above n. 19 at 32.
[65] *Handyside* v *UK*, above n. 1.
[66] *Jersild* v *Denmark*, above n. 46 at 27.

THE STATUS OF THE APPLICANT

The margin of appreciation also varies according to the status of the **12.36** individual applicant. As noted above, journalists are guaranteed special protection because of the vital role which they play in providing accurate and reliable information and promoting political debate. The "duties and responsibilities" of other categories of applicant, for example, civil servants, may also found an argument by the respondent state that the margin of appreciation ought to be a wide one.[67]

THE AIM OF THE RESTRICTION

Certain of the legitimate aims enumerated in Article 10(2) will attract a **12.37** wider margin of appreciation for the state authorities than others.

Protection of public morals

The Court recognises that there is no uniform conception of morality, so **12.38** the content of "public morals" will vary from state to state. Accordingly, the national authorities are permitted to determine which moral principles they wish to protect, and are granted much latitude in deciding how best to protect them.[68] The Court will, of course, scrutinise the legal basis for restrictions adopted to protect public morals but only in exceptional cases has it found such measures to be unnecessary and so outwith Article 10(2). The leading example is the *Open Door Counselling* case, where the Irish courts had imposed an ban on the dissemination by the applicant counselling centres of information regarding the availability of abortion services in English clinics.[69] It was open to the Irish authorities to characterise abortion as one of the moral evils of Irish society, but the Court found that the ban was disproportionate since it was unlimited in time and made no allowance for the age or state of health of the applicants' clients, or their reasons for seeking pregnancy counselling. The ban was also ineffective since the information was available elsewhere in Ireland and it had not prevented large numbers of Irish women from seeking abortions in England.[70]

---

[67] See, for example, *Vogt*, above n. 17 at 235.
[68] For example, *Handyside v UK*, above n. 1.
[69] *Open Door Counselling and Dublin Well Woman v Ireland*, A/246, (1993) 15 EHRR 244.
[70] *Ibid.* at 266–267.

National security

12.39 As in the British courts, a claim by the authorities that national security is at stake will attract an extra degree of deference. In *Brind*, for example, the Commission noted the importance of, and difficulties posed by, the fight against terrorism before rejecting the applications of journalists affected by a ban on broadcasting the voices of representatives of *Sinn Fein* and other specified organisations with links to terrorism.[71] However, whilst the Court may readily accept the premise that national security is at stake, it has become more willing to question the evidential basis for that assertion when it comes to judging whether or not a restriction is necessary.[72]

12.40   In *The Observer and The Guardian* v *UK*, for example, the Court was called upon to assess the necessity of injunctions, both interlocutory and final, which had been obtained by the Attorney-General against the publication of material from *Spycatcher*, a book written by a former secret service agent, Peter Wright.[73] The Court agreed that the injunctions had been motivated in part by concern for national security. However, whilst the interlocutory injunctions were, initially, necessary in order to protect the confidentiality of potentially damaging information, there reached a point where this information had entered the public domain, through the publication of *Spycatcher* in the USA and of extracts from it in newspapers in Britain, the USA and Australia. The continuation of the injunctions beyond that point was not, in the Court's opinion, justified by the need to promote the efficiency and reputation of the secret services, which was the national security justification relied upon by the Government after the information became public.[74]

Protecting the reputation or rights of others

12.41 The protection of the rights of others may also prove a fruitful line of defence, particularly where the rights in question are rights which clearly attract the protection of other articles of the Convention. In *Otto-Pre-minger-Institut*, for example, the Austrian Government successfully relied upon the rights of others to religious freedom under Article 9 to justify a ban upon the showing of a film which could have caused offence to those

---

[71] *Brind* v *UK*, Appl. No. 18714/91, (1994) 77-A D&R 42. See also *Adams* v *UK*, Appl. No. 28979/95, (1997) 23 EHRR CD160 (exclusion order against *Sinn Fein* leader).
[72] See generally Nicol, "National Security Considerations and the Limits of European Supervision" [1996] EHRLR 37.
[73] A/216, (1992) 14 EHRR 153.
[74] *Ibid.* at 190, 195–196.

holding strong religious convictions.[75] Another example of an area where two Convention rights conflict is that of privacy and press freedom: restrictions upon freedom of expression of newspapers and other media organisations may be justified in the interests of protecting the privacy of others.[76] The authorities have a wide margin of appreciation in deciding where exactly to strike the balance between Article 10 rights and the rights of others under Article 8. Hence, in *Neves v Portugal*, the Commission rejected a complaint from a magazine publisher about a draconian penalty — imprisonment, a severe fine and a compensation order — imposed under Portuguese privacy laws following the publication of explicit photographs of a businessman.[77]

The protection of the reputation of others is a legitimate aim which **12.42** appears only in Article 10(2) and not also in Articles 8, 9 and 11. Clearly, the idea is to make special provision for libel laws, whether civil or criminal, which could provide the basis for a prior restraint or subsequent sanction upon freedom of expression. Expansive libel laws provide a very real motivation for self-censorship on the part of media organisations, a "chilling effect" upon freedom of expression, to use the terminology of the Court. As such, the Court has been relatively active in criticising restrictions upon freedom of expression imposed by libel laws, and the margin of appreciation in this area has often appeared slight. This is particularly the case where libel actions have been brought by, or in respect of politicians or public bodies. The Court has stressed that the limits of acceptable criticism are wider as regards politicians than for private individuals since the protection of the reputation of others had, in the case of politicians, to be weighed against the interests of open discussion of political issues. In *Lingens*, for example, the Court found a breach of Article 10 when a journalist fell foul of the Austrian libel laws as a result of two articles which criticised the Austrian Chancellor and accused him of favouritism towards individuals with Nazi connections.[78] In *Derbyshire County Council v Times Newspapers*, the Court of Appeal relied upon Article 10, and upon *Lingens*, in finding that English libel law did not permit a local authority to sue for the purposes of vindicating its governing reputation.[79] However, concerns have been expressed about s. 13 of the Defamation Act 1996, which seeks positively to assist

---

[75] Above n. 25. See also *Wingrove v UK*, above n. 19.
[76] See the views of the Commission in *Spencer v UK*, Appl. No. 28851/95, [1998] EHRLR 348.
[77] See *N v Portugal*, Appl. No. 20683/92, decision of 20 February 1995.
[78] Above n. 5 at 418–419. Similar reasoning was used in *Castells v Spain*, above n. 49, *Oberschlick v Austria*, A/204, (1995) 19 EHRR 389 and *Oberschlick v Austria (No. 2)*, above n. 52.
[79] [1992] QB 770. Its decision was upheld by the House of Lords, although without reliance upon the Convention: [1993] AC 534.

politicians to bring libel claims by permitting them to waive the protection of parliamentary privilege.[80]

Protecting the judiciary

12.43 The aim of protection of the authority and impartiality of the judiciary may warrant a more or less broad margin of appreciation depending upon the particular way in which the applicant is said to have threatened the judicial system. The Court has allowed a wide margin of appreciation, and has proved markedly reluctant to intervene, where the applicant has suffered as a result of a direct attack upon the moral integrity of the judicial system or of particular judges. In *Barfod*, the applicant had accused certain judges of political bias;[81] similarly, in *Prager and Oberschlick*, allegations of illegality and breach of professional standards were levelled against individual judges.[82] The Court rejected both applications. However, in *De Haes and Gijsels* v *Belgium*, the Court upheld an Article 10 complaint in respect of accusations that judges of the Antwerp Court of Appeal had been guilty of bias in favour of a father in custody proceedings on account of their friendship with him, and with each other, and shared, extreme right-wing political views.[83] In contrast to *Prager and Oberschlick*, where the Court criticised the applicants for, in effect, not doing their research properly, in *De Haes and Gijsels* it clearly considered there to have been some foundation for the applicants' views. The Court has also steered clear of intervening in matters arising out of standards of professional conduct of lawyers.[84]

12.44 By contrast, a rather less generous margin of appreciation has been permitted where it is argued that restrictions upon freedom of expression are necessary in order to guarantee a fair trial, or otherwise preserve the integrity of particular legal proceedings. The Court views this goal as one which is objectively determinable, and is willing to second-guess the judgment reached by national courts. A prominent example is the *Sunday Times* case, in which the Court criticised the granting of an injunction to restrain publication of material about the drug thalidomide at a time when a legal claim by parents who had suffered as a result of taking the drug was pending before the English courts. The Court did not accept the

[80] Loveland, "Reforming Libel Law: the Public Law Dimension" (1997) 46 ICLQ 561.
[81] *Barfod* v *Denmark*, A/149, (1991) 13 EHRR 493.
[82] *Prager and Oberschlick* v *Austria*, A/313, (1996) 21 EHRR 1.
[83] Above n. 51.
[84] *Casado Coca* v *Spain*, above n. 57; *Zihlmann* v *Switzerland*, Appl. No. 21861/93, (1995) 82-B D&R 12.

Government's argument that publication of the article in question would have had adverse consequences for the authority of the judiciary.[85] Conversely, in *Worm* v *Austria*, the Court upheld the conviction of a journalist in respect of an article which commented extensively on the evidence given in the trial of a politician after the trial had ended and before a ruling was given.[86] The Commission has also rejected a number of challenges under this heading, particularly where media coverage has been restricted in the interests of ensuring a fair trial.[87]

THE NATURE OF THE RESTRICTION

The nature and extent of the restriction imposed by the authorities is **12.45** relevant to the question of whether or not it is necessary. A basic issue is whether the restriction is a prior restriction on publication or dissemination, or is a penalty imposed afterwards: prior restraints call for "special scrutiny", and "very stringent reasons".[88] Partial or minor restrictions will amount to an interference with freedom of expression but are more easily justified. This was the case in *Brind*, where journalists were permitted to broadcast the words used by representatives of, amongst others, *Sinn Fein*, provided that they were spoken by an actor.[89]

The Commission and the Court will then go on to examine the effect of **12.46** a restriction in the context of deciding whether it is disproportionate, in going further than is necessary to achieve its objectives. An important aspect of the proportionality analysis is whether the legitimate interests at issue could have been protected, or were, in fact, protected, by other, less restrictive measures. In *Goodwin*, for example, the company whose business plan the applicant planned to disclose in a magazine article had obtained an interim injunction to prevent its publication and so had averted the major risk to its commercial interests. Its interest in knowing which of its employees had disclosed the plan was, by comparison, relatively minor.[90] Also, in the *Spycatcher* cases, the Court noted that the Government could have pursued, and was, in fact, in the course of

---

[85] *Sunday Times* v *UK*, above n. 31 at 278–279.
[86] A/801, decision of 29 August 1997.
[87] *Hodgson* v *UK*, Appl. No. 11553/85, (1987) 51 D&R 136; *Channel Four* v *UK*, Appl. No. 14132/88, (1989) 61 D&R 285; *Atkinson vv UK*, Appl. No. 13366/87, (1991) 67 D&R 244.
[88] See *Wingrove* v *UK*, above n. 19; *Otto-Preminger Institut* v *Austria*, above n. 25. The provisions of s. 12 HRA are in line with this principle.
[89] Above n. 71.
[90] Above n. 3 at 144–145.

pursuing, personal remedies against the author of the book. Those alternative remedies could have met some at least of its concerns without placing restrictions upon the freedom of expression of the applicant newspapers.[91] In *Wingrove*, on the other hand, the Court rejected the Applicant's suggestion that his video need not be banned but could be distributed in a box with a warning label. Such a measure would, said the Court, have only limited efficiency and it was not prepared to overturn the judgment of the film censors on that issue.[92]

CONSISTENCY OF LEGAL PRACTICE IN THE STATE CONCERNED

12.47 An important question to be asked of the defence that a restriction is necessary in a democratic society is whether legal practice on the issue in question has been consistent and uniform. If it is not, because, for example, others have done the same as the applicant but have been treated more leniently, it becomes much more difficult for the state to argue that the more severe treatment accorded to the applicant was necessary. In *Vogt*, for example, the applicant teacher had been disciplined for her activities on behalf of the Communist party and it was significant that teachers in other regions of Germany, engaged in similar activities, had not been penalised.[93] Another good example is the *Spycatcher* cases, in which the Government's argument as to the necessity of the injunction against the publication in the UK of Peter Wright's book was undermined by its failure to take any steps to prevent the importation of the book from the US and Australia, or to confiscate copies which had arrived in this country.[94] Similarly, in *Open Door Counselling* v *Ireland*, the Court noted that the information which the applicants had been restrained from disseminating was freely available from other sources.[95]

PRACTICE IN OTHER STATES

12.48 The Court will also take note of practice in other States in making its assessment under Article 10(2). If the respondent state stands alone, or

---

[91] Above n. 30 at 195–196.
[92] Above n. 19 at 32.
[93] Above n. 17 at 238.
[94] *Observer and Guardian* v *UK*, above n. 30 at 194–195.
[95] Above n. 69 at 267.

virtually alone, in its treatment of a particular matter, this will serve to indicate that its measures are not "necessary in a democratic society". In one case, the Court ruled against the Austrian statutory broadcasting monopoly, relying, in part, on the fact that other European states had long since abandoned their similar monopoly systems without the dire consequences predicted by the Austrian Government.[96] Similarly, in *Vogt*, the Court noted that no other state required a duty of loyalty from its civil servants as strict as that required in Germany.[97] Conversely, a state may point to analogous practice in other states in order to support its view that a restriction was necessary in its case. In *Wingrove*, for example, the UK Government defended the existence of the common law offence of blasphemy, in part, by pointing out that a range of other European states retained similar laws.[98] Attention to practice in other states does not mean, however, that the Court will take no account of national diversity. In *Handyside*, the fact that the book in question had been published in a number of other European states did not mean that it could not be banned in the UK.[99]

9. FURTHER READING

Addo, "Are Judges Beyond Criticism under Article 10 of the ECHR?" (1998) 47 KLQ 253

Kentridge, "Freedom of Speech: is it the Primary Right?" (1996) 45 ICLQ 253

Klug, Starmer and Weir, *The Three Pillars of Liberty* (Routledge, 1996), chapter 9

Loveland, "Reforming Libel Law: the Public Law Dimension" (1997) 46 ICLQ 561

Mahoney, "Universality versus Subsidiarity in the Strasbourg Case Law on Free Speech: Explaining Some Recent Judgments" (1997) EHRLR 364

Naismith, "Self-incrimination — Fairness or Freedom" [1997] EHRLR 229

Nicol, "National Security Considerations and the Limits of European Supervision" [1996] EHRLR 37

Tierney, "Press Freedom and Public Interest" [1998] EHRLR 419

---

[96] *Informationsverein Lentia* v *Austria*, above n. 11 at 114.
[97] Above n. 17 at 238.
[98] Above n. 19 at 30.
[99] Above n. 1 at 759.

Chapter 13

FREEDOM OF ASSEMBLY AND ASSOCIATION

Article 11 of the Convention provides: **13.1**

"1. Everyone has the right to freedom of peaceful assembly and to freedom of association with others, including the right to form and join trade unions for the protection of his interests.

2. No restrictions shall be placed on the exercise of these rights other than such as are prescribed by law and are necessary in a democratic society in the interests of national security or public safety, for the protection of health or morals or for the protection of the rights and freedoms of others. This Article shall not prevent the imposition of lawful restrictions on the exercise of these rights by members of the armed forces, of the police or of the administration of the state."

Article 11 protects the related rights of freedom of peaceful assembly and freedom of association. The distinction between the two is perhaps easier to recognise than to define: in essence, freedom of association concerns the formal, organisational structures of political and social activity — trade unions, political parties, pressure groups and the like. Freedom of assembly, on the other hand, covers the actual physical act of meeting together for political and social purposes. Neither freedom of assembly nor freedom of association encompass the right to share, informally, the company of others,[1] although the right to private life and/or freedom of expression may be relevant here.

There is comparatively little case-law under Article 11, due in part to the **13.2** significant overlap between Article 11 rights, and other Convention rights, notably Articles 8–10 on private life, freedom of religion and freedom of expression. Like those provisions, Article 11 aims to protect freedom of personal opinion and decisions under Article 11 will be heavily influenced by the principles established under Articles 8–10.[2] Freedom of

---

[1] *McFeeley* v *UK*, Appl. No. 8317/78, (1980) 20 D&R 44, 98.
[2] See *Young, James and Webster* v *UK*, A/44, (1982) 4 EHRR 38, 55.

association under Article 11, in particular in its application to trade union rights, also overlaps with protection afforded under other international instruments, such as the Council of Europe's European Social Charter and the Conventions promulgated by the International Labour Organisation. The extent of protection under those agreements may be a relevant factor in the Court's consideration of how freedom of association under the Convention ought to be defined.

1. FREEDOM OF ASSEMBLY

THE SCOPE OF FREEDOM OF ASSEMBLY

13.3 Freedom of peaceful assembly, both in private and in public, is a right which goes to the heart of political activity in a democratic society and, as such, is treated as "a fundamental right" deserving of special protection.[3] "Assembly" is a broad concept, encompassing private meetings, public meetings and demonstrations, whether on the highway or otherwise, marches and sit-ins. However, there are two notable qualifications on the ambit of freedom of assembly. Firstly, the assembly must be peaceful if it is to acquire the protection of Article 11, but even this restriction has been narrowly interpreted. An assembly will fail to qualify as a peaceful assembly only if it is organised with the specific intention to commit or provoke violence or disruption to public order, or if the applicant and/or his co-demonstrators have themselves committed acts of violence during the course of it.[4] An assembly which merely results in violence by others is nevertheless a peaceful assembly. In *G v Germany*, for example, the applicant had taken part in a sit-in outside a US military barracks in Stuttgart which had resulted in considerable disruption whilst demonstrators were carried away by the police. The Commission ruled that the demonstration fell within Article 11(1) as a peaceful assembly, even though it had resulted in disruption to public order, because the applicant and the other demonstrators had not been actively violent during the sit-in.[5] Secondly, there is no right merely to pass in public places or to assemble for purely social purposes.[6]

---

[3] *Rassemblement Jurassien Unité v Switzerland*, Appl. No. 8191/78, (1979) 17 D&R 93, 119.
[4] *Christians against Racism and Facism v UK*, Appl. No. 8440/78, (1981) 21 D&R 138, 148.
[5] *G v Germany*, Appl. No. 13079/87, (1989) 60 D&R 256.
[6] *Anderson v UK*, Appl. No. 33689/96, (1998) 25 EHRR CD172.

Not all forms of state control of public assemblies will infringe Article **13.4**
11(1). Clearly, a ban on demonstrating, even if only temporary, will
constitute a restriction which requires justification under Article 11(2), as
will an *ex post facto* penalty imposed upon a participant in a demonstration.[7] However, a requirement merely to notify the police and/or to seek
authorisation for an assembly will not infringe Article 11(1) provided that
the purpose of the requirement is to enable the police to prevent non-
peaceful assemblies, or to take steps to protect an assembly from
disruption.[8]

The importance of freedom of assembly and the extent to which it is **13.5**
vulnerable to attack, not just from the state, but from opposing political
groups, has resulted in the Court finding positive obligations within
Article 11. The state has a negative duty not itself to interfere with
freedom of assembly (save where permitted by Article 11(2)) but it
must also take positive steps to ensure that people can exercise their
right to meet or to march without intimidation or disruption from their
opponents. In *Plattform Ärtze für das Leben* v *Austria*, an anti-abortion
association complained of a lack of police protection during its protest
marches, which had been disrupted by counter-demonstrators protesting
in favour of abortion.[9] The Commission rejected the association's complaint under Article 11 but declared admissible a claim under Article 13,
that the Austrian legal system provided no effective remedy for breach of
its right to freedom of assembly. The Court, echoing its long-established
case-law on freedom of expression, held that even though a demonstration may annoy or cause offence to persons opposed to the ideas it is
seeking to promote, participants must be able to hold the demonstration
without fear of physical violence by their opponents. Such fear would act
as a deterrent upon the expression of opinions about highly controversial
issues affecting the community. This principle would, naturally, affect the
freedoms of counter-demonstrators but, in a democracy, the right to
counter-demonstrate could not extend to a right to inhibit the right to
demonstrate of others. The obligations of the state in this regard could not
be reduced merely to the duty not to interfere: the state had to take
reasonable and appropriate measures to enable lawful demonstrations to
proceed peacefully.[10]

Having made this important statement of principle, the Court then **13.6**
showed itself to be reluctant to interfere with operational policing

---

[7] See *Christians Against Racism and Facism* v *UK*, above n. 4 (ban); *Ezelin* v *France*, A/202, (1992)
14 EHRR 362 (criminal penalty).
[8] *Rassemblement Jurassien Unité* v *Switzerland*, above n. 3.
[9] A/139, (1991) 13 EHRR 204.
[10] *Ibid.* at 210.

decisions. It held that the authorities have a wide discretion in the choice of means used to protect freedom of assembly, and could not guarantee that freedom absolutely. In the instant case, a number of factors militated against a breach of positive obligations under Article 11. In particular, police had been deployed and had sought to protect participants in the marches organised by the applicant, no physical damage was done by the counter-demonstrators, and the marches had been able to proceed to their conclusion.[11]

JUSTIFICATIONS FOR RESTRICTIONS UPON FREEDOM OF ASSEMBLY

13.7 As under Articles 8–10, an authority seeking to justify a restriction upon freedom of assembly must surmount a number of hurdles. It must establish:

- that the restriction pursues a legitimate aim;
- that it is "prescribed by law" in the sense that it is lawful under domestic law, accessible, and foreseeable in its application;[12]
- that it is "necessary in a democratic society" in the sense that it fulfils a pressing social need, and is proportionate in its restrictive effects.

13.8 State justifications for restrictions upon freedom of assembly, generally, focus upon public safety or the prevention of disorder or crime. Such justifications must be treated with caution since, at least where public assemblies are concerned, a degree of disruption to everyday life, is inevitable, and often intended. On a broad view, every demonstration must be restricted in order to prevent disorder, or, on a broader view, to protect the rights and freedoms of others. A distinction may be drawn between prior restrictions, and *ex post facto* penalties imposed upon demonstrators. Where the authorities have banned a demonstration because of a perceived threat to public order, it will be difficult to rebut the argument of justification under Article 11(2). In *Rassemblement Jurassien Unité v Switzerland*, the Commission held that the authorities have a "fairly broad" margin of appreciation once confronted with a foreseeable danger affecting public safety and order so that they must

---

[11] *Ibid.* at 211. See also *Chorherr v Austria*, A/266-B, (1994) 17 EHRR 358.
[12] See chapter 6, paras. 6.32–6.39.

decide, often at short notice, what means to employ to prevent it.[13] In that case, a ban on political meetings was held to be justified in the light of a perceived danger to public order. In considering the proportionality of the ban, the Commission relied upon the fact that it was directed to a defined area and was limited in duration.[14]

Conversely, where an *ex post facto* penalty has been imposed, the **13.9** Court has shown itself willing to take a stand in favour of the right to protest. In *Ezelin*, a lawyer was reprimanded under the professional rules of conduct of the French Bar Council after taking part in a demonstration which had resulted in criminal damage.[15] There was no allegation that he had committed any criminal act himself, merely that he had failed to dissociate himself from the violent acts of others. The Court held that the freedom to take part in a peaceful assembly is of such importance that it cannot be restricted in any way, even for an *avocat*, so long as the person concerned does not himself commit any reprehensible act on such an occasion.[16]

FREEDOM TO ASSEMBLE, AND PROTEST, UNDER ENGLISH LAW

Freedom of assembly, in the sense of a right to assemble and protest in a **13.10** public place, is tightly circumscribed under English law. Indeed, recent authority suggests that it may be misleading to talk of any such freedom. A demonstration on private land may, of course, be a trespass; a demonstration on the highway may be penalised as an obstruction of the highway,[17] and/or as a public nuisance.[18] In *DPP* v *Jones*, however, protestors at Stonehenge were penalised for participating in a peaceful demonstration on the highway which was neither an obstruction of the highway nor a public nuisance.[19] The case arose under s. 14A of the Public Order Act 1986 which empowers the police to prohibit the holding of trespassory assemblies of more than 20 persons. The Divisional Court acknowledged that the public has a limited right to use the highway for

---

[13] Above n. 3 at 120.
[14] *Ibid.* at 121.
[15] *Ezelin* v *France*, above n. 7.
[16] *Ibid.* at 389.
[17] See s. 137 of the Highways Act 1980; *Hirst* v *Chief Constable of West Yorkshire* (1986) 85 Cr App Rep 143.
[18] *R.* v *Clark* [1964] 2 QB 315.
[19] [1997] 2 All ER 119.

the purposes of passing and re-passing but not for any other purpose, including that of holding an assembly or demonstrating. McCowan LJ held that the assembly in question was unlawful and therefore contrary to the order made by the police on the (circular) grounds that the order itself made unlawful an assembly which was otherwise within the law.[20] Collins J added that the English law position was consistent with the Convention because, following the *Rassemblement Jurassien* case, the subjection of meetings in public thoroughfares to an authorisation procedure does not normally encroach upon the essence of right to freedom of peaceful assembly.[21]

13.11   Freedom of peaceful assembly may also be curtailed by the common law of breach of the peace. The police have the power to restrain people from attending a march or demonstration where they fear a breach of the peace, a common law construct to which the courts have attributed various, differing definitions over the years. The most widely used guideline is that "there is a breach of the peace wherever harm is actually done or is likely to be done to a person or, in his presence, to his property or a person is in fear of being so harmed through an assault, an affray, a riot, an unlawful assembly or other disturbance".[22] In *ex parte Ward*, this principle was held to extend to cover protest by animal rights activists which was in itself peaceful, but which was likely to provoke the use of violence against them by others.[23] Further, magistrates have the power to bind people over to keep the peace or to be of good behaviour. An individual will be in breach of a good behaviour order if he conducts himself in a manner which is "*contro bonos mores*", that is "wrong rather than right in the judgment of the vast majority of contemporary citizens".[24] The Law Commission has expressed doubts as to whether the power to bind over for breach of the peace is sufficiently certain in scope as not to fall foul of the "prescribed by law" requirement of Article 11(2). It was certain that the power to bind over to be of good behaviour would not satisfy the certainty requirement.[25] However, in *Steel*, the Court ruled that the concept of breach of the peace, and the power to bind over were sufficiently certain to be "prescribed by law" within the meaning of

---

[20] *Ibid.* at 124.

[21] *Ibid.* at 127.

[22] *R.* v *Howell* [1982] 1 QB 416, 427.

[23] *R.* v *Morpeth Ward Justices ex parte Ward* (1992) 95 Cr. App. Rep. 215; see also *Nicol and Selvanayagam* v *Director of Public Prosecutions* (1996) JP 155.

[24] *Hughes* v *Holley* (1988) 86 Cr. App. Rep. 130, 139.

[25] Law Commission Report No. 222 on Binding Over (Cm. 2439), paras. 5.4–5.7.

Articles 5 and 10(2) (and so also within Article 11(2)) at least in the circumstances of those cases.[26] Other cases are pending.[27]

The right to protest is further challenged by the Protection of Harassment Act 1997. Billed as legislation to combat the problem of "stalking", the Act in fact contains a definition of harassment which is broad enough to cover many forms of public protest. It introduces civil and criminal penalties for pursuing a course of conduct (meaning conduct on more than one occasion), which amounts to harassment. Harassment is not defined but is stated to include alarming a person or causing them distress; the detail with which it is defined by the courts will determine whether the "prescribed by law" standard of Article 11(2) is met. The first reported examples of use of the Act involved the granting of injunctions against animal rights activists. However, in one such case, an injunction was subsequently lifted by Eady J, who held that Parliament had clearly not intended the Act to be used to prevent individuals from exercising their right to protest, and that the courts would resist any attempts to give the statute a broad interpretation.[28] **13.12**

The right to assemble, and to protest, under English law, is one of the prime examples of the residual nature of common law rights. Under the classic common law approach, there is a right to do only that which is not prohibited and, as *DPP* v *Jones* illustrates, there may be precious little room for the freedom of peaceful assembly once all restrictions upon it are taken into account. The enactment of the Human Rights Act will highlight the difference between that approach, and the scheme of Article 11, which sets out a basic right to freedom of peaceful assembly which may be limited only in exceptional circumstances. The domestic courts are certain to be asked whether English law currently gives sufficient weight to the fundamental right to assemble, and to protest. **13.13**

2. FREEDOM OF ASSOCIATION

Freedom of association is not a right to associate with others in the broadest sense,[29] but encompasses the right to establish and to join "associations". No generic definition of this term has been laid down. **13.14**

---

[26] *Steel and others* v *UK*, A/992, decision of 23 September 1998.
[27] *Hashman and Harrup* v *UK*, Appl. No. 25594/94, [1996] EHRLR 667; *Nicol and Selvanayagam* v *UK*, Appl. No. 32213/96.
[28] *Huntingdon Life Sciences* v *Curtin*, *The Times*, 11 December 1997.
[29] See *McFeely* v *UK*, Appl. No. 8317/78, (1980) 20 D&R 44, 98.

Political parties,[30] trade unions, pressure groups and religious bodies .are certainly covered. Professional regulatory bodies, which frequently require membership as a condition of access to the profession (a condition which might otherwise infringe Article 11), are not. Bodies regulating doctors, architects and lawyers, for example, have all been found to be outside Article 11.[31] By contrast, an association of taxi drivers, which did have certain regulatory powers but which had been set up under private law and acted essentially as a representative body for its members, was held to be subject to Article 11.[32] There is an important distinction between freedom of association and freedom for associations. Restrictions upon the rights and activities of associations should be considered under the provision of the Convention which deals with the particular rights and activities in question rather than as constituting a restriction upon the freedom to associate as such. It is only in exceptional cases that a restriction upon the activity of an association will be so fundamental as to amount to a limitation on the right to associate.[33]

13.15   The freedom of association has been found to have both "positive" and "negative" aspects. The positive aspect is the right to form, join, and be active through, associations. The right to form associations requires at least that legal recognition will be afforded to the body so formed. The right to join associations does not, however, imply any positive right to become a member of a particular body: associations are, in principle, free to determine their own membership. This was the view expressed by the Commission in *Cheall*, a case concerning the right to join a trade union which had proceeded through the English courts as *Cheall v APEX*.[34] The TUC had ordered the applicant's expulsion from APEX on the grounds that it had not consulted his previous trade union, in accordance with TUC rules, before admitting him. The applicant complained that the rules were unreasonable and an unjustified restriction upon his freedom of association. The Commission held that the right to associate within a union (or, presumably, any other association) is not a general right to join the union of one's choice irrespective of the union's rules. It noted that the

---

[30] Indeed, political parties qualify for a high level of protection under Article 11 because they are regarded as playing an essential role in ensuring pluralism and the proper functioning of democracy: *United Communist Party of Turkey v Turkey*, A/868, (1998) 26 EHRR 121; *Socialist Party v Turkey*, A/919, decision of 25 May 1998.

[31] *Le Compte, Van Leuven and De Meyere v Belgium*, A/43, (1982) 4 EHRR 1 (doctors); *Revert v France*, Appl. No. 14331/88, (1989) 62 D&R 309 (architects); *A and others v Spain*, Appl. No. 13750/88, (1990) 66 D&R 188 (lawyers).

[32] *Sigurjónsson v Iceland*, A/264, (1993) 16 EHRR 462.

[33] For example, *Sidiropoulos v Greece*, A/934, decision of 10 July 1998 (refusal to register an association).

[34] *Cheall v UK*, Appl. No. 10550/83, (1985) 42 D&R 178.

protection afforded by Article 11 is primarily against interference with freedom of association by the state rather than by private bodies such as unions. However, the state was responsible for protecting individuals against abuse of a dominant position by trade unions which might occur where exclusion or expulsion was not in accordance with union rules, where the rules were wholly unreasonable or arbitrary, or where the consequences of exclusion or expulsion resulted in exceptional hardship, such as job loss. None of those factors were present in Cheall's case, so state responsibility was not engaged.[35]

13.16 The negative right of association, on the other hand, is the right not to join and be active through, associations. It was recognised by the Court for the first time in *Young, James and Webster*, a case arising out of a "closed shop" at British Rail, an arrangement whereby all employees were required to belong to a particular trade union.[36] The Court ignored a passage in the *travaux préparatoires* which clearly indicated that a negative right to resist a closed shop had been specifically excluded from Article 11. However, it did not go so far as to rule in general terms against the closed shop system, noting that compulsion to join a trade union would not always breach Article 11. It found, nevertheless, that the applicants' Article 11 rights had been infringed by the element of compulsion which had resulted in their dismissal.[37] The Court has since confirmed the negative right of association in broader terms. In *Sigur-jónsson*, the Court recognised the applicant's right not to join an association of taxi drivers, on pain of losing his licence, but did not decide, and has not yet decided, whether the negative right should be considered to be of equal importance to the positive right.[38] In determining the scope of negative rights, the starting point must be whether or not an equivalent positive right has been recognised — if it has not, the Court is most unlikely to give effect to the negative right. Hence, in *Gustafsson*, the Court rejected a claim to a negative right not to enter into a collective agreement, relying upon its previous findings that Article 11 confers no positive right to bargain collectively.[39]

13.17 The terminology used here is somewhat confusing since the state may have both positive and negative obligations to secure to its citizens positive and negative freedom of association. Positive obligations, it will be recalled, require the state to actively intervene in relations

---

[35] *Ibid.* at 185–186. See also *Sibson v UK*, A/258-A, (1994) 17 EHRR 193.
[36] *Young, James and Webster v UK*, above n. 2.
[37] *Ibid.* at 53–54.
[38] *Sigurjónsson v Iceland*, above n. 32 at 479. See also *Montion v France*, Appl. No. 28443/95, [1998] EHRLR 503.
[39] *Gustafsson v Sweden*, A/618, (1996) 22 EHRR 409.

between individuals in order to secure Convention rights, and are particularly apposite in this field where many of the practical issues arise in the workplace, between (private) employer and employee. Staying with the trade union analogy, Article 11 may require the state not to interfere with collective trade union rights either through legislation or in its capacity as an employer (negative obligations) and to put in place legislation which ensures that non-state employers are equally respectful of them (positive obligations).

TRADE UNION ACTIVITIES

13.18   The right of individuals to form and join trade unions for the protection of their interests is specifically enshrined within Article 11, although it is treated as merely a species of the more general freedom of association. Before examining the substantive law of the Convention on this issue, it is appropriate to explain in more detail the status and role of the International Labour Organisation, which has developed a corpus of law on trade union activities far more detailed than that of Article 11. The ILO is an agency of the United Nations, based in Geneva, which was established for the purpose of laying down minimum employment standards throughout the world. Its standards are set out in a series of Conventions which, if ratified by a state, become legally binding upon it. Various ILO committees, notably the Committee of Experts on the Application of Conventions and Recommendations (CEACR) and the Conference Committee on the Application of Standards (CCAS) report on compliance by states with those Conventions which are binding upon them. There are, in addition, procedures for complaint against subscribing states by trade unions and employers' organisations, and by other states. Findings on complaints by the Committee on Freedom of Association (CFA) are most relevant. Two ILO Conventions are of particular importance, and have been recognised by the Court as a relevant source upon which it may rely in decision-making under Article 11: Convention No. 87 on the Freedom of Association and Protection of the Right to Organise and Convention No. 98 on The Right to Organise and Collective Bargaining.[40] The Court will not necessarily follow the line suggested by the ILO but recourse to the jurisprudence of the ILO, as contained in the Conventions and in the reports of the CEACR and CCAS is, nevertheless, essential in preparing

---

[40] See, for example, *Sigurjónsson v Iceland*, above n. 32 at 479. Conventions 87 and 98 are Reprinted in Ewing, *Britain and the ILO* (Institute of Employment Rights, 2nd ed., 1994).

arguments as to the protection afforded to trade union rights by Article 11.

Also of relevance is the European Social Charter. This is an international **13.19** agreement which, like the Convention, was formulated and agreed under the aegis of the Council of Europe. It contains a range of economic and social rights including the right to organise (Article 5) and the right to bargain collectively (Article 6). Compliance with its terms is monitored principally by a Committee of Independent Experts which produces periodic reports.[41] The most notable impact of the ESC in English law was the extension of statutory periods of notice of termination of employment so as to comply with Article 4, the right to a fair remuneration.[42] The Court will refer to the Charter as evidence of the extent to which a particular practice has come to be accepted across Europe.

How far then does Article 11 go in securing rights to engage in, or to **13.20** refrain from, collective action through trade unions? The starting point is that individuals must be free to join a trade union, although, as noted above, they cannot insist upon joining a particular union. The right of an individual to join a trade union is stated in Article 11(1) to be for the purpose of protecting his interests, and a number of applications have sought to explore the extent to which trade unions must be permitted to pursue the interests of their members. In general, the Court has been reluctant to lay down firm rules as to what is required, on the basis that Article 11 does not secure any particular treatment of trade unions or their members but lays down only a baseline standard. All that is required is that states protect rights which are "indispensable to the effective enjoyment of trade union freedom".[43] In the *National Union of Belgian Police* case, the Court held that trade unions should be enabled to strive for the protection of their members' interests.[44] That entailed a right to be heard on behalf of their members to which states may give effect in various ways. The right to be heard does not require that a union be entitled to participate in a statutory consultation procedure, or to be recognised for the purpose of collective bargaining.[45]

Unlike the ILO, the Court has not recognised in terms the right to strike **13.21** as one of the essential components of freedom of association. It has indicated that recognition of the right to strike is one of the most important ways (although not, by implication, an indispensable way) in which a

---

[41] See, generally, Harris, *The European Social Charter* (University Press of Virginia, 1984); Samuel, *Fundamental Social Rights: Case-law of the European Social Charter* (Council of Europe, 1997).
[42] Now contained in s. 86 of the Employment Rights Act 1996.
[43] *Swedish Engine Drivers Union* v *Sweden*, A/20, (1979–80) 1 EHRR 617, 628.
[44] *National Union of Belgian Police* v *Belgium*, A/19, (1979–80) 1 EHRR 578, 591.
[45] *Ibid.*; *Swedish Engine Drivers Union* v *Sweden*, above n. 43.

state may implement its obligation to facilitate trade union action and that the exercise of the right to strike may lawfully be restricted in certain instances.[46] The issue has not been directly before the Court for more than two decades, although the recent case of *Gustafsson* may offer trade unions some encouragement. In that case, the Court declined to rule that industrial action designed to force an employer to enter into a collective agreement was a breach of the employer's negative freedom of association; a contrary ruling would have severely emasculated even a right to strike under domestic law.[47] If the right to strike were to be recognised within Article 11, the provisions of English law which treat industrial action as a repudiatory breach of contract by the employee justifying dismissal, and which in many cases prevent dismissed employees from challenging the fairness of their dismissal, may come under threat.[48] It should be noted that the limited degree of protection afforded to striking workers in English law has consistently been criticised by the ILO.[49] The positive right to associate may also have implications for state regulation of internal union affairs. Trade unions are, in principle, entitled under Article 11 to formulate their own rules,[50] and detailed legislative requirements such as were originally introduced by the Employment Act 1988 may ultimately impinge upon this freedom. The ILO has, for example, criticised statutory restrictions upon the power of trade unions to take disciplinary action against their members who refuse to participate in lawful strike action.[51]

13.22   Another important issue is that of discrimination against trade union members. In English law, a trade union member cannot be refused employment on that ground and cannot be victimised or dismissed on grounds of his trade union membership or activities on behalf of his union.[52] However, it remains open to employers to refuse to employ someone on the grounds of their previous trade union activities, and, in certain circumstances, to discriminate against trade union members short of dismissal. Employees have statutory protection from action short of dismissal which is taken for the purposes of preventing or deterring them

---

[46] *Schmidt and Dahlström v Sweden*, A/21, (1979–80) 1 EHRR 632. See, recently, *NATFKE v UK*, Appl. No. 28910/95, (1998) 25 EHRR CD122.

[47] *Gustafsson v Sweden*, above n. 39.

[48] Sections 237–238 of the Trade Union and Labour Relations Consolidation Act 1992.

[49] See ILO, 76th Session, Report of the Committee of Experts on the Application of Conventions and Recommendations, Report III (Part 4A) (1989); ILO, 81st Session, Report of the Committee of Experts on the Application of Conventions and Recommendations, Report III (Part 4A) (1994).

[50] *Cheall v UK*, above n. 34.

[51] Now ss. 64–65 of the Trade Union and Labour Relations Consolidation Act 1992 ("TULRCA"); cf. Art. 3 of ILO Convention No. 87.

[52] TULRCA ss. 137 and 152.

from belonging to a union or benefiting from union membership.[53] In *Associated Newspapers* v *Wilson*, the employers had offered pay rises as an incentive to employees to sign individual contracts rather than contracts negotiated through collective bargaining. The House of Lords held that an omission to offer a pay rise to a union member was not action short of dismissal, and so was not prohibited.[54] A complaint that this state of affairs restricts the lawful exercise of freedom of association has been declared admissible by the Commission after the Government declined to contest it (and the Government has since indicated that it intends to change the law). Should the Government choose to fight the claim, it would have reasonable prospects of success: if it remains the case that there is no right under Article 11 to be permitted to enter into collective bargaining (see above), it is difficult to see how there could be a right not to be discouraged from entering into collective bargaining.[55]

One way in which trade unions may not be permitted to act on behalf **13.23** of their members is in bringing claims before the Court, since the rules of *locus standi* have been interpreted restrictively in this respect. In *Ahmed* v *UK*, for example, the Commission accepted applications by four local government employees who had been prohibited from taking part in political activities including, it was argued, trade union activities.[56] Their trade union, UNISON was not, however, permitted to claim. It could not be considered to be a "victim" of a violation of the Convention because the political restrictions were not addressed to it and did not expressly refer to trade union activities.[57] Conversely, there will be no problem of standing where the rights violated are the collective rights of the union.

As to the negative right of association, the right to join a trade union **13.24** implies, in principle, a correlative negative right not to join.[58] The content of the right is, however, closely circumscribed. First and foremost, it is linked with Articles 9 and 10: only people who have a principled reason for not joining a union, a view or belief which would warrant protection under one or both of those provisions, can rely upon the negative right of association. In *Sibson*, an employee who had left one union to join another, and refused to rejoin the original union unless he received an apology from it, was ruled not to have a conviction worthy of protection.[59] *Young, James and Webster* was also distinguished on the grounds

---

[53] TULRCA s. 146 (formerly s. 23(1) of the Employment Protection (Consolidation) Act 1978).
[54] [1995] 2 AC 454.
[55] See Hendy and Walton, "An Individual Right to Union Representation in International Law" (1997) 26 ILJ 205.
[56] *Ahmed* v *UK*, Appl. No. 22954/93, (1995) 20 EHRR CD72.
[57] *Ibid*. at CD78.
[58] *Young, James and Webster*, above n. 2.
[59] *Sibson* v *UK*, above n. 35.

that those applicants had been dismissed for refusing to join the recognised trade union whereas Mr Sibson was offered a transfer to a nearby site and his livelihood was not threatened.[60] Also, the Court has studiously avoided any finding to the effect that the negative right is to be accorded as much weight as its positive counterpart. If a breach of the negative Article 11 right is found, compulsion upon an individual to join a trade union is likely to be difficult to justify under Article 11(2). In *Young, James and Webster*, the closed shop at British Rail was found to be disproportionate and so not "necessary" because there was no evidence that the unions needed it in order to protect the interests of their members.[61] Similar views were expressed in *Sigurjónsson*.[62]

3. THE EXCEPTION FOR STATE EMPLOYEES

13.25   Article 11(2) provides for special treatment of members of the armed forces, of the police and of the administration of the state, whose rights to assemble, and to associate, may be subject to "lawful restrictions". The leading case on this sentence was brought by representatives of civil servants at General Communications Headquarters (GCHQ) in Cheltenham, whose rights to join a trade union were removed from them on grounds of national security. Their case under English administrative law was rejected by the House of Lords, essentially due to a reluctance to interfere with matters of national security,[63] and thereafter proceeded to Strasbourg where it failed before the Commission.[64] The Commission held that the applicants were "members of the administration of the state" and that "a lawful restriction" in this context is merely one which is in accordance with national law and which is not arbitrary. Further, a "restriction" upon freedom of association included a withdrawal altogether of the right to associate.

13.26   Following the *GCHQ* case, it appeared that states would have a broad discretion to remove trade union rights and other Article 11 rights from the police, the armed forces and members of the administration of the state. However, the Court introduced what appeared to be a new line of

---

[60] See also *Englund v Sweden*, Appl. No. 15533/89, (1994) 77-A D&R 10.
[61] *Ibid.* at 55–58.
[62] Above n. 32 at 480–82.
[63] *Council of Civil Service Unions v Minister for the Civil Service* [1985] AC 374.
[64] *Council of Civil Service Unions v UK*, Appl. No. 11603/85, (1987) 50 D&R 228.

reasoning in *Vogt*, a claim brought by a teacher who had been dismissed on account of her active membership of the German Communist party.[65] It held that regardless of whether or not civil servant teachers fall within the ambit of members of the administration of the state, her dismissal had been a disproportionate penalty and was contrary to Article 11. Taken at its highest, this ruling could nullify the exception altogether since it implies that restrictions upon the excepted categories of state employees will not be saved by the express provision in Article 11(2) where they are not "necessary" in line with the rest of Article 11(2).

On the assumption that the exception is to continue to have some **13.27** force, it is important to know which employees fall into the category of members of the administration of the state. In *Vogt*, the Court held that the category was to be narrowly interpreted, according to the post held by the official concerned.[66] However, as noted above, it did not decide whether civil servant teachers fell within it. In the *GCHQ* case, the UK submitted that the category of "members of the administration of the state" is limited to public servants employed in central government; in *Ahmed*, it argued the opposite, that employees of local government are also included, but the Court did not decide the point.

4. FURTHER READING

Ewing, Britain and the ILO (Institute of Employment Rights, 2nd ed., 1994)

Forde, "The European Convention and Human Rights and Labour Law" (1983) 31 AJCL 301

Klug, Starmer and Weir, *The Three Pillars of Liberty* (Routledge, 1996), chapters 10 and 11

Morris, "Freedom of Association and the Interests of the State" in Ewing, Gearty and Hepple (eds), *Human Rights and Labour Law* (Mansell, 1994)

Samuel, *Fundamental Social Rights: Case-law of the European Social Charter* (Council of Europe, 1997)

Thomas, "Harassment and the Right to Protest" (1998) 142 SJ 304

---

[65] A/323, (1996) 21 EHRR 205.
[66] *Ibid.* at 240.

Chapter 14

THE RIGHT TO PROPERTY

Article 1 of the First Protocol to the Convention (Article 1/1) provides: **14.1**

"Every natural or legal person is entitled to the peaceful enjoyment of his possessions. No one shall be deprived of his possessions except in the public interest and subject to the conditions provided for by law and by the general principles of international law.

   The preceding provisions shall not, however, in any way impair the right of a state to enforce such laws as it deems necessary to control the use of property in accordance with the general interest or to secure the payment of taxes or other contributions or penalties."

   Although it does not say so in terms, Article 1/1 guarantees the right to property.[1] It does so by three distinct but related rules; a basic rule of peaceful enjoyment of possessions and two rules covering particular instances of interference by the state in peaceful enjoyment — deprivation of property and control of the use of property. The dividing line between interference with enjoyment, deprivation and control of use may be difficult to pinpoint, although this will not matter in most cases because similar principles are applied under all three heads. However, the issue of whether a measure is designed to secure "the payment of taxes, or other contributions or penalties" is of importance given the extremely wide powers allowed to the state under the final clause of Article 1/1. Like other Convention rights, the right to property is not absolute but may be limited in certain circumstances. The express limitations set out in Article 1/1, and the limitations which have been implied by the Court, are notable for being considerably broader than those which apply under Articles 8–11. In particular, a state will not have to establish a "pressing social need" in order to justify interfering with property rights.

---

[1] *Marckx v Belgium*, A/31, (1979–80) 2 EHRR 330, 335.

1. THE MEANING OF "POSSESSIONS"

14.2 Article 1 uses the term "possessions" in its first paragraph, and "property" in its second paragraph, but no difference in meaning is to be implied. The scope of Article 1/1 has been interpreted broadly. It covers land, chattels, and all acquired rights which have an economic value, for example, shares,[2] patents,[3] alcohol licences,[4] and planning consents.[5] Rights in contract are included, for example, the right of a party to payment of an arbitral award fixed pursuant to a contractual procedure.[6] In the recent case of *Pressos Compañía Naviera*, the Court found that claims for negligence, which had been retrospectively nullified by the Belgian Government, constituted possessions.[7] In *National Provincial Building Society and others v UK*, the Court assumed that building societies' restitutionary claims to taxes paid to the Treasury under regulations which were subsequently held to be invalid were possessions within Article 1/1 (although it went on to reject the applicants' claims of unlawful interference).[8] These latter examples illustrate how Article 1/1 is likely to be the main port of call for applicants complaining of the retrospective effect of civil legislation. Article 7 of the Convention deals specifically with retrospective laws, but only those which impose criminal liability or penalties.

14.3 The starting point for establishing unlawful interference with a protected property right is the question of whether the entitlement or expectation at issue constitutes a property right under national law. If it does, that will usually be the end of the matter. However, "possessions" has an autonomous Convention meaning which may include items which do not have the requisite status under national law. In *Van Marle*, for example, the applicants were accountants who had been refused registration under a new regulatory system and hence had lost the benefits of the goodwill which they had built up amongst their clientele. That goodwill was not regarded as a property right under Dutch law but the Court held that it was akin to a private right of property and fell within Article 1/1.[9]

---

[2] *Bramelid & Malmström v Sweden*, Appl. No. 8588/79, (1982) 29 D&R 64.
[3] *Smith Kline and French Laboratories v The Netherlands*, Appl. No. 12633/87, (1990) 66 D&R 70.
[4] *Tre Traktörer Aktiebolag v Sweden*, A/159, (1991) 13 EHRR 309.
[5] *Pine Valley Developments v Ireland*, A/222, (1991) 14 EHRR 319.
[6] *Stran Greek Refineries v Greece*, A/301-B, (1995) 19 EHRR 293.
[7] *Pressos Compañía Naviera v Belgium*, A/332, (1996) 21 EHRR 301.
[8] A/845, (1998) 25 EHRR 127.
[9] *Van Marle v The Netherlands*, A/101, (1986) 8 EHRR 483, 491.

Whilst property is broadly defined, Article 1/1 draws a crucial distinc- **14.4**
tion between property which has already been acquired and the hope or
expectation that property will be acquired in the future. In *Marckx*, a
mother and her illegitimate daughter complained about provisions of
Belgian law which placed restrictions upon the rights of illegitimate
children to inherit property. The Court held that the daughter could not
claim under Article 1/1 because that provision only applied to a person's
existing possessions and did not guarantee the right to acquire possessions.[10] The Court went on to find that Belgian law breached the
Convention because of the restrictions placed on the rights of her
mother to dispose of her property as she pleased. Article 1/1 did,
however, apply in *Inze*, another inheritance case, where the applicant's
inheritance rights had accrued upon the death of the testator but the
property in question had not yet been distributed.[11] In *Pressos Compañía
Naviera*, the applicant's negligence claims were within Article 1/1
because in Belgian law they were deemed to have accrued at the time
of the negligent acts complained of and so were in place by the time of the
legislation which prevented claims from being brought. This limitation
upon the scope of Article 1/1 means that it is very unlikely to serve as a
source of socio-economic rights, to food, housing, etc. which are, on
closer analysis, hopes or expectations that property will be acquired or
conferred in the future.

One important grey area is that of social security benefits and pensions: **14.5**
a person may not actually be in receipt of a benefit, or of a pension, but
may expect to become entitled to receive it at some point in the future. A
right to a pension will certainly be considered to be a possession within
Article 1/1 where there is a direct link between contributions and benefits
such that an individual has, at any stage, a share in the fund which can
be valued (a money purchase pension scheme would be a classic
example).[12] Recently, however, the Court has broadened considerably
the application of Article 1/1 in this respect by finding it sufficient that
benefits are linked to contributions in the very basic sense that there
would be no entitlement to benefits at all in the absence of contributions.[13] Non-contributory benefits, such as income support, continue to
be excluded from the scope of Article 1/1.[14]

---

[10] *Marckx v Belgium*, above n. 1 at 350, 355.
[11] *Inze v Austria*, A/126, (1988) 10 EHRR 394.
[12] *Müller v Austria*, Appl. No. 5849/72, (1975) 1 D&R 46.
[13] *Gaygusuz v Austria*, A/655, (1997) 23 EHRR 364. Consequently, a right to a UK State Earnings
Related Pension constitutes a pecuniary right within Article 1/1: *Szraber and Clarke v UK*, Appl.
No. 27004/95, [1998] EHRLR 230.
[14] *G v Austria*, Appl. No. 10094/82, (1984) 38 D&R 84.

14.6   The nature of the property at issue in an Article 1/1 claim may raise an issue of *locus standi*. In general, where the property of a company has been affected, it is the company itself, rather than its shareholders, which must claim.[15] An exception is made for majority shareholders who carry on their own business through the medium of the company and who therefore have a direct personal interest in the subject matter of the complaint.[16] The Commission has also ruled that individuals holding policies issued by insurance companies which had been subjected to a one-off "windfall" tax could not claim under Article 1/1. The tax had a direct impact on the value of their policies but the money actually paid out in tax belonged to the companies themselves, and they were the appropriate "victims".[17]

2. GENERAL PRINCIPLES

14.7   A literal reading of the text of Article 1/1 bears little relation to the way in which it has been applied in practice. Three points, in particular, should be noted:

- Interference with peaceful enjoyment of possessions under the first sentence of Article 1/1 constitutes a separate ground of complaint in itself. It is not simply a standard, the specific derogations from which (deprivation and control of use of property) are actionable, but will found a claim where property has been interfered with in a way which does not amount to either deprivation or control by the state.[18]
- The right of peaceful enjoyment, when it is viewed as a freestanding ground of complaint, is not subject to any express limitations. However, the Court has devised implied limitations, in the form of the "fair balance" test: when interfering with the peaceful enjoyment of property, states must strike a fair balance between the demands of the general interest of the community and the requirements of the protection of the individual's fundamental rights.[19]
- The other limbs of Article 1/1, deprivation of property and control of use of property are both subject to their own express limitations.

---

[15] *Yarrow* v *UK*, Appl. No. 9266/81, (1983) 300 D&R 155.
[16] *Kaplan* v *UK*, Appl. No. 7598/76, (1982) 4 EHRR 64.
[17] *Wasa Liv Ömsesidigt Försäkringsbolarget Valands Pensionsstiftelse and others* v *Sweden*, Appl. No. 13013/87, (1988) 58 D&R 163.
[18] For example, *Sporrong and Lönnroth* v *Sweden*, A/52, (1983) 5 EHRR 35.
[19] *Ibid*. at 52.

Deprivation of property must be in the public interest, and lawful, according to domestic and public international law. State control of the use of property must be in accordance with the general interest or designed to secure the payment of taxes, contributions or penalties. These express limitations are not at all onerous and the Court has, in fact, applied the "fair balance" test to all three limbs of Article 1/1, treating the express limitations as additional requirements.

Measures which interfere with property rights must have a legitimate **14.8** aim, and must be proportionate. They must also strike a fair balance between the rights of the individual and the general interest of the community, in order that no individual bears an "excessive" or "disproportionate" burden. States have a broad margin of discretion both in deciding what are the interests of the community in any given situation, and in striking the appropriate balance. The Court will only intervene where the measures in question are manifestly unreasonable.[20] As a result, findings of violations of Article 1/1 are comparatively rare. The vast majority of violations arise out of two specific components which the Court has recognised to be inherent within the fair balance test: procedures and compensation.

PROCEDURAL RIGHTS

Interference with property rights may involve the determination of civil **14.9** rights and obligations and so raise procedural issues under Article 6(1), but Article 1/1 has been found to impose its own procedural obligations. States have a positive obligation to provide mechanisms whereby measures interfering with property rights may be challenged by the owner ofthe property which has been affected. In *Sporrong and Lönnroth*, for example, the absence of a legal remedy whereby victims of planning blight could end the uncertainty caused by longstanding expropriation permits and prohibitions upon construction was central to the Court's ruling that they had been required to bear an individual and excessive burden.[21]

---

[20] See *James v UK*, A/98, (1986) 8 EHRR 123.
[21] Above n. 18 at 54.

COMPENSATION

14.10   Where a person has been deprived of his possessions, within the second limb of Article 1/1, the striking of a fair balance between individual rights and the interests of the community will require the payment of compensation in all but exceptional circumstances.[22] The Court has not gone quite so far in relation to the other limbs of Article 1/1, but the existence and extent of compensation will undoubtedly be relevant in every case to the outcome of the fair balance test. In *Erkner and Hofauer*, for example, the Court upheld a series of complaints against the operation of a land consolidation scheme under the head of interference with peaceful enjoyment on grounds which included the absence of any provision for financial compensation for loss sustained as a result of compulsory exchange of land.[23] For obvious reasons, the obligation to compensate does not extend to the final limb of Article 1/1, concerning payment of taxes.

14.11   English law does insist upon the payment of compensation, at least where land has been confiscated.[24] Complaints in this country are more likely to centre upon the level of compensation which is paid by the state when it interferes with individual property rights. *Lithgow*, one of the leading cases on Article 1, concerned the allegedly inadequate compensation paid to owners of shares in shipbuilding and aircraft manufacturing companies whose interests were nationalised in 1977.[25] However, Article 1/1 will rarely be of assistance in challenging the amount of compensation paid, since the state authorities enjoy, in principle, a wide discretion in defining the value of property rights and in fixing the level of compensation appropriate to the interference which has taken place.

14.12   In *Lithgow*, the applicants complained about the method of assessment of compensation and, in particular, that it had been based on the value of their shares rather than upon the value of the assets of the companies which were nationalised. The Court held that compensation should be "reasonably related" to the value of the property taken and that Article 1/1 did not guarantee a right to full compensation where there were legitimate public interest reasons for reimbursement at less than full market value.[26] As to the precise method of calculation adopted, the

---

[22] *Lithgow* v *UK*, A/102, (1986) 8 EHRR 329, 371.
[23] *Erkner and Hofauer* v *Austria*, A/117, (1987) 9 EHRR 464.
[24] See, for example, *Prest* v *Secretary of State for Wales* (1982) 81 LGR 193, 198.
[25] Above n. 22.
[26] *Ibid.* at 372.

state had a wide margin of appreciation and its decision as to compensation terms would be respected unless it was "manifestly without reasonable foundation".[27] Few compensation schemes will fail the test, although the Court has recently found against a Greek law on that basis. In *Katikaridis*, the applicants lost part of their property through expropriation for the purposes of constructing a new flyover.[28] There was, in principle, an entitlement to compensation for that loss but what was left of the applicants' property was adjacent to the new road and they were deemed by law to have derived benefit from it. That benefit was then set off against the authorities' liability to pay compensation. The Commission's examination of the facts revealed that the applicants' businesses were now below the flyover, in a worse position than before and the Court found that the compensation system was so inflexible as to be manifestly without reasonable foundation.

POSITIVE OBLIGATIONS

The obligations inherent within Article 1/1 to provide fair procedures, and **14.13** to compensate, are positive obligations as between the state and the individuals whose property rights it has interfered with. The Court has been reluctant to recognise further, positive obligations upon the state to protect private property from interference by other private individuals and groups, preferring to restrict the scope of Article 1/1 to interference with property rights by the state. In the recent case of *Gustafsson*, the applicant hotelier became embroiled in an industrial dispute over his refusal to enter into collective agreements.[29] This resulted in suppliers declining to make deliveries to his restaurant, which he ultimately sold. During the dispute, he had unsuccessfully sought to persuade the Swedish Government to intervene on his behalf. He argued before the Court that his Government's failure to provide protection against the industrial action had caused him financial loss and was in breach of Article 1/1. The Court held, however, that Article 1/1 did not apply because his problems were not the product of the exercise of governmental authority, but concerned exclusively private contractual relationships between the applicant and his suppliers. There could be no state responsibility in those

---

[27] *Ibid.* at 373.
[28] *Katikaridis* v *Greece*, A/690, [1997] EHRLR 198.
[29] *Gustafsson* v *Sweden*, A/618, (1996) 22 EHRR 409.

circumstances.[30] It would be wrong to assume that a state could never be responsible under Article 1/1 for failing to intervene to protect private property. However, *Gustafsson* illustrates not only that serious detriment must be suffered by the applicant if such an argument is to succeed, but also that the authorities must be guilty of an obvious dereliction of duty, rather than, as in that case, a principled political or legal judgment.

3. PEACEFUL ENJOYMENT OF POSSESSIONS

14.14   Interference with the peaceful enjoyment of property is a catch-all category capable of encompassing all measures which affect property, including deprivations and controls upon use falling within the other limbs of Article 1/1. There are, however, the following limitations. First, the first limb of Article 1/1 is a residual category, which potentially includes only those measures which do not fall within the other rules. Therefore, measures will be deemed to interfere with peaceful enjoyment only insofar as they do not amount to a deprivation or a control upon use.[31] Secondly, Article 1/1 is concerned only with those interferences which affect the financial value of property: it does not guarantee a right to peaceful enjoyment of possessions in a pleasant environment. Hence, a complaint of damage to the environment, such as that arising in a case of nuisance at common law, will only be considered under Article 1/1 insofar as the financial value of property has been affected.[32] Loss of personal amenity caused by pollution or other nuisance may, however, fall within Article 8 of the Convention as a breach of the right to respect for private life and/or the home.[33]

14.15   The third important limitation upon the scope of the first limb of Article 1/1 is that interferences with property which arise out of private law rights and obligations are considered to define the scope of the property right, rather than to interfere with it. An example would be matrimonial property which is subject to private law rules which may require its transfer to one spouse or the other upon the dissolution of the marriage.

---

[30] *Ibid.* at 439–441.
[31] See, for example, the expropriation permits in *Sporrong and Lönnroth*, above n. 18.
[32] See *Rayner* v *UK*, Appl. No. 9310/81, (1986) 47 D&R 5; *S* v *France*, Appl. No. 13728/88, (1990) 65 D&R 250.
[33] *López-Ostra* v *Spain*, A/303-C, (1995) 20 EHRR 277, 295. A borderline case is *Wiggins* v *UK*, Appl. No. 7456/76 (1978) 13 D&R 40.

Transfer of such property pursuant to an order of the court is not a breach of Article 1/1.[34] The same principle applies where a property right, such as a licence, is granted by the state on certain terms: those terms cannot constitute an interference with peaceful enjoyment (because they define the scope of the right) although they may amount to a control upon use within the third limb of Article 1/1.[35]

"Enjoyment" is to be interpreted broadly. It rarely gives rise to difficulty,   **14.16** although in one recent case the Court had cause to overrule a narrower approach which had been adopted by the Commission. In *Loizidou*, the Turkish occupation of Northern Cyprus had deprived the applicant of access to land which she owned there.[36] The Commission found that the issue was not one of peaceful enjoyment of possessions, but of freedom of movement (which is covered by Article 2 of the Fourth Protocol to the Convention). The Court disagreed: the applicant's loss of control over her land, and of the opportunity to use and enjoy it, amounted to an interference with peaceful enjoyment. The concept of an "interference" with enjoyment presupposes only a *de minimis* effect. Once the minimum effect has been established, the extent to which a measure does interfere with peaceful enjoyment is a factor which goes only to the validity of the state's justification under the fair balance test.

4. DEPRIVATION OF PROPERTY

Deprivation of property within the second limb of the first paragraph of   **14.17** Article 1/1 has been given a fairly narrow definition by the Court. The second limb will apply where property has been confiscated *de jure* such that the owner is deprived of his legal title,[37] but *de facto* deprivations are, generally, classified as interferences with the enjoyment of property. An example of the Court's restrictive approach is the *Stran Greek Refineries* case, in which the Greek Government had legislated in order to make invalid and unenforceable an arbitral award which the applicant had secured against it.[38] No property had changed hands, so the "deprivation" suffered was only *de facto* and was treated as an interference with enjoyment of the benefits of the award under the first limb of Article 1/1.[39] Confiscation (and/or destruction) of goods, apparently a clear case

---

[34] *Mairitsch v Austria*, Appl. No. 12462/86, (1989) 11 EHRR 46.
[35] *Fredin v Sweden*, A/192, (1991) 13 EHRR 784.
[36] *Loizidou v Turkey*, A/707, (1997) 23 EHRR 513.
[37] *Handyside v UK*, A/24, (1979–80) 1 EHRR 737, 760.
[38] Above n. 6.
[39] *Ibid.* at 326–327. See also *Vasilescu v Romania*, A/915, decision of 22 May 1998.

of deprivation, will be classified as a control upon use of property under the third limb of Article 1/1 where it is effected in order to enforce the terms of a regulatory regime which seeks to restrict the free circulation of certain goods.[40]

14.18   The conditions which must be satisfied in order to justify a deprivation of property are not onerous. Deprivation of property must be "in the public interest" and whether it is or not is really a matter for the state authorities — the Court is highly unlikely to interfere on this ground. A good example is *James* v *UK*, in which the Duke of Westminster and other landlords challenged the Leasehold Reform Act 1967, which gave certain tenants the right to buy the freehold of their property on prescribed terms. The Court rejected arguments to the effect that the Act was not in the public interest, but was in the private interests of a few, or was purely a vote-seeking measure. The belief of the UK Parliament that the Act would remedy social injustice could not be said to be manifestly unreasonable.[41]

14.19   Deprivation of property must also be "subject to the provisions provided for by law" which means the same as "prescribed by law" in Articles 8–10. Deprivation must have a basis in law, it must comply with the conditions laid down by that law, and those conditions should be accessible and foreseeable.[42] The circumstances of deprivation must comply with public international law, meaning the established conditions for the expropriation of property of foreigners which include, notably, the payment of compensation.[43] Public international law has no application where a state confiscates the property of its own nationals. Since the requirements of compensation under public international law are, in some respects, more restrictive than those of Article 1/1, it has been argued, unsuccessfully, that Article 1/1 intends international law principles to apply also to nationals of the state concerned.[44]

5. CONTROL OF THE USE OF PROPERTY

14.20   Control of the use of property is also a wide concept, covering both positive requirements to use property in a certain way, and negative restrictions upon the use of property. An example of a case in the former

---

[40] For example, *AGOSI* v *UK*, A/108, (1987) 9 EHRR 1.
[41] Above n. 20 at 142–144.
[42] See, for example, *Hentrich* v *France*, A/296-A, (1994) 18 EHRR 440.
[43] See Brownlie, *Principles of Public International Law* (Clarendon Press, 4th ed., 1990).
[44] *James* v *UK*, above n. 20 at 148–151.

category is *Denev*, in which the applicant failed in a challenge to Swedish law requiring landowners to plant trees in order to protect the environment.[45] The latter category includes anything from planning regulations to export controls to the confiscation of property under obscenity laws. Measures to control the use of property must be "in accordance with the general interest", again a generous qualification, and must pass the fair balance test.

In *ISKCON* v *UK*, the Krishna Consciousness movement complained **14.21** about a local authority enforcement notice served upon it, which precluded the use of a manor house owned by it as the venue for large religious services.[46] The effect of the notice was to restrict the use of the property to that which was permitted when it was acquired, namely use as a residential theological college. The Commission doubted whether, in the circumstances, there had been any interference with peaceful enjoyment and stated that, as a general principle, Article 1/1 cannot be used to claim planning permission to extend the permitted use of property. If there had been an interference within Article 1/1, the enforcement notice was a control upon the use of property, and could, in any event, be justified. The Commission noted that the authorities have a wide margin of appreciation in planning matters and that the applicant had had the opportunity to challenge the enforcement notice at a planning enquiry. A fair balance had been struck.[47]

Finally, Article 1/1 makes provision for a specific type of control of use **14.22** of property, the "payment of taxes or other contributions or penalties". States are free to introduce such measures to this end as they deem to be necessary and it will be extremely difficult to challenge particular tax-raising measures under Article 1/1. The fair balance principle does apply, but for practical purposes, it is unlikely to be breached save in matters of procedure — the taxpayer must be allowed to ascertain his liability promptly and with reasonable certainty. The substantive decision to introduce a particular taxation measure will only be overturned in the unlikely event that the judgment of the legislature is "devoid of reasonable foundation".[48] In *National Provincial Building Society and others* v *UK*, for example, the applicant societies had been deprived, by retrospective legislation, of the benefit of restitutionary claims to tax paid under void regulations. The Court held that the legislation at issue had been motivated by obvious public interest considerations and had sought

---

[45] *Denev* v *Sweden*, Appl. No. 12570/86, (1989) 59 D&R 127. See also *Moution* v *France*, Appl. No. 28443/95, [1998] EHRLR 503.
[46] Appl. No. 20490/92, (1994) 76-A D&R 90.
[47] *Ibid*. at 108–109.
[48] *Gasus Dosier- und Förder-technik* v *The Netherlands*, A/306-B, (1995) 20 EHRR 403.

merely to re-assert the original intention of Parliament. Moreover, its passage could reasonably have been anticipated by the applicants. In the circumstances, it did not upset the required balance between the protection of applicants' rights to restitution and the public interest in securing payment of taxes due.[49] Tax-raising measures may, however, be more vulnerable to a claim of discrimination under Article 14 (see below).

6. PROPERTY RIGHTS AND DISCRIMINATION

14.23 Potential applicants may find it beneficial to couple a claim for interference with property rights under Article 1/1 with a claim of discrimination under Article 14. This is because the threshold for justification under Article 14 is not nearly so lenient as under Article 1/1, particularly where certain forms of discrimination, notably sex and nationality discrimination, are concerned. In *Darby*, for example, the applicant succeeded in challenging tax legislation, probably the most difficult of all measures to impeach under Article 1/1, on the grounds that it discriminated against him as a non-resident.[50] The specific complaint concerned a special tax payable in Sweden to support the established Church: residents of Sweden who did not belong to the Church could claim exemption from it, but non-residents who were nevertheless subject to Swedish tax laws could not. Similarly, in *Van Raalte*, the Court declared unlawful a Dutch law levying contributions towards child benefit which exempted unmarried childless women over 45, but not unmarried childless men.[51]

14.24   Considerable potential exists for challenging entitlements to social security benefits under Article 14 since many such entitlements were devised on the basis of gender stereotypes which have become outmoded. Very weighty reasons will have to be provided in order to justify a difference in treatment based on gender.[52] However, in the recent case of *Petrovic v Austria*, the Court overruled the Commission and found that the availability of parental leave payments for mothers but not fathers was justified on objective grounds. The Court emphasised that the Contracting States enjoy a certain margin of appreciation in assessing whether and to

---

[49] Above n. 8.
[50] *Darby v Sweden*, A/187, (1991) 13 EHRR 774.
[51] A/732, [1997] EHRLR 449. See also *MacGregor v UK*, Appl. No. 30548/96, [1998] EHRLR 354.
[52] *Schmidt v Germany*, A/291-B, (1994) 18 EHRR 513.

what extent differences in otherwise similar situations justify a different treatment in law. The Austrian Government enjoyed a wide margin of appreciation because, at the material time, there was no common standard in the field, as the majority of the Contracting States did not provide for parental leave allowances to be paid to fathers. Austria was in fact one of the more progressive states and had since amended its legislation so as to avail fathers such as the applicant.[53]

7. FURTHER READING

Jones, "Property Rights, Planning Law and the European Convention" [1996] EHRLR 233

---

[53] A/893, decision of 27 March 1998.

Chapter 15

THE RIGHT TO EDUCATION

Article 2 of the First Protocol states: **15.1**

"No person shall be denied the right to education. In the exercise of any functions which it assumes in relation to education and to teaching, the State shall respect the right of parents to ensure such education and teaching in conformity with their own religious and philosophical convictions."

1. THE SCOPE OF THE RIGHT TO EDUCATION

The right to education in the first sentence of Article 2 refers principally to   **15.2** primary education,[1] but it also extends to secondary and higher education.[2] It is a right conferred upon children (and upon students) not upon parents or educational institutions, who may not, accordingly, claim to be a victim of a violation of Article 2. Parents do have rights, however, under the second sentence of Article 2.

Following the landmark *Belgian Linguistics* cases, the extent of a state's   **15.3** obligations to educate its citizens is severely circumscribed.[3] These were claims by French-speaking parents in Belgium about provisions of Belgian law which regulated the language of instruction in schools, and which prohibited, for example, the operation of French-speaking state schools in an area designated as Flemish-speaking only. The following principles were laid down by the Court.[4]

- Article 1/2 does not require a state to establish at its own expense, or to subsidise, education of any particular type or at any particular

---

[1] *X* v *UK*, Appl. No. 5962/72, (1975) 2 D&R 50.
[2] *X* v *UK*, Appl. No. 8844/80, (1980) 23 D&R 228.
[3] A/6, (1979–80) 1 EHRR 252.
[4] *Ibid.* at 280–282.

level. Pursuant to the second sentence of Article 2, a state is obliged to permit parents to themselves establish a private school of a particular type which will ensure that their children are educated in accordance with their religious and philosophical convictions,[5] but the state does not have to fund or subsidise their efforts.[6]

- The right to education is, thus, the right to avail oneself of the means of instruction existing at any given time.
- Article 1/2 also implies a right to official recognition of the studies which have been completed, in conformity with the rules in force in each state.
- The right to education calls for regulation by the state which may vary in time and place according to the needs and resources of the community and of individuals. However, such regulation may never injure the substance of the right to education or conflict with other rights enshrined in the Convention. Hence, the Commission has decided that states are free to make primary education compulsory,[7] or to require all parents to cooperate in assessing the educational attainments of their children.[8]

15.4   Perhaps the most pressing question raised by Article 2 so far as domestic education law and practice is concerned is whether the basic right to education can found any right to attend the school of one's choice. Legal challenges to the exercise of discretion by schools in refusing to admit applicant pupils, or in excluding pupils who are disruptive, have become increasingly common. It is submitted, however, that the Convention right to education is likely to add little to the existing state of domestic law. In *Campbell and Cosans*, the UK was found to have breached its obligations under the first sentence of Article 2 when a boy was suspended from school for almost a whole academic year for refusing to accept corporal punishment.[9] However, the basis of the Court's decision was not the length of time for which the child had been excluded, but the fact that he was subject to a condition of access which conflicted with the second sentence of Article 2 (in that corporal punishment ran contrary to the philosophical and moral convictions of his parents).[10] As noted above, the right of the state to regulate education is defeated where regulation involves breach of another right conferred by

[5] See *Jordebo* v *Sweden*, Appl. No. 11533/85, (1987) 51 D&R 125.
[6] *W and KL* v *Sweden*, Appl. No. 10476/83, (1985) 45 D&R 143.
[7] *Ibid.* (1984).
[8] *Family H* v *UK*, Appl. No. 10233/83, (1984) 37 D&R 105.
[9] *Campbell and Cosans* v *UK*, A/48 (1982) 4 EHRR 293.
[10] *Ibid.* at 307.

the Convention. Four features of the Commission's case-law would work against claims to access to a particular state school or type of school.

- The state authorities have a legislative and administrative discretion as to how children ought to be educated. In *SP v UK*, for example, the Commission rejected a complaint regarding the failure of a local authority to provide special schooling for a dyslexic child. National education policy was to the effect that children with special needs should be educated, so far as possible, in an ordinary school and the local authority had decided in good faith that the child's needs could be met in the classroom of an ordinary school (although it later had to revise its judgment). Neither national policy nor the decisions of the local authority could be attacked under Article 2.[11] Similarly, the Commission has rejected claims from parents of disabled children who did not wish them to be educated in special schools.[12]
- The ambit of the right to education is subject to limitations upon resources and the discretion of the state authorities to allocate resources as they see fit. Hence, the Commission has ruled in the context of British claims to single-sex, selective education that the authorities could rely in their defence upon the unavailability of places in the selective schools, the maintenance of efficient education in such schools and the efficient use and distribution of resources between selective, single-sex schools and other schools in the area.[13]
- A claim to be educated in a particular school or type of school is unlikely to succeed where other alternatives, including private school education or education at home, are available. The fact that a particular applicant cannot afford private education does not matter for these purposes.[14]
- The Commission has declined to adjudicate upon allegations as to the quality of teaching in a particular school or schools.[15] Whilst education must presumably be effective in a broad sense, Article 2 will not be engaged simply because the quality of education is allegedly better in one school than another.

---

[11] *SP v UK*, Appl. No. 28915/95, (1997) 23 EHRR CD139.
[12] *PD and LD v UK*, Appl. No. 14135/88 (1989) 62 D&R 292; *Graeme v UK*, Appl. No. 13887/88 (1990) 64 D&R 158.
[13] *W & DM and M & HI v UK*, Appl. No. 10228/82, (1984) 37 D&R 96.
[14] *Ibid.* at 100.
[15] *SP v UK*, above n. 11.

15.5   It should also be noted that qualifying conditions for access to educational institutions may vary, depending upon the type of institution: for example, it is open to universities to set academic standards which must be met by prospective entrants.[16] The utility of the right to education under Article 2 may be enhanced where it is cited together with a claim of discrimination under Article 14. Where a state provides a particular benefit or facility, even one which it is not strictly obliged by Article 2 to provide, it must do so on a non-discriminatory basis. An example would be a subsidy to a private school: the state does not have to pay it, but if it chooses to do so, it must make equal subsidies available to other private schools which are in a similar situation, or show a reasonable and objective justification for its failure to do so.[17]

2. RESPECT FOR RELIGIOUS AND PHILOSOPHICAL CONVICTIONS

15.6   The second limb of Article 2 sets out a right of parents to respect, in the education of their children, for their "religious and philosophical convictions". This is, potentially, a right of considerable scope since it is not confined to the issue of religious education but extends to all forms of "education and teaching". It may be used to challenge not only the content of educational instruction or the way in which information is conveyed, but also the organisation and financing of the public education system and questions of discipline, such as corporal punishment.[18] However, like the first sentence of Article 2, the obligations of states to respect parents' religious and philosophical convictions have been narrowly interpreted.

15.7   First, the Court has been keen to limit the types of opinion which will qualify as a religious or philosophical conviction. It rejected the argument of the applicants in the *Belgian Linguistics* cases that philosophical convictions extended to preferences in cultural and linguistic matters. In *Campbell and Cosans*, it held that a conviction was something more cogent, serious and important than an opinion or an idea, and, less helpfully, that a philosophical conviction was a conviction "worthy of respect in a democratic society" which was not itself incompatible with

---

[16] *Patel* v *UK*, Appl. No. 8844/80, (1982) 4 EHRR 256.
[17] See Harris, O'Boyle and Warbrick, *Law of the European Convention on Human Rights* (Butterworths, 1996), at 548; *X* v *UK*, Appl. No. 7782/77, (1979) 14 D&R 179.
[18] *Campbell and Cosans* v *UK*, above n. 9 at 303–304.

human dignity.[19] In that case, the applicants' strongly held views against corporal punishment were held to attract the protection of Article 2.

Secondly, and perhaps more important, the state's obligation under the **15.8** second limb of Article 2 is the relatively mild one of securing respect for religious and philosophical convictions, rather than that of guaranteeing that children can be educated in accordance with the views of their parents. This part of Article 2 seeks, essentially, to prohibit indoctrination and states need only ensure that sensitive information is conveyed in an "objective, critical and pluralistic manner".[20] This is the only apparent restriction imposed by Article 2 upon the academic content of education. The state may respect parents' rights by allowing them to remove their children from the lessons to which they object, but it will not always have to do so. In *Kjeldsen*, the Court upheld a Danish system of compulsory sex education for teenagers, rejecting a complaint of discrimination founded on the fact that children could be removed from religious education but not sex education classes.[21] It may, ultimately, only be possible to achieve "respect" by allowing parents to establish their own private schools. If they do so, Article 2 will not enable them to secure financial or other assistance from the state (save perhaps where there is a basis for a discrimination claim) since, in line with the approach of the Court in the *Belgian Linguistics* cases, it only bites on the way in which existing educational facilities are exploited.[22]

THE UNITED KINGDOM RESERVATION

When it ratified the First Protocol, the UK deposited a reservation to the **15.9** application of Article 2 to the effect that the principle expressed in the second sentence would only apply only "so far as it is compatible with the provision of efficient instruction and training and the avoidance of unreasonable expenditure".[23] That wording reflected the terms of s. 76 of the Education Act 1944 (now s. 9 of the Education Act 1996). The reservation is of limited effect for three reasons. First, under Convention rules, it can only apply in respect of legislation which is in force at the time

---

[19] *Ibid.* at 304–305.
[20] See *Kjeldsen, Busk Madsen and Pedersen* v *Denmark*, A/23, (1979–80) 1 EHRR 711.
[21] *Ibid.*
[22] *PD and LD* v *UK*, above n. 12 at 277.
[23] Reservations to the Convention are discussed briefly in chapter 6. The Human Rights Act makes specific provision for the reservation to Art. 2: ss. 1(2) and 15(1)(a).

when the reservation is made, and any subsequent re-enactments of it. Secondly, the Court will construe reservations narrowly and has shown itself willing to reject arguments that British measures in the field of education are justified according to the criteria of efficient instruction and unreasonable expenditure.[24] Thirdly, the reservation does not, of course, affect the application of the first sentence of Article 2 in the UK.

---

[24] *Campbell and Cosans* v *UK*, above n. 18 at 305–306.

Chapter 16

THE RIGHT TO FREE ELECTIONS

Article 3 of the First Protocol to the Convention states: **16.1**

"The High Contracting Parties undertake to hold free elections at reasonable intervals by secret ballot under conditions which will ensure the free expression of the opinion of the people in the choice of the legislature."

The commitment to free elections contained in Article 3 serves to underline "the prime importance of effective political democracy" to the protection of human rights within the Convention system.[1] The fact that so many states with widely differing political and electoral systems have been able to accept Article 3 implies that it is intended to do little more than establish democracy as a minimum condition of membership of the Council of Europe club. As such, it would do little to enable individuals to challenge the detailed operation of their political systems since all members of the Council of Europe, Britain included, subscribe, on a broad view, to democracy rather than dictatorship. The Commission and the Court have, in fact, found a number of more specific individual rights within Article 3 but, at the same time, have been reluctant to criticise aspects of particular political systems, relying on implied limitations to Article 3 and a wide margin of appreciation.

1. THE LEGISLATURE

Article 3 only applies to elections to "the legislature". The term does not   **16.2**
necessarily refer only to the national parliament but is to be interpreted in the light of the constitutional structure of the state in question. In order to

---

[1] *Mathieu-Mohin and Clerfayt* v *Belgium*, A/113, (1988) 10 EHRR 1, 15.

qualify as part of the legislature, a body must have a primary rule-making power and a high degree of autonomy from the central parliament. State parliaments in federal systems such as Germany and Switzerland fall into this category.[2] British local authorities do not, however, possess the requisite characteristics. They have no inherent primary rule-making power and those powers which are delegated to them are qualified by Parliament and exercised subject to Parliament's ultimate control.[3] The Scottish assembly may well qualify as part of the legislature on the basis of its extensive law-making powers, even though its existence is also contingent upon the will of Parliament. Thus far, the European Parliament has not been recognised as "the legislature". The problem is in part the secondary role which it plays in the EU legislative process,[4] although progressively greater competences have been conferred upon it in recent years and it may now have the necessary legislative powers. In *Matthews v UK*, however, the Commission held that regardless of the extent of the powers of the EU Parliament, it could not fall within Article 3, because the framers of the Convention had intended to refer only to national, and not to supra-national institutions.[5] The restriction of the scope of Article 3 to elections to the legislature also has the effect of excluding referenda.[6]

2. INDIVIDUAL RIGHTS UNDER ARTICLE 3

16.3   The scope of the rights conferred by Article 3 is then determined by what is necessary to "ensure the free expression of the opinion of the people". In *Mathieu-Mohin* the Court recognised that Article 3 confers upon individuals the right to vote in elections and to stand for election to the legislature. At the same time, however, it noted that Article 3 was subject to implied limitations and that states may take steps to restrict the scope of the rights which it confers. Whilst states "have a wide margin of appreciation in this sphere", any measure limiting Article 3 rights must satisfy the following conditions:[7]

---

[2] See, for example, *Timke* v *Germany*, Appl. No. 27311/95, [1996] EHRLR 74.
[3] *Booth-Clibborn* v *UK*, Appl. No. 11391/85, (1985) 43 D&R 236.
[4] *Lindsay* v *UK*, Appl. No. 8364/78, (1979) 15 D&R 247; *Tête* v *France*, Appl. No. 11123/84, (1987) 54 D&R 52.
[5] Appl. No. 24833/94, [1998] EHRLR 340.
[6] *X* v *UK*, Appl. No. 7096/75, (1975) 3 D&R 165.
[7] *Mathieu-Mohin* v *Belgium*, above n. 1 at 16–17; see also *W, X, Y and Z.* v *Belgium*, Appl. No. 6745/74, (1975) 2 D&R 110.

- it must have a legitimate aim, and use means which are not disproportionate to that aim;
- it must not curtail the rights at issue "to such an extent as to impair their very essence and deprive them of their eectiveness";
- it must respect "the principle of equality of treatment of all citizens";
- it must not impose restrictions which are arbitrary.

The Commission has, accordingly, endorsed a number of restrictions on the right to vote, and to stand for election, some of which apply in Britain today. One example is the removal of the franchise from convicted prisoners;[8] another is the system whereby a candidate for election must pay a deposit which will only be returned if a certain amount of votes are received.[9] In *Ahmed*, the Court ruled that British restrictions upon the political activities of local government officers which prohibited the applicants from standing for election to Parliament, did not contravene Article 3. It emphasised the breadth of the margin of appreciation in this field and noted that the applicants were not prevented from resigning from their jobs and then standing for election.[10]

16.4   Article 3 does not appear to guarantee the right to participate in electoral campaigns, short of voting and standing for election (although such a right would fall within the freedom of expression).[11] Nor does it confer a right upon individuals that political parties be given media coverage either at all, or equal to that granted to other parties,[12] a matter which is frequently raised in British election campaigns, usually in the context of party political broadcasts.[13] It is conceivable that a political party itself might have greater rights in this regard, perhaps in conjunction with a discrimination claim under Article 14. However, the Court has been reluctant to find obligations to permit access to the media within the right to freedom of expression under Article 10, and it would be somewhat surprising if it were to do so under Article 3, which allows a more generous discretion to states.

16.5   Article 3 contains certain specific obligations with respect to the conduct of elections: they must be "free", by secret ballot, and at reasonable intervals. In the recent case of *Timke* v *Germany*, the Commission hinted that the interval between elections may be unrea-

---

[8] *H* v *The Netherlands*, Appl. No. 9914/82, (1983) 33 D&R 242.
[9] *Fournier* v *France*, Appl. No. 11406/85, (1988) 55 D&R 130.
[10] *Ahmed* v *UK*, A/966, decision of 2 September 1998.
[11] *Ibid.*
[12] *Purcell* v *Ireland*, Appl. No. 15404/89, (1991) 70 D&R 262.
[13] *Huggett* v *UK*, Appl. No. 24744/94, [1977] EHRLR 449.

sonably short as well as unreasonably long,[14] but such is the breadth of discretion enjoyed by states under Article 3 that this restriction could only bite in extreme cases. The general obligation under Article 3, that conditions governing elections must be such as to secure the free expression of the opinion of the people, is broadly worded and the Commission and the Court have been reluctant to find within it any more specific duties. In particular, Article 3 had been held not to require the adoption of any particular electoral system. For example, the bias against smaller parties which is inherent in the first-past-the-post electoral system, and which is mitigated by a system of proportional representation, did not enable the Liberal Party to mount a successful challenge under Article 3.[15] Any system will be judged according to the particular political circumstances which it is designed to meet; as in *Mathieu-Mohin* itself, and as in the past in Northern Ireland,[16] different rules may be justified in the interests of ensuring representation of minorities.

16.6   Finally, the effect of two other provisions of the Convention should be noted. Article 16 allows the imposition of restrictions upon the political activities of foreigners (and, indeed, foreigners, except for Irish and Commonwealth citizens, cannot vote or stand for election to the Westminster Parliament). Following the *Piermont* case, citizens of other EU countries cannot be considered to be "aliens" within Article 16, and, in any event, Article 8B of the Treaty on European Union specifically permits citizens of any EU Member State to vote in local and European Parliament elections, and to stand for election to the European Parliament, in any other Member State.[17] Article 17 may permit states to place restrictions upon the electoral activities of parties opposed to democracy.

3. FURTHER READING

Klug, Starmer and Weir, *The Three Pillars of Liberty* (Routledge, 1996), chapter 14

---

[14] Above n. 2.
[15] *Liberty Party* , *R and P* v *UK*, Appl. No. 8765/79 (1980) 21 D&R 211.
[16] *A and others* v *UK*, Appl. No. 3625/68, (1970) 13 *Yearbook* 340.
[17] *Piermont* v *France*, A/314, (1995) 20 EHRR 301.

Appendix 1

TEXT OF HUMAN RIGHTS ACT 1998

An Act to give further effect to rights and freedoms guaranteed under the European Convention on Human Rights; to make provision with respect to holders of certain judicial offices who become judges of the European Court of Human Rights; and for connected purposes.

[9th November 1998]

Be it enacted by the Queen's most Excellent Majesty, by and with the advice and consent of the Lords Spiritual and Temporal, and Commons, in this present Parliament assembled, and by the authority of the same, as follows:—

Introduction

1.—(1) In this Act "the Convention rights" means the rights and fundamental freedoms set out in—

    (a) Articles 2 to 12 and 14 of the Convention,

    (b) Articles 1 to 3 of the First Protocol, and

    (c) Articles 1 and 2 of the Sixth Protocol,

as read with Articles 16 to 18 of the Convention.

(2) Those Articles are to have effect for the purposes of this Act subject to any designated derogation or reservation (as to which see sections 14 and 15).

(3) The Articles are set out in Schedule 1.

(4) The Secretary of State may by order make such amendments to this Act as he considers appropriate to reflect the effect, in relation to the United Kingdom, of a protocol.

(5) In subsection (4) "protocol" means a protocol to the Convention—

    (a) which the United Kingdom has ratified; or

    (b) which the United Kingdom has signed with a view to ratification.

(6) No amendment may be made by an order under subsection (4) so as to come into force before the protocol concerned is in force in relation to the United Kingdom.

The Convention Rights.

Interpretation of
Convention rights.

2.—(1) A court or tribunal determining a question which has arisen in connection with a Convention right must take into account any—

(a) judgment, decision, declaration or advisory opinion of the European Court of Human Rights,

(b) opinion of the Commission given in a report adopted under Article 31 of the Convention,

(c) decision of the Commission in connection with Article 26 or 27(2) of the Convention, or

(d) decision of the Committee of Ministers taken under Article 46 of the Convention,

whenever made or given, so far as, in the opinion of the court or tribunal, it is relevant to the proceedings in which that question has arisen.

(2) Evidence of any judgment, decision, declaration or opinion of which account may have to be taken under this section is to be given in proceedings before any court or tribunal in such manner as may be provided by rules.

(3) In this section "rules" means rules of court or, in the case of proceedings before a tribunal, rules made for the purposes of this section—

(a) by the Lord Chancellor or the Secretary of State, in relation to any proceedings outside Scotland;

(b) by the Secretary of State, in relation to proceedings in Scotland; or

(c) by a Northern Ireland department, in relation to proceedings before a tribunal in Northern Ireland—

(i) which deals with transferred matters; and

(ii) for which no rules made under paragraph (a) are in force.

Legislation

Interpretation of
legislation.

3.—(1) So far as it is possible to do so, primary legislation and subordinate legislation must be read and given effect in a way which is compatible with the Convention rights.

(2) This section—

(a) applies to primary legislation and subordinate legislation whenever enacted;

(b) does not affect the validity, continuing operation or enforcement of any incompatible primary legislation; and

(c) does not affect the validity, continuing operation or enforcement of any incompatible subordinate legislation if (disregarding any possibility of revocation) primary legislation prevents removal of the incompatibility.

4.—(1) Subsection (2) applies in any proceedings in which a court determines whether a provision of primary legislation is compatible with a Convention right.

(2) If the court is satisfied that the provision is incompatible with a Convention right, it may make a declaration of that incompatibility.

(3) Subsection (4) applies in any proceedings in which a court determines whether a provision of subordinate legislation, made in the exercise of a power conferred by primary legislation, is compatible with a Convention right.

(4) If the court is satisfied—

(a) that the provision is incompatible with a Convention right, and

(b) that (disregarding any possibility of revocation) the primary legislation concerned prevents removal of the incompatibility,

it may make a declaration of that incompatibility.

(5) In this section "court" means—

(a) the House of Lords;

(b) the Judicial Committee of the Privy Council;

(c) the Courts-Martial Appeal Court;

(d) in Scotland, the High Court of Justiciary sitting otherwise than as a trial court or the Court of Session;

(e) in England and Wales or Northern Ireland, the High Court or the Court of Appeal.

(6) A declaration under this section ("a declaration of incompat-ibility")—

(a) does not affect the validity, continuing operation or enforce-ment of the provision in respect of which it is given; and

(b) is not binding on the parties to the proceedings in which it is made.

5.—(1) Where a court is considering whether to make a declaration of incompatibility, the Crown is entitled to notice in accordance with rules of court.

(2) In any case to which subsection (1) applies—

(a) a Minister of the Crown (or a person nominated by him),

(b) a member of the Scottish Executive,

(c) a Northern Ireland Minister,

(d) a Northern Ireland department,

is entitled, on giving notice in accordance with rules of court, to be joined as a party to the proceedings.

(3) Notice under subsection (2) may be given at any time during the proceedings.

(4) A person who has been made a party to criminal proceedings

Declaration of incompatibility.

Right of Crown intervene.

(other than in Scotland) as the result of a notice under subsection (2) may, with leave, appeal to the House of Lords against any declaration of incompatibility made in the proceedings.

(5) In subsection (4)—

"criminal proceedings" includes all proceedings before the Courts-Martial Appeal Court; and

"leave" means leave granted by the court making the declaration of incompatibility or by the House of Lords.

Public authorities

6.—(1) It is unlawful for a public authority to act in a way which is incompatible with a Convention right.

(2) Subsection (1) does not apply to an act if—

(a) as the result of one or more provisions of primary legislation, the authority could not have acted differently; or

(b) in the case of one or more provisions of, or made under, primary legislation which cannot be read or given effect in a way which is compatible with the Convention rights, the authority was acting so as to give effect to or enforce those provisions.

(3) In this section "public authority" includes—

(a) a court or tribunal, and

(b) any person certain of whose functions are functions of a public nature,

but does not include either House of Parliament or a person exercising functions in connection with proceedings in Parliament.

(4) In subsection (3) "Parliament" does not include the House of Lords in its judicial capacity.

(5) In relation to a particular act, a person is not a public authority by virtue only of subsection (3)(b) if the nature of the act is private.

(6) "An act" includes a failure to act but does not include a failure to—

(a) introduce in, or lay before, Parliament a proposal for legislation; or

(b) make any primary legislation or remedial order.

Proceedings.

7.—(1) A person who claims that a public authority has acted (or proposes to act) in a way which is made unlawful by section 6(1) may—

(a) bring proceedings against the authority under this Act in the appropriate court or tribunal, or

(b) rely on the Convention right or rights concerned in any legal proceedings,

but only if he is (or would be) a victim of the unlawful act.

(2) In subsection (1)(a) "appropriate court or tribunal" means such court or tribunal as may be determined in accordance with rules; and proceedings against an authority include a counterclaim or similar proceeding.

(3) If the proceedings are brought on an application for judicial review, the applicant is to be taken to have a sufficient interest in relation to the unlawful act only if he is, or would be, a victim of that act.

(4) If the proceedings are made by way of a petition for judicial review in Scotland, the applicant shall be taken to have title and interest to sue in relation to the unlawful act only if he is, or would be, a victim of that act.

(5) Proceedings under subsection (1)(a) must be brought before the end of—

    (a) the period of one year beginning with the date on which the act complained of took place; or

    (b) such longer period as the court or tribunal considers equitable having regard to all the circumstances,

but that is subject to any rule imposing a stricter time limit in relation to the procedure in question.

(6) In subsection (1)(b) "legal proceedings" includes—

    (a) proceedings brought by or at the instigation of a public authority; and

    (b) an appeal against the decision of a court or tribunal.

(7) For the purposes of this section, a person is a victim of an unlawful act only if he would be a victim for the purposes of Article 34 of the Convention if proceedings were brought in the European Court of Human Rights in respect of that act.

(8) Nothing in this Act creates a criminal offence.

(9) In this section "rules" means—

    (a) in relation to proceedings before a court or tribunal outside Scotland, rules made by the Lord Chancellor or the Secretary of State for the purposes of this section or rules of court,

    (b) in relation to proceedings before a court or tribunal in Scotland, rules made by the Secretary of State for those purposes,

    (c) in relation to proceedings before a tribunal in Northern Ireland—

        (i) which deals with transferred matters; and

        (ii) for which no rules made under paragraph (a) are in force,

    rules made by a Northern Ireland department for those purposes,

and includes provision made by order under section 1 of the Courts and Legal Services Act 1990.

1990 c. 41.

(10) In making rules, regard must be had to section 9.

(11) The Minister who has power to make rules in relation to a particular tribunal may, to the extent he considers it necessary to ensure that the tribunal can provide an appropriate remedy in relation to an act (or proposed act) of a public authority which is (or would be) unlawful as a result of section 6(1), by order add to—

    (a) the relief or remedies which the tribunal may grant; or

    (b) the grounds on which it may grant any of them.

(12) An order made under subsection (11) may contain such incidental, supplemental, consequential or transitional provision as the Minister making it considers appropriate.

(13) "The Minister" includes the Northern Ireland department concerned.

Judicial remedies.

8.—(1) In relation to any act (or proposed act) of a public authority which the court finds is (or would be) unlawful, it may grant such relief or remedy, or make such order, within its powers as it considers just and appropriate.

(2) But damages may be awarded only by a court which has power to award damages, or to order the payment of compensation, in civil proceedings.

(3) No award of damages is to be made unless, taking account of all the circumstances of the case, including—

    (a) any other relief or remedy granted, or order made, in relation to the act in question (by that or any other court), and

    (b) the consequences of any decision (of that or any other court) in respect of that act,

the court is satisfied that the award is necessary to afford just satisfaction to the person in whose favour it is made.

(4) In determining—

    (a) whether to award damages, or

    (b) the amount of an award,

the court must take into account the principles applied by the European Court of Human Rights in relation to the award of compensation under Article 41 of the Convention.

(5) A public authority against which damages are awarded is to be treated—

1940 c. 42.

    (a) in Scotland, for the purposes of section 3 of the Law Reform (Miscellaneous Provisions) (Scotland) Act 1940 as if the award were made in an action of damages in which the authority has been found liable in respect of loss or damage to the person to whom the award is made;

(b) for the purposes of the Civil Liability (Contribution) Act 1978 as liable in respect of damage suffered by the person to whom the award is made.   1978 c. 47.

(6) In this section—

"court" includes a tribunal;

"damages" means damages for an unlawful act of a public authority; and

"unlawful" means unlawful under section 6(1).

9.—(1) Proceedings under section 7(1)(a) in respect of a judicial act may be brought only—   Judicial acts.

(a) by exercising a right of appeal;

(b) on an application (in Scotland a petition) for judicial review; or

(c) in such other forum as may be prescribed by rules.

(2) That does not affect any rule of law which prevents a court from being the subject of judicial review.

(3) In proceedings under this Act in respect of a judicial act done in good faith, damages may not be awarded otherwise than to compensate a person to the extent required by Article 5(5) of the Convention.

(4) An award of damages permitted by subsection (3) is to be made against the Crown; but no award may be made unless the appropriate person, if not a party to the proceedings, is joined.

(5) In this section—

"appropriate person" means the Minister responsible for the court concerned, or a person or government department nominated by him;

"court" includes a tribunal;

"judge" includes a member of a tribunal, a justice of the peace and a clerk or other officer entitled to exercise the jurisdiction of a court;

"judicial act" means a judicial act of a court and includes an act done on the instructions, or on behalf, of a judge; and

"rules" has the same meaning as in section 7(9).

Remedial action

10.—(1) This section applies if—   Power to take remedial action.

(a) a provision of legislation has been declared under section 4 to be incompatible with a Convention right and, if an appeal lies—

(i) all persons who may appeal have stated in writing that they do not intend to do so;

(ii) the time for bringing an appeal has expired and no appeal has been brought within that time; or

(iii) an appeal brought within that time has been determined or abandoned; or

(b) it appears to a Minister of the Crown or Her Majesty in Council that, having regard to a finding of the European Court of Human Rights made after the coming into force of this section in proceedings against the United Kingdom, a provision of legislation is incompatible with an obligation of the United Kingdom arising from the Convention.

(2) If a Minister of the Crown considers that there are compelling reasons for proceeding under this section, he may by order make such amendments to the legislation as he considers necessary to remove the incompatibility.

(3) If, in the case of subordinate legislation, a Minister of the Crown considers—

(a) that it is necessary to amend the primary legislation under which the subordinate legislation in question was made, in order to enable the incompatibility to be removed, and

(b) that there are compelling reasons for proceeding under this section,

he may by order make such amendments to the primary legislation as he considers necessary.

(4) This section also applies where the provision in question is in subordinate legislation and has been quashed, or declared invalid, by reason of incompatibility with a Convention right and the Minister proposes to proceed under paragraph 2(b) of Schedule 2.

(5) If the legislation is an Order in Council, the power conferred by subsection (2) or (3) is exercisable by Her Majesty in Council.

(6) In this section "legislation" does not include a Measure of the Church Assembly or of the General Synod of the Church of England.

(7) Schedule 2 makes further provision about remedial orders.

Other rights and proceedings

Safeguard for existing human rights.

11.—(A person's reliance on a Convention right does not restrict—

(a) any other right or freedom conferred on him by or under any law having effect in any part of the United Kingdom; or

(b) his right to make any claim or bring any proceedings which he could make or bring apart from sections 7 to 9.

Freedom of expression.

12.—(1) This section applies if a court is considering whether to grant any relief which, if granted, might affect the exercise of the Convention right to freedom of expression.

(2) If the person against whom the application for relief is made ("the

respondent") is neither present nor represented, no such relief is to be granted unless the court is satisfied—

    (a) that the applicant has taken all practicable steps to notify the respondent; or

    (b) that there are compelling reasons why the respondent should not be notified.

(3) No such relief is to be granted so as to restrain publication before trial unless the court is satisfied that the applicant is likely to establish that publication should not be allowed.

(4) The court must have particular regard to the importance of the Convention right to freedom of expression and, where the proceedings relate to material which the respondent claims, or which appears to the court, to be journalistic, literary or artistic material (or to conduct connected with such material), to—

    (a) the extent to which—

        (i) the material has, or is about to, become available to the public; or

        (ii) it is, or would be, in the public interest for the material to be published;

    (b) any relevant privacy code.

(5) In this section—

"court" includes a tribunal; and

"relief" includes any remedy or order (other than in criminal proceedings).

13.—(1) If a court's determination of any question arising under this Act might affect the exercise by a religious organisation (itself or its members collectively) of the Convention right to freedom of thought, conscience and religion, it must have particular regard to the importance of that right.

    Freedom of thought, conscience and religion.

(2) In this section "court" includes a tribunal.

Derogations and reservations

14.—(1) In this Act "designated derogation" means—

    Derogations.

    (a) the United Kingdom's derogation from Article 5(3) of the Convention; and

    (b) any derogation by the United Kingdom from an Article of the Convention, or of any protocol to the Convention, which is designated for the purposes of this Act in an order made by the Secretary of State.

(2) The derogation referred to in subsection (1)(a) is set out in Part I of Schedule 3.

(3) If a designated derogation is amended or replaced it ceases to be a designated derogation.

(4) But subsection (3) does not prevent the Secretary of State from exercising his power under subsection (1)(b) to make a fresh designation order in respect of the Article concerned.

(5) The Secretary of State must by order make such amendments to Schedule 3 as he considers appropriate to reflect—

(a) any designation order; or

(b) the effect of subsection (3).

(6) A designation order may be made in anticipation of the making by the United Kingdom of a proposed derogation.

Reservations.

15.—(1) In this Act "designated reservation" means—

(a) the United Kingdom's reservation to Article 2 of the First Protocol to the Convention; and

(b) any other reservation by the United Kingdom to an Article of the Convention, or of any protocol to the Convention, which is designated for the purposes of this Act in an order made by the Secretary of State.

(2) The text of the reservation referred to in subsection (1)(a) is set out in Part II of Schedule 3.

(3) If a designated reservation is withdrawn wholly or in part it ceases to be a designated reservation.

(4) But subsection (3) does not prevent the Secretary of State from exercising his power under subsection (1)(b) to make a fresh designation order in respect of the Article concerned.

(5) The Secretary of State must by order make such amendments to this Act as he considers appropriate to reflect—

(a) any designation order; or

(b) the effect of subsection (3).

Period for which designated derogations have effect.

16.—(1) If it has not already been withdrawn by the United Kingdom, a designated derogation ceases to have effect for the purposes of this Act—

(a) in the case of the derogation referred to in section 14(1)(a), at the end of the period of five years beginning with the date on which section 1(2) came into force;

(b) in the case of any other derogation, at the end of the period of five years beginning with the date on which the order designating it was made.

(2) At any time before the period—

(a) fixed by subsection (1)(a) or (b), or

(b) extended by an order under this subsection,

comes to an end, the Secretary of State may by order extend it by a further period of five years.

(3) An order under section 14(1)(b) ceases to have effect at the end of the period for consideration, unless a resolution has been passed by each House approving the order.

(4) Subsection (3) does not affect—

    (a) anything done in reliance on the order; or

    (b) the power to make a fresh order under section 14(1)(b).

(5) In subsection (3) "period for consideration" means the period of forty days beginning with the day on which the order was made.

(6) In calculating the period for consideration, no account is to be taken of any time during which—

    (a) Parliament is dissolved or prorogued; or

    (b) both Houses are adjourned for more than four days.

(7) If a designated derogation is withdrawn by the United Kingdom, the Secretary of State must by order make such amendments to this Act as he considers are required to reflect that withdrawal.

17.—(1) The appropriate Minister must review the designated reservation referred to in section 15(1)(a)— *Periodic review of designated reservations.*

    (a) before the end of the period of five years beginning with the date on which section 1(2) came into force; and

    (b) if that designation is still in force, before the end of the period of five years beginning with the date on which the last report relating to it was laid under subsection (3).

(2) The appropriate Minister must review each of the other designated reservations (if any)—

    (a) before the end of the period of five years beginning with the date on which the order designating the reservation first came into force; and

    (b) if the designation is still in force, before the end of the period of five years beginning with the date on which the last report relating to it was laid under subsection (3).

(3) The Minister conducting a review under this section must prepare a report on the result of the review and lay a copy of it before each House of Parliament.

Judges of the European Court of Human Rights

18.—(1) In this section "judicial office" means the office of— *Appointment to European Court of Human Rights.*

    (a) Lord Justice of Appeal, Justice of the High Court or Circuit judge, in England and Wales;

    (b) judge of the Court of Session or sheriff, in Scotland;

(c) Lord Justice of Appeal, judge of the High Court or county court judge, in Northern Ireland.

(2) The holder of a judicial office may become a judge of the European Court of Human Rights ("the Court") without being required to relinquish his office.

(3) But he is not required to perform the duties of his judicial office while he is a judge of the Court.

(4) In respect of any period during which he is a judge of the Court—

(a) a Lord Justice of Appeal or Justice of the High Court is not to count as a judge of the relevant court for the purposes of section 2(1) or 4(1) of the Supreme Court Act 1981 (maximum number of judges) nor as a judge of the Supreme Court for the purposes of section 12(1) to (6) of that Act (salaries etc.);

1981 c. 54.

(b) a judge of the Court of Session is not to count as a judge of that court for the purposes of section 1(1) of the Court of Session Act 1988 (maximum number of judges) or of section 9(1)(c) of the Administration of Justice Act 1973 ("the 1973 Act") (salaries etc.);

1988 c. 36.
1973 c. 15.

(c) a Lord Justice of Appeal or judge of the High Court in Northern Ireland is not to count as a judge of the relevant court for the purposes of section 2(1) or 3(1) of the Judicature (Northern Ireland) Act 1978 (maximum number of judges) nor as a judge of the Supreme Court of Northern Ireland for the purposes of section 9(1)(d) of the 1973 Act (salaries etc.);

1978 c. 23.

(d) a Circuit judge is not to count as such for the purposes of section 18 of the Courts Act 1971 (salaries etc.);

1971 c. 23.

(e) a sheriff is not to count as such for the purposes of section 14 of the Sheriff Courts (Scotland) Act 1907 (salaries etc.);

1907 c. 51.

(f) a county court judge of Northern Ireland is not to count as such for the purposes of section 106 of the County Courts Act (Northern Ireland) 1959 (salaries etc.).

1959 c. 25 (N.I.).

(5) If a sheriff principal is appointed a judge of the Court, section 11(1) of the Sheriff Courts (Scotland) Act 1971 (temporary appointment of sheriff principal) applies, while he holds that appointment, as if his office is vacant.

1971 c. 58.

(6) Schedule 4 makes provision about judicial pensions in relation to the holder of a judicial office who serves as a judge of the Court.

(7) The Lord Chancellor or the Secretary of State may by order make such transitional provision (including, in particular, provision for a temporary increase in the maximum number of judges) as he considers appropriate in relation to any holder of a judicial office who has completed his service as a judge of the Court.

Parliamentary procedure

19.—(1) A Minister of the Crown in charge of a Bill in either House of Parliament must, before Second Reading of the Bill—

    (a) make a statement to the effect that in his view the provisions of the Bill are compatible with the Convention rights ("a statement of compatibility"); or

    (b) make a statement to the effect that although he is unable to make a statement of compatibility the government nevertheless wishes the House to proceed with the Bill.

(2) The statement must be in writing and be published in such manner as the Minister making it considers appropriate.

Statements of compatibility.

Supplemental

20.—(1) Any power of a Minister of the Crown to make an order under this Act is exercisable by statutory instrument.

(2) The power of the Lord Chancellor or the Secretary of State to make rules (other than rules of court) under section 2(3) or 7(9) is exercisable by statutory instrument.

(3) Any statutory instrument made under section 14, 15 or 16(7) must be laid before Parliament.

(4) No order may be made by the Lord Chancellor or the Secretary of State under section 1(4), 7(11) or 16(2) unless a draft of the order has been laid before, and approved by, each House of Parliament.

(5) Any statutory instrument made under section 18(7) or Schedule 4, or to which subsection (2) applies, shall be subject to annulment in pursuance of a resolution of either House of Parliament.

(6) The power of a Northern Ireland department to make—

    (a) rules under section 2(3)(c) or 7(9)(c), or

    (b) an order under section 7(11),

is exercisable by statutory rule for the purposes of the Statutory Rules (Northern Ireland) Order 1979.

(7) Any rules made under section 2(3)(c) or 7(9)(c) shall be subject to negative resolution; and section 41(6) of the Interpretation Act (Northern Ireland) 1954 (meaning of "subject to negative resolution") shall apply as if the power to make the rules were conferred by an Act of the Northern Ireland Assembly.

(8) No order may be made by a Northern Ireland department under section 7(11) unless a draft of the order has been laid before, and approved by, the Northern Ireland Assembly.

Orders etc. under this Act.

S.I. 1979/1573 (N.I. 12).

1954 c. 33 (N.I.).

Interpretation, etc.
21.—(1) In this Act—

"amend" includes repeal and apply (with or without modifications);

"the appropriate Minister" means the Minister of the Crown having charge of the appropriate authorised government department (within the meaning of the Crown Proceedings Act 1947);

1947 c. 44.

"the Commission" means the European Commission of Human Rights;

"the Convention" means the Convention for the Protection of Human Rights and Fundamental Freedoms, agreed by the Council of Europe at Rome on 4th November 1950 as it has effect for the time being in relation to the United Kingdom;

"declaration of incompatibility" means a declaration under section 4;

1975 c. 26.

"Minister of the Crown" has the same meaning as in the Ministers of the Crown Act 1975;

"Northern Ireland Minister" includes the First Minister and the deputy First Minister in Northern Ireland;

"primary legislation" means any—

(a) public general Act;

(b) local and personal Act;

(c) private Act;

(d) Measure of the Church Assembly;

(e) Measure of the General Synod of the Church of England;

(f) Order in Council—

(i) made in exercise of Her Majesty's Royal Prerogative;

1973 c. 36.

(ii) made under section 38(1)(a) of the Northern Ireland Constitution Act 1973 or the corresponding provision of the Northern Ireland Act 1998; or

(iii) amending an Act of a kind mentioned in paragraph (a), (b) or (c);

and includes an order or other instrument made under primary legislation (otherwise than by the National Assembly for Wales, a member of the Scottish Executive, a Northern Ireland Minister or a Northern Ireland department) to the extent to which it operates to bring one or more provisions of that legislation into force or amends any primary legislation;

"the First Protocol" means the protocol to the Convention agreed at Paris on 20th March 1952;

"the Sixth Protocol" means the protocol to the Convention agreed at Strasbourg on 28th April 1983;

"the Eleventh Protocol" means the protocol to the Convention (restructuring the control machinery established by the Convention) agreed at Strasbourg on 11th May 1994;

"remedial order" means an order under section 10;

"subordinate legislation" means any—

(a) Order in Council other than one—

    (i) made in exercise of Her Majesty's Royal Prerogative;

    (ii) made under section 38(1)(a) of the Northern Ireland Constitution Act 1973 or the corresponding provision of the Northern Ireland Act 1998; or

    (iii) amending an Act of a kind mentioned in the definition of primary legislation;

(b) Act of the Scottish Parliament;

(c) Act of the Parliament of Northern Ireland;

(d) Measure of the Assembly established under section 1 of the Northern Ireland Assembly Act 1973;

                                          1973 c. 17.

(e) Act of the Northern Ireland Assembly;

(f) order, rules, regulations, scheme, warrant, byelaw or other instrument made under primary legislation (except to the extent to which it operates to bring one or more provisions of that legislation into force or amends any primary legislation);

(g) order, rules, regulations, scheme, warrant, byelaw or other instrument made under legislation mentioned in paragraph (b), (c), (d) or (e) or made under an Order in Council applying only to Northern Ireland;

(h) order, rules, regulations, scheme, warrant, byelaw or other instrument made by a member of the Scottish Executive, a Northern Ireland Minister or a Northern Ireland department in exercise of prerogative or other executive functions of Her Majesty which are exercisable by such a person on behalf of Her Majesty;

"transferred matters" has the same meaning as in the Northern Ireland Act 1998; and

"tribunal" means any tribunal in which legal proceedings may be brought.

(2) The references in paragraphs (b) and (c) of section 2(1) to Articles are to Articles of the Convention as they had effect immediately before the coming into force of the Eleventh Protocol.

(3) The reference in paragraph (d) of section 2(1) to Article 46 includes a reference to Articles 32 and 54 of the Convention as they had effect immediately before the coming into force of the Eleventh Protocol.

(4) The references in section 2(1) to a report or decision of the Commission or a decision of the Committee of Ministers include references to a report or decision made as provided by paragraphs 3, 4 and 6 of Article 5 of the Eleventh Protocol (transitional provisions).

1955 c. 18.
1955 c. 19.
1957 c. 53.

(5) Any liability under the Army Act 1955, the Air Force Act 1955 or the Naval Discipline Act 1957 to suffer death for an offence is replaced by a liability to imprisonment for life or any less punishment authorised by those Acts; and those Acts shall accordingly have effect with the necessary modifications.

Short title, commencement, application and extent.

22.—(1) This Act may be cited as the Human Rights Act 1998.

(2) Sections 18, 20 and 21(5) and this section come into force on the passing of this Act.

(3) The other provisions of this Act come into force on such day as the Secretary of State may by order appoint; and different days may be appointed for different purposes.

(4) Paragraph (b) of subsection (1) of section 7 applies to proceedings brought by or at the instigation of a public authority whenever the act in question took place; but otherwise that subsection does not apply to an act taking place before the coming into force of that section.

(5) This Act binds the Crown.

(6) This Act extends to Northern Ireland.

(7) Section 21(5), so far as it relates to any provision contained in the Army Act 1955, the Air Force Act 1955 or the Naval Discipline Act 1957, extends to any place to which that provision extends.

1955 c. 18.
1955 c. 19.
1957 c. 53.

SCHEDULES

Section 1(3).

SCHEDULE 1

THE ARTICLES

PART I

THE CONVENTION

RIGHTS AND FREEDOMS

Article 2

Right to life

1. Everyone's right to life shall be protected by law. No one shall be deprived of his life intentionally save in the execution of a sentence of a court following his conviction of a crime for which this penalty is provided by law.

2. Deprivation of life shall not be regarded as inflicted in contravention of this Article when it results from the use of force which is no more than absolutely necessary:

(a) in defence of any person from unlawful violence;

(b) in order to effect a lawful arrest or to prevent the escape of a person lawfully detained;

(c) in action lawfully taken for the purpose of quelling a riot or insurrection.

Article 3

Prohibition of torture

No one shall be subjected to torture or to inhuman or degrading treatment or punishment.

Article 4

Prohibition of slavery and forced labour

1. No one shall be held in slavery or servitude.

2. No one shall be required to perform forced or compulsory labour.

3. For the purpose of this Article the term "forced or compulsory labour" shall not include:

(a) any work required to be done in the ordinary course of detention imposed according to the provisions of Article 5 of this Convention or during conditional release from such detention;

(b) any service of a military character or, in case of conscientious objectors in countries where they are recognised, service exacted instead of compulsory military service;

(c) any service exacted in case of an emergency or calamity threatening the life or well-being of the community;

(d) any work or service which forms part of normal civic obligations.

Article 5

Right to liberty and security

1. Everyone has the right to liberty and security of person. No one shall be deprived of his liberty save in the following cases and in accordance with a procedure prescribed by law:

(a) the lawful detention of a person after conviction by a competent court;

(b) the lawful arrest or detention of a person for non-compliance with the lawful order of a court or in order to secure the fulfilment of any obligation prescribed by law;

(c) the lawful arrest or detention of a person effected for the purpose of bringing him before the competent legal authority on reasonable suspicion of having committed an offence or when it is reasonably considered necessary to prevent his committing an offence or fleeing after having done so;

(d) the detention of a minor by lawful order for the purpose of educational supervision or his lawful detention for the purpose of bringing him before the competent legal authority;

(e) the lawful detention of persons for the prevention of the spreading of infectious diseases, of persons of unsound mind, alcoholics or drug addicts or vagrants;

(f) the lawful arrest or detention of a person to prevent his effecting an unauthorised entry into the country or of a person against whom action is being taken with a view to deportation or extradition.

2. Everyone who is arrested shall be informed promptly, in a language which he understands, of the reasons for his arrest and of any charge against him.

3. Everyone arrested or detained in accordance with the provisions of paragraph 1(c) of this Article shall be brought promptly before a judge or other officer authorised by law to exercise judicial power and shall be entitled to trial within a reasonable time or to release pending trial. Release may be conditioned by guarantees to appear for trial.

4. Everyone who is deprived of his liberty by arrest or detention shall be entitled to take proceedings by which the lawfulness of his detention shall be decided speedily by a court and his release ordered if the detention is not lawful.

5. Everyone who has been the victim of arrest or detention in contravention of the provisions of this Article shall have an enforceable right to compensation.

Article 6

Right to a fair trial

1. In the determination of his civil rights and obligations or of any criminal charge against him, everyone is entitled to a fair and public hearing within a reasonable time by an independent and impartial tribunal established by law. Judgment shall be pronounced publicly but the press and public may be excluded from all or part of the trial in the interest of morals, public order or national security in a democratic society, where the interests of juveniles or the protection of the private life of the parties so require, or to the extent strictly necessary in the

opinion of the court in special circumstances where publicity would prejudice the interests of justice.

2. Everyone charged with a criminal offence shall be presumed innocent until proved guilty according to law.

3. Everyone charged with a criminal offence has the following minimum rights:

    (a) to be informed promptly, in a language which he understands and in detail, of the nature and cause of the accusation against him;

    (b) to have adequate time and facilities for the preparation of his defence;

    (c) to defend himself in person or through legal assistance of his own choosing or, if he has not sufficient means to pay for legal assistance, to be given it free when the interests of justice so require;

    (d) to examine or have examined witnesses against him and to obtain the attendance and examination of witnesses on his behalf under the same conditions as witnesses against him;

    (e) to have the free assistance of an interpreter if he cannot understand or speak the language used in court.

Article 7

No punishment without law

1. No one shall be held guilty of any criminal offence on account of any act or omission which did not constitute a criminal offence under national or international law at the time when it was committed. Nor shall a heavier penalty be imposed than the one that was applicable at the time the criminal offence was committed.

2. This Article shall not prejudice the trial and punishment of any person for any act or omission which, at the time when it was committed, was criminal according to the general principles of law recognised by civilised nations.

Article 8

Right to respect for private and family life

1. Everyone has the right to respect for his private and family life, his home and his correspondence.

2. There shall be no interference by a public authority with the exercise of this right except such as is in accordance with the law and is necessary in a democratic society in the interests of national security, public safety or the economic well-being of the country, for the prevention of disorder

or crime, for the protection of health or morals, or for the protection of the rights and freedoms of others.

Article 9

Freedom of thought, conscience and religion

1. Everyone has the right to freedom of thought, conscience and religion; this right includes freedom to change his religion or belief and freedom, either alone or in community with others and in public or private, to manifest his religion or belief, in worship, teaching, practice and observance.

2. Freedom to manifest one's religion or beliefs shall be subject only to such limitations as are prescribed by law and are necessary in a demo-cratic society in the interests of public safety, for the protection of public order, health or morals, or for the protection of the rights and freedoms of others.

Article 10

Freedom of expression

1. Everyone has the right to freedom of expression. This right shall include freedom to hold opinions and to receive and impart information and ideas without interference by public authority and regardless of frontiers. This Article shall not prevent States from requiring the licensing of broadcasting, television or cinema enterprises.

2. The exercise of these freedoms, since it carries with it duties and responsibilities, may be subject to such formalities, conditions, restrictions or penalties as are prescribed by law and are necessary in a democratic society, in the interests of national security, territorial integrity or public safety, for the prevention of disorder or crime, for the protection of health or morals, for the protection of the reputation or rights of others, for preventing the disclosure of information received in confidence, or for maintaining the authority and impartiality of the judiciary.

Article 11

Freedom of assembly and association

1. Everyone has the right to freedom of peaceful assembly and to freedom of association with others, including the right to form and to join trade unions for the protection of his interests.

2. No restrictions shall be placed on the exercise of these rights other than such as are prescribed by law and are necessary in a democratic society in the interests of national security or public safety, for the prevention of disorder or crime, for the protection of health or morals

or for the protection of the rights and freedoms of others. This Article shall not prevent the imposition of lawful restrictions on the exercise of these rights by members of the armed forces, of the police or of the administration of the State.

Article 12

Right to marry

Men and women of marriageable age have the right to marry and to found a family, according to the national laws governing the exercise of this right.

Article 14

Prohibition of discrimination

The enjoyment of the rights and freedoms set forth in this Convention shall be secured without discrimination on any ground such as sex, race, colour, language, religion, political or other opinion, national or social origin, association with a national minority, property, birth or other status.

Article 16

Restrictions on political activity of aliens

Nothing in Articles 10, 11 and 14 shall be regarded as preventing the High Contracting Parties from imposing restrictions on the political activity of aliens.

Article 17

Prohibition of abuse of rights

Nothing in this Convention may be interpreted as implying for any State, group or person any right to engage in any activity or perform any act aimed at the destruction of any of the rights and freedoms set forth herein or at their limitation to a greater extent than is provided for in the Convention.

Article 18

Limitation on use of restrictions on rights

The restrictions permitted under this Convention to the said rights and freedoms shall not be applied for any purpose other than those for which they have been prescribed.

PART II

THE FIRST PROTOCOL

Article 1

Protection of property

Every natural or legal person is entitled to the peaceful enjoyment of his possessions. No one shall be deprived of his possessions except in the public interest and subject to the conditions provided for by law and by the general principles of international law.

The preceding provisions shall not, however, in any way impair the right of a State to enforce such laws as it deems necessary to control the use of property in accordance with the general interest or to secure the payment of taxes or other contributions or penalties.

Article 2

Right to education

No person shall be denied the right to education. In the exercise of any functions which it assumes in relation to education and to teaching, the State shall respect the right of parents to ensure such education and teaching in conformity with their own religious and philosophical convictions.

Article 3

Right to free elections

The High Contracting Parties undertake to hold free elections at reasonable intervals by secret ballot, under conditions which will ensure the free expression of the opinion of the people in the choice of the legislature.

PART III

THE SIXTH PROTOCOL

Article 1

Abolition of the death penalty

The death penalty shall be abolished. No one shall be condemned to such penalty or executed.

Article 2

Death penalty in time of war

A State may make provision in its law for the death penalty in respect of acts committed in time of war or of imminent threat of war; such penalty shall be applied only in the instances laid down in the law and in accordance with its provisions. The State shall communicate to the Secretary General of the Council of Europe the relevant provisions of that law.

SCHEDULE 2

REMEDIAL ORDERS

Orders

1.—(1) A remedial order may—
- (a) contain such incidental, supplemental, consequential or transitional provision as the person making it considers appropriate;
- (b) be made so as to have effect from a date earlier than that on which it is made;
- (c) make provision for the delegation of specific functions;
- (d) make different provision for different cases.

(2) The power conferred by sub-paragraph (1)(a) includes—
- (a) power to amend primary legislation (including primary legislation other than that which contains the incompatible provision); and
- (b) power to amend or revoke subordinate legislation (including subordinate legislation other than that which contains the incompatible provision).

(3) A remedial order may be made so as to have the same extent as the legislation which it affects.

(4) No person is to be guilty of an offence solely as a result of the retrospective effect of a remedial order.

Procedure

2. No remedial order may be made unless—
- (a) a draft of the order has been approved by a resolution of each House of Parliament made after the end of the period of 60 days beginning with the day on which the draft was laid; or
- (b) it is declared in the order that it appears to the person making it that, because of the urgency of the matter, it is necessary to make the order without a draft being so approved.

Orders laid in draft

3.—(1) No draft may be laid under paragraph 2(a) unless—

(a) the person proposing to make the order has laid before Parliament a document which contains a draft of the proposed order and the required information; and

(b) the period of 60 days, beginning with the day on which the document required by this sub-paragraph was laid, has ended.

(2) If representations have been made during that period, the draft laid under paragraph 2(a) must be accompanied by a statement containing—

(a) a summary of the representations; and

(b) if, as a result of the representations, the proposed order has been changed, details of the changes.

Urgent cases

4.—(1) If a remedial order ("the original order") is made without being approved in draft, the person making it must lay it before Parliament, accompanied by the required information, after it is made.

(2) If representations have been made during the period of 60 days beginning with the day on which the original order was made, the person making it must (after the end of that period) lay before Parliament a statement containing—

(a) a summary of the representations; and

(b) if, as a result of the representations, he considers it appropriate to make changes to the original order, details of the changes.

(3) If sub-paragraph (2)(b) applies, the person making the statement must—

(a) make a further remedial order replacing the original order; and

(b) lay the replacement order before Parliament.

(4) If, at the end of the period of 120 days beginning with the day on which the original order was made, a resolution has not been passed by each House approving the original or replacement order, the order ceases to have effect (but without that affecting anything previously done under either order or the power to make a fresh remedial order).

Definitions

5. In this Schedule—

"representations" means representations about a remedial order (or proposed remedial order) made to the person making (or proposing to make) it and includes any relevant Parliamentary report or resolution; and "required information" means—

(a) an explanation of the incompatibility which the order (or proposed order) seeks to remove, including particulars of the relevant declaration, finding or order; and

(b) a statement of the reasons for proceeding under section 10 and for making an order in those terms.

Calculating periods

6. In calculating any period for the purposes of this Schedule, no account is to be taken of any time during which—

(a) Parliament is dissolved or prorogued; or

(b) both Houses are adjourned for more than four days.

SCHEDULE 3

DEROGATION AND RESERVATION

PART I

DEROGATION

The 1988 notification

The United Kingdom Permanent Representative to the Council of Europe presents his compliments to the Secretary General of the Council, and has the honour to convey the following information in order to ensure compliance with the obligations of Her Majesty's Government in the United Kingdom under Article 15(3) of the Convention for the Protection of Human Rights and Fundamental Freedoms signed at Rome on 4 November 1950.

There have been in the United Kingdom in recent years campaigns of organised terrorism connected with the affairs of Northern Ireland which have manifested themselves in activities which have included repeated murder, attempted murder, maiming, intimidation and violent civil disturbance and in bombing and fire raising which have resulted in death, injury and widespread destruction of property. As a result, a public emergency within the meaning of Article 15(1) of the Convention exists in the United Kingdom.

The Government found it necessary in 1974 to introduce and since then, in cases concerning persons reasonably suspected of involvement in terrorism connected with the affairs of Northern Ireland, or of certain offences under the legislation, who have been detained for 48 hours, to exercise powers enabling further detention without charge, for periods of up to five days, on the authority of the Secretary of State. These powers are at present to be found in Section 12 of the Prevention of Terrorism

(Temporary Provisions) Act 1984 Article 9 of the Prevention of Terrorism (Supplemental Temporary Provisions) Order 1984 and Article 10 of the Prevention of Terrorism (Supplemental Temporary Provisions) (Northern Ireland) Order 1984.

Section 12 of the Prevention of Terrorism (Temporary Provisions) Act 1984 provides for a person whom a constable has arrested on reasonable grounds of suspecting him to be guilty of an offence under Section 1, 9 or 10 of the Act, or to be or to have been involved in terrorism connected with the affairs of Northern Ireland, to be detained in right of the arrest for up to 48 hours and thereafter, where the Secretary of State extends the detention period, for up to a further five days. Section 12 substantially re-enacted Section 12 of the Prevention of Terrorism (Temporary Provisions) Act 1976 which in turn, substantially re-enacted Section 7 of the Prevention of Terrorism (Temporary Provisions) Act 1974.

Article 10 of the Prevention of Terrorism (Supplemental Temporary Provisions) (Northern Ireland) Order 1984 (SI 1984/417) and Article 9 of the Prevention of Terrorism (Supplemental Temporary Provisions) Order 1984 (SI 1984/418) were both made under Sections 13 and 14 of and Schedule 3 to the 1984 Act and substantially re-enacted powers of detention in Orders made under the 1974 and 1976 Acts. A person who is being examined under Article 4 of either Order on his arrival in, or on seeking to leave, Northern Ireland or Great Britain for the purpose of determining whether he is or has been involved in terrorism connected with the affairs of Northern Ireland, or whether there are grounds for suspecting that he has committed an offence under Section 9 of the 1984 Act, may be detained under Article 9 or 10, as appropriate, pending the conclusion of his examination. The period of this examination may exceed 12 hours if an examining officer has reasonable grounds for suspecting him to be or to have been involved in acts of terrorism connected with the affairs of Northern Ireland.

Where such a person is detained under the said Article 9 or 10 he may be detained for up to 48 hours on the authority of an examining officer and thereafter, where the Secretary of State extends the detention period, for up to a further five days.

In its judgment of 29 November 1988 in the Case of *Brogan and Others*, the European Court of Human Rights held that there had been a violation of Article 5(3) in respect of each of the applicants, all of whom had been detained under Section 12 of the 1984 Act. The Court held that even the shortest of the four periods of detention concerned namely four days and six hours fell outside the constraints as to time permitted by the first part of Article 5(3). In addition, the Court held that there had been a violation of Article 5(5) in the case of each applicant.

SCH. 3

Following this judgment, the Secretary of State for the Home Department informed Parliament on 6 December 1988 that, against the background of the terrorist campaign, and the over-riding need to bring terrorists to justice, the Government did not believe that the maximum period of detention should be reduced. He informed Parliament that the Government were examining the matter with a view to responding to the judgment. On 22 December 1988, the Secretary of State further informed Parliament that it remained the Government's wish, if it could be achieved, to find a judicial process under which extended detention might be reviewed and where appropriate authorised by a judge or other judicial officer. But a further period of reflection and consultation was necessary before the Government could bring forward a firm and final view.

Since the judgment of 29 November 1988 as well as previously, the Government have found it necessary to continue to exercise, in relation to terrorism connected with the affairs of Northern Ireland, the powers described above enabling further detention without charge for periods of up to 5 days, on the authority of the Secretary of State, to the extent strictly required by the exigencies of the situation to enable necessary enquiries and investigations properly to be completed in order to decide whether criminal proceedings should be instituted. To the extent that the exercise of these powers may be inconsistent with the obligations imposed by the Convention the Government has availed itself of the right of derogation conferred by Article 15(1) of the Convention and will continue to do so until further notice.

Dated 23 December 1988.

The 1989 notification

The United Kingdom Permanent Representative to the Council of Europe presents his compliments to the Secretary General of the Council, and has the honour to convey the following information.

In his communication to the Secretary General of 23 December 1988, reference was made to the introduction and exercise of certain powers under section 12 of the Prevention of Terrorism (Temporary Provisions) Act 1984, Article 9 of the Prevention of Terrorism (Supplemental Temporary Provisions) Order 1984 and Article 10 of the Prevention of Terrorism (Supplemental Temporary Provisions) (Northern Ireland) Order 1984.

These provisions have been replaced by section 14 of and paragraph 6 of Schedule 5 to the Prevention of Terrorism (Temporary Provisions) Act 1989 which make comparable provision. They came into force on 22 March 1989.

The United Kingdom Permanent Representative avails himself of this opportunity to renew to the Secretary General the assurance of his highest consideration.

23 March 1989.

Part II

Reservation

At the time of signing the present (First) Protocol, I declare that, in view of certain provisions of the Education Acts in the United Kingdom, the principle affirmed in the second sentence of Article 2 is accepted by the United Kingdom only so far as it is compatible with the provision of efficient instruction and training, and the avoidance of unreasonable public expenditure.

Dated 20 March 1952. Made by the United Kingdom Permanent Representative to the Council of Europe.

Section 18(6).

SCHEDULE 4

Judicial Pensions

Duty to make orders about pensions

1.—(1) The appropriate Minister must by order make provision with respect to pensions payable to or in respect of any holder of a judicial office who serves as an ECHR judge.

(2) A pensions order must include such provision as the Minister making it considers is necessary to secure that—

    (a) an ECHR judge who was, immediately before his appointment as an ECHR judge, a member of a judicial pension scheme is entitled to remain as a member of that scheme;

    (b) the terms on which he remains a member of the scheme are those which would have been applicable had he not been appointed as an ECHR judge; and

    (c) entitlement to benefits payable in accordance with the scheme continues to be determined as if, while serving as an ECHR judge, his salary was that which would (but for section 18(4)) have been payable to him in respect of his continuing service as the holder of his judicial office.

Contributions

2. A pensions order may, in particular, make provision—

    (a) for any contributions which are payable by a person who remains a member of a scheme as a result of the order, and which would otherwise be payable by deduction from his salary, to be made otherwise than by deduction from his salary as an ECHR judge; and

(b) for such contributions to be collected in such manner as may be determined by the administrators of the scheme.

Amendments of other enactments

3. A pensions order may amend any provision of, or made under, a pensions Act in such manner and to such extent as the Minister making the order considers necessary or expedient to ensure the proper administration of any scheme to which it relates.

Definitions

4. In this Schedule—

"appropriate Minister" means—

(a) in relation to any judicial office whose jurisdiction is exercisable exclusively in relation to Scotland, the Secretary of State; and

(b) otherwise, the Lord Chancellor;

"ECHR judge" means the holder of a judicial office who is serving as a judge of the Court;

"judicial pension scheme" means a scheme established by and in accordance with a pensions Act;

"pensions Act" means—

(a) the County Courts Act (Northern Ireland) 1959;   1959 c. 25 (N.I.).
(b) the Sheriffs' Pensions (Scotland) Act 1961;   1961 c. 42.
(c) the Judicial Pensions Act 1981; or   1981 c. 20.
(d) the Judicial Pensions and Retirement Act 1993: and   1993 c. 8.

"pensions order" means an order made under paragraph 1.

© Crown Copyright 1998

TEXT OF THE EUROPEAN CONVENTION FOR THE PROTECTION OF HUMAN RIGHTS AND FUNDAMENTAL FREEDOMS

The governments signatory hereto, members of the Council of Europe,

Considering the Universal Declaration of Human Rights proclaimed by the General Assembly of the United Nations on 10th December 1948;

Considering that this Declaration aims at securing the universal and effective recognition and observance of the Rights declared;

Considering that the aim of the Council of Europe is the achievement of greater unity between its members and that one of the methods by which that aim is to be pursued is the maintenance and further realisation of human rights and fundamental freedoms;

Reaffirming their profound belief in those fundamental freedoms which are the foundation of justice and peace in the world and are best maintained on the one hand by an effective political democracy and on the other by a common understanding and observance of the human rights upon which they depend;

Being resolved, as the governments of European countries which are like-minded and have a common heritage of political traditions, ideals, freedom and the rule of law, to take the first steps for the collective enforcement of certain of the rights stated in the Universal Declaration,

Have agreed as follows:

Article 1

Obligation to respect human rights

The High Contracting Parties shall secure to everyone within their jurisdiction the rights and freedoms defined in Section I of this Convention.

SECTION 1—RIGHTS AND FREEDOMS

Article 2

Right to life

1. Everyone's right to life shall be protected by law. No one shall be deprived of his life intentionally save in the execution of a sentence of a court following his conviction of a crime for which this penalty is provided by law.

2. Deprivation of life shall not be regarded as inflicted in contravention of this Article when it results from the use of force which is no more than absolutely necessary:

    (a) in defence of any person from unlawful violence;

    (b) in order to effect a lawful arrest or to prevent the escape of a person lawfully detained;

    (c) in action lawfully taken for the purpose of quelling a riot or insurrection.

Article 3

Prohibition of torture

No one shall be subjected to torture or to inhuman or degrading treatment or punishment.

Article 4

Prohibition of slavery and forced labour

1. No one shall be held in slavery or servitude.

2. No one shall be required to perform forced or compulsory labour.

3. For the purposes of this Article the term 'forced or compulsory labour' shall not include:

    (a) any work required to be done in the ordinary course of detention imposed according to the provisions of Article 5 of this Convention or during conditional release from such detention;

    (b) any service of a military character or, in the case of conscientious objectors in countries where they are recognised, service exacted instead of compulsory military service;

    (c) any service exacted in case of an emergency or calamity threatening the life or well-being of the community;

    (d) any work or service which forms part of normal civic obligations.

Article 5

Right to liberty and security

1. Everyone has the right to liberty and security of the person. No one shall be deprived of his liberty save in the following cases and in accordance with a procedure prescribed by law:

(a) the lawful detention of a person after conviction by a competent court;

(b) the lawful arrest or detention of a person for non-compliance with the lawful order of a court or in order to secure the fulfilment of any obligation prescribed by law;

(c) the lawful arrest or detention of a person effected for the purpose of bringing him before the competent legal authority on reasonable suspicion of having committed an offence or when it is reasonably considered necessary to prevent his committing an offence or fleeing after having done so;

(d) the detention of a minor by lawful order for the purpose of educational supervision or his lawful detention for the purpose of bringing him before the competent legal authority;

(e) the lawful detention of persons for the prevention of the spreading of infectious diseases, of persons of unsound mind, alcoholics or drug addicts or vagrants;

(f) the lawful arrest or detention of a person to prevent his effecting an unauthorised entry into the country or of a person against whom action is being taken with a view to deportation or extradition.

2. Everyone who is arrested shall be informed promptly, in a language which he understands, of the reasons for his arrest and of any charge against him.

3. Everyone arrested or detained in accordance with the provisions of paragraph (1)(c) of this Article shall be brought promptly before a judge or other officer authorised by law to exercise judicial power and shall be entitled to trial within a reasonable time or to release pending trial. Release may be conditioned by guarantees to appear for trial.

4. Everyone who is deprived of his liberty by arrest or detention shall be entitled to take proceedings by which the lawfulness of his detention shall be decided speedily by a court and his release ordered if the detention is not lawful.

5. Everyone who has been the victim of arrest or detention in contravention of the provisions of this Article shall have an enforceable right to compensation.

Article 6

Right to a fair trial

1. In the determination of his civil rights and obligations or of any criminal charge against him, everyone is entitled to a fair and public hearing within a reasonable time by an independent and impartial tribunal established by law. Judgment shall be pronounced publicly but the press and public may be excluded from all or part of the trial in the

interests of morals, public order or national security in a democratic society, where the interests of juveniles or the protection of the private life of the parties so require, or to the extent strictly necessary in the opinion of the court in special circumstances where publicity would prejudice the interests of justice.

2. Everyone charged with a criminal offence shall be presumed innocent until proved guilty according to law.

3. Everyone charged with a criminal offence has the following minimum rights:

    (a) to be informed promptly, in a language which he understands and in detail, of the nature and cause of the accusation against him;

    (b) to have adequate time and facilities for the preparation of his defence;

    (c) to defend himself in person or through legal assistance of his own choosing or, if he has not sufficient means to pay for legal assistance, to be given it free when the interests of justice so require;

    (d) to examine or have examined witnesses against him and to obtain the attendance and examination of witnesses on his behalf under the same conditions as witnesses against him;

    (e) to have the free assistance of an interpreter if he cannot understand or speak the language used in court.

Article 7

No punishment without law

1. No one shall be held guilty of any criminal offence on account of any act or omission which did not constitute a criminal offence under national or international law at the time when it was committed. Nor shall a heavier penalty be imposed than the one that was applicable at the time the criminal offence was committed.

2. This Article shall not prejudice the trial and punishment of any person for any act or omission which, at the time when it was committed, was criminal according to the general principles of law recognised by civilised nations.

Article 8

Right to respect for private and family life

1. Everyone has the right to respect for his private and family life, his home and his correspondence.

2. There shall be no interference by a public authority with the exercise of this right except such as is in accordance with the law and is necessary in a democratic society in the interests of national security, public safety or

the economic well-being of the country, for the prevention of disorder or crime, for the protection of health or morals, or for the protection of the rights and freedoms of others.

Article 9

Freedom of thought, conscience and religion

1. Everyone has the right to freedom of thought, conscience and religion; this right includes freedom to change his religion or belief and freedom, either alone or in community with others and in public or private, to manifest his religion or belief, in worship, teaching, practice and observance.

2. Freedom to manifest one's religion or beliefs shall be subject only to such limitations as are prescribed by law and are necessary in a democratic society in the interests of public safety, for the protection of public order, health or morals, or for the protection of the rights and freedoms of others.

Article 10

Freedom of expression

1. Everyone has the right to freedom of expression. This right shall include freedom to hold opinions and to receive and impart information and ideas without interference by public authority and regardless of frontiers. This Article shall not prevent States from requiring the licensing of broadcasting, television or cinema enterprises.

2. The exercise of these freedoms, since it carries with it duties and responsibilities, may be subject to such formalities, conditions, restrictions or penalties as are prescribed by law and are necessary in a democratic society, in the interests of national security, territorial integrity or public safety, for the prevention of disorder or crime, for the protection of health or morals, for the protection of the reputation or rights of others, for preventing the disclosure of information received in confidence, or for maintaining the authority and impartiality of the judiciary.

Article 11

Freedom of assembly and association

1. Everyone has the right to freedom of peaceful assembly and to freedom of association with others, including the right to form and to join trade unions for the protection of his interests.

2. No restrictions shall be placed on the exercise of these rights other than such as are prescribed by law and are necessary in a democratic society in the interests of national security or public safety, for the protection of health or morals or for the protection of the rights and freedoms of others. This Article shall not prevent the imposition of lawful restrictions on the exercise of these rights by members of the armed forces, of the police or of the administration of the State.

Article 12

Right to marry

Men and women of marriageable age have the right to marry and to found a family, according to the national laws governing the exercise of this right.

Article 13

Right to an effective remedy

Everyone whose rights and freedoms as set forth in this Convention are violated shall have an effective remedy before a national authority notwithstanding that the violation has been committed by persons acting in an official capacity.

Article 14

Prohibition of discrimination

The enjoyment of the rights and freedoms set forth in this Convention shall be secured without discrimination on any ground such as sex, race, colour, language, religion, political or other opinion, national or social origin, association with a national minority, property, birth or other status.

Article 15

Derogation in time of emergency

1. In time of war or other public emergency threatening the life of the nation any High Contracting Party may take measures derogating from its obligations under this Convention to the extent strictly required by the exigencies of the situation, provided that such measures are not inconsistent with its other obligations under international law.

2. No derogation from Article 2, except in respect of deaths resulting from lawful acts of war, or from Articles 3, 4 (paragraph 1) and 7 shall be made under this provision.

3. Any High Contracting Party availing itself of this right of derogation shall keep the Secretary General of the Council of Europe fully informed of the measures which it has taken and the reasons therefor. It shall also inform the Secretary General of the Council of Europe when such measures have ceased to operate and the provisions of the Convention are again being fully executed.

Article 16

Restriction on political activity of aliens

Nothing in Articles 10, 11 and 14 shall be regarded as preventing the High Contracting Parties from imposing restrictions on the political activities of aliens.

Article 17

Prohibition of abuse of rights

Nothing in this Convention may be interpreted as implying for any State, group or person any right to engage in any activity or perform any act aimed at the destruction of any of the rights and freedoms set forth herein or at their limitation to a greater extent than is provided for in the Convention.

Article 18

Limitation on use of restrictions on rights

The restrictions permitted under this Convention to the said rights and freedoms shall not be applied for any purpose other than those for which they have been prescribed.

SECTION II—EUROPEAN COURT OF HUMAN RIGHTS

Article 19
Establishment of the Court

To ensure the observance of the engagements undertaken by the High Contracting Parties in the Convention and the protocols thereto, there shall be set up a European Court of Human Rights, hereinafter referred to as 'the Court'. It shall function on a permanent basis.

Article 20

Number of judges

The Court shall consist of a number of judges equal to that of the High Contracting Parties.

Article 21

Criteria for office

1. The judges shall be of high moral character and must either possess the qualifications required for appointment to high judicial office or be jurisconsults of recognised competence.

2. The judges shall sit on the Court in their individual capacity.

3. During their term of office the judges shall not engage in any activity which is incompatible with their independence, impartiality or with the demands of a full-time office; all questions arising from the application of this paragraph shall be decided by the Court.

Article 22

Election of judges

1. The judges shall be elected by the Parliamentary Assembly with respect to each High Contracting Party by a majority of votes cast from a list of three candidates nominated by the High Contracting Party.

2. The same procedure shall be followed to complete the Court in the event of the accession of new High Contracting Parties and in filling casual vacancies.

Article 23

Terms of office

1. The judges shall be elected for a period of six years. They may be re-elected. However, the terms of office of one-half of the judges elected at the first election shall expire at the end of three years.

2. The judges whose terms of office are to expire at the end of the initial period of three years shall be chosen by lot by the Secretary General of the Council of Europe immediately after their election.

3. In order to ensure that, as far as possible, the terms of office of one-half of the judges are renewed every three years, the Parliamentary Assembly may decide, before proceeding to any subsequent election, that the term or terms of office of one or more judges to be elected shall be for a period other than six years but not more than nine and not less than three years.

4. In cases where more than one term of office is involved and where the Parliamentary Assembly applies the preceding paragraph, the allocation of the terms of office shall be effected by a drawing of lots by the Secretary General of the Council of Europe immediately after the election.

5. A judge elected to replace a judge whose term of office has not expired shall hold office for the remainder of his predecessor's term.

6. The terms of office of judges shall expire when they reach the age of 70.

7. The judges shall hold office until replaced. They shall, however, continue to deal with such cases as they already have under consideration.

Article 24

Dismissal

No judge may be dismissed from his office unless the other judges decide by a majority of two-thirds that he has ceased to fulfil the required conditions.

Article 25

Registry and legal secretaries

The Court shall have a registry, the functions and organisation of which shall be laid down in the rules of the Court. The Court shall be assisted by legal secretaries.

Article 26

Plenary Court

The Plenary Court shall:
(a) elect its President and one or two Vice-Presidents for a period of three years; they may be re-elected;
(b) set up Chambers, constituted for a fixed period of time;
(c) elect the Presidents of the Chambers of the Court; they may be re-elected;
(d) adopt the rules of the Court; and
(e) elect the Registrar and one or more Deputy Registrars.

Article 27

Committees, Chambers and Grand Chamber

1. To consider cases brought before it, the Court shall sit in committees

of three judges, in Chambers of seven judges and in a Grand Chamber of seventeen judges. The Court's Chambers shall set up committees for a fixed period of time.

2. There shall sit as an *ex officio* member of the Chamber and the Grand Chamber the judge elected in respect of the State Party concerned or, if there is none or if he is unable to sit, a person of its choice who shall sit in the capacity of judge.

3. The Grand Chamber shall also include the President of the Court, the Vice-Presidents, the Presidents of the Chambers and other judges chosen in accordance with the rules of the Court. When a case is referred to the Grand Chamber under Article 43, no judge from the Chamber which rendered the judgment shall sit in the Grand Chamber, with the exception of the President of the Chamber and the judge who sat in respect of the State Party concerned.

Article 28

Declaration of inadmissibility by committees

A committee may, by a unanimous vote, declare inadmissible or strike out of its list of cases an individual application submitted under Article 34 where such a decision can be taken without further examination. The decision shall be final.

Article 29

Decisions by Chambers on admissibility and merits

1. If no decision is taken under Article 28, a Chamber shall decide on the admissibility and merits of individual applications submitted under Article 34.

2. A Chamber shall decide on the admissibility and merits of inter-State applications submitted under Article 33.

3. The decision on admissibility shall be taken separately unless the Court, in exceptional cases, decides otherwise.

Article 30

Relinquishment of jurisdiction to the Grand Chamber

Where a case pending before a Chamber raises a serious question affecting the interpretation of the Convention or the protocols thereto or where the resolution of a question before it might have a result inconsistent with a judgment previously delivered by the Court, the Chamber may, at any time before it has rendered its judgment, relinquish jurisdiction in favour of the Grand Chamber, unless one of the parties to the case objects.

Article 31

Powers of the Grand Chamber

The Grand Chamber shall
   (a) determine applications submitted either under Article 33 or Article 34 when a Chamber has relinquished jurisdiction under Article 30 or when the case has been referred to it under Article 43; and
   (b) consider requests for advisory opinions submitted under Article 47.

Article 32

Jurisdiction of the Court

1. The jurisdiction of the Court shall extend to all matters concerning the interpretation and application of the Convention and the protocols thereto which are referred to it as provided in Articles 33, 34 and 47.

2. In the event of dispute as to whether the Court has jurisdiction, the Court shall decide.

Article 33

Inter-State cases

Any High Contracting Party may refer to the Court any alleged breach of the provisions of the Convention and the protocols thereto by another High Contracting Party.

Article 34

Individual applications

The Court may receive applications from any person, non-govern-mental organisation or group of individuals claiming to be the victim of a violation by one of the High Contracting Parties of the rights set forth in the Convention and the protocols thereto. The High Contracting Parties undertake not to hinder in any way the effective exercise of this right.

Article 35

Admissibility criteria

1. The Court may only deal with the matter after all domestic remedies have been exhausted, according to the generally recognised

rules of international law, and within a period of six months from the date on which the final decision was taken.

2. The Court shall not deal with any individual application submitted under Article 34 that

(a) is anonymous; or

(b) is substantially the same as a matter that has already been examined by the Court or has already been submitted to another procedure of international investigation or settlement and contains no relevant new information.

3. The Court shall declare inadmissible any individual application submitted under Article 34 which it considers incompatible with the provisions of the Convention or the protocols thereto, manifestly ill-founded, or an abuse of the right of application.

4. The Court shall reject any application which it considers inadmissible under this Article. It may do so at any stage of the proceedings.

Article 36

Third-party intervention

1. In all cases before a Chamber or the Grand Chamber, a High Contracting Party one of whose nationals is an applicant shall have the right to submit written comments and to take part in the hearings.

2. The President of the Court may, in the interest of the proper administration of justice, invite any High Contracting Party which is not a party to the proceedings or any person concerned who is not the applicant to submit written comments or take part in the hearings.

Article 37

Striking out applications

1. The Court may at any stage of the proceedings decide to strike an application out of its list of cases where the circumstances lead to the conclusion that

(a) the applicant does not intend to pursue his application; or

(b) the matter has been resolved; or

(c) for any other reason established by the Court, it is no longer justified to continue the examination of the application.

However, the Court shall continue the examination of the application if respect for human rights as defined in the Convention and the protocols thereto so requires.

2. The Court may decide to restore an application to its list of cases if it considers that the circumstances justify such a course.

Article 38

Examination of the case and friendly settlement proceedings

1. If the Court declares the application admissible, it shall
(a) pursue the examination of the case, together with the representatives of the parties, and if need be, undertake an investigation, for the effective conduct of which the States concerned shall furnish all necessary facilities;
(b) place itself at the disposal of the parties concerned with a view to securing a friendly settlement of the matter on the basis of respect for human rights as defined in the Convention and the protocols thereto.
2. Proceedings conducted under paragraph 1(b) shall be confidential.

Article 39

Finding of a friendly settlement

If a friendly settlement is effected, the Court shall strike the case out of its list by means of a decision which shall be confined to a brief statement of the facts and the solution reached.

Article 40

Public hearings and access to documents

1. Hearings shall be public unless the Court in exceptional circumstances decides otherwise.
2. Documents deposited with the Registrar shall be accessible to the public unless the President of the Court decides otherwise.

Article 41

Just satisfaction

If the Court finds that there has been a violation of the Convention or the protocols thereto, and if the internal law of the High Contracting Party concerned allows only partial reparation to be made, the Court shall, if necessary afford just satisfaction to the injured party.

Article 42

Judgments of Chambers

Judgments of Chambers shall become final in accordance with the provisions of Article 44, paragraph 2.

Article 43

Referral to the Grand Chamber

1. Within a period of three months from the date of the judgment of the Chamber, any party to the case may, in exceptional cases, request that the case be referred to the Grand Chamber.

2. A panel of five judges of the Grand Chamber shall accept the request if the case raises a serious question affecting the interpretation or application of the Convention or the protocols thereto, or a serious issue of general importance.

If the panel accepts the request, the Grand Chamber shall decide the case by means of a judgment.

Article 44

Final judgments

1. The judgment of the Grand Chamber shall be final.
2. The judgment of a Chamber shall become final
(a) when the parties declare that they will not request that the case be referred to the Grand Chamber; or
(b) three months after the date of the judgment, if reference of the case to the Grand Chamber has not been requested; or
(c) when the panel of the Grand Chamber rejects the request to refer under Article 43.
3. The final judgment shall be published.

Article 45

Reasons for judgments and decisions

1. Reasons shall be given for judgments as well as for decisions declaring applications admissible or inadmissible.

2. If a judgment does not represent, in whole or in part, the unanimous opinion of the judges, any judge shall be entitled to deliver a separate opinion.

Article 46

Binding force and execution of judgments

1. The High Contracting Parties undertake to abide by the final judgment of the Court in any case where they are parties.

2. The final judgment of the Court shall be transmitted to the Committee of Ministers, which shall supervise its execution.

Article 47

Advisory opinions

1. The Court may, at the request of the Committee of Ministers, give advisory opinions on legal questions concerning the interpretation of the Convention and the protocols thereto.

2. Such opinions shall not deal with any question relating to the content or scope of the rights or freedoms defined in Section I of the Convention and the protocols thereto, or with any other question which the Court or the Committee of Ministers might have to consider in consequence of any such proceedings as could be instituted in accordance with the Convention.

3. Decisions of the Committee of Ministers to request an advisory opinion of Court shall require a majority vote of the representatives entitled to sit on the Committee.

Article 48

Advisory Jurisdiction of the Court

The Court shall decide whether a request for an advisory opinion submitted by the Committee of Ministers is within its competence as defined in Article 47.

Article 49

Reasons for advisory opinions

1. Reasons shall be given for advisory opinions of the Court.

2. If the advisory opinion does not represent, in whole or in part, the unanimous opinion of the judges, any judge shall be entitled to deliver a separate opinion.

3. Advisory opinions of the Court shall be communicated to the Committee of Ministers.

Article 50

Expenditure on the Court

The expenditure on the Court shall be borne by the Council of Europe.

Article 51

Privileges and immunities of judges

The judges shall be entitled, during the exercise of their functions, to the privileges and immunities provided for in Article 40 of the Statute of the Council of Europe and in the agreements made thereunder.

SECTION III—MISCELLANEOUS PROVISIONS

Article 52

Enquiries by the Secretary General

On receipt of a request from the Secretary General of the Council of Europe any Contracting Party shall furnish an explanation of the manner in which its internal law ensures the effective implementation of any of the provisions of the Convention.

Article 53

Safeguard for existing human rights

Nothing in this Convention shall be construed as limiting or derogating from any of the human rights and fundamental freedoms which may be ensured under the laws of any High Contracting Party or under any other agreement to which it is a Party.

Article 54

Powers of the Committee of Ministers

Nothing in this Convention shall prejudice the powers conferred on the Committee of Ministers by the Statute of the Council of Europe.

Article 55

Exclusion of other means of dispute settlement

The High Contracting Parties agree that, except by special agreement, they will not avail themselves of treaties, conventions or declarations in force between them for the purpose of submitting, by way of petition, a dispute arising out of the interpretation or application of this Convention to a means of settlement other than those provided for in this Convention.

Article 56

Territorial application

1. Any State may at the time of its ratification or at any time thereafter declare by notification addressed to the Secretary General of the Council of Europe that the present Convention shall, subject to paragraph 4 of this

Article, extend to all or any of the territories for whose international relations it is responsible.

2. The Convention shall extend to the territory or territories named in the notification as from the thirtieth day after the receipt or this notification by the Secretary General of the Council of Europe.

3. The provisions of this Convention shall be applied in such territories with due regard, however, to local requirements.

4. Any State which has made a declaration in accordance with paragraph 1 of this Article may at any time thereafter declare on behalf of one or more of the territories to which the declaration relates that it accepts the competence of the Court to receive applications from individuals, non-governmental organisations or groups of individuals as provided in Article 34 of the Convention.

Article 57

Reservations

1. Any State may, when signing this Convention or when depositing its instrument of ratification, make a reservation in respect of any particular provision of the Convention to the extent that any law then in force in its territory is not in conformity with the provision. Reservations of a general character shall not be permitted under this Article.

2. Any reservation made under this Article shall contain a brief statement of the law concerned.

Article 58

Denunciation

1. A High Contracting Party may denounce the present Convention only after the expiry of five years from the date on which it became a party to it and after six months' notice contained in a notification addressed to the Secretary General of the Council of Europe, who shall inform the other High Contracting Parties.

2. Such a denunciation shall not have the effect of releasing the High Contracting Party concerned from its obligations under this Convention in respect of any act which, being capable of constituting a violation of such obligations, may have been performed by it before the date at which the denunciation became effective.

3. Any High Contracting Party which shall cease to be a member of the Council of Europe shall cease to be a Party to this Convention under the same conditions.

4. The Convention may be denounced in accordance with the

provisions of the preceding paragraphs in respect of any territory to which it has been declared to extend under the terms of Article 56.

Article 59

Signature and ratification

1. This Convention shall be open to the signature of the members of the Council of Europe. It shall be ratified. Ratifications shall be deposited with the Secretary General of the Council of Europe.

2. The present Convention shall come into force after the deposit of ten instruments of ratification.

3. As regards any signatory ratifying subsequently, the Convention shall come into force at the date of the deposit of its instrument of ratification.

4. The Secretary General of the Council of Europe shall notify all the members of the Council of Europe of the entry into force of the Convention, the names of the High Contracting Parties who have ratified it, and the deposit of all instruments of ratification which may be effected subsequently.

Done at Rome this 4th day of November 1950, in English and French, both texts being equally authentic, in a single copy which shall remain deposited in the archives of the Council of Europe. The Secretary General shall transmit certified copies to each of the signatories.

Protocol No. 1

The governments signatory hereto, being members of the Council of Europe.

Being resolved to take steps to ensure the collective enforcement of certain rights and freedoms other than those already included in Section I of the Convention for the Protection of Human Rights and Fundamental Freedoms signed at Rome on 4 November 1950 (hereinafter referred to as 'the Convention'),

Have agreed as follows:

Article 1

Protection of property

Every natural or legal Person is entitled to the peaceful enjoyment of his possessions. No one shall be deprived of his possessions except in the public interest and subject to the conditions provided for by law and by the general principles of international law.

The preceding provisions shall not, however, in any way impair the right of a State to enforce such laws as it deems necessary to control the use of property in accordance with the general interest or to secure the payment of taxes or other contributions or penalties.

Article 2

Right to education

No person shall be denied the right to education. In the exercise of any functions which it assumes in relation to education and to teaching, the State shall respect the right of parents to ensure such education and teaching in conformity with their own religious and philosophical convictions.

Article 3

Right to free elections

The High Contracting Parties undertake to hold free elections at reasonable intervals by secret ballot, under conditions which will ensure the free expression of the opinion of the people in the choice of the legislature.

Article 4

Territorial application

Any High Contracting Party may at the time of signature or ratification or at any time thereafter communicate to the Secretary General of the Council of Europe a declaration stating the extent to which it undertakes that the provisions of the present Protocol shall apply to such of the territories for the international relations of which it is responsible as are named therein.

Any High Contracting Party which has communicated a declaration in virtue of the preceding paragraph may from time to time communicate a further declaration modifying the terms of any former declaration or terminating the application of the provisions of this Protocol in respect of any territory.

A declaration made in accordance with this Article shall be deemed to have been made in accordance with paragraph 1 of Article 56 of the Convention.

Article 5

Relationship to the Convention

As between the High Contracting Parties the provisions of Articles 1, 2, 3 and 4 of this Protocol shall be regarded as additional articles to the Convention and all the provisions of the Convention shall apply accordingly.

Article 6

Signature and ratification

This Protocol shall be open for signature by the members of the Council of Europe, who are the signatories of the Convention; it shall be ratified at the same time as or after the ratification of the Convention. It shall enter into force after the deposit of ten instruments of ratification. As regards any signatory ratifying subsequently, the Protocol shall enter into force at the date of the deposit of its instrument of ratification.

The instruments of ratification shall be deposited with the Secretary General of the Council of Europe, who will notify all members of the names of those who have ratified.

Done at Paris on the 20th day of March 1952, in English and French, both texts being equally authentic, in a single copy which shall remain deposited in the archives of the Council of Europe. The Secretary General shall transmit a certified copy to each of the signatory governments.

[Protocol No. 2 becomes otiose, since the provisions on the Court's competence to give advisory opinions is incorporated in Articles 47 to 49 of the Convention.]

[Protocol No. 3 has become otiose; it modified the procedure of the Commission by abolishing the system of sub-commissions.]

Protocol No. 4 to the Convention for the Protection of Human Rights and Fundamental Freedoms securing certain Rights and Freedoms other than those already included in the Convention and in the First Protocol thereto

The governments signatory hereto, being members of the Council of Europe

Being resolved to take steps to ensure the collective enforcement of certain rights and freedoms other than those already included in Section I of the Convention for the Protection of Human Rights and Fundamental Freedoms signed at Rome on 4 November 1950 (hereinafter referred to as 'the Convention') and in Articles 1 to 3 of the First Protocol to the Convention, signed at Paris on 20 March 1952,

Have agreed as follows:

Article 1

Prohibition of imprisonment for debt

No one shall be deprived of his liberty merely on the ground of inability to fulfil a contractual obligation.

Article 2

Freedom of movement

1. Everyone lawfully within the territory of a State shall, within that territory, have the right to liberty of movement and freedom to choose his residence.

2. Everyone shall be free to leave any country, including his own.

3. No restrictions shall be placed on the exercise of these rights other than such as are in accordance with law and are necessary in a democratic society in the interests of national security or public safety, for the maintenance of the *ordre public*, for the prevention of crime, for the protection of health or morals, or for the protection of the rights and freedoms of others.

4. The rights set forth in paragraph 1 may also be subject, in particular areas, to restrictions imposed in accordance with law and justified by the public interest in a democratic society.

Article 3

Prohibition of expulsion of nationals

1. No one shall be expelled, by means either of an individual or of a collective measure, from the territory of the State of which he is a national.

2. No one shall be deprived of the right to enter the territory of the State of which he is a national.

Article 4

Prohibition of collective expulsion of aliens

Collective expulsion of aliens is prohibited.

Article 5

Territorial application

1. Any High Contracting Party may, at the time of signature or ratification of this protocol, or at any time thereafter, communicate to the Secretary General of the Council of Europe a declaration stating the extent to which it undertakes that the provisions of this Protocol shall apply to such of the territories for the international relations of which it is responsible as are named therein.

2. Any High Contracting Party which has communicated a declaration in virtue of the preceding paragraph may, from time to time, communicate a further declaration modifying the terms of any former declaration or terminating the application of the provisions of this Protocol in respect of any territory.

3. A declaration made in accordance with this Article shall be deemed to have been made in accordance with paragraph 1 of Article 56 of the Convention.

4. The territory of any State to which this Protocol applies by virtue of ratification or acceptance by that State, and each territory to which this Protocol is applied by virtue of a declaration by that State under this Article, shall be treated as separate territories for the purpose of the references in Articles 2 and 3 to the territory of a State.

5. Any State which has made a declaration in accordance with paragraph 1 or 2 of this Article may at any time thereafter declare on behalf of one or more of the territories to which the declaration relates that it accepts the competence of the Court to receive applications from individuals, non-governmental organisations or groups of individuals as provided in Article 34 of the Convention in respect of all or any of Articles 1 to 4 of this Protocol.

Article 6

Relationship to the Convention

As between the High Contracting Parties the provisions of Articles 1 to 5 of this Protocol shall be regarded as additional Articles to the Convention, and the provisions of the Convention shall apply accordingly.

Article 7

Signature and ratification

1. This Protocol shall be open for signature by the members of the Council of Europe who are signatories of the Convention; it shall be ratified at the same time as or after the ratification of the Convention. It shall enter into force after the deposit of five instruments of ratification. As regards any signatory ratifying subsequently, the Protocol shall enter into force at the date of the deposit of its instrument of ratification.

2. The instruments of ratification shall be deposited with the Secretary General of the Council of Europe, who will notify all members of the names of those who have ratified.

In witness whereof the undersigned, being duly authorised thereto, have signed this Protocol.

Done at Strasbourg, this 16th day of September 1963, in English and in French, both texts being equally authoritative, in a single copy which shall remain deposited in the archives of the Council of Europe. The Secretary General shall transmit certified copies to each of the signatories.

[Protocol No. 5 has become otiose; it concerned the procedure for the election of members of the Commission and Court.]

Protocol No. 6 to the Convention for the Protection of Human Rights and Fundamental Freedoms concerning the abolition of the death penalty

The member States of the Council of Europe, signatory to this Protocol to the Convention for the Protection of Human Rights and Fundamental Freedoms, signed at Rome on 4 November 1950 (hereinafter referred to as 'the Convention'),

Considering that the evolution that has occurred in several member States of the Council of Europe expresses a general tendency in favour of the abolition of the death penalty;

Have agreed as follows:

Article 1

Abolition of the death penalty

The death penalty shall be abolished. No one shall be condemned to such penalty or executed.

Article 2

Death penalty in time of war

A State may make provision in its law for the death penalty in respect of acts committed in time of war or of imminent threat of war; such penalty shall be applied only in the instances laid down in the law and in accordance with its provisions. The State shall communicate to the Secretary General of the Council of Europe the relevant provisions of that law.

Article 3

Prohibition of derogations

No derogation from the provisions of this Protocol shall be made under Article 15 of the Convention.

Article 4

Prohibition of reservations

No reservation may be made under Article 57 of the Convention in respect of the provisions of this Protocol.

Article 5

Territorial application

1. Any State may at the time of signature or when depositing its instrument of ratification, acceptance or approval, specify the territory or territories to which this Protocol shall apply.

2. Any State may at any later date, by a declaration addressed to the Secretary General of the Council of Europe, extend the application of this Protocol to any other territory specified in the declaration. In respect of such territory the Protocol shall enter into force on the first day of the month following the date of receipt of such declaration by the Secretary General.

3. Any declaration made under the two preceding paragraphs may, in respect of any territory specified in such declaration, be withdrawn by a notification addressed to the Secretary General. The withdrawal shall become effective on the first day of the month following the date of receipt of such notification by the Secretary General.

Article 6

Relationship to the Convention

As between the States Parties the provisions of Articles 1 to 5 of this Protocol shall be regarded as additional articles to the Convention and all the provisions of the Convention shall apply accordingly.

Article 7

Signature and ratification

The Protocol shall be open for signature by the member States of the Council of Europe, signatories to the Convention. It shall be subject to ratification, acceptance or approval. A member State of the Council of Europe may not ratify, accept or approve this Protocol unless it has, simultaneously or previously, ratified the Convention. Instruments of ratification, acceptance or approval shall be deposited with the Secretary General of the Council of Europe.

Article 8

Entry into force

1. This Protocol shall enter into force on the first day of the month following the date on which five member States of the Council of Europe have expressed their consent to be bound by the Protocol in accordance with the provisions of Article 7.

2. In respect of any member State which subsequently expresses its consent to be bound by it, the Protocol shall enter into force on the first day of the month following the date of the deposit of the instrument of ratification, acceptance or approval.

Article 9

Depositary functions

The Secretary General of the Council of Europe shall notify the member States of the Council of:
  (a) any signature;
  (b) the deposit of any instrument of ratification, acceptance or approval;
  (c) any date of entry into force of this Protocol in accordance with Articles 5 and 8;
  (d) any other act, notification or communication relating to this Protocol.

In witness whereof the undersigned, being duly authorised thereto, have signed this Protocol.

Done at Strasbourg, this 28th day of April 1983, in English and in French, both texts being equally authentic, in a single copy which shall be deposited in the archives of the Council of Europe. The Secretary General of the Council of Europe shall transmit certified copies to each member State of the Council of Europe.

Protocol No. 7 to the Convention for the Protection of Human Rights and Fundamental Freedoms

The member States of the Council of Europe signatory hereto,

Being resolved to ensure the collective enforcement of certain rights and freedoms by means of the Convention for the Protection of Human Rights and Fundamental Freedoms signed at Rome on 4 November 1950 (hereinafter referred to as 'the Convention'),

Have agreed as follows:

Article 1

Procedural safeguards relating to expulsion of aliens

1. An alien lawfully resident in the territory of a State shall not be expelled therefrom except in pursuance of a decision reached in accordance with law and shall be allowed:
    (a) to submit reasons against his expulsion;
    (b) to have his case reviewed; and
    (c) to be represented for these purposes before the competent authority or a person or persons designated by that authority.

2. An alien may be expelled before the exercise of his rights under paragraph 1 (a), (b) and (c) of this Article, when such expulsion is necessary in the interests of public order or is grounded on reasons of national security.

Article 2

Right of appeal in criminal matters

1. Everyone convicted of a criminal offence by a tribunal shall have the right to have his conviction or sentence reviewed by a higher tribunal. The exercise of this right, including the grounds on which it may be exercised, shall be governed by law.

2. This right may be subject to exceptions in regard to offences of a minor character, as prescribed by law, or in cases in which the person concerned was tried in the first instance by the highest tribunal or was convicted following an appeal against acquittal.

Article 3

Compensation for wrongful conviction

When a person has by a final decision been convicted of a criminal offence and when subsequently his conviction has been reversed, or he has been pardoned, on the ground that a new or newly discovered fact shows conclusively that there has been a miscarriage of justice, the person who has suffered punishment as a result of such conviction shall be compensated according to the law or the practice of the State concerned, unless it is proved that the non-disclosure of the unknown fact in time is wholly or partly attributable to him.

Article 4

Right not to be tried or punished twice

1. No one shall be liable to be tried or punished again in criminal proceedings under the jurisdiction of the same State for an offence for which he has already been finally acquitted or convicted in accordance with the law and penal procedure of that State.

2. The provisions of the preceding paragraph shall not prevent the reopening of the case in accordance with the law and penal procedure of the State concerned, if there is evidence of new or newly discovered facts, or if there has been a fundamental defect in the previous proceedings, which could affect the outcome of the case.

3. No derogation from this Article shall be made under Article 15 of the Convention.

Article 5

Equality between spouses

Spouses shall enjoy equality of rights and relationships of a private law character between them, and in their relations with their children, as to marriage, during marriage and in the event of its dissolution. This Article shall not prevent States from taking such measures as are necessary in the interests of the children.

Article 6

Territorial application

1. Any State may at the time of signature or when depositing its instrument of ratification, acceptance or approval, specify the territory or territories to which the Protocol shall apply and state the extent to which it undertakes that the provisions of this Protocol shall apply to such territory or territories.

2. Any State may at any later date, by a declaration addressed to the Secretary General of the Council of Europe, extend the application of this Protocol to any other territory specified in the declaration. In respect of such territory the Protocol shall enter into force on the first day of the month following the expiration of a period of two months after the date of receipt of such notification by the Secretary General.

3. Any declaration made under the preceding two paragraphs may, in respect of any territory specified in such declaration, be withdrawn or modified by a notification addressed to the Secretary General. The withdrawal or modification shall become effective on the first day of the month following the expiration of a period of two months after the date of receipt of such notification by the Secretary General.

4. A declaration made in accordance with this Article shall be deemed to have been made in accordance with paragraph 1 of Article 56 of the Convention.

5. The territory of any State to which this Protocol applies by virtue of ratification, acceptance or approval by that State, and each territory to which this Protocol is applied by virtue of a declaration by that State under this Article, may be treated as separate territories for the purpose of the reference in Article I to the territory of a State.

6. Any State which has made a declaration in accordance with paragraph 1 or 2 of this Article may at any time thereafter declare on behalf of one or more of the territories to which the declaration relates that it accepts the competence of the Court to receive applications from individuals, non-governmental organisations or groups of individuals as provided in Article 34 of the Convention in respect of Articles 1 to 5 of this Protocol.

Article 7

Relationship to the Convention

As between the States Parties, the provisions of Articles 1 to 6 of this protocol shall be regarded as additional Articles to the Convention, and all the provisions of the Convention shall apply accordingly.

Article 8

Signature and ratification

This Protocol shall be open for signature by member States of the Council of Europe which have signed the Convention. It is subject to ratification, acceptance or approval. A member State of the Council of Europe may not ratify, accept or approve this Protocol without previously or simultaneously ratifying the Convention. Instruments of ratification, acceptance or approval shall be deposited with the Secretary General of the Council of Europe.

Article 9

Entry into force

1. This Protocol shall enter into force on the first day of the month following the expiration of a period of two months after the date on which

seven member States of the Council of Europe have expressed their consent to be bound by the Protocol in accordance with the provisions of Article 8.

2. In respect of any member State which subsequently expresses its consent to be bound by it, the Protocol shall enter into force on the first day of the month following the expiration of a period of two months after the date of the deposit of the instrument of ratification, acceptance or approval.

Article 10

Depositary functions

The Secretary General of the States of the Council of Europe shall notify all the member States of the Council of Europe of:

(a) any signature;
(b) the deposit of any instrument of ratification, acceptance or approval;
(c) any date of entry into force of this protocol in accordance with Articles 6 and 9;
(d) any other act, notification or declaration relating to this Protocol.

In witness whereof the undersigned, being duly authorised thereto, have signed this Protocol.

Done at Strasbourg, this 22nd day of November 1984, in English and French, both texts being equally authentic, in a single copy which shall be deposited in the archives of the Council of Europe. The Secretary General of the Council of Europe shall transmit certified copies to each member State of the Council of Europe.

[Protocol No. 8 has become otiose; it amended certain provisions relating to the Commission and the Court.]

[Protocol No. 9 has become otiose; it amended certain provisions of the Convention to improve the position of individual applicants.]

[Protocol No. 10 has become otiose; it changed the majority required for a decision of the Committee of Ministers under the original Article 32.]

Protocol No. 11 to the Convention for the Protection of Human Rights and Fundamental Freedoms, restructuring the control machinery established thereby

The member States of the Council of Europe, signatories to this Protocol to the Convention for the Protection of Human Rights and Fundamental Freedoms, signed at Rome on 4 November 1950 (hereinafter referred to as 'the Convention'),

Considering the urgent need to restructure the control machinery established by the Convention in order to maintain and improve the efficiency of its protection of human rights and fundamental freedoms, mainly in view of the increase in the number of applications and the growing membership of the Council of Europe;

Considering that it is therefore desirable to amend certain provisions of the Convention with a view, in particular, to replacing the existing European Commission and Court of Human Rights with a new permanent Court;

Having regard to Resolution No. 1 adopted at the European Ministerial Conference on Human Rights, held in Vienna on 19 and 20 March 1985;

Having regard to recommendation 1194 (1992), adopted by the Parliamentary Assembly of the Council of Europe on 6 October 1992;

Having regard to the decision taken on reform of the Convention control machinery by the Heads of State and Government of the Council of Europe member States in the Vienna Declaration on 9 October 1993,

Have agreed as follows:

Article 1

[Replaces the text of Sections II to IV of the Convention and of Protocol No. 2; the amendments have been incorporated in the text set out above.]

Article 2

[Amends the text of other provisions of the Convention and Protocols; the amendments have been incorporated in the text set out above.]

Article 3

1. This Protocol shall be open for signature by member States of the Council of Europe signatories to the Convention, which may express their consent to be bound by
   (a) signature without reservation as to ratification, acceptance or approval; or
   (b) signature subject to ratification, acceptance or approval, followed by ratification, acceptance or approval.
2. The instruments of ratification, acceptance or approval shall be deposited with the Secretary General of the Council of Europe.

Article 4

This Protocol shall enter into force on the first day of the month following the expiration of a period of one year after the date on which all Parties to the Convention have expressed their consent to be bound by the Protocol in accordance with the provisions of Article 3. The election of new judges may take place, and any further necessary steps may be taken to establish the new Court, in accordance which the provisions of this Protocol from the date on which all Parties to the Convention have expressed their consent to be bound by the Protocol.

Article 5

1. Without prejudice to the provisions in paragraphs 3 and 4 below, the terms of office of the judges, members of the Commission, Registrar and Deputy registrar shall expire at the date of entry into force of this Protocol.

2. Applications pending before the Commission which have not been declared admissible at the date of the entry into force of this Protocol shall be examined by the Court in accordance with the provisions of this Protocol.

3. Applications which have been declared admissible at the date of the entry into force of this Protocol shall continue to be dealt with by members of the Commission within a period of one year thereafter. Any applications the examination of which has not been completed within the aforesaid period shall be transmitted to the Court which shall examine them as admissible cases in accordance with the provisions of this Protocol.

4. With respect to applications in which the Commission, after the entry into force of this Protocol, has adopted a report in accordance with former Article 31 of the Convention, the report shall be transmitted to the parties, who shall not be at liberty to publish it. In accordance with the provisions applicable prior to the entry into force of this Protocol, a case may be referred to the Court. The panel of the Grand Chamber shall determine whether one of the Chambers or the Grand Chamber shall decide the case. If the case is decided by a Chamber, the decision of the Chamber shall be final. Cases not referred to the Court shall be dealt with by the Committee of Ministers acting in accordance with the provisions of former Article 32 of the Convention.

5. Cases pending before the Court which have not been decided at the date of entry into force of this Protocol shall be transmitted to the Grand Chamber of the Court, which shall examine them in accordance with the provisions of this Protocol.

6. Cases pending before the Committee of Ministers which have not been decided under former Article 32 of the Convention at the date of entry into force of this Protocol shall be completed by the Committee of Ministers acting in accordance with that Article.

Article 6

Where a High Contracting Party had made a declaration recognising the competence of the Commission or the jurisdiction of the Court under former Article 25 or 46 of the Convention with respect to matters arising after or based on facts occurring subsequent to any such declaration, this limitation shall remain valid for the jurisdiction of the Court under this Protocol.

Article 7

The Secretary General of the Council of Europe shall notify the member States of the Council of:

(a) any signature;

(b) the deposit of any instrument of ratification, acceptance or approval;

(c) the date of entry into force of this Protocol or of any of its provisions in accordance with Article 4; and

(d) any other act, notification or communication relating to this Protocol.

In witness whereof the undersigned, being duly authorised thereto, have signed this Protocol.

Done at Strasbourg, this 11th day of May 1994 in English and French, both texts being equally authentic, in a single copy which shall be deposited in the archives of the Council of Europe. The Secretary General of the Council of Europe shall transmit certified copies to each member State of the Council of Europe.

INDEX